The Stranger Beside Me

ANN RULE

sphere

SPHERE

First published in the USA in 1980 by W. W. Norton and Company, Inc.
First published in Great Britain in 1994 by Warner Books
This edition published in 2019 by Sphere

1 3 5 7 9 10 8 6 4 2

A CIP catalogue record for this book
is available from the British Library.

ISBN 978-0-7515-7809-6

Typeset by Hewer Text UK Ltd, Edinburgh
Printed and bound in Great Britain by Clays Ltd, Elcograf S.p.A

Papers used by Sphere are from well-managed forests and other responsible sources.

MIX
Paper from
responsible sources
FSC
www.fsc.org   FSC® C104740

Sphere
An imprint of
Little, Brown Book Group
Carmelite House
50 Victoria Embankment
London EC4Y 0DZ

An Hachette UK Company
www.hachette.co.uk

www.littlebrown.co.uk

This book is dedicated to my parents:
Sophie Hansen Stackhouse and the late Chester
R. Stackhouse . . . for their unfailing love and
support, and because they always believed . . .

And tortures him now more, the more he sees
Of pleasure not for him ordained: then soon
Fierce hate he recollects, and all his thoughts
Of mischief, gratulating, thus excites:
"Thoughts, whither have ye led me? with what sweet
Compulsion thus transported to forget
What hither brought us? hate, not love, nor hope
Of Paradise for Hell, hope here to taste
Of pleasure, but all pleasure to destroy,
Save what is in destroying; other joy
To me is lost. . . ."

Paradise Lost: Book IX
(Lines 469–79)

Preface

This book began a half dozen years ago as an entirely different work. It was to have been a crime reporter's chronicling of a series of inexplicable murders of beautiful young women. By its very nature, it was to have been detached, the result of extensive research. My life, certainly, would be no part of it. It has evolved instead into an intensely personal book, the story of a unique friendship that has somehow transcended the facts that my research produced. As the years passed, I learned that the stranger at the very vortex of an ever-spreading police probe was not a stranger at all; he was my friend.

To write a book about an anonymous murder suspect is one thing. To write such a book about someone you have known and cared for for ten years is quite another. And yet, that is exactly what has happened. My contract to write this book was signed many months before Ted Bundy became the prime suspect in more than a dozen homicide cases. My book would not be about a faceless name in a newspaper, about one unknown out of the over one million people who live in the Seattle area. It would be about my friend, Ted Bundy.

We might never have met at all. Logically, statistically, demographically, chance that Ted Bundy and I should meet and become fast friends is almost too obscure to contemplate. We have lived in the same states at the same time—not once but many times—but the fifteen years between our ages precluded our meeting for many years.

When we did meet in 1971, I was a plumpish mother of four, almost forty, nearing divorce. Ted was twenty-four, a brilliant, handsome senior in psychology at the University of Washington. Chance made us partners on the crisis lines at Seattle's Crisis Clinic on the Tuesday night late shift. Rapport, an almost instant rapport, made us friends.

I was a volunteer on the phones, and Ted earned two dollars an hour as a work-study student. He looked forward to law school, and I hoped that my fledgling career as a free-lance writer might grow into something that would provide a fulltime income for my family. Although I had a bachelor's degree in creative writing from the University of Washington, I had done little writing until 1968 when I'd become the Northwest correspondent for *True Detective Magazine* and her sister publications, all specializing in fact-detective stories. My beat was major crime stories in a territory extending from Eugene, Oregon to the Canadian border.

It proved to be a field for which I was well suited. I'd been a Seattle policewoman in the 1950s and the combination of my interest in law enforcement and my education in writing worked. I had minored in abnormal psychology at the University and had gone on to obtain an associate degree in police science to enable me to write with some expertise about the advances in scientific criminal investigation. By 1980, I would have covered more than 800 cases, principally homicides, all up and down the Northwestern coast, gaining the trust of hundreds of homicide detectives—one of whom would give me the somewhat unsettling accolade, "Ann you're just like one of the boys."

I'm sure that our mutual interest in the law drew Ted and me together, gave us some common ground for discussion—just as our interest in abnormal psychology did. But there has always seemed to be something more, something almost ephemeral. Ted himself referred to it once in a letter mailed from a jail cell, one of the many cells he would occupy.

"You've called it Karma. It may be. Yet whatever super-natural force guides our destinies, it has brought us together in some mind-expanding situations. I must believe this invisible hand will pour more chilled Chablis for us in less treacherous, more tranquil times to come. Love, ted."

The letter was dated March 6, 1976, and we were never to come face to face again outside prison walls or a tightly secured courtroom. But a curious bond remains.

And so Ted Bundy was my friend, through all the good times and the bad times. I stuck by him for many years, hoping that none of the innuendo was true. There are few who will understand my decision. I'm sure that it will anger many. And, with it all, Ted Bundy's story must be told, and it must be told in its entirety if any good can evolve from the terrible years: 1974–1980.

I have labored for a long time with my ambivalence about Ted. As a professional writer, I have been handed the story of a lifetime, a story any author prays for. Probably there is no other writer so privy to every facet of Ted's story. I did not seek it out, and there have been many, many, long nights when I wished devoutly that things might have been different—that I *was* writing about a complete stranger whose hopes and dreams were no part of my own. I have wanted to go back to 1971, to erase all that has happened, to be able to think of Ted as the open, smiling young man I knew then.

Ted knows I am writing this book. He has always known, and he has continued to write to me, to call me. I suspect that he knows I will try to show the whole man.

Ted has been described as the perfect son, the perfect student, the Boy Scout grown to adulthood, a genius, as hand-some as a movie idol, a bright light in the future of the Republican Party, a sensitive psychiatric social worker, a budding lawyer, a trusted friend, a young man far whom the future could surely hold only success.

He is all of these things, and none of them.

Ted Bundy fits no pattern at all; you could not look at his record and say: "See, it was inevitable that he would turn out like this."

In fact, it was incomprehensible.

ANN RULE
January 29, 1980

1

No one glanced at the young man who walked out of the Trailways Bus Station in Tallahassee, Florida at dawn on Sunday, January 8, 1978. He looked like a college student—perhaps a bit older—and he blended in smoothly with the 30,000 students who had arrived in Florida's capital city that week. He had planned it that way. He felt at ease in a campus atmosphere, at home.

In truth, he was almost as far away from home as he could get and still remain in the United States. He had planned that too, just as he planned everything. He had accomplished the impossible, and now he would begin a new life, with a new name, a contrived, "stolen" background, an entirely different pattern of behavior. By doing this, he felt confident that his heady sense of freedom would continue forever.

In Washington State, or Utah, or Colorado, he would have been recognized instantly by even the most desultory of media watchers and readers. But here in Tallahassee, Florida, he was anonymous, only another handsome young man with a ready smile.

He had been Theodore Robert Bundy. But Ted Bundy would be no more. Now he was Chris Hagen. That would do until he decided who he would be next.

He had been cold for so long. Cold in the frigid night air of Glenwood Springs, Colorado as he emerged undetected from the Garfield County Jail. Cold on New Year's Day as he mingled with the tavern crowd in Ann Arbor, Michigan, cheering for the Rose Bowl game on TV. Cold when he decided that he would head south. Where he went didn't really matter as long as the sun was hot, the weather mild, and he was on a college campus.

Why had he chosen Tallahassee? Chance more than anything. Looking back, we see it is often casual choices which chart a path to tragedy. He had been enthralled with the University of Michigan campus, and he could have stayed there. There'd been enough money left from the stash he'd hidden in jail to pay for a twelve-dollar room at the YMCA but Michigan nights in January can be unrelentingly icy, and he didn't have warm clothing.

He'd been to Florida before. Back in the days when he was an energetic young worker for the Republican Party he'd received a trip to the 1968 convention in Miami as part of his reward. But, as he pored over college catalogues in the University of Michigan Library, he wasn't thinking of Miami.

He looked at the University of Florida in Gainesville and dismissed it summarily. There was no water around Gainesville, and, as he would say later, "It didn't look right on the map—super-stition, I guess."

Tallahassee, on the other hand, "looked great." He had lived the better part of his life on Washington's Puget Sound and he craved the sight and smell of water: Tallahassee was on the Ochlockonee River which led to the Apalachee Bay and the vastness of the Gulf of Mexico.

He knew he couldn't go home again, ever, but the Florida Indian names reminded him a little of the cities and rivers of Washington with their Northwestern tribal names.

Tallahassee it would be.

He had traveled comfortably up until New Year's Day. The first night out was a little hard, but walking free was enough in itself. When he'd stolen the "beater" off the streets in Glenwood Springs, he'd known it might not be up to making the snow-clogged pass into Aspen, but he'd had little choice. It had burned out thirty miles from Vail—forty miles from Aspen—but a good Samaritan had helped him push the car off the road, and given him a ride back to Vail.

From there, there was the bus ride to Denver, a cab to the airport, and a plane to Chicago, even before they'd discovered he was gone. He hadn't been on a train since he was a child and he'd enjoyed the Amtrak journey to Ann Arbor, having his first drinks in two years in the club car as he thought of his captors searching the snowbanks further and further behind him.

In Ann Arbor, he'd counted his money and realized that he would have to conserve it. He'd been straight since leaving

Colorado, but he decided one more car theft didn't matter. He left this one in the middle of a black ghetto in Atlanta with the keys in it. Nobody could ever tie it to Ted Bundy—not even the FBI (an organization that he privately considered vastly overrated) who had just placed him on their Ten-Most-Wanted List.

The Trailways bus had delivered him right into the center of downtown Tallahassee. He'd had a bit of a scare as he got off the bus. He thought he'd seen a man he'd known in prison in Utah, but the man had looked right through him, and he realized he was slightly paranoid. Besides, he didn't have enough money to travel any further and still afford a room to rent.

He loved Tallahassee. It was perfect, dead, quiet—a hick town on Sunday morning. He walked out onto Duval Street, and it was glorious. Warm. The air smelled good and it seemed right that it was the fresh dawn of a new day. Like a homing pigeon, he headed for the Florida State University campus. It wasn't that hard to find. Duval cut across College and he turned right. He could see the old and new capitol buildings ahead, and, beyond that, the campus itself.

The parking strips were planted with dogwood trees—reminiscent of home—but the rest of the vegetation was strange, unlike that in the places from which he'd come. Live oak, water oak, slash pine, date palms, and towering sweet gums. The whole city seemed to be sheltered by trees. The sweet gum branches were stark and bare in January, making the vista a bit like a northern winter's, but the temperature was nearing 70 already. The very strangeness of the landscape made him feel safer, as if all the bad times were behind him, so far away that everything in the previous four years could be forgotten, forgotten so completely that it would be as if it had never happened at all. He was good at that; there was a place he could go to in his mind where he truly *could* forget. Not erase; forget.

As he neared the Florida State campus proper, his euphoria lessened; perhaps he'd made a mistake. He'd expected a much bigger operation in which to lose himself, and a proliferation of For Rent signs. There seemed to be very few rentals, and he knew the classifieds wouldn't help him much; he wouldn't be able to tell which addresses were near the university.

The clothing that had been too light in Michigan and Colorado was beginning to feel too heavy, and he went to the campus bookstore where he found lockers to stow his sweaters and hat.

He had $160 left, not that much money when he figured he had to rent a room, pay a deposit, and buy food until he found a job. He found that most of the students lived in dormitories, fraternal houses, and in a hodge-podge of older apartment and rooming houses bordering the campus. But he was late in arriving; the term had started, and almost everything was already rented.

Ted Bundy had lived in nice apartments, airy rooms in the upper stories of comfortable older homes near the University of Washington and the University of Utah campuses, and he was less than enchanted with the pseudo-Southern-mansion facade of "The Oak" on West College Avenue. It drew its name from the single tree in its front yard, a tree as disheveled as the aging house behind it. The paint was fading, and the balcony listed a bit, but there was a For Rent sign in the window.

He smiled ingratiatingly at the landlord and quickly talked his way into the one vacancy with only a $100 deposit. As Chris Hagen, he promised to pay two months rent—$320—within a month. The room itself was as dispirited as the building, but it meant he was off the streets. He had a place to live, a place where he could begin to carry out the rest of his plans.

Ted Bundy is a man who learns from experience—his own and others'. Over the past four years, his life had changed full circle from the world of a bright young man on his way up, a man who might well have been Governor of Washington in the foreseeable future, to the life of a con and a fugitive. And he had, indeed, become con-wise, gleaning whatever bits of information he needed from the men who shared his cell blocks. He was smarter by far than any of them, smarter than most of his jailers, and the drive that had once spurred him on to be a success in the straight world had gradually redirected itself until it focused on only one thing: escape—permanent and lasting freedom, even though he would be, perhaps, the most hunted man in the United States.

He had seen what happened to escapees who weren't clever enough to plan. He knew that his first priority would have to be identification papers. Not one set, but many. He had watched the less astute escapees led back to their prisons, and had deduced that their biggest mistake had been that they were stopped by the law and had been unable to produce I.D. that would draw no hits on the "big-daddy" computers of the National Crime Information Center in Washington D.C.

He would not make that fatal error; his first chore would be to research student files and find records of several graduates, records without the slightest shadows on them. Although he was thirty-one, he decided that in his new lives, he would be about twenty-three, a graduate student. Once he had that secure cover, he would find two other identities that he could switch to if his antennae told him he was being observed too closely.

He also had to find work—not the kind of job for which he was infinitely qualified: social service, mental health counselor, political aide, legal assistant—but a blue collar job. He would have to have a social security number, a driver's license, and permanent address. The latter, he had; the rest he would obtain. After the rental deposit, he had only $60 left, and he'd been shocked already to see the inroads inflation had made into the economy while he'd been incarcerated. He'd been sure that the several hundred dollars he'd begun his escape with would last him a month or two, but now it was almost gone.

He would rectify that. The program was simple. First the I.D., next the job, and last, but most important, he would be the most law-abiding citizen who ever walked a Florida street. He promised himself that he would never get so much as a jaywalking ticket, nothing whatever that would cause law enforcement officers to ever glance his way.

He was now a man without any past at all. Ted Bundy was dead.

As all of his plans had been, it was a good plan. Had he been able to carry it out to the letter, it is doubtful that he would ever have been apprehended. Florida lawmen had homicide suspects of their own to keep tabs on, and crimes as far afield as Utah or Colorado held little interest for them.

Most young men, among strangers, in a strange land, with only $60 to their names, jobless, and in need of $320 within the month, might be expected to feel a stirring of panic at the unknown quality of the days ahead.

"Chris Hagen" felt no panic. He felt only a bubbling elation and a vast sense of relief. He had done it. He was free, and he no longer had to run. Whatever lay ahead paled in comparison with what the morning of January 9th had meant to him as 1977 drew to a close. He was relaxed and happy as he fell asleep in his narrow bed in the Oak in Tallahassee.

He had good reason to be. For Theodore Robert Bundy—the man who was no more—had been scheduled to go on trial for first degree murder in Colorado Springs, Colorado at 9 A.M. on January 9th. Now that courtroom would be empty.

The defendant was gone.

2

The Ted Bundy who "died" and was reborn as Chris Hagen in Tallahassee on January 8, 1978 had been a man of unusual accomplishment. While much of his life had seemed to fit into the flat wasteland of the middle class, there was also much that did not.

His very birth stamped him as different. The mores of America in 1946 were a world removed from the attitudes of the '70s and '80s. Today, illegitimate births make up a substantial proportion of deliveries, despite legalized abortions, vasectomies, and birth control pills. There is only token stigma toward unwed mothers and most of them keep their babies, merging smoothly into society.

It was not that way in 1946. Premarital sex surely existed—as it always has—but women didn't talk about it if they indulged, not even to their best friends. Girls who engaged in sex before marriage were considered promiscuous, though men could brag about it. It wasn't fair, and it didn't even make much sense, but that's the way it was. A liberal at that time was someone who pontificated that "only good girls get caught." Programmed by anxious mothers, girls never doubted the premise that virginity was an end in itself.

Eleanor Louise Cowell was twenty-two, a "good girl," raised in a deeply religious family in northwest Philadelphia. One can only imagine her panic when she found she had been left pregnant by a man she refers to today only as "a sailor." He left her, frightened and alone, to face her strict family. They rallied around her, but they were shocked and saddened.

Abortion was out of the question. It was illegal—carried out in murky rooms on dark streets by old women or doctors who'd lost their licenses. Furthermore, her religious training forbade it. Beyond that, she already loved the baby growing within her. She couldn't bear the thought of putting the child up for adoption. She did the only thing she could; when she was seven months pregnant, she left home and entered the Elizabeth Lund Home for Unwed Mothers in Burlington, Vermont.

The maternity home was referred to by waggish locals as "Lizzie Lund's Home for Naughty Ladies." The girls who came there in trouble were aware of that little joke, but they had no choice but to live out their days until labor began in an atmosphere which was—if not unfriendly—seemingly heedless of their feelings.

After sixty-three days of waiting there, Theodore Robert Cowell was born on November 24, 1946.

She took her son back to her parents' home in Philadelphia and began a hopeless charade. As the baby grew, he would hear Eleanor referred to as his older sister, and was told to call his grandparents "Mother" and "Father." Already showing signs of brilliance, the slightly undersized little boy whose crop of curly brown hair gave him a faunlike appearance did as he was told, and yet he sensed that he was living a lie.

Ted adored his grandfather-father Cowell. He identified with him, respected him, and clung to him in times of trouble.

But, as he grew older, it was clear that remaining in Philadelphia would be impossible. Too many relatives knew the real story of his parentage, and Eleanor dreaded what his growing-up years would be like. It was a working-class neighborhood where children would listen to their parents' whispered remarks and mimic them. She never wanted Ted to have to hear the word "bastard."

There was a contingent of Cowells living in Washington State, and they offered to take Eleanor and the boy in if they came west. To insure Ted's protection against prejudice, Eleanor—who would henceforth be called Louise—went to court on October 6, 1950 in Philadelphia and had Ted's name legally changed to Theodore Robert Nelson. It was a common name, one that should give him an anonymity, that would not draw attention to him when he began school.

And so, Louise Cowell and her son, four-year-old Ted Nelson, moved 3,000 miles away to Tacoma, Washington where they moved in with her relatives until she could get a job. It was a tremendous wrench for Ted to leave his grandfather behind, and he would never forget the old man. But he soon adjusted to the new life. He had cousins, Jane and Alan Scott, who were close to his age and they became friends.

In Tacoma, Washington's third largest city, Louise and Ted started over. The beauty of Tacoma's hills and harbor was often obscured by smog from industry, and the downtown streets infiltrated by honky-tonk bars, peep shows, and pornography shops catering to soldiers on passes from Fort Lewis.

Louise joined the Methodist Church, and there at a social function she met Johnnie Culpepper Bundy—one of a huge clan of Bundys who reside in the Tacoma area. Bundy, a cook, was as tiny as Louise, neither of them standing an inch over five feet. He was shy, but he seemed kind. He seemed solid.

It was a rapid courtship, marked principally by attendance at other social functions at the church. On May 19, 1951, Louise Cowell married Johnnie Bundy. Ted attended the wedding of his "older sister" and the little cook from the army base. He was not yet five when he had a third name: Theodore Robert Bundy.

Louise continued working as a secretary and the new family moved several times before finally buying their own home near the soaring Narrows Bridge.

Soon, there were four half-siblings, two girls and two boys. The youngest boy, born when Ted was fifteen, was his favorite. Ted was often pressed into babysitting chores, and his teen-age friends recall that he missed many activities with them because he had to babysit. If he minded, he seldom complained.

Despite his new name, Ted still considered himself a Cowell. It was always the Cowell side of the family to which he gravitated.

He *looked* like a Cowell. His features were a masculinized version of Louise Bundy's, his coloring just like hers. On the surface, it seemed the only genetic input he'd received from his natural father was his height. Although still smaller than his peers in junior high school, Ted was already taller than Louise and Johnnie. One day he would reach six feet.

Ted spent time with his stepfather only grudgingly. Johnnie tried. He had accepted Louise's child just as he had accepted her, and he'd been rather pleased to have a son. If Ted seemed increasingly removed from him, he put it down to burgeoning adolescence. In discipline, Louise had the final word, although Johnnie sometimes applied corporal punishment with a belt.

Ted and Johnnie often picked beans in the acres of verdant fields radiating out through the valleys beyond Tacoma. Between the two of them, they could make five to six dollars a day. If Bundy worked the early shift at Madigan Army Hospital as a cook—5 A.M. to 2 P.M.—they would hurry out to the fields and pick during the heat of the afternoon. If he worked a late shift, he would get up early anyway and help Ted with his paper route. Ted had seventy-eight customers along his early morning route and it took him a long time to work it alone.

Johnnie Bundy became a Boy Scout leader, and he frequently organized camping trips. More often than not, however, it was other peoples' sons who went on the outings; Ted always seemed to have some excuse to beg off.

Oddly, Louise had never directly confirmed to Ted that she was, in fact, his mother and not his older sister. Sometimes he called her Mother, and sometimes just Louise.

Still, it was clear to everyone who knew them that this was the child she felt had the most potential. She felt he was special, that he was college material, and urged him on to start saving for college when he was only thirteen or fourteen.

Although Ted was growing like a weed, he was very slender—too light for football in junior high. He attended Hunt Junior High, and did turn out for track where he had some minor successes in the low hurdles.

Scholastically, he did much better. He usually managed to maintain a B average, and would stay up all night to finish a project if need be.

It was in junior high that Ted endured some merciless teasing from other boys. Some who attended Hunt Junior High recall that Ted invariably insisted on showering in privacy in a stall, shunning the open showers where the rest of his gym class whooped and hollered. Scornful of his shyness, the other boys delighted in creeping up to the single shower stall and pouring cold water down on him. Humiliated and furious, he chased them away.

Ted attended Woodrow Wilson High School in Tacoma and became a member of the largest graduating class of that school to date; the class of 1965 had 740 members. Any search of records on Ted Bundy at Woodrow Wilson is fruitless; they have disappeared, but many of his friends remember him.

A young woman, now an attorney, recalls Ted at seventeen. "He was well known, popular, but not in the top crowd—but then neither was I. He was attractive, and well dressed, exceptionally well mannered. I know he must have dated, but I can't ever remember seeing him with a date. I think I remember seeing him at the dances—especially the TOLOS, when the girls asked the boys to dance—but I can't be sure. He was kind of shy—almost introverted."

Ted's best friends in high school were Jim Paulus, a short, compact young man with dark hair and horn-rimmed glasses who was active in student politics, and Kent Michaels, vice-president of the student council, a reserve football team member, and now an attorney in Tacoma. Ted often skiied with them, but, despite his awakening interest in politics himself, he did not hold a student body office.

In a class with almost 800 members, he was a medium-sized fish in a large pond; if not among the most popular, he at least moved near those at the top and he was well liked.

Scholastically, he was getting better. He consistently drew a B plus average. At graduation, he was awarded a scholarship to the University of Puget Sound in Tacoma.

Ted wrote an unusual note in a classmate's copy of "The Nova," Wilson High's yearbook:

Dearest V.,
    The sweetness of the spring time rain runs down the window pain (sic.) (I can't help it. It just flows out)
                                Theodore Robert Bundy Peot(sic)

The only fact that might mar the picture of the clean-cut young graduate in the spring of 1965 was that Ted had been picked up at least twice by juvenile authorities in Pierce County for suspicion of auto theft and burglary. There is no indication that he was ever confined, but his name was known to juvenile caseworkers. The records outlining the details of the incidents have long been shredded—procedure when a juvenile reaches eighteen. Only a card remains with his name and the offenses listed.

Ted spent the summer of 1965 working for Tacoma City Light to save money for college, and he attended the University of Puget Sound for the school year 1965–66.

After working in the sawmill the next summer, Ted transferred to the University of Washington where he began a program of intensive Chinese. He felt that China was the country that we would one day have to reckon with, and that a fluency in the language would be imperative.

Ted moved into McMahon Hall, a dormitory on the University campus. He had yet to have a serious involvement with a woman, although he had yearned for one, held back by his shyness and his feeling that he was not socially adept, that his background was stultifyingly middle class, that he had nothing to offer the kind of woman he wanted.

When Ted met Stephanie Brooks in the spring of 1967 at McMahon Hall, he saw a woman who was the epitome of his dreams. Stephanie was like no girl he had ever seen before, and he considered her the most sophisticated, the most beautiful creature possible. He watched her, saw that she seemed to prefer football jocks, and hesitated to approach her. As he would write a dozen years later, "She and I had about as much in common as Sears and Roebuck does with Saks. I never considered S. with any more romantic interest than I considered some elegant creature on the fashion page."

But they did share one common interest—skiing. Stephanie had her own car, and he managed to hitch a ride to the mountain summits east of Seattle with her. As they rode back from a day's skiing, he studied the beautiful, dark-haired girl behind the wheel. He had told himself that Stephanie out-classed him, and yet he realized that he was infatuated with her. He was both bemused and thrilled when she began to spend more and more time with him. His preoccupation with intensive Chinese was pushed temporarily into the background.

"It was at once sublime and overpowering," he recalled. "The first touch of hands, the first kiss, the first night together. . . . For the next six years, S. and I would meet under the most tentative of circumstances."

Ted had fallen in love. Stephanie was a year or so older, the daughter of a wealthy California family, and she was, quite possibly, the first woman to initiate him into physical lovemaking. He was twenty years old. He had very little to offer her, a young woman who'd been raised in an atmosphere where money and prestige were taken for granted. And yet she stayed with him for a year, a year that may have been the most important in his life.

Ted worked a series of menial, low-paying jobs to pay his way through college: in a posh Seattle yacht club as a bus boy, at Seattle's venerable Olympic Hotel as a busboy, at a Safeway store stocking shelves, in a surgical supply house as a stockboy, as a legal messenger, as a shoe clerk. He left most of these jobs of his own accord— usually after only a few months. Safeway personnel files evaluated him as "only fair," and noted that he had simply failed to come to work one day. Both the surgical supply house and the messenger service hired him twice, however, and termed him a pleasant, dependable employee.

Ted became friends in August of 1967 with sixty-year-old Beatrice Sloan, who worked at the yacht club. Mrs. Sloan, a widow, found the young college student a lovable rascal, and Ted could talk her out of almost anything when they worked at the yacht club together for the next six months and then for many years after. She arranged for his job at the Olympic Hotel, a job that lasted only a month; other employees reported they suspected he was rifling lockers. Mrs. Sloan was somewhat shocked when Ted showed her a uniform that he had stolen from the hotel, but she put it down as a boyish prank as she would rationalize so many of his actions.

Beatrice Sloan heard all about Stephanie, and understood Ted's need to impress this marvelous girl. She loaned him her car often and he returned it in the wee hours of the morning. Once, Ted told her he was going to cook a gourmet meal for Stephanie and the widow loaned him her best crystal and silver so that he could create the perfect setting. She laughed as he imitated the precise English accent he planned to use as he served the meal he'd cooked himself.

She felt that Ted needed her. He'd explained that his family life had been very strict, and that he was on his own now. She allowed him to use her address when he applied for jobs and as a reference; sometimes he had no place to sleep except in the lounge of

McMahon Hall, a dormitory he still had a key for. He was a "schemer," she knew, but she thought she could understand why; he was only trying to survive.

Ted entertained her. Once, he put on a black wig and he seemed to take on an entirely different appearance. Later, she would catch a glimpse of him on television during Governor Rosellini's campaign and he was wearing that same wig.

Even though Mrs. Sloan suspected that Ted was sneaking girls up into the "crow's nest" at the yacht club for what she called hanky-panky, and even though she also suspected him of taking money sometimes from the drunken patrons of the club who had to be driven home, she couldn't help liking the young man. He took the time to talk to her, and bragged to her that his father was a famous chef, that he planned to go to Philadelphia to visit an uncle who was high up in politics. She even loaned him money once—and then wished that she hadn't. When he wouldn't pay it back, she called Louise Bundy and asked that she remind Ted. Louise had laughed, according to Mrs. Sloan, and said, "You're a fool to loan him money. You'll never get it back. He's a stranger around here."

Stephanie Brooks was a junior when she met Ted in the spring of 1967, and she was in love with Ted through the summer and into 1968. But not as much in love as he was. They dated often—dates that did not require much money: walks, movies, hamburger dinners, sometimes skiing. His lovemaking was sweet and gentle, and there were times when she thought it might really work out.

But Stephanie was pragmatic. It was wonderful to be in love, to have a college romance, to stroll through the wooded paths of the campus hand-in-hand as the Japanese cherry blossoms gave way to the rhododendrons and then to the brilliant orange of the vine maples. The skiing trips up to the Cascades were fun, too, but she sensed that Ted was foundering, that he had no real plans, no real prospects for the future. Consciously or unconsciously, Stephanie wanted her life to continue as it always had; she wanted a husband who would fit into her world in California. She just didn't believe that Ted Bundy fit that picture.

Stephanie found Ted very emotional, unsure of himself. He didn't seem to have the capacity to decide what his major was going to be. But, more than that, she had a niggling suspicion that he used people, that he would become close to people who might do favors for him, and that he took advantage of them. She was sure that he had lied to her, that he had made up answers that sounded good.

That bothered her. It bothered her more than his indecision, and his tendency to use people.

Stephanie graduated from the University of Washington in June, 1968, and it seemed that that might be a way to ease out of the romance. Ted still had years to go, and she would be in San Francisco, starting a job, back among her old friends. The affair might just die of lack of nourishment due to time and distance.

But Ted won a scholarship to Stanford in intensive Chinese for the summer of 1968. He was only a short drive down the Bayshore Highway from her parents' home, and so they continued to date throughout the summer. Stephanie was adamant when the time came for Ted to return to the University of Washington. She told him that their romance was over, that their lives were headed on divergent paths.

He was devastated. He could not believe that she was really through with him. She was his first love, the absolute personification of everything he wanted. And now she was willing to walk away from him. He had been right in the first place. She was too beautiful. Too rich. He should never have believed he could have her.

Ted returned to Seattle. He no longer cared about intensive Chinese. Indeed, he cared about very little. Yet, he still had a toehold on the political scene. In April of 1968, he'd been appointed Seattle chairman and assistant state chairman of the New Majority for Rockefeller, and he'd won a trip to the Miami convention. His mind filled with his break with Stephanie Brooks, Ted went to Miami, only to see his candidate plowed under.

Back at the University, he took courses—not in Chinese, but in urban planning and sociology. He didn't come close to his previous excellence, and he dropped out of college.

During the fall of 1968, Ted had worked as a driver for Art Fletcher, a popular black candidate for Lieutenant Governor. When there were death threats against Fletcher, the candidate was housed in a secret penthouse location. Ted became not only a driver, but a bodyguard, sleeping in a room close by. He wanted to carry a gun, but Fletcher vetoed that.

Fletcher lost the election.

It seemed that everything Ted had counted on was crumbling. In early 1969, he set out on travels that might help him understand his roots. He visited relatives in Arkansas and in Philadelphia where he took some classes at Temple University. Yet all the while the real purpose of his trip burned in his mind.

His cousins, Alan and Jane Scott, with whom he'd grown up in Tacoma, had hinted at it; he himself had always known it, sensed the truth hidden there in memories from his earliest years. He had to know who he was.

Ted went to Burlington, Vermont, after checking records in Philadelphia. His birth certificate was in the files there, stamped with the archaic and cruel "Illegitimate." He had been born to Eleanor Louise Cowell. The name of the father was given as Lloyd Marshall, a graduate of Pennsylvania State University, an Air Force veteran, a salesman born 1916.

So his father had been thirty years old when he was born, an educated man. Why had he left them alone? Had he been married? What had become of him? There is no information on whether Ted tried to find that man who had gone out of his life before he was even born. But Ted knew. He knew that what he had always sensed was true: Louise was, of course, his mother. Johnnie Bundy wasn't his father, and his beloved grandfather wasn't his father either. He had no father.

Ted had continued to write to Stephanie, with only sporadic response. He knew she was working for a brokerage firm in San Francisco. As he headed back toward the West Coast, he was obsessed with getting to Stephanie. The knowledge that his mother had lied to him wasn't a complete surprise. It wasn't a surprise at all—and yet it hurt. All those years.

It was a bright spring day in 1969 when Stephanie walked out of her office building. She didn't see Ted. There was suddenly someone behind her, someone putting his hands on her shoulders. She turned around and there he was . . .

If he had expected that she would be delighted to see him, that their romance could be resumed, he was to be harshly disappointed. She was moderately glad to see him, but nothing more than that. Ted seemed to be the same drifting young man she'd always known. He wasn't even enrolled in college anymore.

Had she accepted him back at that point, some of his humiliation might have been tempered. But she couldn't. She asked how he had gotten to San Francisco, and he was vague, mumbled something about hitchhiking. They talked for awhile, and then she sent him away, for the second time.

She never expected to see him again.

3

Somehow the revelation about his parentage and the final rejection from the lost Stephanie, coming so close together in 1969, did not bury Ted Bundy. Instead, he became possessed of a kind of icy resolve. By God, if it took whatever he had, he was going to change. By sheer force of will, he would become the kind of man that the world—and particularly Stephanie—saw as a success. The years that followed would see an almost Horatio Alger-like metamorphosis in Ted.

He didn't want to go back to McMahon Hall; the memories there were too filled with Stephanie. Instead, he walked the streets of the University District, knocking on doors of older homes that flanked the streets just west of the campus. At each door, he would smile and explain he was looking for a room, that he was a student in psychology at the University.

Freda Rogers, an elderly woman who, along with her husband Ernst, owned the neat, white two-story frame house at 4143 12th N.E. was quite taken with Ted. She rented him a large room in the southwest corner of the home. He would live there for five years and become more of a son than a son than a tenant to the Rogers family. Ernst Rogers was far from well, and Ted promised to help with heavy chores and the gardening—a promise he kept.

Ted also called Beatrice Sloan, his old friend from the Seattle yacht club. She found him the same as he'd always been full of plans and adventures. He told her he'd been to Philadelphia where he'd seen his rich uncle, and that he was on his way to Aspen, Colorado to become a ski instructor.

"Then I'll knit you a ski hat," she replied promptly.

"No need. I already have a ski mask. But I do need a ride to the airport."

Mrs. Sloan did drive him to the airport and saw him off on his trip to Colorado. She wondered a little at the expensive ski gear he carried. She knew he'd never had any money, and the equipment was clearly the best.

Why he went to Colorado at that point is unclear. He did not have a job or even the promise of a job as a ski instructor. Perhaps, he only wanted to see the skiing hamlet that Stephanie had raved about. He was back by the time the fall quarter started at the University of Washington.

In a psychology curriculum, Ted seemed to have found his niche. He pulled down mostly A's with a sprinkling of B's, in courses like physiological psychology, social psychology, animal learning, statistical methods, developmental psychology, deviant personality, and deviant development. The boy who had seemed to be without direction or plans now became an honors student.

His professors liked him, particularly Patricia Lunneborg, Scott Fraser, and Ronald E. Smith. Smith, who three years later would write Ted a glowing letter of recommendation to the University of Utah Law School which read in part:

> Mr. Bundy is undoubtedly one of the top undergraduate students in our department. Indeed, I would place him in the top 1% of undergraduate students with whom I have interacted both here at the University of Washington and at Purdue University. He is exceedingly bright, personable, highly motivated, and conscientious. He conducts himself more like a young professional than like a student. He has the capacity for hard work and because of his intellectual curiosity is a pleasure to interact with. . . . As a result of his undergraduate psychology major, Mr. Bundy has become intensely interested in studying psychological variables which influence jury decisions. He and I are currently engaged in a research project in which we are attempting to study experimentally some of the variables which influence jury decisions.
>
> I must admit that I regret Mr. Bundy's decision to pursue a career in law rather than to continue his professional training in psychology. Our loss is your gain. I have no doubt that Mr. Bundy will distinguish himself as a law student and as a professional and I recommend him to you without qualification.

Ted needed nothing more than his scholastic excellence to stand him in good stead with his professors. It was somewhat odd then that he should tell Professor Scott Fraser that he had been a foster child, raised in one foster care home after another during his childhood. Fraser accepted this information as fact and was surprised later to find that it had not been true.

Ted often frequented University District taverns, drinking beer and occasionally scotch. It was in the Sandpiper Tavern on September 26, 1969 that he met the woman who would be a central force in his life for the next seven years.

Her name was Meg Anders. Like Stephanie, Meg was a few years older than Ted. She was a young divorcee with a three-year-old daughter named Liane. Meg was a diminutive woman with long brown hair—not pretty, but with a win-someness that made her seem years younger than she was. The daughter of a prominent Utah doctor, she was on the rebound from a disastrous marriage which had foundered when she learned that her husband was a convicted felon. Meg had divorced him and taken her daughter to Seattle to make a new life. Working as a secretary at a Seattle college, she knew no one in Seattle except for Lynn Banks, a childhood friend from Utah, and the people she worked with.

A little hesitant at first, she had finally allowed Ted to buy her a beer and had been fascinated with the good-looking young man who talked about psychology and his plans for the future. When she gave him her phone number, she really hadn't expected that he would call her. When he did, she was thrilled.

They began a friendship, and then an affair. Although Ted continued to live at the Rogers home and Meg kept her apartment, they spent many nights together. She fell in love with him; given her situation, it would have been almost impossible not to. She believed totally in his ability to succeed—something Stephanie had never done—and Meg often loaned Ted money to help with his schooling. Almost from the start, she wanted to marry him but understood when he told her that would have to be a long time in the future; he had much to accomplish first.

Ted continued to work at part-time jobs—selling shoes for a department store, working again for the surgical supply house. When he couldn't make ends meet, Meg helped out.

Sometimes she worried that it was her family's money and position that attracted Ted to her. She'd seen his appraising glance around their home in Utah when she took him home for Christmas in 1969. But it had to be more than that. He was good to her, and he was as devoted as a father to Liane. Liane always got flowers from him on her birthday, and Ted always sent Meg a single red rose on September 26th to commemorate their first meeting.

She sensed that he sometimes saw other women, knew that he and a friend would occasionally drop into the Pipeline Tavern or Dante's or O'Bannion's and pick up girls. She tried not to think about it. Time would take care of that.

What she did not know was that Stephanie existed, that Stephanie lived in Ted's mind as strongly as she always had. Although Stephanie had felt relieved when she said goodbye to Ted in the spring of 1969, she had not dropped him completely. The California woman who had wrought such a cataclysmic change in Ted Bundy's life had relatives in Vancouver, British Columbia, and she had taken to calling Ted to say "Hi" when her travels brought her through Seattle from time to time.

As 1969 and 1970 passed, Ted's path was straight upward, excelling in everything he put his hand to; he was becoming more urbane, superbly educated, socially adept. He was an ideal citizen. He even drew a commendation from the Seattle Police Department when he ran down a purse snatcher and returned the stolen bag to its owner. In the summer of 1970, it was Ted Bundy who saved a three-and-a-half-year-old toddler from drowning in Green Lake in Seattle's north end. No one had seen the child wander away from her parents—no one but Ted—and he had dashed into the water to save the youngster.

Ted kept up his contacts with the Republican Party. He was a precinct committeeman and would become more involved in the party work as the years progressed.

To those closest to him, Meg was definitely Ted's girl. He took her to meet Louise and Johnnie Bundy in their rambling blue and white house in Tacoma, and they liked her. Louise was relieved to see that he'd apparently gotten over his disappointment over the end of his romance with Stephanie.

From 1969 onward, Meg was a welcome visitor at both the Bundys' Tacoma home and at the A-frame cabin they'd built at Crescent Lake near Gig Harbor, Washington. Meg, Ted, and Liane often went camping, rafting, sailing, and took more trips to Utah and to Ellensburg, Washington to visit Ted's highschool friend, Jim Paulus.

Everyone they visited found Meg gentle and bright, devoted to Ted, and it seemed only a matter of time until they married.

4

The Seattle Crisis Clinic's offices were housed in 1971 in a huge old Victorian mansion on Capitol Hill. Once the area where Seattle's richest pioneering fathers settled, Capitol Hill today has the second highest crime rate in the city. Many of these old houses remain, scattered willy-nilly among apartment houses and Seattle's main hospital district. When I signed on as a volunteer at the Crisis Clinic, I felt some trepidation about working a night shift, but with four children at home that was the only time I had free.

Ted Bundy became a paid work-study student at about the time I became a volunteer. While I worked a four-hour shift one night a week from 10 P.M. to 2 A.M., Ted worked from 9 P.M. to 9 A.M. several nights a week. There were fifty-one volunteers and a dozen work-study students manning the crisis lines around the clock. Most of us never met because of the staggered schedules, and the circumstances that made Ted and me partners were purely coincidental. I have pondered on that coincidence in the years since, wondered why I should have been the one out of fifty-one to spend so much time with Ted Bundy.

None of those on the phone were professional psychiatric social workers, but we were people who were empathetic and who sincerely tried to help the clients who called in in crisis. All of the volunteers and work-study students had to pass muster first during interviews with Bob Vaughn, the protestant minister who directed the Crisis Clinic and Bruce Cummins who had a Masters in psychiatric social work. Through the three-hour intake interviews, we had "proved" that we were essentially normal, concerned, and capable people who were not likely to panic in emergencies. It was a favorite joke among the crew that dealing with other peoples' problems.

After going through a forty-hour course which featured psychodramas with would-be volunteers answering staged calls which represented the more common problems we might expect, we were trained by experienced volunteers in the phone rooms themselves—allowed to listen in on calls through auxilliary receivers. Ted and I were trained by Dr. John Eshelman, a brilliant and kind man who is now head of the economics department at Seattle University.

I remember the first night I met Ted. John gestured toward a young man sitting at a desk in the phone room which adjoined ours with only an arch separating us, "This is Ted Bundy. He'll be working with you."

He looked up and grinned. He was twenty-four then, but he seemed younger. Unlike most of the other male college students of that era who wore long hair and often beards, Ted was clean-shaven and his wavy brown hair was cut above the ears, exactly the style that the male students had worn when I had attended the University fifteen years before. He wore a tee shirt, jeans, and sneakers, and his desk was piled with textbooks.

I liked him immediately. It would have been hard not to. He brought me a cup of coffee and waved his arm over the awesome banks of phone lines, "You think we can handle all this? John's going to turn us loose alone after tonight."

"I hope so," I answered. And I did devoutly hope so. Suicides-in-progress seemed to make up only about ten percent of the calls coming in, but the range of crises was formidable. Would I say the right thing? Do the right thing?

As it turned out, we made a good team. Working side by side in the cluttered two rooms on the top floor of the building, we seemed to be able to communicate in emergencies without even having to speak. If one of us got a caller on the line who was actually threatening suicide, we would signal the other to call the phone company and put a trace on the line.

The wait always seemed endless. In 1971 it took almost an hour to get a trace and an address if we had no hint about the area of town from which the call was coming. The one of us who was on the line with the would-be suicide would attempt to maintain a calm, caring tone while the other raced around the offices making calls to get help to the caller.

We had callers who became unconscious from overdoses many times, but we always managed to keep the lines open. Then there would be the welcome sound of Medic I crews breaking in, sounds of their voices in the room with the caller, and finally, the phone would be picked up and we would hear "It's O.K. We've got him; we're on the way to Harbor-view."

If, as many people believe today, Ted Bundy took lives, he also saved lives. I know he did, because I was there when he did it.

I can picture him today as clearly as if it were only yesterday, see him hunched over the phone, talking steadily, reassuringly—see him look up at me, shrug, and grin. I can hear him agreeing with an elderly woman that it must have been beautiful indeed when Seattle was lit only by gas lights, hear the infinite patience and caring in his voice, see him sigh and roll his eyes while he listened to a penitent alcoholic. He was never brusque, never hurried.

Ted's voice was a strange mixture of a slightly western drawl and the precise clipped phraseology of an English accent. I might describe it as courtly.

Shut off from the night outside—with doors locked to protect us from the occasional irrational caller who tried to break in—there was an insular feel to those two offices where we worked. The two of us were all alone in the building, connected to the outside world only by the phone lines. Beyond the walls, we could hear sirens screaming as police units and Medic I rigs raced up Pine Street a block away toward the county hospital. With the blackness outside our windows broken only by the lights in the harbor far below us, the sound of rain and sleet against the panes, those sirens seemed to be the only thing reminding us that there was a world of people out there. We were locked in a boiler room of other people's crises.

I don't know why we became such close friends so rapidly. Perhaps it was because we dealt with so many life-and-death situations together, making our Tuesday nights intense situations that bound us together the way soldiers in battle often are. Perhaps it was the isolation, and the fact that we were constantly talking to other people about their most intimate problems.

And so, when the quiet nights came, the nights when the moon was no longer full, when the welfare money had run out with no money left to buy liquor, and when the street people and the callers seemed to be enjoying a spate of serenity, Ted and I talked for hours to each other.

On the surface, at least, it seemed that I had more problems than Ted did. He was one of those rare people who listen with full attention, who evince a genuine caring by their very stance. You could tell things to Ted that you might never tell anyone else.

Most of the Crisis Clinic volunteers gave our time because we had endured crises ourselves, tragedies that made us more able to understand those who called in. I was not an exception. I had lost my only brother to suicide when he was twenty-one, a Stanford senior about to enter Harvard Medical School. I had tried vainly to convince him that life was worthwhile and precious, and I had failed because I'd been too close to him and had felt his pain too acutely. If I could save someone else, I think I felt that it might help me to expiate some of the guilt I still carried.

Ted listened quietly as I told him about my brother, of the long night's wait while sheriffs deputies looked for Don, finally finding him too late in a deserted park north of Palo Alto, dead of carbon monoxide poisoning.

In 1971 my life was not without problems. My marriage was in deep trouble, and I was again trying to cope with guilt. Bill and I had agreed to a divorce only weeks before he'd been diagnosed as having malignant melanoma, the deadliest of skin cancers.

"What can I do?" I asked Ted. "How can I leave a man who may be dying?"

"Are you sure he's dying?" Ted responded.

"No. The first surgery seems to have caught all the malignancy, and the skin grafts have finally held. He wants to end the marriage. He says he wants to, but I feel as if I'm really running away from a sick man who needs me."

"But it's his choice, isn't it? If he seems well, and if your being together is an unhappy situation for both of you, then you have no guilt. He's made the decision. It's his life, and, especially when he might not have that many years ahead, it's his right to decide how he wants to spend them."

"Are you talking to me as if I were a crisis caller?" I smiled.

"Maybe. Probably. But my feelings would be the same. You both deserve to get on with your lives."

Ted's advice proved to be the right advice. Within a year, I would be divorced, and Bill would remarry, would have four good years doing what he wanted.

What was happening in my life in 1971 is unimportant to the story of Ted Bundy, save for the fact that Ted's incisive viewpoint on my problems, his unfailing support and belief in my capabilities as a writer who could earn a living on her own, demonstrate the kind of man I knew. It was that man I would continue to believe in for many years.

Because I had opened up my life to him, Ted seemed to feel at ease in talking about the vulnerable areas in his world, although it was not until many weeks after I met him that he did so.

One night, he moved his chair through the alcove that separated our desks and sat beside me. Behind him one of the posters that were plastered over most of the walls in our offices was in my direct line of vision. It was a picture of a howling kitten clinging to a thick rope, and it read, "When you get to the end of your rope . . . tie a knot and hang on."

Ted sat there silently for a moment or two as we sipped coffee companionably. Then he looked down at his hands and said, "You know, I only found out who I really am a year or so ago. I mean, I always knew, but I had to prove it to myself."

I looked at him, a little surprised, and waited for the rest of the story.

"I'm illegitimate. When I was born, my mother couldn't say that I was her baby. I was born in a home for unwed mothers and, when she took me home, she and my grandparents decided to tell everyone that I was her brother, and that they were my parents. So I grew up believing that she was my sister, that I was a 'late baby' born to my grandparents."

He paused, and looked at the sheets of rain that washed over the windows in front of us. I didn't say anything; I could tell he had more to say.

"I knew. Don't tell me how I knew. Maybe I heard conversations. Maybe I just figured out that there couldn't be twenty years' difference in age between a brother and a sister, and Louise always took care of me. I just grew up knowing that she was really my mother."

"Did you ever say anything?"

He shook his head. "No. It would have hurt them. It just wasn't something you talked about. When I was little, we moved away—Louise and I—and left my grandparents behind. If they were my mother and father, we wouldn't have done that. I went back east in 1969. I needed to prove it to myself, to know for sure. I traced my birth to Vermont, and I went to the city hall, and I looked at the records. It wasn't difficult; I just asked for my birth certificate under my mother's name—and there it was."

"How did you feel? Were you shocked, or upset?"

"No. I think I felt better. It wasn't a surprise at all. It was like I had to know the truth before I could do anything else. And when I saw it there on the birth certificate, then I'd done that. I wasn't a kid. I was twenty-two when I found out for certain."

"They lied to you. Did it seem like they'd deceived you?"

"No. I don't know."

"People lie out of love too, you know," I said. "Your mother could have let you go—but she didn't. She did the best she could. It must have seemed the only thing she could do to keep you with her. She must have loved you very much."

He nodded, and said softly, "I know . . . I know."

"And look at you now. You turned out pretty good. In fact, you turned out great."

He looked up and smiled. "I hope so."

"I know so."

We never talked about it again. It was funny. In 1946, when Ted's mother had found out she was pregnant in Philadelphia, I had been a high school student thirty miles away in Coatesville. I remember that when the girl who sat next to me in physics class became pregnant, it was the talk of the school. That's the way things were in 1946. Could Ted understand that in 1971? Could he even fathom what his mother had gone through to keep him?

He certainly seemed to have made the most of his considerable assets. He was brilliant, and making almost straight A's in psychology in his senior year, even though most of his studying had to be done between calls during his all-night shifts at at the Crisis Clinic. I had never brought up any facet of psychology that Ted wasn't fully conversant with. During that autumn quarter of 1971, Ted was taking ecological biology, adaptation of man, laboratory of human performance, and an honors seminar.

He was handsome, although the years of adversity ahead would somehow see him become even handsomer, as if his features were being honed to a fine edge.

And Ted was physically strong, much stronger than I had thought when I saw him for the first time. He had seemed slender, almost frail, and I had made it a habit to bring cookies and sandwiches to share with him each Tuesday night; I thought he might not be getting enough to eat. I was surprised one warm night when he'd bicycled to the clinic wearing cut-off blue jeans. His legs were as thickly muscled and powerful as a professional athlete's. He *was* slender, but he was whipcord tough.

As far as his appeal for women, I can remember thinking that, if I were younger and single—or if my daughters were older—this would be almost the perfect man.

Ted talked quite a bit about Meg and Liane; I assumed that he was living with Meg, although he never actually said he was.

"She's really interested in your work," he said one night. "Could you bring in some of your detective magazines so I can take them home to her?"

I did bring in several, and he took them with him. He never commented on them, and I assumed that he hadn't read them.

We were talking one night about his plans to go to law school. It was almost spring then, and, for the first time, he told me about Stephanie.

"I love Meg, and she really loves me," he began. "She's helped me with money for school. I owe her a lot. I don't want to hurt her, but there's somebody else I can't stop thinking about."

Again, he had surprised me. He'd never mentioned anyone but Meg.

"Her name is Stephanie, and I haven't seen her for a long time. She's living near San Francisco, and she's completely beautiful. She's tall, almost as tall as I am, and her parents are wealthy. She's never known anything but being rich. I just couldn't fit in with that world."

"Are you in touch with her at all?" I asked.

"Once in a while. We talk on the phone. Every time I hear her voice, it all comes back. I can't settle for anything else unless I try one more time. I'm going to apply for law school anyplace I can get in around San Francisco. I think the problem now is that we're just too far apart. If we were both in California, I think we could get back together."

I asked him how long it had been since he'd gone with Stephanie, and he said they'd broken up in 1968, but that Stephanie was still single.

"Do you think she might love me again if I sent her a dozen red roses?"

It was such a naive question that I looked up to see if he was serious. He was. When he talked about Stephanie in the spring of 1972, it was as if the intervening years hadn't happened at all.

"I don't know, Ted." I ventured. "If she feels the same way you do, the roses might help—but they wouldn't make her love you if she's changed."

"She's the one woman, the only woman I ever really loved. It's different from the way I feel about Meg. It's hard to explain. I don't know what to do."

Seeing the glow in his eyes when he talked about Stephanie, I could envision the heartbreak ahead for Meg. I urged him not to make promises to Meg he couldn't keep.

"At some point, you're going to have to choose. Meg loves you. She's stood by you when the going is rough, when you don't have any money. Yon say that Stephanie's family makes you feel poor, as if you don't fit in. It might be that Meg's real, and Stephanie's a dream. I guess the real test is—how would you feel if you didn't have Meg? What would you do if you knew she had someone else, if you found her with another man?"

"I did once. It's funny you should bring it up, because it just made me wild. We'd had a fight, and I saw some guy's car parked outside her apartment. I raced around the alley and stood up on a garbage can to look in the window. The sweat was just pouring off me and I was like a crazy man. I couldn't stand to think of Meg with another man. I couldn't believe the effect it had one me . . ."

He shook his head, bemused by the violence of his jealousy.

"Then maybe you care more about Meg than you realize."

"That's the problem. One day I think I want to stay here, marry Meg, help bring Liane up, have more children—that's what Meg wants. Sometimes it seems like that's all I want. But I don't have any money. I won't have any money for a long time. And I can't see myself being tied down to a life like that just when I'm getting started. And then I think about Stephanie, and the life I could have with her. I want that too. I've never been rich, and I want to be. But how can I say 'thanks a lot and goodbye' to Meg?"

The phones rang then, and we left the problem in midair. Ted's turmoil didn't seem that bizarre or desperate for a man of twenty-four; in fact, it seemed quite normal. He had some maturing to do. When he did, I thought he would probably make the right decision.

When I arrived for work a few Tuesdays later, Ted told me he had applied for admittance to law school at Stanford and at the University of California at Berkeley.

Ted seemed to be a prime candidate for law school; he had the incisive mind for it, the tenacity, and he believed totally in the orderly progression of changes in the system of government through legislation. His stance made him something of a loner among the work-study students working at the Crisis Clinic. They were semihippies, both in their garb and their political views, and he was a conservative Republican.

I could see that they considered him a rather odd duck as they argued about the riots that were constantly erupting on the University campus.

"You're wrong, man," a bearded student told him. "You aren't going to change Vietnam by sucking up to the old fogies in Congress. All they care about is another big contract for Boeing. You think they give a shit about how many of us get killed?"

"Anarchy isn't going to solve anything. You just end up scattering your forces and getting your head broken," Ted responded.

They snorted in derision. He was anathema to them.

The student riots, and the marches blocking the I-5 Freeway enraged Ted. On more than one occasion, he had tried to block the demonstrations, waving a club and telling the rioters to go home. He believed there was a better way to do it, but his own anger was, strangely, as intense as those he tried to stop.

I never saw that anger. I never saw any anger at all. I cannot remember everything that Ted and I talked about, try as I might, but I do know we never argued. Ted's treatment of me was the kind of old-world gallantry that he invariably showed toward any woman I ever saw him with, and I found it appealing. He always insisted on seeing me safely to my car when my shift at the Crisis Clinic was over in the wee hours of the morning. He stood by until I was safely inside my car, doors locked and engine started, waving to me as I headed for home twenty miles away. He often told me, "Be careful. I don't want anything to happen to you."

Compared to my old friends, the Seattle homicide detectives, who routinely saw me leave their offices after a night's interviewing, at midnight in downtown Seattle with a laughing, "We'll watch out the window and if anyone mugs you, we'll call 911," Ted was a like a knight in shining armor!

5

I had to drop my volunteer work at the Crisis Clinic in the spring of 1972. I was writing six days a week, and, beyond that, I was getting stale—a little jaded on the phones. After a year and a half, I had heard the same problems too many times. I had problems of my own. My husband had moved out, we had filed for divorce, and I had two teenagers and two preteens at home who provided their own crises for me to cope with. Ted graduated from the University in June. We had never seen each other outside the Crisis Clinic, and now we kept in touch with infrequent phone calls. I didn't see him again until December.

My divorce was final on December 14th. On December 16th all current and former clinic personnel were invited to a Christmas party at Bruce Cummins's home on Lake Washington. I had a car—but no escort—and I knew Ted didn't have a car, so I called and asked him if he would like to attend the party with me. He seemed pleased, and I picked him up at the Rogers's rooming house on 12th N.E. Freda Rogers smiled at me and called up the stairs to Ted.

On the long drive from the University District to the south end, we talked about what had happened in the intervening months since we'd seen each other. Ted had spent the summer working as an intern in psychiatric counseling at Harbor-view, the huge county hospital complex. As a policewoman in the 1950s, I had taken a number of mentally deranged subjects—220s in police lingo—to the fifth floor of Harborview and knew the facilities there well. But Ted talked little about his summer job. He was far more enthusiastic about his activities during the governor's campaign in the fall of 1972.

He had been hired by the Committee to Re-Elect Dan Evans, Washington's Republican Governor. Former Governor Albert

Rosellini had made a comeback try, and it had been Ted's assignment to travel around the state and monitor Rosellini's speeches, taping them for analysis by Evans's team.

"I just mingled with the crowds and nobody knew who I was," he explained.

He'd enjoyed the masquerade, sometimes wearing a false moustache, sometimes looking like the college student he'd been only a short time before, and he'd been amused at the way Rosellini modified his speeches easily for the wheat farmers of eastern Washington and the apple growers of Wenatchee. Rosellini was a consummate politician, the opposite of the up-front, All-American Evans.

All this was heady stuff for Ted, to be on the inside of a statewide campaign, to report to Governor Evans himself and his top aides with the tapes of Rosellini's speeches.

On September 2nd, Ted—driving Governor Evans and other dignitaries in the lead limousine—had been the first man to traverse the North Cascades Highway that winds through spectacular scenery at the northern boundaries of Washington State.

"They thought that President Nixon was going to show up," Ted recalled. "And they had secret service men checking everybody out. His brother came instead, but I didn't care. I got to lead 15,000 people in a sixty-four-mile parade across the mountains."

The Evans campaign for re-election had been successful, and now Ted was in good standing with the administration in power. At the time of the Christmas party, he was employed by the City of Seattle's Crime Prevention Advisory Commission and was reviewing the state's new hitchhiking law, a law which made thumbing a ride legal again.

"Put me down as being absolutely against hitchhiking," I said. "I've written too many stories about female homicide victims who met their killers while they were hitchhiking."

Although Ted still looked forward to law school, he had his sights on the position as director of the Crime Prevention Advisory Commission, was among the final candidates, and felt optimistic about getting the job.

We went our separate ways at the party; I danced with Ted once or twice and noticed that he seemed to be having a good time, talking with several women. He seemed to be completely entranced with a young woman who belonged to Seattle's Junior League, a Crisis Clinic volunteer whom neither of us had happened to meet before. Since some shifts never coincided, it wasn't unusual that volunteers' paths didn't cross. The woman was married to a young lawyer with a "future," a man who is now one of Seattle's most successful attorneys.

Ted didn't talk to her; in fact, he seemed in awe of her, but he pointed her out to me and asked about her. She was a beautiful woman with long dark hair, straight and parted in the middle, and dressed in a way that spoke of money and taste. She wore a black, long-sleeved blouse, a straight white silk evening skirt, solid gold chains, and earrings.

I doubt that she was even aware of Ted's fascination with her, but I caught him staring at her several times during the evening. With the others at the party, he was expansive, relaxed, and usually the center of conversation.

Since I was the driver, Ted drank a good deal during the evening, and he was quite intoxicated when we left at 2:00 A.M. He was a friendly, relaxed drunk, and he settled into the passenger seat and rambled on and on about the woman at the party who had impressed him so much.

"She's just what I've always wanted. She's perfect—but she didn't even notice me . . ."

And then he fell sound asleep.

When I delivered Ted back to the Rogers's that night, he was almost comatose, and it took me ten minutes of shaking him and shouting to wake him up. I walked him to the door and said goodnight, smiling as he bumbled in the door and disappeared.

A week later, I received a Christmas card from Ted. The block print read, "O. Henry wrote the 'Gift of the Magi,' a story of two lovers who sacrificed for each other their greatest treasures. She cut her long hair to buy her lover a watch chain. He sold his watch to buy her combs for her hair. In acts that might seem foolish these two people found the spirit of the Magi."

It was my favorite Christmas story. How had he known?

Inside, Ted printed his own wishes: "The New Year should be a good one for a talented, delightful, newly liberated woman. Thank you for the party. Love, ted."

I was touched by the gesture. It was typical of Ted Bundy; he knew I needed the emotional support of those sentiments.

Seemingly, there wasn't a thing in the world I could do for him. He wasn't interested in me romantically, I was just about as poor as he was, hardly influential. He sent that card simply because we were friends.

When I look at that card today and compare it with the signatures on the dozens of letters I would receive later, I am struck with the difference. Never again would he sign with the jaunty flourish he did then.

Ted didn't get the job as director of the Crime Prevention Advisory Commission and he resigned in January, 1973. I saw him again on a rainy day in March. An old friend whom I'd known since my days on the police department, Joyce Johnson—a detective for eleven years in the Sex Crimes Unit—and I emerged from the police-jail elevator in the Public Safety Building on our way to lunch, and there was Ted. Bearded now, he looked so different that I didn't recognize him at first. He called my name and grabbed my hand. I introduced him to Joyce, and he told me enthusiastically that he was working for King County Law and Justice Planning Office.

"I'm doing a study on rape victims," he explained. "If you could get me some back copies of the stories you've done on rape cases, it would help my research."

I promised to go through my files and cull some of the accounts—many of them written about cases in which Joyce Johnson had been the principal detective—and get them to him. But, somehow, I never got around to it, and I eventually forgot that he'd wanted them.

Ted had applied, for the second time, to the University of Utah's Law School, largely at Meg's urging. Her father was a wealthy physician, her siblings professionals in Utah, and she hoped that she and Ted would eventually end up in the Mormon state.

He was quickly accepted, although he had been rejected in a previous application to the University of Utah in 1972, despite his degree from the University of Washington "With Distinction." Ted's gradepoint average from the University was 3.51, a GPA that any student might have aspired to, but his legal aptitude test scores had not been high enough to meet Utah's standards for entry.

In 1973, he bombarded the admissions department at Utah with letters of recommendation from professors and from Governor Dan Evans. Not content with the restrictions of a standard application form, he had résumés printed up listing his accomplishments since graduation from the University of Washington, and wrote a six-page personal statement on his philosophies on law.

It made an impressive packet.

Under postgraduate employment Ted listed:

Criminal Corrections Consultant: January, 1973. Currently retained by the King County Office of Law and Justice Planning to identify recidivism rates for offenders who have been found guilty of misdemeanors and gross misdemeanors in the twelve county District Courts. The purpose of the study is to determine the nature and number of offenses committed subsequent to a conviction in District Court.

Crime Commission Assistant Director: October, 1972 to January, 1973. As assistant to the Director of the Seattle Crime Prevention Commission, suggested and did the preliminary investigation for the Commission's investigations into assaults against women, and "white collar" (economic) crime. Wrote press releases, speeches, and newspaper articles for the Commission. Participated extensively in the planning of the Commission's activities for 1973.

Psychiatric Counselor: June, 1972 to September, 1972. Carried a full case-load of twelve clients during a four-month internship in Harborview Hospital's Outpatient Clinic. Held periodic sessions with clients; entered progress reports in hospital charts, continually re-evaluated psychiatric diagnoses, and referred clients to physicians for medical and psychotherapeutic medication evaluations. Participated in numerous training sessions conducted by staff psychiatrists.

Ted went on:

I apply to law school because my professional and community activities demand daily a knowledge of the law I do not have. Whether I am studying the behavior of criminal offenders, examining bills before the legislature, advocating court reform, or contemplating the creation of my own corporation, I immediately become conscious of my limited understanding of the law. My life style requires that I obtain a knowledge of the law and the ability to practice legal skills. I intend to be my own man. It's that simple.

I could go on at great length to explain that the practice of law is a life-long goal, or that I do not have great expectations that a law degree is a guaranty of wealth and prestige. The important factor, however, is that law fulfills a functional need which my daily routine has forced me to recognize.

I apply to law school because this institution will give me the tools to become a more effective actor in the social role I have defined for myself,

T.R.B.

Ted's personal statement was most erudite and filled with quotes from experts ranging from Freud to the President's Committee on Law Enforcement, and the Administration of Justice Report. He began with a discussion of violence: "You begin with the relation between might and right, and this is the assuredly proper starting point for our inquiry. But for the term 'might,' I would substitute a tougher and more telling word: 'violence.' In right and violence, we have today an obvious antimony."

He had not softened his position against riots, student insurrections, and anarchy. The law was right; the rest was violence.

Ted stated his current involvement in a series of studies of jury trials. "Using computer-coded data collected on 11,000 felony cases by the Washington State Criminal Justice Evaluation Project, I am writing programs designed to isolate what I hope to be tentative answers . . . to questions regarding the management of felony cases."

He talked of a study he had undertaken to equate the racial composition of a jury with its effect on the defendant.

Ted's thoroughly impressive application to the University of Utah Law School in early 1973 worked, and over-shadowed his mediocre Law School Aptitude Test scores. But, oddly, he chose not to enter their law school in the fall of 1973, and the reason given to the Dean of Admissions was a curious lie.

He wrote "with sincere regret" a week before classes were to begin, that he had been injured severely in an automobile accident and was hospitalized. He explained that he had hoped that he would be physically strong enough to attend the fall quarter, but found he was not able to, apologizing for waiting so long to let the University know and saying he hoped that they could find someone to fill his place.

In truth, Ted had been in an extremely minor accident, spraining his ankle, had not been hospitalized, and was in perfect condition. He had, however, wrecked Meg's car. Why he chose not to go to Utah in 1973 remains a mystery.

There were discrepancies too in his almost flamboyant dossier. Both the study on rape that he told me he was writing and the racial significance in jury composition study were only ideas; he had not actively begun work on either.

Ted did begin law school in the fall of 1973—at the University of Puget Sound in his home town, Tacoma. He attended night classes on Mondays, Wednesdays and Fridays, riding from the Rogers's rooming house to U.P.S., twenty-six miles south, in a car pool with three other students. After the night classes, he often stopped for a few beers with his car pool members at the Creekwater Tavern.

Ted may have elected to remain in Washington because he had been awarded a plum political job in April, 1973—as assistant to Ross Davis, chairman of the Washington State Republican Party. His $1,000 a month salary was more money than he'd ever made. The "perks" that came with the job were something that a man who had struggled for money and recognition most of his life could revel in: the use of a Select Credit Card issued to the Republican Party, attendance at meetings with the "big boys," and occasional use of a flashy car. There was statewide travel, with all expenses paid.

Davis and his wife thought highly of Ted. He ate dinner with their family at least once a week, and often babysat for their children. Davis recalls Ted as "smart, aggressive,—exceptionally so, and a believer in the system."

Despite his work for the Republican Party, Ted managed to keep up a good gradepoint average in his night law classes at U.P.S. He continued to live at Freda and Ernst Rogers's home in the University

District in Seattle. Ernst's health was no better, and, when he had free time, Ted helped to keep the house in repair.

There had been great upheavals in Ted's life during 1973, but I had seen him only once during that year—the brief meeting in the Public Safety Building in March. It was that kind of friendship where you touch base with someone rarely, you are pleased to see each other, and they are, at least on the surface, the same people you have always known.

I saw Ted again in December of 1973—again at a Crisis Clinic Christmas party. It was held at a board member's house in the Laurelhurst section in Seattle's north end, and, this time, Ted brought Meg Anders with him, and I met her for the first time.

In one of those crystalline flashes that float to the surface of memory, I can recall standing in the host's kitchen, talking to Ted and Meg. Someone had placed a giant bowl of fried chicken wings on the counter, and Ted munched on them as we talked.

Ted had never described Meg to me. I had heard his detailed recollection of Stephanie Brooks's beauty, and I had seen his reaction to the tall, dark-haired woman at last year's party. Meg was nothing like either of them. She seemed very small, very vulnerable, and her long light brown hair over-powered her facial features. Clearly, she adored Ted, and she clung to him, too shy to mingle.

I commented that Ted and I had attended the last Crisis Clinic Christmas party together, and her face lit up.

"*Really*? It was you?"

I nodded. "I didn't have a date, and Ted didn't have a car, so we decided to pool our resources."

Meg seemed vastly relieved. I was clearly no threat to her, a nice, middle-aged lady with a bunch of kids. I wondered then why he had let her agonize over it for a whole year when he could easily have explained our friendship to her.

I spent most of that evening talking with Meg because she seemed so intimidated by the mass of strangers milling around us. She was very intelligent and very nice. But her focus of attention was Ted. When he wandered off into the crowd, her eyes followed him; she was trying very hard to be casual, but for her there was no one else there at all.

I could understand her feelings only too well. Three months before, I had fallen in love with a man who wasn't free, would never be free, and I could empathize with Meg's insecurity. Still, Ted had been with her for four years, and he seemed devoted to her and to Liane. There seemed a good possibility that they might marry one day.

Seeing Meg and Ted together, I assumed that he had given up his fantasy about Stephanie. I could not have been more wrong. Neither Meg nor I knew that Ted had just spent several days with Stephanie Brooks, that he was, in fact, *engaged* to Stephanie, and that he was looking forward to seeing her again within a week.

Ted's life was so carefully compartmentalized that he was able to be one person with one woman, and an entirely different man with another. He moved in many circles, and most of his friends and associates knew nothing of the other areas in his life.

When I said goodbye to Ted and Meg in December, 1973, I truly didn't expect to see him again; our bond had been through the Crisis Clinic and we were both moving away from that group. I had no way of knowing that Ted Bundy would one day change *my* life profoundly.

It would be almost two years before I heard from Ted again, and, when I did, it would be under circumstances that would shock me more than anything ever has—or possibly ever will again.

6

Most of us have harbored a fantasy wherein we return to confront a lost first love, and, in that reunion, we have become better looking, thinner, richer, utterly desirable—so desirable that our lost love realizes instantly that he has made a terrible mistake. It seldom occurs in real life, but it is a fantasy that helps to relieve the pain of rejection. Ted had tried once, in 1969, to reach out to Stephanie Brooks, to rekindle a seemingly extinguished flame, and it hadn't worked.

But, by the late summer of 1973, Ted Bundy had begun to be somebody. He had worked, planned, groomed himself to be the kind of man that he thought Stephanie wanted. Although his relationship with Meg Anders had been a steady and, to Meg, a committed one for four years, Ted had had no one but Stephanie on his mind when he arrived in Sacramento on a business trip for the Washington Republican Party. He contacted Stephanie in San Francisco and she was amazed at the changes four years had wrought in him. Where he had been a boy, uncertain and wavering, with no foreseeable prospects, he was now urbane, smooth, and confident. He was nearing twenty-seven, and he seemed to have become an imposing figure in political circles in Washington State.

When they went out to dinner, she marveled at his new maturity, the deft manner with which he dealt with the waiter. It was a memorable evening and when it was over, Stephanie agreed readily to make a trip soon to Seattle to visit him, to talk about what the future might hold for them. He did not mention Meg; he seemed as free to make a commitment as Stephanie was.

Stephanie had flown to Seattle during her vacation in September, and Ted met her at the airport, driving Ross Davis's car, and whisked her to the University Towers Hotel. He took her to dinner at the Davis's home. The Davises seemed to approve heartily of her, and she didn't demur when Ted introduced her as his fiancée.

Ted had arranged for a weekend in a condominium at Alpental on Snoqualmie Pass, and, still using Davis's car, he drove them up to the Cascade Pass, up through the same mountain foothills they'd traversed when they'd gone on skiing trips in their college days. Looking at the luxurious accommodations, she wondered how he had paid for it, but he explained that the condo belonged to a friend of a friend.

It was an idyllic time. Ted was talking marriage seriously, and Stephanie was listening. She had fallen in love with him, a love that was much stronger than the feeling she'd had for him in their college romance. She was confident that they would be married within the year. She would work to pay his way through law school.

Back at the Davises' home, Stephanie and Ted posed for a picture together, smiling, their arms around each other. And then Mrs. Davis drove her to the airport for the flight to San Francisco as Ted had an important political meeting to attend.

Stephanie flew back to Seattle in December, 1973, and spent a few days with Ted in the apartment of a lawyer friend of his who was in Hawaii. Then she went further north to Vancouver, B.C. to spend Christmas with friends. She was very happy. They would be together again for several days after Christmas and she was sure they could firm up their wedding plans then.

Ted, then, even as he introduced me to Meg at that Christmas party in 1973 had apparently been marking time until Stephanie returned.

During those last days of 1973, Ted wined and dined Stephanie royally. He took her to Tai Tung's, the Chinese restaurant in the international district where they had eaten during their first courtship. He also took her to Ruby Chow's, a posh oriental restaurant, run by a Seattle city council-woman, telling her that Ruby was a good friend of his.

But something had changed. Ted was evasive about marriage plans. He told her that he'd become involved with another woman—a woman who had had an abortion because of him. "That's over. But she calls every so often, and I just don't think it's going to work out for us."

Stephanie was stunned. Ted told her he was trying to "get loose" of this other girl—a girl whose name he never mentioned—but that things were just too complicated. Where he had been so loving and affectionate, he now seemed cold and distant. They had such a little time to spend together, and yet he left her alone for an entire day while he worked on a "project" at school that she felt sure could have waited. He didn't buy her anything at all for Christmas, although he showed her an expensive chess set that he'd bought for his lawyer friend. She had brought him an expensive Indian print sad a bow tie, but he showed little enthusiasm for her gifts.

His lovemaking, which had been ardent, had became perfunctory, what she termed a "Mr. Cool" performance, rather than a spontaneous show of passion. In fact, she felt he was no longer attracted to her at all.

Stephanie wanted to talk about it, to talk about their plans, but Ted's conversation was a bitter diatribe about his family. He talked about his illegitimacy, stressing over and over that Johnnie Bundy wasn't his father, wasn't very bright, and didn't make much money. He seemed angry at his mother because she had never talked to him about his real father. He was scornful of what he called the "lack of I.Q." of the whole Bundy clan. The only member of the extended family that he seemed to care about was his grandfather Cowell, but the old man was dead, leaving Ted with no one.

Something had happened to change Ted's whole attitude toward her, and Stephanie was a very confused and upset woman when she flew back to California on January 2, 1974. Ted had not even made love to her on their last night together. He had chased after her for six years. Now, he seemed uninterested, almost hostile. She had thought they were engaged, and yet he had acted as if he could hardly wait to be rid of her.

Back in California she waited for a call or a letter from him, something that might explain his radical change of heart. But there was nothing. Finally, she went to a counselor to try to sort out her own feelings.

"I don't think he loves me. It seems as though he just stopped loving me."

The counselor suggested that she write to Ted, and she did, saying that she had questions that had to be answered. Ted didn't answer that letter.

In mid-February, Stephanie called Ted. She was angry and hurt, and she started to yell at him for dropping her without so much as an explanation. His voice was flat, calm, as he said, "Stephanie, I have no idea what you mean . . ."

Stephanie heard the phone click and the line went dead. At length, she concluded that Ted's high-power courtship in the latter part of 1973 had been deliberately planned, that he had waited all those years to be in a position where he could make her fall in love with him, just so that he could drop her, reject her, as she had rejected him. In September, 1974, she wrote to a friend, "I don't know what happened. He changed so completely. I escaped by the skin of my teeth. When I think of his cold and calculating manner, I shudder."

She was never to have an explanation. She never heard from him again and she married someone else at Christmas, 1974.

7

During December 1973 I had participated in a different kind of writing project. I carried many deputy sheriff commissions in my wallet; they had been given to me by various counties around Washington State as a P.R. gesture, and made me more of a "Kentucky Colonel" than a bonafide law officer. I'll admit I got a kick out of having the badges, but I didn't do any real law enforcement work. Then on Thursday, December 13th, I had been asked to help with an investigation in Thurston County sixty miles south of Seattle.

Sheriff Don Redmond called and asked if I would attend a briefing on a homicide case his county was investigating. "What we want to do, Ann," he explained, "is fill you in on where we are with the Devine case, get your impressions. Then we need a comprehensive narrative of everything we've got so far. It may be rushing you, but we'd like about thirty pages covering the case that we can hand to prosecuting attorney on Monday morning. Could you do that?"

I drove to Olympia the next day and met with Sheriff Redmond, Chief Criminal Deputy Dwight Caron, and Detective Sergeant Paul Barclift. We spent the day going over follow-up reports, looking at slides, and reading the medical examiner's autopsy reports in the case involving the murder of fifteen-year-old Katherine Merry Devine.

Kathy Devine had vanished from a street corner in Seattle's north end on November 25th. The pretty teenager—who had looked closer to eighteen than fifteen—had last been seen alive hitchhiking. She had told friends that she was running away to Oregon. They had seen her, in fact, get into a pickup truck with a male driver. She had waved goodbye, and then she had disappeared. She never arrived at her Oregon destination.

On December 6th, a couple, hired to clean up litter in McKenny Park near Olympia, had found Kathy's body. She lay on her face in the sodden forest. She was fully clothed, but her jeans had been slit in the back seam with a sharp instrument from her waist to the crotch. Decomposition was far advanced, due to an unusually warm winter, and ravaging animals had carried away her heart, lungs, and liver.

The pathologist's tentative conclusion was that she had been strangled, perhaps had her throat cut; the primary wounds had been to the neck. The condition of her clothing suggested also that she had been sodomized. She had been dead since shortly after she was last seen.

Sheriff Redmond and his investigators were left with the girl's body, the mock suede coat with fur trim, the blue jeans, a white peasant blouse, waffle stomper boots, and some cheap costume jewelry. The time lapse between her disappearance and the discovery of her body made it next to impossible to get a handle on the man who had killed her.

"It's that damned new hitchhiking law," Redmond said. "Kids can stick their thumbs out and get in a car with anybody."

There was so little to go on, but I took copious notes and spent the weekend putting the Devine case in chronological order, listing what was known and concluding that Kathy Devine had probably been killed by the man who gave her the ride. It seemed an isolated case; I had not written up any similar homicides in several years.

I spent that whole weekend—with the exception of Saturday night when I attended the Crisis Clinic party—working on my thirty-page report for Redmond. On Sunday evening, two deputies were sent up from Olympia to pick it up. As a special deputy on assignment, I was paid $100 from the department's investigative funds. I didn't forget the Devine case; a few months later, I wrote it up as an unsolved case for *True Detective*, asking that anyone with information contact the Thurston County Sheriff's Office. But no one did, and the case remained unsolved.

With the new year, 1974, I was aware that, if I was going to support four children, I would have to step up my writing sales. Although their father's cancer had seemingly been arrested, I remembered the first surgeon's prognosis that Bill's life expectancy could range anywhere from six months to five years.

Most of my cases came from the Seattle Police and the King County Police homicide units. Those detectives were exceptionally kind to me, allowing me to interview them when crime in Seattle was at a low ebb. Far from being the tough, hard-bitten detectives depicted on television and in fiction, I found them to be highly sensitive men—men who understood that if I didn't find enough cases to write up, my kids might not eat. I formed some of the strongest friendships of my life with those men.

For my part, I never "burned" them, never took anything "off the record" and used it in a story. I waited until trials were ended, or until a defendant had pleaded guilty, careful that my reporting would in no way prejudice a prospective jury before trial.

They trusted me, and I trusted them. Because they knew I was trying to learn everything I could in the field of homicide investigations, I was often invited to attend seminars given by experts in law enforcement and, once, a two-week homicide crime scene course given as part of the King County Police basic police school. I rode shifts with the Washington State Patrol, the K-9 units, Seattle Police and King County patrol units, Medic I paramedics, and spent 250 hours with Marshal 5, the Seattle Fire Department's arson team.

I suppose it was an odd career for a woman, but I enjoyed it thoroughly. Half the time I was an everyday mother; the other half I was learning about homicide investigative techniques and how to spot an arson fire. My grandfather and uncle had been sheriffs in Michigan, and my own years as a policewoman had only enhanced my belief that lawmen were "good guys." Nothing I saw as a crime reporter tarnished that image, even though in the early 1970s policemen were frequently referred to as pigs.

Because in a sense I had become one of them again, I was privy to information on cases being actively worked—as I had been with the Devine homicide. I didn't discuss this information with anyone outside the police world, but I was aware of what was happening in 1974.

The year had barely begun when there was a shocking attack on a young woman who lived in a basement room of a big old house at 4325 8th N.E., near the University of Washington. It happened sometime during the night of January 4th, and it was bizarre enough that

Detective Joyce Johnson mentioned it to me. Johnson, with twenty-two years on the force, dealt with crimes every day that would upset most laymen, but this assault had disturbed her mightily.

Joni Lenz, eighteen, had gone to sleep as usual in her room, a room located in a basement accessible from the outside by a side door that was usually kept locked. When she didn't appear for breakfast the next morning, her housemates assumed she was sleeping in. By midafternoon, however, they went down to check on her. Joni didn't respond to their calls. As they approached her bed, they were horrified to see that her face and hair were covered with clotted blood. She was unconscious. Joni Lenz had been beaten with a metal rod wrenched from the bed frame, and when they pulled the covers away, they were stunned to see that the rod had been jammed viciously into her vagina, doing terrible damage to her internal organs.

"She's still unconscious," Joyce Johnson told me a week later. "It breaks my heart to see her parents sitting by her bed, praying she'll come out of it. Even if she does, the doctors think she'll have permanent brain damage."

Joni did beat the odds. She survived, but she had no memory of events from ten days before the attack until she awoke from her coma, and she was left with brain damage that will stay with her for the rest of her life.

She had not been raped—except for the symbolic rape with the bed rod. Someone in the grip of a maniacal rage had found her asleep and vented that anger. Detectives could find no motive at all; the victim was a friendly, shy girl who had no enemies. She had to have been a chance victim, attacked simply because someone who knew she slept alone in her basement room, had perhaps seen her through a window, found the basement door unlocked.

Joni Lenz was lucky; she lived. She was one of the very few who did.

"Hi, this is Lynda with your Cascade Ski Report: Snoqualmie Pass is 29 degrees with snow and ice patches on the road; Stevens Pass is 17 degrees and overcast with packed snow on the roadway . . ."

Thousands of western Washington radio listeners had heard twenty-one-year-old Lynda Ann Healy's voice without really knowing who she was. It was a sexy-sweet voice, the kind of voice that disc jockeys could talk back to, that commuters driving to work at 7 A.M. could enjoy. The last names of the girls who gave the pass reports were never revealed, no matter how many interested men might call in, however. They were anonymous, the vocal personification of the All-American girl.

Lynda was as beautiful as she sounded, tall, slender, with chestnut hair that fell almost to her waist, clear blue eyes fringed with dark lashes. A senior majoring in psychology at the University of Washington, she shared an older green frame house with four other students. Marti Sands, Jill Hodges, Lorna Moss, and Barbara Little split the rent at 5517 12th N.E.

Lynda had grown up in a sheltered, upper-middle-class home in Newport Hills on the east side of Lake Washington from Seattle. Gifted musically, she had played Fiona in Newport High's production of *Brigadoon*, and she been a soloist in the Congregational Church's "Winds of God" folk mass. But it was psychology—particularly working with retarded youngsters—that interested her most. Certainly, in her years at the University, she had had ample opportunity to study the deviant mind. Study, not know.

None of the five roommates in the big old house was particularly naive, and they were all cautious young women. Jill's father was the prosecuting attorney in an eastern Washington county, and, as a criminal lawyer's daughter, she had been aware of violent crime, but none of the girls had ever been exposed personally to violence. They had read of the attack a few blocks away on January 4th, and they had heard rumors of a prowler in their own neighborhood. They took the proper precautions, locked their doors, went out in pairs after dark, discouraged men who seemed odd.

Still, with five of them living in the same house, they felt safe.

Lynda's job at Northwest Ski Reports meant that she had to get up at 5:30 in the morning, and bike over to the office a few blocks away, so she rarely stayed up past midnight. Thursday, January 31st, began routinely for her. She'd recorded the ski report, gone to classes, and then come home to write a letter. She hadn't a problem in the world—other than the fact that her boyfriend worked such long hours that they had little time together, and some vague stomach pains that had been bothering her. She wrote a note to a friend, the last letter she would ever write:

"Just thought I'd drop a line to say 'Hello.' It's snowing outside so I'm writing this letter bundled up in my blue afghan. You wouldn't believe how comfortable it makes studying, or napping. Everyone at my house is fine. I've invited Mom and Dad, Bob and Laura to dinner. I think I'll make Beef Stroganoff. I've been doing a lot of skiing, some working, and studying . . . not necessarily in that order."

At 2:30 that afternoon, Jill Hodges drove Lynda to the University for chorus practice, and returned at five to pick up Lynda and Lorna Moss. They ate dinner and afterward Lynda borrowed Marti Sands's car to go to the grocery store, returning at 8:30.

Lynda, Lorna, Marti and a male friend then walked to Dante's, a tavern popular with University students, located at Fifty-third and Roosevelt Way. The foursome shared two pitchers of beer, and the girls talked to no one, although Lorna and Marti would later recall that their friend Pete had visited briefly with some people who were playing a dice game at a nearby table.

They were home in an hour and Lynda received a call from a former boyfriend in Olympia. Her roommates remember that she spoke with him for about an hour. The girls then watched "Miss Jane Pittman" on television before retiring.

When Lynda left to go to her basement room, she wore blue jeans, a white blouse, and boots.

Barbara Little had been at the library that Thursday evening, and went to her room in the basement—a room separated from Lynda's by only a thin plywood wall—at a quarter to one. Lynda's light was out, and all was quiet.

At 5:30 A.M., Barbara heard Lynda's alarm radio go off as usual, and she went back to sleep. At 6:00 her own alarm sounded and she was somewhat surprised to hear the insistent buzzing of Lynda's alarm still sounding.

The phone rang—Lynda's employer at the ski report company inquiring why Lynda hadn't arrived at work. Barbara went to Lynda's room and switched on the light; the room was immaculate, the bed perfectly made without a wrinkle. This was a bit unusual as Lynda's habit was to make her bed after she returned from classes, but Barbara wasn't particularly concerned. She turned off the alarm, and assumed that Lynda was already on her way to work.

Lynda Ann Healy was not on her way to work, or to school. She was gone without a struggle, and without a trace.

The green ten-speed bike that Lynda routinely used for transportation was still in the basement, but her roommates noted something alarming. The side door which led into the basement was unlocked. *They never left it unlocked*. Indeed, the door was very difficult—almost impossible—to unlock from the outside, so they always opened it from the inside when they wanted to push their bikes out and then locked it from the inside again, going around the house to reach their bikes. The single window with its transparent curtain next to the concrete interior steps had long since been painted shut.

The girls who lived in the shared home met on campus that afternoon and compared notes. Each assumed that one of the others had seen Lynda at classes during the day, yet none had. When her family arrived that evening for the dinner she'd planned, they were frightened; Lynda was the last person in the world who would fail to show up for work, class, and, most particularly, for a supper where she'd invited her family.

They called the Seattle Police and reported her as a missing person.

Detectives Wayne Dorman and Ted Fonis of the Homicide Unit arrived to talk to Lynda's worried parents and housemates. They were led to her neat room in the basement. It was a happy-looking room, painted a sunny yellow, its walls festooned with posters and photographs—many of Lynda and friends skiing, several of the retarded youngsters from the experimental school, Camelot House, where the missing girl volunteered her time. Lynda's bed was next to the plywood wall; Barbara's was just on the other side.

The detectives pulled the spread back. The caseless pillow was stained crimson with dried blood, and a great splotch had soaked through the sheets into the mattress. Whoever had shed that blood would have had to have been seriously injured, perhaps unconscious—but there was not enough blood present to indicate that the victim had bled to death.

Lorna and Marti pointed out to the investigators that the bed had been made differently than Lynda would have done it. "She always pulled the sheet up over the pillow, and now it's tucked underneath."

Lynda had had a pink satin pillowcase on her bed. It was gone; its mate was in her dresser drawer. Her nightgown was located in the back of the closet, the neck area stiffened with dried blood.

A reasonable supposition was that someone had entered Lynda's room as she lay sleeping, beaten her into unconsciousness before she could cry out, and carried her away.

Her roommates looked through her closet and found the only clothing missing were the jeans, blouse, and boots she'd worn the night before.

"And her backpack is gone," Marti said. "It's red with gray straps. She usually kept books in it, and maybe her yellow ski cap and gloves . . . and yes, she had a whole bunch of tickets to the Youth Symphony and some checks for tickets in there."

Lynda's nightgown had been stained with blood which surely indicated she'd worn it when she was attacked. The only conclusion the detectives could reach was that her abductor had taken time to dress her before he took her away. Yet all her coats were in her room; had it been too late for her to ever need a coat again? And why the backpack? Why the pillowcase?

The owner of the house told Detectives Fonis and Dorman that he routinely changed all the locks on outer doors to the house when new tenants moved in. This might have been a prudent safeguard, save for the fact that the five girls had left an extra key in the mailbox on the front porch. Furthermore, both Lynda and Marti had lost their keys and had duplicates made.

Any man, watching, waiting, aware that five women lived in the home could have charted their movements, seen them retrieving the extra key from the mailbox.

Now, filled with dread, the remaining four tenants moved out of the green house, and some young male friends moved in to monitor any strange activities. But what had happened had happened. The last peculiar incidents the other four girls could remember was that there had been three phone calls on the afternoon after Lynda vanished. Each time they answered, they could hear only breathing on the other end and then the line had gone dead.

Every inch of the neighborhood was searched, all the dark leafy ravines of nearby Ravenna Park, both by officers and by K-9 dogs. But Lynda Ann Healy was gone, and the man who had taken her away had left no trace of himself, nothing. Not so much as a hair, a drop of blood or semen. He had either been very clever, or very, very lucky. It was the kind of case that homicide detectives dread.

On February 4th, a male voice called the police emergency number 911. "Listen. And listen carefully. The person who attacked that girl on 8th last month and the person who took Lynda Healy away are one in the same. He was outside both houses. He was seen."

"Who is calling?" the operator asked.

"No way are you going to get my name," the man answered and hung up.

Both Lynda's current and former boyfriends volunteered to take a lie-detector test-and both passed without question.

As the days and then weeks passed, it was painfully clear that Lynda Ann Healy was dead, her body hidden so carefully that only her killer and God knew where she was. The Seattle Police crime lab had a pitifully short list of physical evidence items to work with. "One white sheet (bloodstained—type A positive), one yellow pillow (bloodstained—type A positive), one short cream-colored nightgown with brown and blue flowered trim (bloodstained—type A positive). Area of bloodstain on white sheet shows distinct 'ribbed' pattern at edges." This was all that remained of the vibrant girl who had bade goodnight to her friends on January 31st and walked away into oblivion.

To solve a homicide—and Lynda Healy's disappearance was surely a homicide—detectives must find some common threads, something linking the victim to the killer, a similar method of operation in a series of crimes, physical evidence, links between the victims themselves.

Here, they were stymied. There were no connections at all between Lynda Healy and Joni Lenz except that they had both been attacked as they slept in basement rooms in communal houses less than a mile apart. Joni had suffered head wounds, and, from the blood pattern on Lynda's pillow and the stains on her nightgown, it would seem that she too had been struck violently on the skull. But none of the residents of the two houses knew each other; they hadn't even attended the same classes.

February slipped into March, and Lynda didn't come home, nor was there even one sighting of the possessions missing with her-the backpack; her peasant blouse; her old jeans with the funny triangular patch in the back; her two turquoise rings, distinctive round flat rings with tiny, turquoise nuggets "floating" on the silver circles on top.

Just two more quarters and Lynda would have graduated from the University, would have taken a job where she would have been of infinite help to the retarded children whose lives had not been blessed as hers had been with brains, beauty, a loving and nurturing home.

While Seattle Police detectives wrestled with the inexplicable disappearance of Lynda Ann Healy, Sheriff Don Redmond in Thurston County and his detectives were having problems of their own. A female student was missing from Evergreen State College whose campus is just southwest of Olympia.

Evergreen is a relatively new college in Washington with great, soaring precast concrete buildings rising improbably from the dense forest of fir trees. It is a school much maligned by traditional educators because it eschews required courses, accepted grading scales, and embraces a "do your own thing" philosophy. Students choose what they want to learn—everything from cartoon animation to ecology—and draw up contracts that they promise to fulfill each quarter for credit. Its detractors claim that a graduate of Evergreen has no real skills or educational background to offer an employer, calling it a "toy college." Nevertheless, Evergreen attracts some of the brightest and the best.

Nineteen-year-old Donna Gail Manson was a typical Evergreen student, a highly intelligent girl who marched to a different drummer. Her father taught music in the Seattle public schools, and Donna shared his talent and interest in music. She was a flutist, expert enough to play in a symphony.

With the news that a second young woman had undoubtedly come to harm within Thurston County, I drove once again to

Olympia and conferred with Sheriff Redmond and Sergeant Paul Barclift. Barclift explained the circumstances of Donna's vanishing to me.

On the rainy Tuesday night of March 12, 1974, Donna had planned to attend a jazz concert on campus. Her dormitory mates recalled that she'd changed clothes several times, studying her image in the mirror before she was satisfied with the red, orange, and green striped top, blue slacks, a fuzzy black maxi-coat. She'd worn an oval brown agate ring and a Bulova wristwatch.

And then she'd set out—alone—to walk to the concert shortly after 7:00 P.M.

"She was not seen at the concert," Redmond said. "She probably didn't get that far."

Lynda Ann Healy and Katherine Merry Devine had been tall and willowy; Donna Manson was only five feet tall, and weighed 100 pounds.

The Thurston County detectives and Rod Marem, Chief Security Officer for Evergreen State College, were not notified that Donna was missing for six days. Donna's lifestyle was such that she often took off on a moment's notice, only to reappear with tales of a hitchhiking trip—sometimes to points as far away as Oregon. When the report on her absence came in from another student, it was only a "Please attempt to contact" request. But the days passed with no word of her, and her disappearance took on an ominous tone.

Barclift began to contact everyone who knew Donna, followed up every possible lead. He talked to her best friend, Teresa Olsen, and her ex-roommate Celia Dryden, and several other girls who had lived in the dormitory with her.

Donna Manson, despite her I.Q., had not been a good student. She had attended Green River Community College in Auburn before she'd come to Evergreen, and had entered with a cumulative 2.2 (C plus) grade point.

She had chosen a rather broad curriculum—PORTELS (Personal Options Toward Effective Learning Skills). However, Donna had fallen behind even at Evergreen because she consistently stayed out all night, returning at dawn to ask Celia, to cover for her in class, and then going to bed for most of the day. This had bothered Celia, as had Donna's obsession with death, magic, and alchemy. Donna had seemed to be weighed down with depression, and her constant scribblings about alchemy troubled her room-mate too.

Celia had asked to be moved to another room shortly before Donna vanished.

Alchemy is an ancient pseudoscience: ". . . the preparation of an elixir of longevity . . . any seemingly magical power or process of transmuting." Practiced first in ancient Egypt, it was not the curriculum that might be offered at a more conventional college.

"We thought she might have committed suicide," Barclift said. "But we had her writings evaluated by a psychiatrist and he felt they were not particularly significant for a girl of that age. If she had been afraid of anything specific, he thought she would have written it down—and we didn't find anything like that in her writings."

The investigators had found several slips of paper in Donna's room. One listed "Thought Power Inc." A preliminary check by the detectives showed this to be a licensed business in Olympia, located in a neat older home. Seminars on positive thinking and mind discipline were held there. The owners had changed the name to the "Institute of ESP" just before Donna disappeared.

Donna Manson had used marijuana almost daily, and her friends thought she might also have tried other drugs. She had dated four men. They were checked out and all were cleared.

Donna had hitchhiked to Oregon in November, but most of her trips away from campus were to visit friends in Selleck, a tiny mining hamlet located along the road that led up to Issaquah and North Bend and then connected to the main freeway which wound over Snoqualmie Pass. "We checked with the people there and they hadn't seen her since February 10th," Barclift said.

As caught up as she was in her search for what she termed "that other world you can't explain," Donna had remained close to her parents. She had spent the weekend of February 23–24 with them, had called them on March 9th, and written them a letter on March 10th. She'd been in good spirits and was planning a trip to the beach with her mother.

Barclift drove me around the Evergreen campus. He pointed out the lights that stood next to the pathways, but the campus seemed to retain many elements of the original wilderness it had been. In spots, the winding paths disappeared into tunnels of lowering fir boughs. The forest primeval. "Most of the girls walk in pairs or groups after dark," he commented.

The campus was sodden with spring rains. It had been searched in a grid pattern by men and tracking dogs. If Donna was there—her body hidden in a morass of salal, Oregon Grape, sword ferns, and deadfall firs—they would have found her. But Donna was gone, just as completely as Lynda Healy was. The things she'd left behind in her room—her backpack, her flute, suitcases, all her clothing, even the camera she invariably carried—were turned over to her parents.

In the end the Thurston County investigators were left with Donna's writings on death and magic, and the x-rays they had obtained from her physician of her spine, left ankle, and left wrist. If they found her now, they feared it might be the only way to identify her.

8

During that spring of 1974, I had rented a houseboat in Seattle to use as an office, subletting the creaky little one-room structure that floated precariously on logs in Lake Union—a mile south of the University District. I was fully aware now that two college girls were missing, that Kathy Devine had been murdered, and I was beginning to sense that police felt a pattern was emerging, but the public remained unaware. Seattle averages about sixty homicides a year, King County vacillates from two or three to a dozen annually, and Thurston County rarely exceeds three. Not a bad percentage for areas highly populated, and things appeared to be normal. Tragic, but normal.

My ex-husband had suffered a sudden grand mal epileptic seizure; his cancer had metastasized to the brain. He underwent surgery and was hospitalized for several weeks. My youngest daughter, Leslie, then sixteen, took a bus to Seattle every day after school to care for her father; she didn't think the nurses were attentive enough. I worried. She was so lovely, looked so much like the girls who were disappearing, and I was frightened to have her walk even half a block alone in the city. She was insistent that it was something she had to do, and I held my breath each day until she was home safe. I was experiencing the king of dread that soon every parent in the area would feel. As a crime writer, I had seen too much violence, too much tragedy, and I saw "suspicious men" wherever I went. I have never been afraid for myself. But for my daughters, oh yes, for my daughters. I warned them so much that they finally accused me of getting paranoid.

I gave up the houseboat. I didn't want to be that far away from my children, not even during the daytime hours.

On April 17th, it happened again. This time the girl who vanished was 120 miles away from Seattle, far across the looming

Cascade Mountains that separate the verdant coastland of Washington from the arid wheatfields of the eastern half of the state.

Susan Elaine Rancourt was a freshman at Central Washington State College in Ellensburg, a rodeo town that has retained the flavor of the old west. One of six children in a close family, Susan had been a cheerleader and homecoming queen in La Conner, Washington, High School.

She differed from the other missing girls in that she was a blonde, a blonde with long hair, blue eyes. She had the sort of stunning figure that most teenaged girls pray for, not to mention teenaged boys. Perhaps her early development had contributed to her shyness and eclipsed the fact that Susan had a superior, scientifically oriented intelligence.

When the rest of her family moved to Anchorage, Alaska, it took courage on Susan's part to stay behind to attend college in Ellensburg. She'd known she'd have to pay most of her own way; with five other siblings to raise, her family just didn't have the money to foot all her college bills.

The summer before her freshman year, Susan worked *two* full-time jobs—seven days a week—to save money for tuition. She'd always known that her career would be in the field of medicine, and her high school grades—straight A's—and her college aptitude scores verified that she was a natural. At Ellensburg, Susan Rancourt was majoring in biology, still getting a straight 4.0 point, and working a full-time job in a nursing home. She was a young woman any family could be proud of.

Where Lynda Healy had been cautious, and Donna Manson had been heedless of danger, Susan Rancourt was frankly afraid of the dark, of being out alone. She *never* went anywhere without her roommate after the sun had set.

Never, until the evening of April 17th. It had been a busy week for her; midterm finals were being held, but she learned of an opportunity open for would-be dorm advisors. With that job, her expenses could be cut a great deal; besides it would give her a chance to meet more students, to break out of her self-imposed shell of shyness.

So she took a chance.

Susan was only five feet two and weighed 120 pounds, but she was strong. She jogged every morning and she'd gone to Karate classes. Perhaps she'd been foolish to think she couldn't protect herself on a crowded campus even if someone did approach her.

At eight o'clock that evening, she took a load of clothing to a wash room in one of the campus dorms, and walked off to the advisors' meeting. The meeting was over at nine, and she planned to meet a friend to see a German film and then return to the laundromat to put her clothes in the dryer at ten o'clock.

But no one saw Susan after she left the meeting. Her friend waited and waited, and then finally went into the film alone, looking back toward the entrance several times for the familiar sight of Susan's figure.

Susan's clothes remained in the washer, until another student who needed to use it impatiently removed them and set them on a table, where they were discovered a day later.

Susan Rancourt's failure to return to her dorm was reported at once. Susan had a boyfriend, but he was far away at the University of Washington in Seattle, and she dated no one else. She just wasn't the type not to come home at night, and she surely wouldn't have missed a final exam; she'd never even skipped a class.

Campus police officers noted down the outfit she'd worn when she had last been seen: gray corduroy slacks, a short-sleeved yellow sweater, a yellow coat, and brown "hush puppy" shoes. And then they attempted to retrace the route she would have taken from the advisors' meeting back to the dormitories a quarter mile away.

The quickest and most common route led up the Mall past a construction area, across a footbridge over a pond—and then under a railroad trestle near a student parking lot.

"If someone watched her, followed her, and meant to grab her," one officer commented, "it would have been here—under the trestle; it's dark as Hell for about twenty feet."

But there should have been something left of Susan there. For one thing, she'd been carrying a folder full of loose papers that would have scattered in every direction in a struggle. And, shy as she was, Susan Rancourt was a fighter, adept at Karate. Her friends insisted that there was no way she would have given up quietly.

Beyond that, the path back to Barto Hall where the film was being shown was the route most students took. At nine at night, there would have been steady light traffic. Someone should have seen something unusual—but not one had.

Susan had had only one physical imperfection; she was very nearsighted. On the night of April 17th, she had worn neither her glasses nor her contact lenses. She could have seen well enough to make her way around the campus, but she would have had to walk up quite close to someone to recognize them, and she might well have missed a subtle movement in the shadows beneath the trestle.

With the disappearance of Susan Rancourt, other coeds came forward with descriptions of incidents that had vaguely disturbed them. One girl said she'd talked to a tall, handsome man in his twenties outside the campus library on April 12th, a man who had one arm in a sling and a metal brace on his finger. He'd had trouble managing his armload of books and had dropped several. "Finally, she asked me if I'd help him carry them to his car," she recalled.

The car, a Volkswagen bug, was parked about 300 yards from the railroad trestle. She'd carried his books to the car, and then noticed that the passenger seat was missing. Something—she couldn't even say what—had caused the hairs on the back of her neck to stand on end, something about that missing seat. He seemed nice enough, and they'd talked about how he'd been injured skiing at Crystal Mountain, but, suddenly, she just wanted to be away from him. "I put the books on the hood of his car, and I ran . . ."

A second girl told a story very like the first. She had met the man with an injured arm on the 17th, and had carried some packages wrapped in butcher paper to his car for him. "Then he told me that he was having trouble getting it started, and asked me to get in and try the ignition while he did something under the hood. I didn't know him. I didn't want to get in his car, and I just made some excuse about being in a hurry and I left."

The son of an Oregon district attorney, visiting on campus, remembered seeing a tall man with his arm in a sling standing in front of Barto Hall around 8:30 on the evening of the 17th.

The reports didn't seem all that ominous; any time a crime or a disappearance occurs, ordinary incidents take on an importance for "witnesses" who want to help. The statements were typed, filed away, and the search for Susan Rancourt continued.

In this case, as in many others, a minute detail would provide mute testimony to the fate of the missing girls. With Donna Manson, it had been her camera left behind; with Susan, it was her contact lenses and her glasses, glasses that she'd probably meant to carry with her to the movie on the night she vanished, and her dental floss. When her mother looked into her medicine cabinet and saw the dental floss, she felt her heart thud. "She was such a creature of habit. She never went anywhere overnight without dental floss . . ."

Captain Herb Swindler, a massive bulldog of a cop, a veteran in homicide investigations, had taken over command of the Crimes Against Persons Unit of the Seattle Police Department in the spring of 1974. I had known Herb for twenty years; in 1954 he was the patrol officer who had responded first to a complaint of indecent liberties by the mother of a small girl in West Seattle, and I was the most-rookie of policewomen who was called in to question the child. I'd been twenty-one then, and admittedly somewhat embarrassed at the questions I had to ask the little girl about the "nice old man" who boarded with the family.

I remember how Herb teased me because I'd blushed—the standard razzing that new policewomen received—but he'd been gentle with the child, with her mother. He was a good cop, and a thorough investigator and he'd moved up rapidly through the ranks. Now, the buck stopped in Herb's office; most of the missing girls' cases had seemingly originated in Seattle, and he was wrestling day and night with the mysteries that seemed to have no clues, no answers. It was as if the man responsible was taunting the police, laughing at the ease with which he'd abducted the women, leaving no trace of himself.

Swindler is a talkative man, and he needed a sounding board. I filled that need. He knew I wouldn't talk to anyone outside the department, knew I'd followed the cases as meticulously as any detective. Certainly, I was a writer looking for *the* big story; but I was also the mother of two teenaged daughters, and the horror of it all, the agony of the parents, kept me awake nights. He was confident I wouldn't publish a word until the time was right—if ever.

During those months of 1974, I talked to Swindler almost every day—listening, trying to find some common denominator. My territory took me up and down the coast, and I often knew of cases in other cities, cases 200 miles away in Oregon, and I reported any disappearance that might tie in to the Seattle Police.

The next girl to walk away forever lived in Oregon. Nineteen days after Susan Rancourt vanished—on May 6th—Roberta Kathleen "Kathy" Parks had spent an unhappy and guilt-ridden day in her room in Sackett Hall on the Oregon State University campus in Corvallis, 250 miles south of Seattle. I knew Sackett Hall; I'd lived there myself when I attended one term at O.S.U. back in the 1950s, a huge, modern dormitory complex on a campus that was then considered a "cow college." Even then, when the world didn't seem to be so fraught with danger, none of us would ever go to the snack machines in the cavernous basement corridors alone at night.

Kathy Parks wasn't very happy at Oregon State. She was homesick for Lafayette, California, and she'd broken up with her boyfriend who'd left for Louisiana. On May 4th, Kathy had argued in a phone call with her father, and, on May 6th, she learned that he'd suffered a massive heart attack. Her sister had called her from Spokane, Washington with the news of their father's coronary, and then called back some hours later to say that it looked as though he would survive.

Kathy, whose major was world religions, felt a little better after the second call, and she agreed to join some of the other residents of Sackett Hall in an exercise session in the dorm lounge.

Shortly before eleven, the tall slender girl with long ash-blonde hair left Sackett Hall to meet some friends for coffee in the Student Union Building. She promised her roommate she would be back within the hour. Wearing blue slacks, a navy blue top, a light green jacket, and platform sandals, she left Sackett for the last time.

Kathy never made the Student Union Building. Like the others, all of her possessions were left behind: her bike, clothing, cosmetics.

This time, no one had seen anyone suspicious. No man with his arm in a sling. No Volkswagen bugs. Kathy had never talked of being afraid or of receiving obscene phone calls. She had been a girl so subject to wide mood swings that the question of suicide arose. Had she felt so guilty about fighting with her father, perhaps believing that she had caused his heart attack? Guilty enough to have taken her own life?

The Willamette River, which wends its way near Corvallis, was dragged, and nothing was found. Had she chosen another means of self destruction, her body would surely be located soon, but it was not.

Lieutenant Bill Harris, of the Oregon Sate Police Criminal Investigation Unit, was stationed on the O.S.U. campus and he headed the probe in Oregon. He had had a tragic homicide in Sackett Hall a few years before, where a coed was found stabbed to death in her room, but his successful investigation had resulted in the arrest of a male student who lived on an upper floor. That youth was still in the Oregon State Penitentiary.

After a week-long search, Harris was convinced that Kathy Parks had been abducted, probably seized as she walked between the great masses of lilac bushes blooming along the path between Sackett Hall and the Student Union Building. Gone, like all the others, without a single cry for help.

Police bulletins with pictures of the four missing girls were tacked up side by side on the office walls of every law enforcement agency in the Northwest, smiling faces that looked enough alike to be sisters. Yet only Herb Swindler was absolutely convinced that Kathy Parks was part of the pattern; other detectives felt Corvallis was too far away for her to be a victim of the same man who prowled Washington campuses.

There was to be only a short respite. Twenty-six days later, a casual acquaintance of my elder daughter, Brenda Carol Ball, twenty-two, who lived with two roommates in the south King County suburb of Burien, disappeared. Brenda had been a Highline Community College student, until two weeks before. She was five feet three, 112 pounds, and her brown eyes sparkled with her zest for life.

On the night of May 31–June 1, Brenda went alone to the Flame Tavern at 128th South and Ambaum Road South. Her roommates had seen her last at 2 P.M. that Friday afternoon and she told them that she planned to go to the tavern, and mentioned that she might catch a ride afterward to Sun Lakes State Park in eastern Washington and meet them there.

She did go to the Flame and was seen there by several people who knew her. No one remembers exactly what she was wearing, but her usual garb was faded blue jeans and long-sleeved turtleneck tops. She seemed to be having a good time, and stayed until closing at 2 A.M.

Brenda asked one of the musicians in the band for a ride home, but he explained he was heading in another direction. The last time anyone remembers seeing Brenda Ball, she was talking in the parking lot with a handsome, brown-haired man who had one arm in a sling. . .

Because Brenda—like Donna Manson—was a free spirit, given to impulsive trips, there was a long delay before she was officially reported missing. Nineteen days passed before her roommates became convinced that something had happened to her. They'd checked with her bank and become alarmed when they learned that her savings account hadn't been touched. All of her clothing was still in their apartment. Her parents, who lived nearby, hadn't heard from her either.

At twenty-two, Brenda was the oldest of all the missing women, an adult, who had proved herself capable and cautious in the past. But not now. It seemed that Brenda too had met someone she should not have trusted. Brenda was gone.

But the stalking was far from over. Even before Brenda Ball was reported as a missing person to King County Police, the man law enforcement officers sought was on the prowl again, about to strike audaciously, virtually in full view of dozens of witnesses—and still remain only a phantom figure. He would thumb his nose at police, leaving them as frustrated as they had ever been in the series of crimes that had already both galled and horrified them; many of the detectives searching for the missing girls had daughters of their own.

It was almost as if it were some kind of perverse game of challenge on the part of the abductor, as if, each time, he would come a little further out of the shadows, take more chances, to prove that he could do what he wanted and still not be caught, or even seen.

Georgeann Hawkins, at eighteen, was one of those golden girls for whom luck or fate had dealt a perfect hand—until the inexplicable night of June 10th. Raised in the Tacoma suburb of Sumner, she'd been a Daffodil Princess, and, like Susan Rancourt, a cheerleader, an honor student at Lakes High School. She had a vivacious, pixie-like quality to her loveliness, glossy long brown hair, and lively brown eyes. She was tiny—five feet, two inches tall, 115 pounds—healthy in a glowing way, the youngest of two daughters of the Warren B. Hawkins family.

While many good students in high school tend to find the University of Washington's curriculum much more difficult and drop to a comfortable C average, Georgeann had continued to maintain a straight A record. Her biggest worry during that finals week of June, 1974 was that she was having a difficult time with Spanish. She considered dropping the course, but, on the morning of June 10th, she had phoned her mother and said she was going to cram for the next day's final as hard as she could, and she thought she could handle it.

She already had a summer job lined up—with Pierce County in Tacoma—and she'd discussed it by phone with her parents at least once a week.

During rush week in September of 1973, Georgeann had been tapped by one of the top sororities on campus, Kappa Alpha Theta, and lived in the big house among several other Greek houses along 17th Avenue N.E.

Residents of the sororities and fraternities along Greek Row visit back and forth much more freely than they did back in the fifties when it was strictly forbidden for members of the opposite sex to venture above the formal living rooms on the first floor. Georgeann frequently dropped in to see her boyfriend, who lived in the Beta Theta Pi House six houses down from the Theta House.

During the early evening hours of Monday, June 10th, Georgeann and a sorority sister had gone to a party where they'd had one or two mixed drinks. Georgeann explained that she had to get back to study for her Spanish exam. But, first, she was going to stop by the Beta House and say goodnight to her boyfriend.

Georgeann was cautious; she rarely went anywhere on campus alone at night, but the area along 17th Avenue N.E. was so familiar, so well-lighted, and there was always someone around she knew. The fraternal organizations front the street on each side, with a grassy island running down the middle. Trees, in full leaf in June, do block out some of the street lights; they've grown so tall since they were planted back in the twenties.

The alley that runs in back of the Greek houses from 45th N.E. to 47th N.E. is as bright as day, lit by street lights every ten feet or so. June 10th was a warm night, and every window opening onto the alleyway was open. It is doubtful that any of the student residents were asleep, even at midnight; most of them were cramming for finals with the aid of black coffee and No-Doz.

Georgeann did go to the Beta House, a little before 12:30 A.M. on June 11th. She visited with her steady boyfriend for a half hour or so, borrowed some Spanish notes, and then said goodnight and left by the back door to walk the ninety feet down to the back door of the Theta House.

One of the other Betas heard the door slam and stuck his head out his window, recognizing Georgeann.

"Hey George!" he called loudly. "What's happening?"

The pretty, deeply tanned, girl wearing blue slacks, a white backless teeshirt, and a sheer red, white, and blue top, craned her neck and looked back. She smiled and waved, talked for a moment or two about the Spanish exam, and then, laughing called "Adios."

She turned and headed south toward her residence. He watched her for about thirty feet. Two other male students who knew her recall that they saw her traverse the next twenty feet.

She had forty feet to go—forty feet in the alley brightly lit. Certainly, there were some murky areas between the big houses, filled with laurel hedges, blooming rhododendrons, but Georgeann would have stayed in the middle of the alley.

Her roommate, Dee Nichols, waited for the familiar sound of pebbles hitting their window; Georgeann had lost her key to the back door, and the sorority sister would have to run down the stairs and let her in.

There was no rattling of pebbles. There was no sound, no outcry, nothing.

An hour passed. Two hours. Worried, Dee called the Beta House and learned Georgeann had left for home a little after 1:00 A.M. She awoke the housemother, and said softly, "Georgeann's gone. She didn't come home."

They waited through the night, trying to find some reasonable explanation for why Georgeann might be gone, not wanting to alarm her parents at three A.M.

In the morning, they called the Seattle Police.

Detective "Bud" Jelberg of the Missing Persons Unit took the report, and rechecked with the fraternity house where she'd been seen last, then called her parents. Usually, any police department will wait twenty-four hours before beginning a search for a missing adult but, in view of the events of the first half of 1974, the disappearance of Georgeann Hawkins was treated very, very seriously immediately.

At 8:45 A.M. Detective Sergeant Ivan Beeson, and Detectives Ted Fonis and George Cuthill of the Homicide Unit arrived at the Theta House, 4521 17th N.E. They were accompanied by George Ishii, one of the most renowned criminalists in the Northwest. Ishii, who heads the Western Washington State Crime Lab, is a brilliant man, a man who probably knows more about the detection, preservation, and testing of physical evidence than any other criminalist in the western half of the United States. He was my first teacher of crime scene investigation. In two quarters, I learned more about physical evidence than I ever had before.

Ishii believes implicitly in the theories of Dr. E. Locarde, a pioneer French criminalist who states, "Every criminal leaves something of himself at the scene of a crime—something, no matter how minute—and always takes something of the scene away with him." Every good detective knows this; this is why they search so intensely at a crime scene for that small part of the perpetrator that he was left behind: a hair, a drop of blood, a thread, a button, a finger or palm print, a footprint, traces of semen, tool marks, shell casings. And, in most instances, they find it.

The criminalist and the three homicide detectives covered that alleyway behind 45th and 47th N.E.—that ninety feet—on their hands and knees.

And found nothing at all.

Leaving the alley cordoned off, and guarded by patrolmen, they went into the Theta House to talk with Georgeann's sorority sisters and her housemother.

Georgeann lived in Number Eight in the house, a room she shared with Dee Nichols. All of her possessions were there, everything but the clothes she'd been wearing and her leather purse, a tan "sack" bag with reddish stains on it. In that purse she had carried her I.D., a few dollars, a bottle of "Heaven Sent" perfume with angels on the label, and a small hair brush.

"Georgeann never went anyplace without leaving me the phone number where she'd be," Dee said. "I know she intended to come back here last night. She had one more exam and then she was going home for the summer on the 13th. The blue slacks—the ones she was wearing—were missing three buttons; there was only one left. I can give you one of the buttons like it from our room."

Like Susan Rancourt, Georgeann was very myopic. "She wasn't wearing her glasses or her contacts last night," her roommate recalled. "She'd worn her contacts all day to study, and after you've worn contact lenses for a long time, things look blurry when you put glasses on, so she wasn't wearing them either."

The missing girl could have seen well enough to negotiate the familiar alley, but she would have seen nothing more than a vague outline of a figure more than ten feet away. If someone had been lurking in the alley, someone who had learned Georgeann's name after hearing the youth call to her from the Beta House window, he could easily have used a soft "George—" to call her close to him. And she would have had to walk very close indeed in order to recognize the man who beckoned to her.

Perhaps so close that she could have been seized, gagged, and carried off before she had a chance to cry out?

Surely, anyone looking down the alley would have been alerted at the sight of a man carrying her away. Or would they? There are always high jinks during finals week, anything to break the tension, and strong young men frequently pick up giggling, squealing girls, playing "cave man."

But no one had seen even that. Georgeann Hawkins may have been knocked out with one blow, chloroformed, injected with a swift-acting nervous system depressant, or just pinioned in powerful arms, a hand held tightly over her mouth so that she couldn't even scream.

"She was afraid of the dark," Dee said quietly. "Sometimes, we would walk all the way around a block just to avoid a dark spot along the sidewalk. When *he* got her, I know that she was hurrying back here. I don't think she had a chance."

The sorority sister who had attended the party earlier in the evening with Georgeann, remembered that they'd parted on the corner of 47th N.E. and N.E. 17th. "She stood and waited while I walked to our house, and I yelled to her that I was O.K., and she yelled back that she was O.K. All of us kind of checked on each other like that. She went into the Beta House and that's the last time I ever saw her."

It was incomprehensible then, and it is still incomprehensible to Seattle homicide detectives, that Georgeann Hawkins could vanish so completely within a space of forty feet. Of all the cases of missing girls, it is the Hawkins case that baffles them the most. It was something that couldn't have happened, and yet it did.

When the news of Georgeann's disappearance hit the media, two witnesses came forward with stories of incidents on June 11th that were amazingly similar. An attractive sorority girl said that she'd been walking in front of the Greek houses on 17th N.E. at about 12:30 A.M. when she'd seen a young man on crutches just ahead of her. One leg of his jeans had been cut up the side and he appeared to have a full cast on that leg.

"He was carrying a briefcase with a handle, and he kept dropping it. I offered to help him, but I told him I had to go into one of the houses for a few minutes, and, if he didn't mind waiting, I'd come out and help him get his stuff home."

"And did you?"

"No. I was inside longer than I thought, and he was gone when I came out."

A male college student also had seen the tall, good-looking man with the briefcase and crutches. "A girl was carrying his case for him, and, later on, after I'd taken my girl home, I saw the girl again, walking alone."

He looked at a picture of Georgeann Hawkins, but said he was positive she wasn't the girl he'd seen.

At this time, the notation in the Susan Rancourt file in Ellensburg about the man with his arm in a sling was not generally known.

Only after publicity about the man with his leg in the cast was disseminated would the two incidents so far apart be coordinated. Coincidence, or part of a sly plan to throw young women off guard?

Detectives canvassed every house on each side of 17th N.E. At the Phi Sigma Sigma fraternity at 4520—just across from the Theta House—they found that the housemother recalled being awakened from a sound sleep between one and two on the morning of June 11th.

"It was a scream that wakened me. It was a high-pitched scream . . . a terrified scream. And then it just stopped, and everything was quiet. I figured it was just kids horsing around, but now I wish . . . I wish I'd. . ."

No one else heard it.

Lynda . . . Donna . . . Susan . . . Kathy . . . Brenda . . . Georgeann. All gone as completely as if a seam in the backdrop of life itself had opened, drawn them in, and closed without leaving so much as a mended tear in the tapestry.

Georgeann Hawkins' father, his voice breaking, summed up the feelings of all the desperately worried parents who waited for some word. "Every day, I'm a little bit lower. You'd like to hope, but I'm too realistic. She was a very friendly, very involved, youngster. I keep saying 'was.' I shouldn't say that. It's a job raising kids. You steer them along, and we figured we had both our kids over the hump."

Any homicide detective who has ever tried to cope with the anguish of parents who realize intuitively that their children are dead, but have not even the faint comfort of knowing where their bodies are, can attest to the fact that this is the worst. One weary investigator commented to me, "It's rough. It's damn rough, when you have to tell them that you've found a body, that it's their kid. But it's never over for the parents who just don't know. They can't really have a funeral, they can't know that their children aren't being held and tortured someplace, they can't face their grief and get it over. Hell, you never get over it, but, if you know, you can pick your life up again, somehow."

The girls were gone, and each set of parents tried to deal with it, brought in the records that would mean the identification one day, perhaps, of a decomposed body. Dental records, all the years of paying for fillings and orthodontics so that their daughters would have good teeth to last a lifetime. The x-rays from Donna Manson's broken bones, set clean and strong again. And, for Georgeann, x-rays taken when she'd suffered from Osgood-Schlatter's Disease as a teenager, an inflammation of the tibia near the knee. After months of concern, her legs had grown long and shapely, marked only by slight bumps just below the knee.

Any of us who have raised children know, as John F. Kennedy once said, that "to have children is to give hostages to fate." To lose a child to an illness, or even an accident, can be dealt with during the passage of time. To lose a child to a predator, an insanely brilliant killer, is almost more than any human should have to bear.

When I began writing fact-detective stories, I promised myself that I would always remember I was writing about the loss of human beings, that I was never to forget that. I hoped that the work I did might somehow save other victims, might warn them of the danger. I never wanted to become tough, to seek out the sensational and the gory, and I never have. I have joined the Committee of Friends and Families of Missing Persons and Victims of Violent Crimes, at the invitation of the group. I have met many parents of victims, cried with them, and yet I have somehow felt guilty—because I make my living from other peoples' tragedies. When I told the Committee how I felt, they put their arms around me and said, "No. Keep on writing. Let the public know how it is for us. Let them know how we hurt, and how we try to save other parents' children by working for new legislation that requires mandatory sentencing and the death penalty for killers."

They are far stronger than I could ever be.

And so, I kept on, trying to find the answer to the awful puzzle, believing that the killer, when he was found, would prove to be a man with a record of violence, a man who should never have been allowed to walk the streets, someone who must surely have shown signs of a deranged mind in the past, someone who had been let out of prison too soon.

9

I happened to be sitting in Captain Herb Swindler's office one afternoon in late June of 1974 when Joni Lenz and her father came into the Homicide Unit. Herb had a montage of the victims' pictures on his wall; he kept them there as a reminder that the investigation must continue with no let-up in intensity. Joni had volunteered to come in and look at the other girls' pictures, to see if she recognized any of them, even though their names were completely unfamiliar to her.

"Joni," Herb said gently. "Look at these girls. Have you ever seen any of them? Maybe you've been in a club together, worked together, had a class or something with them."

With her father standing protectively beside her, the victim of the January 4th bludgeoning studied the photographs. The slender girl was still recovering from the brain damage she'd suffered, and she spoke with a hesitancy, a vagueness, but she was trying very hard to help. She moved closer to the wall, studied each photo carefully, and then she shook her head.

"N-n-n-o-o," she stuttered. "I never saw them. I didn't know them. I can't remember—a lot of things I can't remember, but I know I never knew the girls."

"Thank you, Joni," Herb said. "We appreciate your coming in."

It had been a long shot the slight possibility that the one living victim would prove to be a link. Herb glanced at me, and shook his head as Joni Lenz limped out of the room. If she had known any of the others, so much of her memory of the past year had been battered out of her brain cells.

Now, in the early summer of 1974, the reading public knew of the pattern of missing girls; it was no longer a matter that concerned only detectives and the principals involved. And the public was terrified. Hitchhiking among young women dropped sharply, and women from fifteen to sixty-five jumped at shadows.

Stories began, the kind of stories that can never be traced directly to the source. I heard variations on the same theme a dozen times. But they always came from a friend of a friend of a friend of someone whose cousin, or sister, or wife had been involved.

Sometimes the attacks were said to have happened in a shopping mall, sometimes in a restaurant, sometimes a theater. It went like this: "This man and his wife (or sister, daughter, etc.) went to Southcenter Mall to shop, and she went back to their car to get something. Well, she didn't come back for a long time, and he got worried and went looking for her. He got there just in time to see some guy carrying her away. The husband yelled, and the guy dropped her. He'd given her some kind of shot that made her pass out. It was really lucky that he got there in time, because, you know, with everything that's been happening, it was probably that killer."

The first few times I heard versions of the "true" story, I attempted to trace it back to its origin, but I found it was impossible to do so. I doubt that any of the incidents ever happened at all; it was the reaction of the public, mass hysteria. If the girls who were gone could disappear the way they had, then anyone could, and there seemed to be no way to prevent it.

The pressure on law enforcement of course, was tremendous. On July 3rd, more than a hundred representatives from departments all over Washington and Oregon met in Olympia at Evergreen State College for a day-long brainstorming conference. Perhaps if they pooled their information, they might find the common denominator that would break the seemingly inscrutable mysteries.

I was invited to attend, and felt a kind of eerie oppressiveness as I walked along the fir shrouded paths to the conference. Donna Manson had walked here four months before, headed for the same building. Now, the rains had given way to bright sunshine and the birds called from the trees above me, but the feeling of dread was still there.

Sitting among the investigators from the Seattle Police Department, the King County Police Department the Washington State Patrol, the U.S. Army's C.I.D., the University of Washington

Police, the Central Washington Security Force, the Tacoma Police Department, the Pierce County Sheriff's Office, the Multnomah (Oregon) County Sheriff's department, the Oregon State Police, and dozens of smaller police departments, I found it almost impossible to believe that all these men, with scores upon scores of years of training and experience could not find out more about the suspect they sought.

It was not from lack of trying; every single department involved wanted him, and they were willing to explore any avenue—no matter how bizarre—to accomplish an arrest, a good arrest that would stick.

Sheriff Don Redmond of Thurston County summed up the feeling in his opening remarks, "We want to show parents we really care. We want to find their children. The people of the State of Washington are going to have to give us a hand. So many times people could volunteer information. We need the eyes and ears of the people out there."

Redmond's department, located in Washington's capital city, was still searching for the killer of Katherine Merry Devine, and the whereabouts of Donna Manson. Now, they had another homicide of a teenager to contend with. Brenda Baker had been fifteen years old, a hitchhiker like Kathy and Donna, and she'd run away from home on May 25th. Oa June 17th, her badly decomposed body was found at the edge of Millersylvania State Park. It was too late to determine cause of death or to make a quick identification. At first, it was thought that it might have been the body of Georgeann Hawkins. Denial charts proved, however, that it was Brenda Baker. The Baker girl's body was found several miles away from McKenny Park where Kathy Devine had been found. However, both sites were the same distance from I-5, the freeway that runs between Seattle and Olympia.

Looking at the cases of the missing girls side by side, some striking similarities could not be ignored; it was as if the man who'd taken them away had chosen a certain type he wanted, picked his quarry with care:

* Each had long hair, parted in the middle.
* Each was Caucasian, fair-complexioned.

* Each was of much more than average intelligence.
* Each was slender, attractive, highly talented.
* Each had vanished within a week of midterm or final exams at local colleges.
* Each came from a stable, loving family.
* Each disappearance took place during the hours of darkness.
* Each girl was single.
* Each girl had been wearing slacks or jeans when she disappeared.
* In each case, detectives had not one piece of physical evidence that might have been left by the abductor.
* Construction work was going on on each campus where the girls were missing.

And, in two instances—Susan Rancourt in Ellensburg, and Georgeann Hawkins in Seattle—a man wearing a cast on his arm or leg had been seen close to where they had vanished.

They were all young girls; none of them could be considered a mature woman.

It was weird, perverted, insane, and, for the detectives trying to get a fix on the man, skin to working their way through a maze, starting up each new path only to find it blocked. The victims certainly did not appear to have been selected by random choice, and they wondered about that.

They even wondered if it might not be *more* than one man they were seeking—a cult choosing maidens to be sacrificed in deadly rituals? During that spring of 1974, a rash of reports had come in from northwestern states on the mutilation of cattle, found in fields with only their sexual organs missing. All this smacked of devil worship; the natural (or unnatural) progression of such mutilations would be human sacrifice.

For the detectives gathered at Evergreen College, all men whose work and life styles made them think in rational, concrete terms, the occult was a foreign concept. I believe in the efficacy of ESP, but I was most certainly not conversant with astrology beyond reading the daily syndicated columns. However, I had had a phone call a few days before that Olympia conference and a meeting with a woman who *was* an astrologer.

My friend, who uses the initials "R.L." when she charts astrology, is a woman who had worked at the Crisis Clinic while I did. In her late thirties, she was in her senior year at the University of Washington as a history major. I had not heard from her in some time when she'd called in late June.

"Ann, you're close to the police," she began. "I've found something that I think they should know about. Could we talk?"

I met with R.L. in her North End apartment and she led me to her office where the desk, floors, and furniture were buried in charts with strange symbols. She had been trying to find a pattern—an astrological pattern—in the case of the missing girls.

"I've come across something. Look at these," she said.

I was completely at a loss. I could make out my sign—Libra's scales—but the rest was only so much scribbling to me. I told her so.

"O.K. I'll give you a crash course. You probably know about the sun signs. There are twelve and last approximately a month each year. That's what people mean when they say 'I'm an Aquarian, or a Scorpio, etcetera.' But the *moon* passes through each of these signs every month."

She showed me an Ephemeris (an astrological almanac) and I could see that the phases of the moon signs seemed to last about forty-eight hours each month.

"All right, I understand that much. But I can't see what it has to do with the cases," I argued.

"There's a pattern. Lynda Healy was taken when the moon was going through a Taurus phase. From that point on, the girls vanished alternately in Pisces and Scorpio moon phases. The chances against that happening—the odds—are almost impossible."

"You think someone is deliberately abducting those girls, maybe killing them, because he knows the moon is going through a certain sign? I can't comprehend that."

"I don't know if he knows anything about astrology," she said. "He might not even be aware of the forces of the moon."

She pulled out a sealed envelope. "I want you to give this to someone who's in charge. It's not to be opened until after the weekend of July 13th to 15th."

"Come on! They'd laugh me out of their offices."

"What else do they have to go on? I've seen this pattern. I've worked it out several times, and there it is. If I could tell you who, or where, or when it's going to happen again, I would—but I can't do that. It's happened once when the moon was in Taurus, and then a half dozen times back and forth between Pisces and Scorpio. I think he's going to go back to Taurus and start a new cycle."

"All right," I finally said. "I'll take the envelope, but I won't promise I'll give it to anyone. I don't know who I could give it to."

"You'll find someone," she said firmly.

I had that envelope in my purse as I attended the law enforcement conference at Evergreen. I was still undecided about mentioning it, or the predictions of R.L.

Herb Swindler took over the lectern after the lunch break. He threw out a startling question and drew some guffaws from his fellow lawmen.

"Anybody have any ideas? Is there some pattern coming down that we haven't considered? Anybody here know anything about numerology, anybody psychic?"

I figured Herb was kidding, but he wasn't. He began to write on the blackboard, listing the dates of the girls' disappearances in an attempt to find a numerological link.

But there seemed to be nothing that could be called a pattern. From Lynda's disappearance to Donna's, there had been a forty-two day interim; from Donna's to Susan's—36 days; from Susan's to Kathy Parks'—19 days; from Kathy's to Brenda's—25 days, and from Brenda's to Georgeann's—11 days. The only thing immediately apparent was that the abductions were getting closer and closer together.

"O.K." Herb said, "Any other suggestions? I don't care how crazy it might sound. We'll kick it around."

The letter was burning a hole in my purse. I raised my hand.

"I haven't heard anything about numerology, but my friend, an astrologer, says there's an astrological pattern."

There were some eyes raised to the ceiling, some chuckles, but I plunged ahead, explaining what R.L. had told me. "He's only taking the girls away when the moon is moving through Taurus, Pisces, or Scorpio."

"Your friend thinks this is unusual," Swindler smiled.

"She says it defies the laws of probability."

"Then she can tell us when it might happen again?"

"I'm not sure. She gave me a sealed envelope. You can have it if you like. You're not to open it until July 15th."

I could sense that my audience was getting restless, that they thought we were wasting time.

I passed the envelope up to Herb, and he weighed it in his hand.

"So she thinks that's the next time a girl's going to vanish, does she?"

"I don't know. I don't know what's in that envelope. She wants to test her theory, and she only said not to open the letter until then."

The discussion moved into other areas. I suspected that most of the investigators present thought I was a "crazy reporter," and I wasn't too sure myself that it wasn't really reaching to make a pattern where there was none.

The general consensus of opinion was that it was only one man who was responsible for the girls' vanishing, and we were trying to figure out what rose he could use that would put the women at ease enough so that they would drop their natural caution.

Who would most young women trust automatically? What guise could he have assumed that would make them feel he was safe? Since childhood, most of us have been trained to believe we can trust a minister, a priest, a fireman, a doctor, ambulance attendant, and a policeman. The last thought was one that couldn't be overlooked, abhorrent as it was to these men who were policemen themselves. A rogue cop, maybe? Or someone in a policeman's uniform?

The next safe assumption was that most young women would have helped a handicapped person—a blind man, someone taken suddenly ill, *someone on crutches or in a cast*.

So what do you do? Infiltrate every campus in the North-west with policemen, tell them to stop every man who's dressed like a cop, fireman, ambulance attendant, priest, every man with a cast? There wasn't enough manpower in Oregon and Washington law enforcement agencies to even dream of doing that.

In the end, the only thing to do was to warn the public with as much media saturation as possible, to ask for information from citizens, and to keep on working the slightest tip that came in. Surely, the man, or the group, that was seizing the girls would make a slip-up; surely, he would leave some clue that would lead back to him. The officers at that July 3rd conference said a prayer that no more girls would have to suffer before that happened.

Tragically, it seemed that the press coverage of the conference served only as a gauntlet thrown down, a challenge to the man who watched and waited, who felt that he was above the law, too cunning ever to he caught, no matter how blatant he might be.

Lake Sammamish State Park edges the east side of the lake for which it is named. The park, twelve miles east of Seattle, and almost adjacent to Interstate 90 which leads up into Snoqualmie Pass, draws summertime crowds not only from Seattle itself, but from nearby Bellevue, the city's largest suburb. Bellevue is a booming bedroom city of 75,000 people, and the hamlets of Issaquah and North Bend are also close to the state park.

Lake Sammamish State Park is level, a sweep of meadow land dotted in the spring with buttercups, in summer with field daisies. There are trees, but no dark copses, and a ranger's residence is on the property. Lifeguards watch the swimmers, and warn pleasure boats away, and picnickers can look to the east and watch the billowing chutes of skydivers who jump from the small planes which circle constantly.

When my children were small and we lived in Bellevue, we spent almost every warm summer evening at Lake Sammamish State Park. The kids learned to swim there, and I often went there alone with them during the day; it seemed the safest place in the world.

July 14th, 1974 was one of those glorious brilliant days that Washingtonians look forward to during the endless rainy days of winter and early spring. The sky was a clear blue, and temperatures crept up into the eighties before noon, threatening to hit 90 before the day was over. Such days are not commonplace, even in summer in western Washington, and Lake Sammamish State Park was packed to overflowing that Sunday—40,000 people jockeying for a spot to spread their blankets and enjoy the sun.

Besides individual family groups, the Rainier Brewery was holding its annual "beer bust" in the park, and there was a Seattle

Police Athletic Association picnic; the asphalt parking lot was jammed early in the day.

A pretty young woman arrived at the park around 11:30 that morning, and was approached by a young man wearing a white tee-shirt and blue jeans.

"Say, could you help me a minute?" he asked, smiling.

She saw that one of his arms was suspended in a beige sling, and she answered, "Sure what do you need?"

He explained that he wanted to load his sailboat on his car and he couldn't manage it with his bum arm. She agreed to help him and walked with him to a metallic brown VW bug in the parking lot.

There was no sailboat anywhere around.

The woman looked at the handsome young man—a man she later described as having sandy blond hair, being about five feet, ten inches tall, and weighing 160 pounds—and asked where his boat was.

"Oh. I forgot to tell you. It's up at my folks' house—just a jump up the hill."

He motioned to the passenger door, and she stopped, wary. She told him her parents were waiting for her and that she was already late.

He took her refusal with good will, "That's O.K. I should have told you it wasn't in the parking lot. Thanks for bothering to come to the car."

It was 12:30 when she glanced up and saw the man walking toward the parking lot with a pretty young woman, a woman wheeling a bike and engaged in an animated conversation with the man. And then she forgot about the incident—forgot until she read the papers the next day.

July 14th had been a lonely day for twenty-three-year-old Janice Ott, a probation case worker at the King County Youth Service Center in Seattle, the county's juvenile detention hall and court. Her husband, Jim, was 1,400 miles away in Riverside, California, completing a course in the design of prosthetic devices for the handicapped. The job with the Juvenile Court—a job Janice had waited a long time for—had kept her from going to California with her husband. It meant a separation of several months, and they'd only been married a year and a half. She would join him in September for a reunion; for now calls and letters would have to suffice.

Janice Anne Ott was a tiny girl, weighing only 100 pounds, and barely topping five feet. She had long blonde hair, parted in the middle, and startling gray-green eyes. She looked more like a high school girl than a mature young woman who had graduated from Eastern Washington State College in Cheney with a straight A average. Janice's father in Spokane, Washington was an assistant director of public schools in that city and had once been an associate of the State Board of Prison Terms and Paroles; the family orientation was decidedly toward public service.

Like Lynda Ann Healy, Janice was well-educated in the theoretical approaches to antisocial behavior and disturbed minds, and, like Lynda, she was idealistic. Her father would say later, "She thought that some people were sick or misdirected, and felt that she could help them through her training and personality."

It was just after noon when Janice, riding her ten-speed bike from her Issaquah home, arrived at Lake Sammamish State Park. She had left a note for the girl she shared her small house with, saying she would he back around four that afternoon.

She found a spot to spread her blanket about ten feet away from three other groups. She wore cut-off jeans and a white shirt tied in front; beneath it, she had on a black bikini, and she stripped to that and lay down to take advantage of the sun.

It was only minutes later when she felt a shadow and opened her eyes. A good-looking man, a man wearing a white tee-shirt, white tennis shorts, and white tennis shoes looked down at her. He had a sling on his right arm.

The picnickers nearby couldn't help but overhear their conversation, as Janice sat up, blinking in the bright sun.

They would remember that the man had a slight accent—perhaps Canadian, perhaps British—as he said, "Excuse me. Could you help me put my sailboat onto my car? I can't do it by myself. I've got this broken arm."

Janice Ott had told the man to sit down, and they'd talk about it. She told him her name, and those close by heard him say his name was "Ted."

"See, my boat's up at my parents' house in Issaquah . . ."

"Oh really? That's where I live too," she'd smiled.

"You think you could come with me and help me?"

"Sailing must be fun," she said to him. "I never learned how."

"It will be easy for me to teach you," he responded.

Janice had explained that she had her bike with her, and she didn't want to leave it on the beach for fear it might be stolen, and he'd answered easily that there was room for it in the trunk of his car.

"Well. . . . O.K., I'll help you."

They'd chatted for about ten minutes before Janice stood up, slipped back into her shorts and shirt, and then she'd left the beach with "Ted," pushing her bike toward the parking lot.

No one ever saw Janice Ott alive again.

Eighteen-year-old Denise Naslund went to Lake Sammamish State Park on that Sunday in July too, but she wasn't alone. She was accompanied by her boyfriend and another couple, arriving in Denise's 1963 Chevrolet. Denise, dark-haired, dark-eyed, and startlingly attractive, was exactly two days older than Susan Elaine Rancourt, who had been gone now three months; maybe she had read about Susan, but it's doubtful. Denise was five feet four, weighed 120 pounds, and she matched the pattern so well.

She once babysat for a good friend of mine, who remembers her as an unfailingly cheerful dependable girl. Her mother, Mrs. Eleanor Rose, would recall later that Denise often said, "I want to live. There is so much in this beautiful world to do and to be seen."

Denise was studying to be a computer programmer, working part-time as a temporary office helper to pay her own way through night school, and the picnic on July 14th was a welcome vacation from her busy schedule. The afternoon had started out well, and then been somewhat marred by an argument with her boyfriend, an argument quickly resolved. The four young people in her group had stretched out on blankets in the sun, eyes closed, the voices of the swimmers and other picnickers a pleasant cacophony in the background.

A little before four P.M.—hours after Janice Ott had vanished—a sixteen-year-old girl, walking back to her friends after a stop at the park's restroom, was approached by a man with his arm in a sling. "Excuse me, young lady—could you help me launch my sailboat?"

She shook her head, but he was insistent. He tugged on her arm, "Come on."

She quickly walked off.

At 4:15 another young woman in the park saw the man with his arm in the sling.

"I need to ask a really big favor of you," he began. He needed help in launching his boat, he explained.

The woman said that she was in a hurry, that her friends were waiting for her to leave for home.

"That's O.K.," he said with a smile. But he stood staring at her for a few moments before he walked away. He'd been wearing a white tennis outfit, had looked like a nice guy, but she *was* in a hurry.

Denise and her friends roasted hotdogs around four, and then the two men had promptly fallen asleep. About 4:30, Denise got up and strolled toward the women's restroom.

One of the last people known to have seen her alive was a woman who saw Denise talking to another girl in the cinder-block structure, saw them walk out of the building together.

Back at their campsite, Denise's friends began to get restless; she'd been gone such a long time when she should have returned within a few minutes. Her purse, car keys, her woven leather sandals still rested on the blanket. It hardly seemed likely that she'd decided to walk away from the park wearing just her cut-off shorts, her blue halter top. And she hadn't mentioned that she was going swimming.

They waited, and waited, and waited, until the sun began to dip low, casting shadows over the area, and it began to grow chilly.

They didn't know, of course, about the man with the injured arm. They didn't know that he had approached yet another woman a little before five P.M., asked her the same favor, "I was wondering if you could help me put my sailboat on my car?"

That twenty-year-old woman had just arrived at the park, via her bike, and she'd seen the man staring at her. She hadn't wanted to go anywhere with him, and she'd explained that she really wasn't very strong, and that, besides that, she was waiting for someone. He had quickly lost interest in her and turned away.

The timing was about right. Denise was the kind of girl who would help someone, particularly someone who was handicapped—however temporarily.

As the evening wore on, the park emptied, and there was only Denise's car left in the lot, only her worried friends who had searched the whole park without a sign of her. They had hoped that she might have gone off to search for her dog which had wandered off.

They found the dog, alone.

Denise's boyfriend couldn't believe what was happening. He and Denise had been together for nine months. They loved each other; she would never have left him like this.

They reported her disappearance to the park ranger at 8:30 that night. It was too late to drag the lake, or even search the park thoroughly. The next day, one of the most extensive searches ever carried out in King County would begin.

Back at the little house at 75 Front Street in Issaquah, where Janice Ott lived in a basement apartment, her phone had begun to ring at four. Jim Ott had waited for his wife's call—the call she'd promised to make when he talked to her the night before, the call that was never to come. Jim dialed her number repeatedly all evening, hearing only the futile rings of a phone in an empty house.

Jim Ott waited by his phone on Monday night, too. He didn't know that his wife had never come back to her apartment.

I talked to Jim Ott a few days later after he'd caught a plane for Seattle, and he told me of a strange series of almost extrasensory communications he'd received during the days after July 14th.

"When she called me on Saturday night—the 13th—I remember that she was complaining about how long it took for mail to get from Washington to California. She said she'd just mailed me a letter, but she thought she'd call because it took five days for me to receive it. In that letter, she'd written 'Five days! Isn't that a drag? Someone could *expire* before you ever got wind of it!'"

When Jim Ott got that letter, there was every indication that Janice had indeed expired.

He paused, getting a grip on his feelings. "I didn't know she was gone on Monday night and I waited by the phone until I fell asleep. I woke up suddenly and I looked at the clock; it said 10:45. And I heard her voice. I heard it as clearly as if she was in the room with me. She was saying. 'Jim . . . Jim . . . come help me. . . .' "

The next morning, Jim Ott had learned that his wife was missing.

"It's funny, I'd sent Janice a card that crossed in the mails with her letter. It was one of those sentimental cards with a guy and a girl on it, kind of walking into the sunset. It said, 'I wish we were together again . . . much too long without you.' And then, I wrote at the bottom—and I don't know why I chose just those words, 'Please take care of yourself. Be careful about driving. Be careful of people you don't know. I don't want anything to happen to you; you're my source of peace of mind.' "

Ott said that he and his wife had always been close, had often shared the same thoughts at the same time, that he was now waiting for some other message, some sign of where she might be, but after those clear words in the stillness of his room on July 15th, "Jim . . . Jim . . . come help me. . . ." there had been only silence.

In Seattle, in his offices at the Seattle Police Department, Captain Herb Swindler opened the sealed envelope I'd delivered from the astrologer. A slip of paper read, "If the pattern continues, the next disappearance will occur on the weekend of July 13th to 15th."

He felt a chill. It had come true—twice.

10

"Ted" had surfaced, allowed himself to be seen in broad day-light, approached a half dozen young women at least, beyond the missing pair. He'd given his name. His true name? Probably not, but, for the media who pounced on the incredible disappearances it was something to headline. *Ted. Ted. Ted.*

Indeed, the dogged pursuit of reporters seeking something new to write was going to interfere mightily with the police investigation. The frantic families of the missing girls from Lake Sammamish were besieged by some of the most coercive tactics any reporter can use. When families declined to be interviewed, there were some reporters who hinted that they might have to print unsavory rumors about Janice and Denise unless they could have interviews, or that, even worse, families' failure to tell of their exquisite pain in detail might mean a lessening of publicity needed to find their daughters.

It was ugly and cruel, but it worked; the grieving parents allowed themselves to be photographed, and gave painful interviews. Their daughters had been good girls—not casual pick-ups—and they wanted that known. And they wanted the girls' pictures shown in every paper, on every TV news show; maybe that way, they could be found.

The police investigators had little time to spend giving out interviews.

Technically, the missing girls' investigations fell within several different jurisdictions: Lynda Ann Healy and Georgeann Hawkins within Seattle's city limits and that probe headed by Captain Herb Swindler and his unit; Janice Ott, Denise Naslund, and Brenda Ball had gone missing in King County, and Captain J. N. "Nick" Mackie's men were now under the heaviest stress in looking for a solution to the latest vanishing. Thurston County's Sheriff Don Redmond was responsible for the Donna Manson case, in conjunction with Rod Marem of the Evergreen College Campus Police. Susan Rancourt's case was still being actively worked by Kittitas County and the Central Washington University Campus Police, and Roberta Kathleen Parks's disappearance was being investigated by the Oregon State Police and the Corvallis, Oregon City Police.

The hue and cry from the public to produce, and produce some answers quickly, grew every day and the impact on the detectives was tremendous. If there could not be an arrest—or many arrests— the layman, bombarded with nightly television updates and front page stories, failed to understand why, at the very least, the bodies of the missing girls could not be found.

For the King County Police, the abductions and probable murders of three girls in the county meant thirty-five percent of their average yearly workload occurring in one month. Although the county population equals Seattle's half million people, it is a spread-out population, most of it small towns, rural, and sylvan, not as catalytic to violent crimes as the crowded city.

There were only eleven homicides in the county in 1972—nine closed successfully by year's end; in 1973, there had been five—all cleared. Although the homicide unit in 1974 handled armed robberies in addition to murder cases, a field-working sergeant and six detectives had been able to deal effectively with the case load. The disappearance of first Brenda Ball, and six weeks later, Janice Ott and Denise Naslund would force drastic restructuring of the unit.

Mackie was a highly competent administrator. He was not yet forty when he took over as head of the Major Crimes Unit. He had reorganized the jail's administration, and accomplished much, but his background was not heavily oriented toward actual investigative work. The field detectives were headed by Sergeant Len Randall, a soft-spoken blond bear of a man who made it a practice to join his men at major crime scenes.

For the main part, the King County detectives were a young group; the only man in the unit over thirty-five was Ted Forrester who wore his appellation "Old Man," with grudging good nature. He handled the southeast end of the county—farmland, old mining towns, woods and the foothills of Mount Rainier. Rolf Grunden had the south end, urban, part of the future megalopolis of Seattle–Tacoma. Mike Baily and Randy Hergesheimer shared the south-west, also principally urban. Roger Dunn's sector was the north end of the county—the area between Seattle's city limits and the Snohomish County line.

The newest man in the unit was Bob Keppel, a slender, almost boyish looking, man. It was in Keppel's sector that the Lake Sammamish disappearances had occurred—the territory east of Lake Washington. Until July 14, 1974, Keppel had handled only one homicide investigation.

In the end, as the years passed, the "Ted" case would weigh most heavily on Bob Keppel's shoulders. He would come to know more about "Ted," more about his victims, than any of the other investigators in the county, with the possible exception of Nick Mackie.

By 1979, Bob Keppel's hair would be shot with grey, and Captain Mackie invalided out of law enforcement with two crippling coronaries. Captain Herb Swindler would undergo critical open heart surgery. It is impossible to pinpoint just how much stress comes to bear on detectives involved in an investigation of the scope of the missing girls' cases, but anyone who is close to homicide detectives sees the tension, the incredible pressure brought on by their responsibility. If a corporation president carries the responsibility of bringing in or losing profits, homicide detectives—particularly in cases like the "Ted" disappearances—are truly dealing with life and death, working against time and almost impossible odds. It is a profession that brings with it the occupational hazards of ulcers, hypertension, coronary disease, and, on occasion, alcoholism. The public, the victims' families, the press, superiors—all demand immediate action.

The scope of the search for Denise Naslund and Janice Ott drew all of the King County's Major Crimes Unit's manpower into the eastside area, along with Seattle detectives, and personnel from the smalltown police departments near Lake Sammamish State Park: Issaquah and North Bend.

In a sense, they had a place to start now—not for Janice and Denise alone—but for the six other girls they felt sure were part of the deadly pattern. "Ted" had been seen; perhaps a dozen people came forward when the story hit the papers on July 15th: the other girls who had been approached, who shuddered to think that they had come so close to death, and the people at the park who had seen "Ted" talk to Janice Ott before she'd walked away with him.

Ben Smith, a police artist, listened to their descriptions and drew a composite picture of a man said to resemble the stranger in the white tennis outfit. He erased, drew again, tediously trying to capture on paper what was in the minds of the witnesses. It was not an easy task.

As soon as the composite appeared on television, hundreds of calls came in. But then "Ted" seemed to have had no particularly unusual characteristics. A good-looking young man appearing to be in his early twenties, blondish-brown hair, a little wavy, even features, no scars, no outstanding differences that might set him apart from hundreds, thousands of young men at the beach. The broken arm—yes—but the detectives doubted that it was really broken. They were sure the sling was off now, thrown away, after it had served its purpose.

No. "Ted" apparently was so average looking that he, perhaps, had counted on his prosaic appearance, allowed himself to be seen, and was now taking a perverse pleasure in the publicity.

Again and again, the detectives probed. "Think. Try to picture something special about him, something that stands out in your mind."

The witnesses tried. Some even underwent hypnosis in the hope they would remember more. The accent, yes, slightly English. Yes, he'd spoken of playing racquet ball while he chatted with Janice Ott. His smile, his smile was something special. He spoke with excellent grammar; he'd sounded well-educated. Good. What else? Tan, he was tan. Good. What else?

But there was nothing else, nothing beyond the strange way he had stared at a few of the almost-victims.

There was the car, the off-shaded brown VW bug of indeterminate vintage. All bugs looked alike; who could tell? And the one witness who had walked out to the parking lot with "Ted," hadn't actually seen him get into the bug. He'd leaned against it as he explained that his sailboat wasn't at the park. It could have been anyone's car. No, wait, he had gestured toward the passenger door. It must have been his car.

No one at all had seen Janice Ott get into any car on the lot.

There was Janice Ott's ten-speed bike, yellow "Tiger" brand. It wasn't the kind of bike that could be quickly disassembled for ease of transporting. A full-size ten-speed would not fit into the trunk of a VW without sticking out. Surely someone must have noticed the car with the bike—either on a rack or protruding awkwardly from the car.

But no one had.

The lakefront park was closed to the public as police divers, looking like creatures from another planet, dove again and again beneath the surface of Lake Sammamish, coming to the top each time shaking their heads. The weather was hot, and, if the girls' bodies *were* in the lake, they would have bloated and surfaced, but they did not.

County patrolmen, Issaquah police, and eighty volunteers from the Explorer Scouts Search and Rescue teams, both on foot and on horseback, combed the 400-acre park, finding nothing. Seattle police helicopters circled over the area, spotters looking down vainly for something that would help: a brilliant yellow bike or the bright blue backpack Janice had borrowed to use on Sunday, the girls themselves, their bodies lying unseen by ground parties in the tall vegetation east of the parking lot.

Sheriff's patrol cars cruised slowly along all the back roads wending through the farmland beyond, stopped to check old barns, sagging deserted sheds, empty houses.

In the end, they found nothing.

There were no ransom notes; their abductor had not taken the women away because he wanted money. It became more and more apparent as the week passed that the man in white was probably a sexual psychopath. The other women had vanished at long intervals. Many detectives believe that the male too operates under a pseudo-menstrual cycle, that there are times when the perverse drives of marginally normal men become obsessive and they are driven out to rape, or kill.

But two women in one afternoon? Was the man they sought so highly motivated by sexual frenzy that he would need to seize two victims within a four-hour time span? Janice had vanished at 12:30; Denise around 4:30. It would seem that even the most maniacally potent male might have been exhausted and satiated after one attack. Why then would he return to the same park and take away another woman only four hours later?

The pattern of attacks had appeared to be escalating, the abductions coming closer and closer together, as if the awful fixation of the suspect needed more frequent stimulus to give him relief. Perhaps the elusive "Ted" had had to have more than one victim to satisfy him. Perhaps Janice had been held captive somewhere, tied up and gagged, while he went back for a second woman. Perhaps he had needed the macabre thrill of a double sexual attack and murder—with one victim forced to wait and watch as he killed the other. It was a theory that many of us could scarcely bear to contemplate.

Every experienced homicide detective knows that if a case is not resolved within twenty-four hours, the chances of finding the killer diminish proportionately with the amount of time that passes. The trail grows colder and colder.

The days and weeks passed without any new developments. The investigators didn't even have the victims' bodies. Denise and Janice could be anywhere—100, 200 miles away. The little brown VW had only a quarter of a mile to travel before it reached the east, or into the densely populated city of Seattle to the west. It was akin to looking for two needles in a million haystacks.

On the chance that the women had been killed and buried somewhere in the vast acres of semi-wild land around the park, planes went aloft and took films with infrared film. It had worked in Houston in 1973 when Texas investigators searched for the bodies of teenage boys slain by mass killer Dean Coril. If earth and foliage have been recently over-turned, the already dying vegetation will appear bright red in the finished print, long before a human eye can detect any change at all in trees or bushes. There were some suspicious areas, and deputies dug delicately, carefully. They found only dead trees, nothing beneath them in the ground.

Film taken at several of the big company picnics held at Lake Sammamish on July 14th was quickly developed and detectives watched the subjects in the foreground—but mostly what was going on in the background, hoping to catch a glimpse of the man with his arm in a sling. They didn't smile at the laughter and playfulness on the screen, the happy faces; they kept watching for the man who might have been just out of focus. He wasn't there.

Reporters checked out Lake Sammamish State Park on the Sunday following the abductions. They found, in spite of the spectacularly sunny day—a day much like the Sunday of a week before—that there were few picnickers or swimmers. Several of the women they talked to who *were* there pointed out guns hidden under their beach towels, switchblades, whistles. Women went to the restroom in teams of two or more. Park Rangers Donald Simmons remarked that the crowd was about a twentieth the size he expected.

But, as the weeks passed, people forgot, or put the two disappearances out of their minds. The park filled up again, and the ghosts of Denise Naslund and Janice Ott didn't seem to be haunting anyone.

No one that is, but the King County Police detectives. Cases Number 74-96644; 74-95852; and 74-81301 (Janice, Denise and Brenda) would haunt them for the rest of their lives.

Dr. Richard B. Jarvis, a Seattle psychiatrist specializing in the aberrations of the criminal mind, drew a verbal picture of the man now known as "Ted," a profile based on his years of experience. He felt that, if the eight missing girls' cases were interrelated, if the girls had been harmed, that the assailant was probably between twenty-five and thirty-five, a man mentally ill, but not the type who would draw attention to himself as a potential criminal.

Jarvis felt that "Ted" feared women and their power over him, and that he would also evince at times "socially isolative" behavior.

Jarvis could see many parallels between the man in the park and a twenty-four-year-old Seattle man who had been convicted in 1970 for the murders of two young women, rape and attempted rape involving other girls. That man, designated a sexual psychopath, was currently serving a life term in prison.

The man Jarvis referred to had been a star athlete all through school, popular, considerate and respectful of women, but he had changed markedly after his high school girlfriend of longstanding had rejected him. He later married, but began his sexual prowlings after his wife filed for divorce.

A sexual psychopath, according to Dr. Jarvis, is not *legally* insane, and does know the difference between right and wrong. But he is driven to attack women. There is usually no deficiency in intelligence, no brain damage, or frank psychosis.

Jarvis' statements made an interesting side-bar in the Seattle paper that ran the story; later, much later, I would re-read that story and realize how close he had come to describing the real killer.

During the very few moments when detectives working on the cases had time to talk, we tossed back and forth possible evaluations of who "Ted" might be. He obviously had to be quite intelligent, attractive, and charming. None of the eight girls would have gone with a man who had not seemed safe, whose manner was not so urbane and ingratiating that their normal caution, all the warnings since childhood, would have been ignored. Even though force—and probably violence—came later, he must have, in most of the cases, gained their confidence in the beginning. It seemed likely that he was—or had recently been—a college student; he was apparently familiar with campuses, and the way of life there.

The device used to gain the girls' trust—beyond his appearance and personality—was certainly his illusion of comparative helplessness. A man with one arm broken, or a leg in a full cast, would not seem much of a threat.

Who would have access to casts, slings, crutches? Anyone perhaps, if he sought them out—but a medical student, a hospital orderly, an ambulance attendant, a medical supplies firm employee seemed the most apparent.

"He's got to be someone who seems above suspicion," I mused. "Someone that even the people who spend time with him would never connect to 'Ted.'"

It was a great theory, and yet it made finding that man even more impossible.

The astrology pattern, even though it had accurately predicted the weekend that the next disappearances would occur, was too ephemeral to trace. Maybe the man *didn't* know that he was being affected by those moon signs, if, indeed he was.

I was now shuttling charts full of strange symbols to Herb Swindler from R.L. Herb was taking a lot of ribbing from detectives who didn't believe in "any of that hocus pocus."

Both the King County Police and the Seattle Police were being deluged with communications from psychics, but none of their "visions" of the spots where the girls would be found proved accurate. A search for "a little yellow cottage near Issaquah" proved fruitless, as did the effort to locate a "house full of sex cultists in Wallingford" and a "huge red house in the South End full of blood." Still, the information from clairvoyants was about as helpful as the tips coming in from citizens. "Ted" had been seen here, there, everywhere—and nowhere.

If the astrological moon pattern was to be believed, the next disappearance was slated to occur between 7:25 P.M. on August 4th, 1974 and 7:12 P.M. on August 7th—when the moon was moving through Pisces again.

It did not.

In fact, the cases in Washington stopped as suddenly as they had begun. In a sense, it was over; in another sense, it would never be over.

11

I can remember standing in the Homicide Unit of the Seattle Police Department during August of 1974 and looking at a computer print-out, single spaced, that the detectives had taped to the twelve-foot ceiling of their office; it reached the floor and overflowed. On it were the names of suspects turned in by citizens, names of men they thought might be the mysterious "Ted." Just locating and questioning each of the "suspects" could take years, *if* there was enough manpower to do it, and, of course, there wasn't. There probably wasn't a police department in the country with enough investigators to go through that awesome list of suspects precisely. All King County and Seattle police could do was to cull out those that looked the most likely, and check those men out.

One of the reports that had come in, on August 10th, had a familiar, ominous sound to detectives; a young woman related an encounter that she had had in the University District a few blocks from where Georgeann Hawkins vanished. "I was walking near 16th N.E. and 50th on July 26th at 11:30 in the morning. There was this man—five foot nine or ten, good build, with brown hair to his collar—and he was wearing blue jeans, but one leg was cut off because he had a cast on his leg all the way up to his hip. He was on crutches, and he was carrying a kind of old fashioned briefcase. It was black, round on the top, with a handle. He kept dropping it, picking it up, and then dropping it again."

The girl stated that she had passed him, and looked back when she heard the briefcase thud to the sidewalk. "He smiled at me. He looked like he wanted me to help him and I was almost going to . . . until I noticed his eyes . . . they were very weird and they gave me the creeps. I began walking very rapidly away until I got to the 'Ave' (the main business thoroughfare in the University District). He was very clean-cut, and his cast was white and fresh; it looked like it had just been put on."

She'd never seen him before, and she hadn't seen him again.

Police patrol units out of the Wallingford Precinct in the city's North End watched constantly for men with broken arms, men with legs in full casts, but they found few, and those they did stop to question proved to have real injuries.

Something had been bothering me for two weeks as August drew to a close. I'd kept going back to the composite picture of the "Ted" in Lake Sammamish State Park, reading over the physical description, the references to a "slight English, or English type accent." And I saw a resemblance to someone I knew. I put it in the back of my mind, told myself that I too was being caught up in the hysteria of that long, terrible summer.

I knew a lot of men named Ted—including two homicide detectives—but the only Ted I knew who fit the description was Ted Bundy. I hadn't seen him or talked to him for eight months and, for all I knew, he had left Seattle. But, the last time I'd seen him, I knew that he'd lived at 4123 12th Avenue N.E., only blocks from so many of the missing girls.

I felt guilty that a friend I'd known for three years should even come to mind. You didn't go running to the police to turn in the name of a good friend, a friend who seemed the very antithesis of the man they sought. No, it couldn't be. It was ridiculous. Ted Bundy would never hurt a woman; he wouldn't even make an off-color remark to one. A man whose life's work was oriented toward helping people, toward eliminating that very sexual violence that marked the crimes, couldn't be involved, no matter how much he resembled the composite.

I went through periods where I didn't think about it, and then, usually just before I dropped off to sleep at night, Ted Bundy's face would flash through my mind. A long time later, I would learn that I wasn't the only one who wrestled with such indecision that August, that there were others with much more insight into Ted Bundy than I had who were torn.

Finally, I decided that I could do something that would erase my doubts. As far as I knew, Ted didn't even have a car, much less a VW bug. If I could check to see that that was still true, then I could forget it. If, by the furthest stretch of my imagination, Ted Bundy had had anything to do with the missing girls, I had an obligation to come forward.

I chose to contact Seattle Homicide detective Dick Reed. Reed, a tall, lean man with the irrepressible humor of a practical joker, had been in the homicide unit longer than any of the other seventeen detectives. He'd become a close friend. I knew I could count on him to be discreet, to run a Motor Vehicles Department check on the computer on Ted without making a big deal out of it.

I called him and began haltingly, ". . . I don't really think this is anything, but it's bugging me. I have a good friend named Ted; he's about twenty-seven, and he matches the description, and he used to live out by the University, but I don't know where he is now. Listen, I don't even think he *has* a car because I used to give him rides. And I don't want this to be like I'm turning him in or anything. I just want to know if he has a car now. Can you do that?"

"Sure," he answered. "What's his name? I'll run it through the computer. If he has a car registered to him, it will show."

"His name is Ted Bundy. B-u-n-d-y. Call me back. O.K.?"

My phone rang twenty minutes later. It was Dick Reed.

"Theodore Robert Bundy. 4123 12th Avenue N.E. Would you believe a 1968 bronze Volkswagen bug?"

I thought he was teasing me. "Come on, Reed. What does he really drive? He doesn't even have a car, does he?"

"Ann, I'm serious. He's currently listed at that address, and he drives a bronze bug. I'm going to go out and drive around the block and see if I can spot it."

Reed called me back later that afternoon and said he hadn't been able to find the car parked near the house on 12th N.E. He said he would go a step further. "I'm going to send to Olympia and get a driver's license picture of him. I'll pass it on to the County."

"But my name doesn't have to be on the information, does it?"

"No problem. I'll put it down as anonymous."

Reed did put Ted Bundy's picture into that vast hopper with some 2400 other "Ted's"—and nothing came of it. The King County detectives couldn't possibly show mug "lay-downs" of each of those 2400 "suspects" to the witnesses at Lake Sammamish State Park. Just the sheer number of faces would tend to confuse them, and there was nothing about Ted Bundy at that time that would mark him as a likely suspect. The computer check on Ted drew no "hits" at all that would make them suspect him.

I forgot about it. I didn't lend much weight to the fact that Ted had acquired a Volkswagen. A lot of people drove VWs, and I heard nothing more to indicate that Ted Bundy was a viable suspect.

I hadn't seen Ted since the Christmas party at the end of 1973. I had tried to call him once or twice when I was living on the houseboat to invite him down, but I'd never found him home.

Ted's job with the Republican Party had phased out, but he'd been busy attending law school at U.P.S. in Tacoma for most of the school year 1973–74. He'd been receiving unemployment insurance at the beginning of spring, 1974, and his attendance at U.P.S. had become desultory at best. On April 10th, he dropped out of law school altogether. He had received a second acceptance from the Registrar at the University of Utah Law School for the coming fall. He hadn't even taken his final exams at U.P.S., although he wouldn't admit it to the students in his car pool. When they asked about his grades, he'd sloughed the question off with, "I can't remember."

He may have felt that U.P.S. was not up to his standards, that Utah had much more to offer him. His last application to Utah had contained the information that he was to be married to a former Utah resident, Meg Anders, by the time he entered law school in the fall, and a notation on his application made by the registrar read, "Very anxious to attend University of Utah—will be married before quarter starts. Recommend acceptance."

One of Ted's statements accompanying his application gives an interesting insight into his self confidence:

I do not believe this is the time to be timid, and I shall not be. I have planned too long for a career in law to allow vanity or a poor performance on the LSAT to prevent me from making every effort to plead my case for admission to law school. Therefore, I say to you now, with the greatest confidence, that the file you have before you is not just the file of a 'qualified student,' but the file of an individual who is obstinate enough to want to become a critical and tireless student and practitioner of the law, and qualified enough to succeed. My grades these past two years, my recommendations, and my personal statement speak of Ted Bundy, the student, the worker, and researcher in pursuit of a legal education; the LSAT does not and cannot reveal this.

Sincerely,
Theodore R. Bundy

Ted's signature is a masterpiece of swirls and flourishes, and he had inserted a card asking that this statement be read before any of the many other forms in his application.

Not the least of the documents in Ted's file at the University of Utah Dean of Admissions' office was a letter from Governor Dan Evans, a letter he had written on behalf of Ted in 1973.

Dean of Admissions
College of Law
University of Utah
Salt Lake City, Utah 84112

Dear Dean,
I write to you in support of the application of Theodore Bundy to your law school. Ted has expressed a desire to attend the University of Utah. It is my pleasure to support him with this letter of recommendation.

I first met Ted after he had been selected to join my campaign staff in 1972. It was the consensus among those of us who directed the operation that Ted's performance was outstanding. Given a key role in the issues, research, and strategy section, he demonstrated an ability to define and organize his own projects, to effectively synthesize and clearly communicate factual information, and to tolerate uncertain and sometimes critical situations. In the end, it was probably his composure and discretion that allowed him to successfully carry out his assignments. These qualities made his contributions to strategy and policy dependable and productive.

If, however, you are concerned that a political campaign is not the measure of a prospective law student, then I am sure you will look, as I have, at Ted's other achievements and activities. Look at his academic record in his last two years of college; look at his impressive community involvements; and look at the several law-related positions he has held since graduation. I believe he is qualified to and intent upon pursuing a career in law.

I strongly recommend the admission of Ted Bundy to your law school. You would be accepting an exceptional student.

Sincerely,
Daniel J. Evans

Utah had been willing to accept Ted in 1973; he was a student they wanted, and, in 1974, he was recovered from his "serious accident" that had prevented his going to Utah the year before.

With U.P.S. behind him and Utah ahead in September, Ted had a new job in May of 1974. He was hired on May 23, 1974 to work on the budget for the Washington State Department of Emergency Services, a many-armed agency responsible for quick action in natural disasters, forest fires, enemy attack, and even plague (if such a catastrophe should occur). In 1974, the first of the nation's gas shortages was at its peak. Fuel allocation would be part of the D.E.S. duties.

Ted worked five days a week—from eight to five—and overtime if a need arose in the D.E.S. headquarters in Olympia. He commuted the sixty miles from the Rogers's rooming house, although, occasionally, he stayed in Olympia with friends or stopped in Tacoma to spend the night with his family.

It seemed an excellent interim job for Ted while he marked time before moving to Salt Lake City. His salary was $722 a month, not as much as he'd made as Ross Davis's side, and the job wasn't as prestigious, but it would give him a chance to save for tuition and to see the red tape of a state governmental office from the inside.

Around the Rogers's rooming house, newer residents saw Ted so rarely that summer of 1974 that they dubbed him "The

Phantom." They saw him mostly either coming or going, sometimes watching television. He was often away for several days at a stretch.

Ted's attitude at the Department of Emergency Services drew mixed reviews from his fellow workers. Some of them liked him; others thought he was gold-bricking. His work was erratic. It was not unusual for him to work through the night on fuel allocation projects, but he also often arrived for work very late in the morning. If he missed a day's work, he never bothered to call in to inform his supervisors he would be out; he would simply appear the next day saying he'd been ill.

Ted did sign up for the office softball team, and went to parties given by fellow workers. Carole Ann Boone Anderson, Alice Thissen, and Joe McLean liked Ted very much. Some of his other co-workers deemed him something of a con man, a manipulator, and a man who talked as if he worked hard, but who actually produced little.

Ted's longest absence from the job, according to Neil Miller, administrative officer for the D.E.S. office, had been between Thursday, July 11th and Wednesday, July 17th. This time, he *had* phoned in to say he was sick, but Miller cannot recall what his illness was. Ted had sick pay accumulated to cover the first day, but lost three days' pay.

Ted had taken a lot of kidding after the double disappearances at Lake Sammamish on July 14th, and the avalanche of publicity about the mysterious "Ted" which followed. Carole Ann Boone Anderson razzed him unmercifully about it, although they were great friends and Ted had been very considerate with her as she debated ending a relationship with a man she'd been seeing.

The head of the Search and Rescue group for Washington State also teased Ted about his being a "look-alike" for the "Ted" the police were looking for.

But nobody meant it seriously.

12

In all, there would be four individuals who would suggest the name "Ted Bundy" to the homicide probers. At about the same time I had had Dick Reed check on whether Ted drove a car—possibly a Volkswagen—a professor from the University of Washington, and a woman employed at the Department of Emergency Services in Olympia had called the King County Police to say that Ted Bundy resembled the artist's depiction of the man seen at Lake Sammamish on July 14th. Just as I had, each of them noted that there was nothing about Ted's personality or activities that would make him a suspect; it was just similarity in appearance and the name "Ted."

Meg Anders had studied the drawing that appeared in so many papers and on the nightly television news broadcasts. She saw the resemblance too, and—just as I had—she put it out of her mind at first. For me, it had been vaguely disturbing; for Meg, it could mean the end of all her dreams.

Meg had only one close friend other than Ted, a woman. That was Lynn Banks, the woman she had grown up with in Utah, the woman who had moved to Seattle about the same time Meg had. Lynn would not let Meg forget the picture of the man the police sought, even though Meg tried to ignore it. She thrust a newspaper in front of Meg's eyes and demanded, "Who does this look like? It's someone we know, isn't it?"

Meg looked away. "It does look like him, doesn't it? Very much . . ."

Lynn didn't like Ted. She had felt that his treatment of Meg was cavalier, that he was not dependable. More than that, she distrusted him. She had come upon him once, late at night, as he crept through the backyard of the house where she lived, and he hadn't had a good explanation for being there. Now, she insisted that Meg go to the police and tell them how much Ted Bundy looked like the composite picture.

"No," Meg said firmly. "I can't do that, and I don't want to talk about it anymore."

Meg Anders could not really believe that her Ted could be the Ted the police wanted. She still loved him so much, despite the way he had changed during the summer of 1974. She blocked all of Lynn's arguments. She didn't want to think about it.

Meg still had no knowledge of Ted's "engagement" to Stephanie Brooks the previous winter, had no idea how close she had come to losing him. She was concerned about the things she did know about. She and Ted were about to be separated, physically—if not emotionally—by the miles between Seattle and Salt Lake City. He planned to leave on Labor Day for law school. She had wanted him to go to Utah for his law education, but she dreaded the years ahead without him. There would be visits, of course, but it wouldn't be the same.

Ted had begun to pack up his belongings, cleaning out the room where he'd lived for almost five years. He packed up the raft hanging over his bed, the raft that had often startled the women he brought home, his plants, the bicycle wheel that hung by chains and a meat hook from the ceiling, records, books, clothes. He had an old white pickup truck he could move with, and he would haul the VW bug behind it.

Ted had become sexually cold to Meg during the summer, blaming his lack of interest in sex on job pressures and what he called "too high a peak of frustration." Meg had been hurt and confused; she was convinced that there were other women who were fulfilling his sexual drives in the way she once had.

Meg threw a small going away party for Ted, and she'd expected that they would make love afterward. But they did not, and Ted left her with only a kiss.

It was not a happy parting. Meg decided that when Ted returned to Seattle in a few weeks to sell his car so that he could repay Freda Rogers $500 he owed her, she would tell him that she wanted to break off their relationship. It didn't look like there was going to be a marriage; it didn't seem to her that they even had a relationship any longer. She was going through the same conflicting emotions that Stephanie Brooks had the January before.

And yet Meg still loved him. She had loved him for so long.

Driving the pickup with the VW trailing behind, Ted set off for Salt Lake City on the Labor Day weekend. I thought of Ted only once during the fall of 1974. In cleaning out some old files, I came across the Christmas card he'd sent me two years before. I read the front, and then, suddenly, something struck me. There had been so much stress placed on the fact that all the missing women had had beautiful long hair. I looked at the card in my hand, "She cut her long hair to buy her lover a watch chain. He sold his watch to buy her combs for her hair."

No, that was really embroidering on my imagination. It was simply a nice card, something Ted had undoubtedly picked out at random. The mention of long hair was a coincidence.

Nothing had come of my giving Ted's name to Dick Reed. If Ted had become a suspect, I would have been told. Obviously, my fears had been needless. I thought about throwing the card away, but I kept it, tucking it in with a bunch of old letters. I doubted that I would ever see Ted again.

Early in August of that uncharacteristically hot summer of 1974, a King County road worker had paused on a service road two miles east of Lake Sammamish State Park to eat his lunch. As he unwrapped a sandwich, his appetite vanished when his nostrils were assailed with a carrionlike odor. He'd glanced down the brush-strewn bank beside the road, looking for the source of the smell and seen what he took to be a deer carcass discarded by a poacher.

The man had walked back to his truck and moved to a more pleasant spot. He'd quickly forgotten the incident, but he remembered it when he picked up a newspaper on September 8th.

It is now a matter of academic conjecture whether an earlier report by that road worker would have helped detectives. It might well have been vital to the investigation, because that witness had seen not a deer carcass, but a human body, a *complete* human body, and the grouse hunters who crashed through the brush in the same region a month later stumbled across only bones.

Elzie Hammons, a Seattle construction worker, found the scattered remains on September 6th: a lower jaw, a rib cage, a spinal column.

Finally, tragically, the first solid evidence in any of the eight missing girls' disappearances had surfaced, eight months after Lynda Healy had vanished. Hammons knew instinctively what he had found, and he raced into Issaquah to find a phone.

Immediately, King County police deputies and detectives responded, and the area was cordoned off. Reporters chafed at the restriction, and cameramen tried to get something they could show on the evening news. The public was clamoring for news of the find and very little was being released.

Captain Nick Mackie, Sergeant Len Randall and their six detectives, dressed in coveralls, moved past the ropes often, carrying the bits of bone found among the sword fern and brush in over thirty locations. For four days, they worked in daylight and under powerful kleig lights as the sun set.

Coyotes had done their work well; in the end, the detectives, the two hundred Explorer Scouts, deputies, and tracking dogs had literally sifted the earth and drying ground cover in a 300-foot circle, and yet they found so little. The burning heat of July and August had accelerated decomposition, and the foraging animals had reduced the bodies to skulls and bare bones.

There were eight tufts of hair, some of it still long swatches of luxuriant dark brown, some of it blondish-red. There was one skull, the rib cage, the spinal column, a lower mandible (jaw) of another skull, numerous small bones, *but there were five femur (thigh) bones.*

There was no clothing, no jewelry, no bicycle parts, no backpack; the bodies tossed there so carelessly had been naked, and none of the victims' possessions accompanied them.

Now the grim task of identifying the remains began. Dr. Daris Swindler (no relation to Herb Swindler), a physical anthropologist from the University of Washington, studied the femur bones. Dental charts from all the missing women were compared to the skull and the lower mandible. Hair samples gleaned from the brushes the women had left behind were compared microscopically to the tufts found near Issaquah.

Captain Nick Mackie called a press conference, and the dark circles under his eyes, his tired voice, were indicative of the strain he was under. "The worst we feared is true," he announced. "We have identified the remains of Janice Ott and Denise Naslund. They were found approximately 1.9 miles from Lake Sammamish State Park where they vanished on July 14th."

He did not speak of Dr. Swindler's other findings, of the anthropologist's feeling that perhaps the femur bones had come from not two, but three or four different bodies. If there had been more skulls lying there among the alder saplings and ferns, they were gone, carried off by animals.

Who were the other two girls who had been brought there?

It was impossible to tell. It wasn't even possible to identify the sex of those thigh bones. All Dr. Swindler could determine was that they were the thigh bones of persons "under thirty," and probably between five feet and five feet five inches tall.

A search for whatever bones might remain on the hillside was hampered by the fact that the slope is crisscrossed with coal mines and shafts, left when mining in the area was suspended in 1949. Many of those mines are filled with water, and far too dangerous to even attempt to search. Mines toward the top of the hill *were* searched and nothing was found.

Memorial services were held for Denise and Janice, and the search for their killer went on.

Winter comes early to the foothills of the Cascade Mountains, and by late October, the region was blanketed with snow. If the land there had more secrets to give up, there was nothing to do but wait until spring thawing.

In the meantime, a task force of top detectives from both the Seattle Police Department and the King County Police Department, set up headquarters in a windowless room hidden between the first and second floors in the county court house. There, the walls were covered with maps of Lake Sammamish, the University District, flyers bearing the missing girls' pictures, and composite drawings of "Ted." The phone jangled continually. Thousands of names, thousands of tips; somewhere in that plethora of information, there might be the one lead to the real "Ted." But where?

Captain Nick Mackie took a brief vacation, a two-day hunting trip. As he climbed a hill in eastern Washington, he was felled by the first of the heart attacks which would eventually mean the end of his career in law enforcement; no one who had watched him agonize over the girls' disappearances, who had seen him work ten-hour days, doubted that the strain had contributed to his coronary. He was only forty-two.

Mackie recovered and was back to work within a few weeks, and the search for the smiling, tanned man in the white tennis outfit continued without let-up.

Ted Bundy had returned to Seattle in mid-September, and was back in Utah within a few days, ready to begin law classes at the University of Utah. He'd found an apartment in a big, old dormered house at 565 First Avenue in Salt Lake City, a house quite similar to the Rogers's where he'd lived in Seattle. He moved into Number 2, and soon had it decorated to his satisfaction. He got a job as a night dormitory manager on campus, and his new life had begun. He could make ends meet by getting a partial rent decrease for managing the building where he lived, and he drew $2.10 an hour at the dorm. Soon, he had a better paying job as a campus security officer at the University of Utah.

He still phoned Meg often, but he met many new women in Utah. There was Callie Fiore, a fey, almost-kooky freckled girl who lived in the house on First Avenue; Sharon Auer, who was a law student; another pretty girl who lived in Bountiful, just north of Salt Lake City. Much later, when I would see him again, when he had become the number one suspect in so many killings and disappearances, he asked me, "Why should I want to attack women? I had all the female companionship I wanted. I must have slept with at least a dozen women that first year in Utah, and all of them went to bed with me willingly."

I didn't doubt it. Women had always liked Ted Bundy. Why indeed would he have needed to take any woman by force?

During that fall of 1974, I had no knowledge whatsoever of criminal activity in Utah. It was hundreds of miles from my "territory," and I was kept busy dealing with cases in the Northwest. I had learned that I would have to have major surgery—elective, but something that couldn't wait. It would mean that I wouldn't be able to work for at least a month. I had no choice but to write twice as many stories so that I could bank enough to see us through.

Had I had either the inclination, the opportunity, or the time to investigate events around Salt Lake City during that fall, I would have read about cases that bore an eerie parallel to those seemingly ended in Washington. The siege of horror *did* seem to be over; by October three months had passed and there had been no more disappearances of young women. Detectives doubted that the killer had overcome his compulsion, had exorcized the devils that drove him. Rather, they felt that he was either dead, incarcerated in some other area, or that he had moved on.

13

It was October 18, 1974, a Friday evening, when seventeen-year-old Melissa Smith, daughter of Midvale's Police Chief, Louis Smith, prepared to attend a slumber party. Melissa was a little girl, five feet three, 105 pounds, very pretty, and she wore her long light brown hair parted in the middle. She was a cautious girl, more so because of her father's profession. She had been warned again and again; Louis Smith had seen too much violence and tragedy not to be afraid for Melissa and her sister.

Melissa had planned to leave for the all-night party at a girl-friend's home early in the evening, but, when she phoned her friend's home, there was no answer. So she was still at home when another friend called her in distress over a lovers' spat. The friend was at work at a pizza parlor, and Melissa promised to walk over and talk to her. Wearing blue jeans, a blouse with a blue flowered pattern, and a navy blue shirt, Melissa left home, alone.

Midvale is a hamlet of 5,000 people, located just south of Salt Lake City, a quiet, solidly Mormon community. It's a good place to raise kids, and Melissa, although warned, had never had reason to be afraid.

The walk to the pizza parlor meant negotiating short cuts—down a dirt road and a dirt bank, under a highway overpass and a railroad bridge, and across a school playfield.

Melissa arrived to comfort her friend, and stayed at the restaurant until a little after ten. She had planned to return home, pick up her nightclothes, and go to the slumber party. Her chosen route home would be the same short cut she'd taken hours before.

Melissa never reached home. No one saw her after she walked out of the lighted parking lot of the pizza parlor. It would be nine days before her body was found near Summit Park, many miles east of Salt Lake City in the Wasatch Mountains, long since discarded by her killer.

Pathologist Serge Moore performed the autopsy on the battered body found nude in the lonely mountains. She had been beaten savagely, possibly with a crowbar, about the head. Melissa had sustained depressed fractures on the left side and back of her head and massive subdural hemorrhages. Her body was covered with bruises which had occurred prior to death.

She had also been strangled, by ligature. Someone had tightened her own dark blue stocking around her neck so cruelly that the hyoid bone was fractured. Melissa had been raped and sodomized.

Sheriff Delmar "Swede" Larson of Salt Lake County, and Captain N.D. "Pete" Hayward, a longtime homicide detective and now chief of his unit, assigned principal responsibility for the Melissa Smith murder investigation to Detective Jerry Thompson.

It was not an easy case; no one had actually seen Melissa walk off into the shadows beyond the parking lot. No one had seen anyone with her or near her. And she had not been found for nine days. Her killer could be halfway around the world. As far as physical evidence, they had only the girl's body. There had been so little blood beneath it that it was probable she had been killed elsewhere—but where?

The investigation into Melissa's murder was still a night-and-day probe on Halloween, four days after her body was found. On October 31st, some twenty-five miles south in Lehi, Utah, seventeen-year-old Laura Aime, disappointed at the lack of excitement on Halloween night, left a café and headed for a nearby park. It was a little after midnight.

Laura Aime was almost six feet tall and weighed only 115 pounds. Her model-like slimness seemed to her to be awkward skinnyness instead. She'd dropped out of school and had moved in with friends in American Fork, working at one low-paying job after another. But she had maintained almost daily contact with her family who lived in Salem, Utah.

When Laura vanished on Halloween night, her parents didn't even know she was missing. They didn't know for four days—not until they called her friends' home to see why she hadn't been in touch with them.

"Laura isn't here," was the response. "We haven't seen her since she left on Halloween."

The Aimes were frightened. Her mother had warned her to be careful, that she must stop her practice of hitchhiking, when the news of Melissa Smith's murder had filled the headlines, and Laura had assured her that she was quite capable of taking care of herself.

Now, Laura herself was missing. The pretty, long-haired girl, the drifter in search of something to hold onto, had walked off into the night wearing only blue jeans and a sleeveless striped sweater.

Had it been a normally cold winter, the place where they found Laura Aime would have long since been covered by a blanket of snow. But it was a mild Thanksgiving Day when hikers set out through American Fork Canyon on November 27th. They found her body there in the Wasatch Mountains on a river's bank below a parking lot. She was naked, battered so that her face was unrecognizable. Her father identified her on that bleak Thanksgiving Day in the morgue. He recognized some old scars on her forearm, scars left from the time her horse tossed her into some barbed wire when she was eleven.

The post-mortem exam of Laura Aime's body, performed by Dr. Moore, elicited conclusions much like those in the autopsy on Melissa Smith. Laura Aime had depressed skull fractures on the left side and back of her head, and she had been strangled. The necklace she had worn when she vanished was caught in the nylon stocking that had been used as a ligature and was still cinched tightly around her neck. She had countless facial contusions, and her body bore deep abrasions where it had been dragged. The weapon used to inflict the skull fractures appeared to have been an iron crowbar or pry bar.

Laura Aime had also been sexually assaulted; swabs taken from her vagina and anus showed the presence of nonmotile sperm. It was far too late to determine the blood type of the man who had killed her by the dead ejaculate that he had left.

Blood tests indicated no sign of drugs, but did show that the teenager might have been under the influence of alcohol at the time of her death. The reading was just over .1—a legal indicator of intoxication, but not necessarily so profound that she would have been unable to protect herself, run, or scream.

But a scream on Halloween night might have gone unnoticed. If Laura Aime had called for help, no one had heard her.

Ted Bundy's Seattle girlfriend, Meg Anders, and her friend, Lynn Banks, had both been raised in Ogden, Utah, and Lynn had been home for a visit during the fall of 1974. She'd read of the two murdered women, looked at their pictures, and seen the physical resemblance to the Washington victims. When she got back to Seattle, she confronted Meg with her suspicions.

Meg looked through the newspaper clippings that Lynn had brought back with her, and she drew a sigh of relief when she read that Melissa Smith had disappeared on the night of October 18th.

"There, see? October 18th. I talked to Ted that night about eleven o'clock. He was looking forward to going hunting with my dad the next day. He was in a good mood."

Lynn, a tiny woman—inches under five feet—was far more persuasive than her diminutive size would indicate, and she was frightened enough to be insistent this time.

"You *have* to go to the police! There are too many things that you and I both know. You can't keep hiding from it any longer."

Meg Anders did contact the King County Police in the fall of 1974; her information about Ted Bundy resulted in the fourth listing of his name among the thousands turned in. Mine had been the first, and, like mine and the others, the information did not warrant particular scrutiny. Meg had kept most of her fears to herself in her first call to the detectives.

It was Lynn's urging which made Meg turn on her lover, but that friendship with Lynn also ended because of Lynn's animosity toward Ted. Ted himself had no idea that Meg had contacted the investigators.

Melissa Smith's body had been found, and Laura Aime was still missing on Friday evening, November 8th, 1974. It was raining that night in the Salt Lake City area, a fine misty rain that promised to become a prolonged downpour. It wasn't a particularly propitious night for a shopping trip, but eighteen-year-old Carol DaRonch headed toward the Fashion Place Shopping Mall in suburban Murray, Utah anyway. She drove her new Camaro, leaving home a little after 6:30 P.M.

Carol had graduated from high school in the spring of 1974 and taken a job with the Mountain Bell Telephone Company; she still lived at home with her parents, A frequent shopper at the mall, she had nothing to fear as she parked her car in the parking lot. She was going to shop at Auerbach's, and just browse.

She ran into some cousins, chatted with them for a while, made her purchase at Auerbach's, and was leafing through some books at Walden's Book Store when she looked up to see a handsome man standing beside her. He was well-dressed in a sports jacket, green slacks, and cordovan colored patent leather shoes. He had wavy brown hair and a moustache.

He asked her if she had parked her car in the lot near the Sears store, and she nodded. Then he inquired as to her license number and she gave it to him. He seemed to recognize it. He told her that a shopper had reported that someone had been trying to break into her car, using a wire coathanger. "Would you mind coming with me so we can check to see if anything has been stolen?"

She was taken by surprise. It didn't occur to her to wonder how the man with the moustache had found her, how he could have known that she was the owner of the Camaro. His manner was such that she assumed he must be a security guard or a policeman. She followed him meekly through the lighted central corridor of the mall and out into the rainy night. She became apprehensive as they walked through the parking lot, but the man seemed so in control, explaining that his partner probably already had the thief in custody. "Perhaps you'll recognize him if you see him," he told her easily.

She asked to see his identification, and he only chuckled. Carol DaRonch had been trained to trust police officers, and she felt somewhat foolish for having questioned the man. She opened her car with her keys, and glanced around the interior. "It's all here. There's nothing missing. I don't think he managed to get in," she told him.

The man wanted her to open the passenger door too, and she demurred; there was nothing missing, and she saw no need. She was surprised when he tried that door anyway, shrugged and led her back to the mall, telling her that they would confer with his partner.

He glanced around. "They must have gone back to our substation. We'll meet them there and identify him."

"How would I know him?" she argued. "I wasn't even there. I was inside shopping."

The man brushed off her objections, hurrying faster now, past many stores, and out into the darkness of the north parking lot. She asked his name, growing impatient and wary. She hadn't lost anything, and she had better things to do than follow this man on a wild goose chase.

"Officer Roseland. Murray Police Department," he answered shortly. "We're almost there."

They stood outside a door with "139" on it. He knocked, waited, and no one answered. He tried the door and found it locked. (The door was a back entrance to a laundromat; it was not a police substation, but Carol didn't know that.)

Now the man insisted that she accompany him to head-quarters to sign a complaint. He said he would drive her down in his car. She expected to see a squad car. Instead, he led her to a battered Volkswagen bug. She had heard of unmarked cars, even "sneaker" cars, but this didn't look like any police vehicle she'd ever seen. She demanded to see I.D.

Looking at her as if she were a hysterical female, the man grudgingly flashed his wallet and she caught only a glimpse of a small gold badge. He put it back in his pocket so quickly that she hadn't been able to see the name of a department, or even a number.

He opened the passenger door and waited for her to get in. She debated refusing, but the man was impatient, and she got into his car. The moment the doors were closed, she caught the strong odor of alcohol on his breath. She didn't think policemen were allowed to drink on duty. When he instructed her to fasten her seat belt, she said "No." She was poised, ready for flight, but the car had already pulled out of the lot and was accelerating.

The driver didn't head in the direction of the Murray Police Department. He was driving in the opposite direction. She looked at cars passing by them, wondered if she should scream, wondered if she should try to jump out, but they were going too fast, and no one seemed to be noticing them at all.

And then the car stopped, so suddenly that it ran over a curb near the McMillan Grade School. She turned to look at "Officer Roseland" and saw that he was no longer smiling. His jaw was set, and he seemed removed somehow from her. When she asked him what he was doing, he didn't answer her.

Carol DaRonch reached for the door handle on her side, and started to jump out, but the man was too quick for her. In an instant, he had clapped a handcuff on her right wrist. She fought him, kicking, screaming, as he struggled to get the cuffs on her other wrist. He missed, and managed only to get the second cuff on the same wrist. She continued to fight, scratching him, screaming at the top of her lungs, screams that went unheard in the quiet neighborhood. He was getting angrier and angrier with her.

Suddenly, there was a small, black gun in his hand. He held it next to her head and said, "If you don't stop screaming, I'm going to kill you. I'll blow your brains out."

She fell backward out of the car, onto the sodden parking strip, saw the pistol drop to the floor of the car. Now he had a crowbar of some kind in his hand, and he threw her up against his car. She put up one hand, and with the strength borne of desperation, managed to keep it away from her head. She kicked at his genitals, and broke free. Running. She didn't see or care where. She had to get away from him.

Wilbur and Mary Walsh were driving down Third Avenue East when a figure was suddenly caught in their headlights. Walsh threw on his brakes, barely missing it, and his wife fumbled with the door locks. They couldn't see who it was trying to get into their car, expecting a maniac at the very least. Then they saw that it was only a young girl, a terribly frightened girl who sobbed, "I can't believe it. I can't believe it."

Mrs. Walsh tried to comfort her, telling her that she was safe, that nothing was going to harm her now.

"He was going to kill me. He said he was going to kill me if I didn't stop screaming."

The Walshes drove Carol DaRonch to the Murray Police Station on State Street. She was unable to walk, and Wilbur Walsh carried the slender girl inside, their entrance drawing startled looks from the men on duty there.

As her sobs subsided to gasps, Carol told the policemen that one of their men—Officer Roseland—had attacked her. Of course, there was no Officer Roseland in the department, and no one used an old Volkswagen while on duty. They listened as she described the car, the man, the iron bar he'd used against her. "I didn't really see it. I felt it in my hand as he tried to hit me with it. It had a lot of sides on it, more than four, I think."

She held up her right wrist still bearing the two handcuffs. Carefully, the officers removed the cuffs, dusted them for latent prists, and came up with only useless smudges. They were not the Smith and Wesson brand usually favored by policemen, but a foreign brand: Gerocal.

Patrolmen were dispatched to the site of the attack near the grade school. They found Carol DaRonch's shoe, lost in the struggle, but nothing more. The Volkswagen was, predictably, long gone.

Patrol units cruised the mall, looking for a light colored bug with dents and rust spots, with a tear in the upholstery of the rear seat. They didn't find it, nor was Murray Detective Joel Reed successful in trying to lift prints from the door knob on door 139. Exposure to rain, even dew, can eradicate fingerprints quickly.

Carol DaRonch looked through a pile of mug books and recognized no one. She had never seen the man before, and devoutly hoped never to see him again. Three days later, she discovered two small drops of blood staining the light fake fur of her jacket collar and brought the jacket in for lab testing. The blood was not hers; it was type O, but there was not enough of it to differentiate for RH positive or negative factors.

Murray detectives had a description of a man, a car, an M.O., and, Thank God, a live victim. The similarities between the DaRonch almost-successful kidnaping and the murder of Melissa Smith could not be denied. Melissa had vanished from the parking lot of the pizza parlor, a restaurant only a mile away from the Fashion Place Mall, but no one knew what ruse had been used to entice her from that lot without a struggle. Her father was a policeman. Would she have gone willingly with a policeman?

Probably.

Whatever "Officer Roseland's" mission had been on the rainy night of November 8th, he had been frustrated. Carol DaRonch had escaped. If he had intended to rape her—or worse—his appetite had only been honed to a keener edge. He had more to do that night.

Seventeen miles from Murray, Bountiful, Utah is a northern suburb of the Mormon city, a suburb that lives up to its name with its natural beauty and its recreational opportunities. On November 8th, the Dean Kents of Bountiful prepared to attend a musical presented at Viewmont High School. Dean Kent had been ill, but he was feeling better, and he and his wife, Belva, and their oldest daughter, seventeen-year-old Debby, headed for the premiere performance of "The Redhead."

Debby Kent's younger brother, Blair, didn't care about seeing the play; he was dropped off at a roller rink and his mother promised to pick him up at 10 P.M. Shortly before eight, they arrived at the high school. They knew most of the crowd in the auditorium; high school drama productions tend to appeal principally to the families of the performers, classmates, and friends who have been prevailed upon to buy tickets.

While the audience waited in hushed expectation, Viewmont High School's drama teacher, Jean Graham, a young woman only a few years out of college herself, was approached by a stranger backstage. She was busy, distracted, trying to coordinate last minute preparations for the performance, and she paused only briefly as the tall, slim man with the moustache called to her. She remembers that he wore a sports jacket, dress slacks, and patent leather shoes, and that he was very handsome.

He was courteous, almost apologetic, as he asked her if she would accompany him to the parking lot to identify a car. She shook her head, scarcely wondering why he needed such help. She was just too busy.

"It will only take a minute," he urged.

"No, I can't. I'm in charge of the play," she said briskly, and hurried past him in the darkened hallway. He was still lingering in the hall when she headed toward the front of the auditorium twenty minutes later.

"Hi," she said. "Did you find anyone to help you yet?"

He didn't speak, but stared at her strangely, his eyes boring into her. Odd, she thought. But she was used to men staring at her.

Her duties required that she go backstage again some minutes later and the man was still there. He walked toward her, smiling.

"Hey, you look really nice," he complimented her. "Come on, give me a hand with that car. Just a couple of minutes will do it." His manner was easy, cajoling.

And yet she was on guard. She tried to get past him, told him that maybe her husband could help him. "I'll go find him." She was frightened, but that was ridiculous, she told herself. There were several hundred people close by. The man stepped to the side, blocking her way. They jockeyed for position in a peculiar side-to-side dance step, and then she was free of him. Who *was* he? He wasn't on the staff, too old to be a student, and too young to be a parent. She hurried backstage.

Debby Kent left at intermission to phone her brother and tell him that the play wouldn't be over by ten, and then returned for the second act. One of her girlfriends, Jolynne Beck, noticed the handsome stranger pacing at the rear of the auditorium. Jean Graham saw him there too, and felt curiously disturbed when she saw him for the last time, before the play had concluded.

Debby Kent volunteered to drive over to the roller rink and pick up her brother. "I'll be back to pick you up," she promised her parents.

Several residents of an apartment complex across from the high school remember hearing two short, piercing screams coming from the west parking lot between 10:30 and 11 that night. They hadn't sounded like horseplay; they'd sounded like someone in mortal terror, screams so compelling that the witnesses had walked outside to stare over at the dark lot.

They had seen nothing at all.

Debby's brother waited in vain at the bowling alley. Her parents stood impatiently in front of the high school while the crowd thinned. Finally, no one was left, but their car was still in the lot. Where was Debby? It was midnight, and they couldn't find their daughter anywhere. It seemed she'd never arrived at the car at all. They notified the Bountiful Police Department, described their daughter: seventeen years old, with long brown hair parted in the middle.

"She just wouldn't have left us stranded," her mother said nervously. "Her father's just getting over a heart attack. And the car's still in the school lot. It doesn't make sense."

Bountiful police had the radio report on the attempted abduction in Murray; they were all too aware of the Melissa Smith case, and of the disappearance of Laura Aime. The neighborhood around Viewmont High School had the school itself opened and each room checked on the off chance that Debby might have been accidentally locked in a room. Her parents frantically called all her friends. But no one had seen Debby Kent.

No one has ever seen Debby Kent again.

With the first thin wash of daylight the next morning, a police investigative crew searched the Viewmont High School parking lot, canvassed the neighborhood, looking for some clue to the inexplicable vanishing of Debby Kent.

They learned of the screams heard the night before, but found no actual witnesses to an abduction. There had been so many cars in the lot that no one could pick out one, perhaps a tannish old Volkswagen bug?

Bountiful detectives Ira Beal and Ron Ballantyne hunkered down to search the now empty lot. And there, between an exterior door to the school and the parking lot, they found the little key. They knew what it was—a handcuff key.

They took the key at once to the Murray Police Department, inserted it in the lock of the handcuffs removed from Carol DaRonch. It slid in perfectly; the cuffs opened. Still, they knew that some handcuff keys are interchangeable. The key wouldn't open their Smith and Wesson cuffs, but it would work on several brands of small cuffs. It could not be considered positive physical evidence connecting the two cases, but it most certainly was alarming. Carol DaRonch had escaped. Apparently, Debby Kent had not.

Just as in Washington State earlier in the year, the Utah law enforcement officers were inundated with calls. The last call that appeared to have any real bearing on the case came in mid-December. A man who had arrived at Viewmont High School to pick up his daughter after the play reported that he had seen an old, beat-up Volkswagen—a light colored bug—racing from the parking lot just after 10:30 on the night of November 8th.

There was no more. Debby Kent's parents were left to face a bleak, tragic Christmas season, just as Melissa Smith's and Laura Aime's were. Carol DaRonch was afraid to go out alone, even in the daylight.

14

Ted Bundy was not doing as well in his first year at the University of Utah's law school as he had done in his earlier college career. He was having difficulty maintaining a C average, and finished the quarter with two incompletes—Ted who had breezed through courses at the University of Washington and graduated "with distinction," Ted who had assured the Director of Admissions at Utah that he was not "just a qualified student, but . . . an individual who is obstinate enough to want to become a critical and tireless student and practitioner of the law, and qualified enough to succeed."

Certainly, he had to work to pay his way through and that would cut into his studying time, but he was also drinking a great deal more than he had in the past. He called Meg frequently and was very disturbed when he did not find her at home. Strangely, while he was being continuously unfaithful himself, he expected—demanded—that she be totally loyal to him. According to Lynn Banks, Meg's close friend, he would dial Lynn's number if he failed to find Meg at home, insisting on being told where she was.

On November 18, 1974, I entered Group Health Hospital in Seattle to be prepped for surgery the next morning. I had had four babies without anesthetic, but this surgery proved to be more painful than anything in my memory, and I was sedated heavily for two days. I remember calling Joyce Johnson sometime in the late afternoon of November 19th, telling her that I was all right, and I remember my mother—who had come up from Salem, Oregon to stay with my children—sitting beside my bed.

I also remember the deluge of flowers I received from various police departments. The Seattle homicide detectives sent me a dozen red roses, and Herb Swindler appeared carrying a pot of yellow mums, followed by Ted Forrester from the King County major crimes unit with a huge planter. I don't know what the nurses thought as they saw the steady parade of visiting detectives with ill-hidden gun belts at their waists. They must have thought I was a girlfriend of the Mafia under surveillance.

Of course it was only a bunch of "tough" cops being kind. They knew I was alone and worried about getting back on my feet and able to work, and they were showing the sentimental side they usually keep hidden. Within a few days, I felt much better and rather enjoyed my notoriety.

My mother visited me. She seemed worried as she remarked, "I'm glad I'm up here with the kids. You got a really strange phone call last night."

"Who was it?"

"I don't know. It sounded like it was long distance. Some man called you a little before midnight and he seemed terribly upset that you weren't home. I asked if there was any message, but he wouldn't leave any and he wouldn't say who he was."

"Upset? How upset?"

"It's hard to describe. He might have been drunk, but he seemed disoriented, panicky, and he talked rapidly. It bothered me."

"It was probably a wrong number."

"No, he asked for 'Ann.' I told him you were in the hospital and that I could have you call him back in a day or so, but he hung up."

I had no idea who it might have been, and I would not remember the call at all until I was reminded of it almost a year later.

The Intermountain Crime Conference was held at State-line, Nevada on December 12, 1974, and law enforcement officers met to discuss those cases which seemed to have indicators that other states might be involved. Washington detectives presented their missing and murdered girls cases, and Utah lawmen discussed Melissa Smith, Laura Aime, Debby Kent, Carol DaRonch. There were similarities, certainly, but there are, sadly, hundreds of young women killed each year in the United States. Many of them are strangled, bludgeoned, and raped. The method of murder was not enough to assume that any one man was responsible for a particular group of victims.

Ted's name was now listed—four times—in that endless computer read-out is the Washington State Task Force Office. But he was still one among several thousand, a man with no adult criminal record at all, and certainly a man whose job record and educational background did not stamp him as a "criminal type."

He had been in Washington, and now he was in Utah. His name was Ted, and he drove a Volkswagen. His girlfriend, Meg, had been suspicious enough to turn him in, but Meg was a very jealous woman, a woman who had been lied to; there were a score or more jealous women who had turned their boyfriends' names in as possible "Teds."

It was after that 1974 Intermountain Conference, after more urging from Lynn Banks, that Meg Anders had gone a step further. She placed a call to the Salt Lake County Sheriff's Office, and repeated her suspicious about Ted Bundy. Her voice had had a near-hysterical edge to it, and Capt. Hayward too suspected that this woman on the long distance line from Seattle was exaggerating, was allowing herself to see connections that were, at best, tenuous. He wrote down the name "Ted Bundy" and gave it to Jerry Thompson to add to the burgeoning list of Utah suspects.

Without physical evidence, without solid information, detectives cannot rush out and arrest a man. It goes against the grain of our whole philosophy of justice. It would be eight months before Ted Bundy would, through his own actions, place himself squarely in the eye of the law, would almost challenge police to stop him.

What do I remember of the Christmas season of 1974? Very little; there was no reason to. I remember that I was back at work two weeks after surgery, a recuperation compounded by a bout with the flu. I couldn't drive yet, but a few of the detectives had taken their free time to tape the vital information on some of their cases which had already been to trial, and they drove out to bring me the tapes so that I could type stories at home.

I remember that the following January brought one wailing wind storm, a storm that whipped across Puget Sound and hit our old beach house with such force that the living room window all across the southern wall was blown in, scattering plants, lamps, and glass shards twenty feet into the room. It looked like a tornado had danced through, and we froze until we could get someone out to put in a new window. That was the month the basement flooded, and the roof started to leak in several spots. I can remember being very discouraged, but I can't remember once thinking about Ted Bundy.

Ted came back to Seattle in January of 1975, and spent more than a week with Meg, from January 14th to 23rd, after he had finished his final exams in Utah. Meg didn't tell him that she had turned his name into the police, and she carried a heavy burden of guilt, although no officer had yet approached him. He was so nice to her, was seriously talking marriage again, and her doubts of the fall just past now seemed to be only a nightmare. This was the old Ted, the man she had loved for so many years. She was able to put her fears somewhere far back in her mind. The only woman in Utah that he mentioned to her was Callie Fiore, whom he described as "flaky." He said that there'd been a goodbye party for Callie sometime after Christmas of 1974, that they'd seen her off on a plane.

He didn't mention that Callie hadn't left for good, that she was coming back to Salt Lake City.

When Ted left to go back to law school, Meg felt much better. There were plans for her to visit him in Salt Lake City that summer, and he promised to come back to Seattle as soon as he could.

Caryn Campbell had vacationed in Aspen, Colorado in January of 1975. Caryn, a registered nurse, was engaged to Dr. Raymond Gadowski of Farmington, Michigan and the pair, along with Gadowski two children by a prior marriage, were combining a pleasure trip with a medical symposium on cardiology that Gadowski was scheduled to attend in Aspen.

The group checked into the plush Wildwood Inn on January 11th, and was given a room on the second floor. At twenty-three, Caryn was nine years younger than Gadowski, but she loved him and she got along well with his son, Gregory, eleven, and his daughter, Jenny, nine. She wanted to get married, and soon. When the couple argued that day, it was because Gadowski was not particularly anxious to rush into a second marriage.

Caryn Campbell was suffering with a slight case of the flu when they arrived, but she was able to take the youngsters skiing and sightseeing while Gadowski attended seminars. On January 12th, they ate dinner with friends at the Stew Pot, and Caryn ordered beef stew. The others had cock-tails but Caryn, still feeling queasy, drank only milk.

And then Caryn, Gadowski and the youngsters returned to the cozy lounge at the Wildwood Inn. Gadowski picked up the evening paper, and Caryn remembering that she'd left a new magazine in their room, headed toward the elevator to get it. She carried with her the only key to Room 210. All things being equal, she should have returned to the lounge within ten minutes.

Caryn got off the elevator on the second floor and spoke to several other physicians waiting there, doctors she'd met at the convention. They watched her walk down the hall toward her room.

Downstairs, Gadowski finished the paper, and glanced around. His children were playing contentedly, but Caryn hadn't come back. He looked toward the elevators, expecting to see her emerge at any moment. The minutes dragged, and she didn't appear.

Warning the youngsters to stay in the lounge, the young cardiologist went up to their room, and then remembered that Caryn had the key. He knocked, and waited for her to cross the room and open the door. She didn't.

He knocked again, thinking that perhaps she was in the bathroom and hadn't heard him, knocked louder. Still, she didn't open the door. He felt a prickling of alarm; if she had gotten sicker, perhaps fainted inside, she might have hit her head on something, might be unconscious.

He sprinted down to the desk, obtained a duplicate key, and ran back to the second floor. The door swung open and the room before him looked exactly as it had when they'd left before dinner. There was no sign of Caryn's purse, and the magazine that she'd meant to get was still on the stand beside the beds. Obviously, she hadn't come up to the room at all.

Puzzled and indecisive, he stood in the empty room, the key in his hand. Then he turned, and walked out into the hallway, locking the door behind him. There were a lot of parties going on that Sunday night, and he figured that fiancée had probably run into some of their friends, been enticed to stop someplace "for just one drink." She wasn't usually inconsiderate, and she must have known he'd be worried, but then the atmosphere in the lodge was an easy-going one. He checked back in the lounge, and found the children still alone.

Gadowski paced, hurrying faster and faster, from one bar in the sprawling building to another, listening for the sound of Caryn's laughter, looking for the familiar way she tossed back her hair. The din and the ebullient spirits of the people around him seemed to mock him. Caryn was gone, simply gone, and he couldn't understand it.

He gathered up his youngsters and took them to the room. It was 10 P.M. now, and, outside the big warm lodge, it was freezing cold. All Caryn had been wearing when she'd strolled toward the elevator were blue jeans, her light brown wooly jacket and boots. That was warm enough during the day, but it was inconceivable that she'd gone out into the January Colorado night like that.

Gadowski called the Aspen Police Department shortly after ten. The patrolmen who arrived took a missing report, but they assured the Michigan doctor that almost everybody who "disappeared" showed up after the bars and parties broke up.

Gadowski shook his head impatiently. "No, she isn't like that. She was ill. She may have gotten sicker."

A description of the nurse was broadcast to patrolmen on duty in Aspen: twenty-three-year-old woman, five feet, four inches tall, brown shoulder-length hair, the clothes she was wearing. Many times during the night, patrol units would pull up to a young woman wearing jeans, a wooly jacket, only to find that it was someone else; it was never Caryn Campbell.

By morning, Gadowski was distraught after a sleepless night, the children crying and upset. Aspen police detectives moved through the Wildwood Inn, searching room by room, storerooms, closets, even the kitchens, and up through crawl spaces, peering down into the elevator shafts. The pretty nurse wasn't anywhere in the lodge.

They questioned every guest, but no one had seen Caryn Campbell after she'd said "Hi" to the group at the elevator on the second floor and walked down the hall toward her room.

Finally, Dr. Gadowski packed up their bags and flew home with his children, hoping each time the phone rang that it would, somehow, be Caryn, with a logical explanation of why she had walked away from him.

The call never came.

On February 18th, a recreational employee working along the Owl Creek road a few miles from the Wildwood Inn, noticed a flight of squawking birds that were circling something in a snow-bank twenty-five feet off the road. He walked through the melting drifts and turned away, sickened.

What remained of Caryn Campbell's nude body lay there in the snow, stained crimson with her blood.

Pathologist Dr. Donald Clark performed a post mortem examination on the body that dental records verified was Caryn's. She had died of repeated blunt instrument blows to her skull and had, in addition, suffered deep cuts from a sharp weapon. A knife? An axe? There was not enough tissue left in the neck area to say whether she had been strangled, but her hyoid bone had been cracked.

It was much too late to tell if she had been subjected to a sexual attack, but the nude condition of her body pointed to rape as a strong motive.

Undigested bits of stew and milk were easily identifiable in her stomach; Caryn Campbell had been killed within hours after she had eaten on January 12th, which would make time-of-death shortly after she had left the lounge of the Wildwood Inn to go up to her room.

She had never made it to her room, or, if she had, someone had waited inside for her. That seemed unlikely; the room had shown no signs of struggle at all. Somewhere, along that well-lighted corridor on the second floor of the Wildwood Inn, somewhere between the elevators and Room 210, Caryn had met her killer, and had, seemingly, gone with him without a fight.

It was a disappearance reminiscent of the Georgeaann Hawkins case in June of 1974. Less than fifty feet to walk to safety, and then, gone.

One California woman tourist had been in that corridor of the Wildwood Inn on the night of January 12th and she had seen a handsome young man who had smiled at her, but she'd thought nothing of it. She had left for home before Caryn Campbell's disappearance became known to other hotel guests.

The winter waned, and back in Washington State the snows had begun to melt and slough off in the foothills of the Cascade

Mountains. On Saturday, March 1, 1975, two Green River Community College students were working on a forestry survey project on Taylor Mountain, a thickly wooded "mini" mountain east of Highway 18, a two lane highway that cuts through forests between Auburn and North Bend, Washington. The site is about ten miles from the hillside where the remains of Janice Ott, Denise Naslund, and an unidentified third person (perhaps fourth) were located in September of 1974. It was slow going through the moss shrouded alders, the ground carpeted with sword ferns and fallen leaves.

One of the forestry students looked down. A human skull rested at his feet.

Brenda Ball had been found at last, although it would take dental records to verify that. As they had six months before, King County Police detectives immediately ordered the lonely area cordoned off, and again, Detective Bob Keppel led over two hundred searchers into the area. Men and dogs moved with painstaking slowness through the dank forest, turning over piles of leaves, rotten stumps.

Denise and Janice had been found only a few miles from the park where they vanished; Brenda's skull was discovered thirty miles away from the Flame Tavern. This could, perhaps, be explained by the fact that she'd intended to hitchhike to Sun Lakes State Park east of the mountains. Highway 18 would have been a likely alternate route to Snoqualmie Pass. Had she gotten into a car with the stranger with a sling on his arm, grateful that she had a ride all the way to Sun Lakes? And had he then pulled over, stopped in this desolate region, and stared at her with the pitiless eyes of a killer?

The discovery of the skull on Taylor Mountain made some kind of macabre sense, but that was all there was to be found of the dark-eyed girl. Even if animals had scattered the remainder of her skeleton, there should have been something more and there was nothing. No more bones, not so much as a tattered rag of her clothing.

Cause of death was impossible to determine, but the skull was fractured on the left side, smashed by a blunt instrument.

The grim search went on for two more days.

Early on March 3rd, Bob Keppel slipped and fell as he made his way down a slimy incline. He had stumbled—literally—over another skull one hundred feet away from that of Brenda Ball.

Dental records would confirm that Keppel had found all that was left of Susan Rancourt, the shy blonde coed who had vanished from Ellensburg, *eighty-seven miles away!* There was no reason at all for Susan to be here in this lonely grove. It appeared that the killed had established his own graveyard, bringing only his victims' severed heads with him, month after month. It was an ugly supposition to contemplate, but one that could not be ignored.

Susan's skull, too, had been brutally fractured.

As the search went on, the other families waited, dreading that their daughters might be up on Taylor Mountain, that they would hear a knock on their door at any time.

Fifty feet more of the tedious sifting of wet leaves, brushing aside dripping sword ferns. And there was yet another skull. Dental records confirmed this victim was a girl that detectives hadn't expected to find so far away from home. It was that of Roberta Kathleen Parks, missing since the previous May from Corvallis, Oregon—262 miles away. As with the others, it bore the crushing damage of a blunt instrument.

The first to vanish was the last to be found. Lynda Ann Healy, the teacher of retarded youngsters, gone fourteen months from the basement room in the University District, could be identified only by her lower mandible. The fillings in the jaw bone matched Lynda's dental charts. Lynda's skull, too had been carried to Taylor Mountain.

Although the search continued from dawn until sunset for another week, no more skulls were found, no clothes, no jewelry.

There had been a few dozen small bones, neck bones, but not nearly enough to indicate that the victims' complete bodies had been carried into the forest, and the realization that only the girls' heads had been brought there one at a time over a six months period brought forth more rumors of cults, witchcraft, and satanism.

Seattle Police had a file, File 1004, a file on occult happenings. Reports came into the beleaguered Task Force—reports from people who thought they'd seen "Ted" at cult gatherings. In any case with such widespread publicity, a number of "kooks" will surface advancing theories that make an ordinary man's hair stand up on the back of his neck. There were totally unsubstantiated rumors that the missing and murdered girls had been sacrificed and their headless bodies dumped, weighted, into the almost bottomless waters of Lake Washington.

A psychic from eastern Washington contacted Captain Herb Swindler and prevailed upon him to meet with her at dawn on the Taylor Mountain site where the woman pierced the ground with a stick and attempted to deduce information from the way it cast shadows. It was an eerie scene, and it produced no new theories.

Swindler was soon besieged by messages from those who claimed direct contact with "that other world," and almost as many requests from other departments with crimes they felt might have resulted from devil worship. The man was a no-nonsense cop, and he was hassled by his detectives who thought the psychic angle was ridiculous.

But Swindler kept remembering the astrological prediction that had come true on July 14th. Asked if he felt the occult was involved, he shook his head, "I don't know; I've never known."

Psychiatrists were more inclined to believe that the killer was a man obsessed by a terrible compulsion, a compulsion that forced him to hunt down and kill the same type of woman, over, and over, and over again, that he could never be able to murder her enough times to find surcease.

Over at County Police headquarters, Captain Nick Mackie admitted that the crimes might never be solved. The probers knew now that Lynda, Susan, Kathy, Brenda, Denise and Janice were dead. As to the fate of Donna and Georgeann, they were in the dark. There were still the extra femur bones found with Denise and Janice; they probably belonged to the missing women. It was all they were ever to know. Donna Manson and Georgeann Hawkins may never be found. In Utah, it is the same with Debby Kent. Gone.

"The name of the game is tenacity," Mackie remarked. "We have looked at 2,247 'Ted' lookalikes, 916 vehicles . . ."

Mackie said that there were 200 suspects left after the winnowing out, but 200 is still an impossibly large number of men to learn *everything* about. "We have no crime scene evidence, no positive means of death," Mackie said. "It's the worst case I've ever been on. There's just nothing."

Mackie added that a psychological profile of the killer indicated that he would probably have criminal behavior in his background, was probably a sexual psychopath. "You go up to a certain point in your investigation," the weary detective chief commented. "Then you stop, and start all over again."

Ted Bundy's name remained on the roster of 200 suspects. But Ted Bundy had no criminal background; he was squarely on the other side of the law from all the information the Task Force had uncovered on him. His juvenile records were shredded, and they didn't know of his long-ago arrests for car theft and burglary. Meg hadn't told them that she knew Ted had stolen television sets, even while he was an honor student at the University. There was a great deal she hadn't yet told them.

Just as the crimes had stopped in Washington, they stopped in Utah. The murder of Caryn Campbell in Aspen was another state away, and appeared to be an isolated instance. Detective Mike Fisher in Aspen was busy checking out local suspects, eliminating every man who had known the pretty nurse. He could see no link with the Utah cases, and Washington Stats was a long, long way away.

Crime news was about to escalate in Colorado.

Vail, Colorado is one hundred miles away from Aspen, a booming ski resort town, but without the flash, money, the drugs, and the "laissez faire" attitude of Aspen. Jerry Ford keeps a vacation condo in Vail, and Cary Grant occasionally flies in quietly with his daughter, Jennifer, to ski.

Jim Stovall, Chief of Detectives of the Salem, Oregon Police Department, takes his winter vacation there, working as a ski instructor. His daughter lives there, also a ski instructor.

Stovall drew a deep breath as he recalled to me that twenty-six-year-old Julie Cunningham was a good friend of his daughter, and Stovall, who has solved so many Oregon homicides, was at a loss to know what had happened to Julie on the night of March 15th.

At twenty-six, Julie Cunningham should have had the world by the tail. She was very attractive and she had silky dark hair, parted in the middle. She shared a pleasant apartment in Vail with a girl-friend, and worked as a clerk in a sporting goods store, and as a part-time ski instructor. But Julie wasn't happy; she was searching for the one man she could really love and trust, someone to settle down with. She'd done the ski-bum bit, but she was growing out of that; she wanted marriage and children.

Julie was not the best judge of men. She believed their lines, and she was becoming disillusioned. She'd heard, "It's been great; I'll give you a call some day" much too often. Maybe Vail was the wrong place for her to be; maybe the aura of a ski town didn't lend itself to permanent relationships.

In early March of 1975, Julie was to suffer her last heartbreak. She thought she had met the man she wanted, and she was thrilled when he invited her to go to Sun Valley with him for a vacation. But she'd been "dumped on" again when they reached the resort made famous by Sonja Henie movies in the thirties. The man had never had any intention of a committed relationship, and she returned to Vail, crying and depressed.

On the Saturday night of March 15th, Julie didn't have a date. She called her mother that evening, feeling a little better when she hung up just before nine. She decided to get out of her apartment, and, wearing blue jeans, a brown suede jacket, boots, and a ski cap, headed for a tavern a few blocks away. Her roommate was there; she could have a beer or two. There was always tomorrow.

Only there wasn't. There were no more tomorrows for Julie Cunningham. She didn't arrive at the tavern, and, when her roommate came home in the early morning hours, Julie wasn't there. Julie's clothes, books, records, make-up—everything but what she'd worn when she walked out—were there, but their owner never returned.

Julie Cunningham's disappearance was soon eclipsed in the news by an event in Aspen. Claudine Longet, the divorced wife of singer Andy Williams, was arrested for the March 19th slaying of her lover, "Spider" Sabich, a former world champion skier. The lovers' quarrel, the notoriety of the principals, made much bigger headlines than the disappearance of an unknown ski instructor.

But the pattern was repeating, just as it had in Washington a year earlier. A victim in January. No victim in February. A victim in March.

Would there be a victim in April in Colorado?

Denise Oliverson was twenty-five years old that spring, married, and living in Grand Junction, Colorado, a town just east of the Utah-Colorado border on Highway 70. Denise argued with her husband on Sunday afternoon, April 6th, and left their home, riding her yellow bike, headed for her parents' home. She may have grown less angry with each mile that passed; it was a wonderful spring day, and perhaps she realized that their fight had been silly. Maybe she planned to go home and make up that night.

It was a warm day, and Denise wore jeans, and a print, green long-sleeved blouse; if anyone saw the pretty, dark-haired woman peddling her ten-speed that afternoon, they have never come forward to report it.

Denise didn't arrive at her folks' place, but they hadn't been expecting her. She didn't come home that night either, and her husband figured she was still angry with him. He would give her time to cool off, and then call.

On Monday, he called her parents and was startled to learn she had never arrived at their home. A search of the route she had probably taken was instituted and police discovered her bike—and her sandals—beneath a viaduct near a railroad bridge close by the Colorado River on U.S. 50. The bike was in good working order; there would have been no reason to leave it there.

Like Julie Cunningham, Denise Oliverson had disappeared.

There would be other girls who would vanish in Colorado during that bright spring of 1975.

Eighteen-year-old Melanie Cooley, who looked enough like Bountiful Utah's Debby Kent to have been a twin, walked away from her high school in Nederland, a tiny mountain hamlet fifty miles west of Denver on April 15th. Eight days later, county road workers found her battered body on the Coal Creek Canyon road twenty miles away. She had been bludgeoned on the back of the head—probably with a rock—and her hands were tied. A filthy pillowcase, perhaps used as a garotte, perhaps as a blindfold, was still twisted around her neck.

On July 1st, Shelley K. Robertson, twenty-four, failed to show up for work in Golden, Colorado. Her family checked around and discovered she had been seen alive on Monday, June 30th, by friends. A police officer had seen her in a service station in Golden on July 1st, in the company of a wildhaired man driving an old pickup truck. No one saw her after that.

Shelley had been a hitchhiker, and her family tried to believe that she had decided to take off on a whim for a visit to another state. But, as the summer passed with no word from her at all, that seemed unlikely.

On August 21, Shelley's nude body was discovered 500 feet inside a mine at the foot of Berthoud Pass by two mining students. Decomposition was far advanced, making cause of death impossible to determine. Almost 100 miles from Denver, the mine is quite close to Vail. The mine was searched on the possibility that Julie Cunningham's body might be hidden inside, but she was not found.

And then it was over. There were no more victims,, or, if there were, they were young women whose vanishing was not reported to police. In each jurisdiction, the detectives had checked out relatives, friends, known sex criminals, and eliminated them all, through polygraph examinations or alibis.

Of all the Western victims, there was not one who had short hair, not one who could be described as anything but beautiful. And not one who would have gone away willingly with a complete stranger; even the girls who had been known to hitchhike had been cautious. Yet there is a common denominator in almost every instance. Something in the victims' lives had gone awry on the days they vanished, something that would tend to make them distracted, and therefore easy prey for a clever killer.

Brenda Baker and Kathy Devine were both running away from home; Lynda Ann Healy had been ill; Donna Manson was suffering from depression; Susan Rancourt was alone on campus at night for the very first time, ever; Roberta Kathleen Parks was depressed and upset over her father's illness; Georgeann Hawkins was extremely worried about passing her Spanish final; Janice Ott was lonely for her husband and depressed on that Sunday in July; Denise Naslund had had a fight with her boyfriend. Of the

Washington women, only Brenda Ball had been her usual good-natured self the last time her friends saw her, yet patrons at the Flame Tavern recall that she was worried because she'd been unable to find a ride home that night.

In Utah, Carol DaRonch was a naive, too-trusting girl; Laura Aime was a little drunk, disappointed at the fizzle of her party plans for Halloween; Debby Kent was worried about her father's recent heart attack and anxious to protect him from worry; Melissa Smith was concerned about her friend's "broken heart" and probably was thinking about their conversation as she left the pizza parlor.

The Colorado victims too had other things on their minds. Caryn Campbell had had an argument with her fiancé over their prolonged engagement, and she was ill. Julie Cunningham was depressed over a failed romance; Denise Oliverson had had a fight with her husband; and Shelley K. Robertson had argued with *her* boyfriend the weekend before she vanished. The thoughts of Melanie Cooley are not known.

The most basic bit of advice given to women who have to walk alone at night is, "Look alert. Be aware of your surroundings and walk briskly. You will be safer if you know where you are going, and if anyone who observes you senses that."

Had the man who approached these young women divined somehow that he had come upon his victims at a time when they were particularly vulnerable, when they were not thinking as clearly as they usually did? It would almost seem so. The stalking, predatory animal cuts the weakest from the pack, and then kills at his leisure.

15

In May of 1975, Ted Bundy had invited some old friends from the Washington State Department of Emergency Services to visit him at his apartment on First Avenue in Salt Lake City. Carole Ann Boone Anderson, Alice Thissen, and Joe McLean spent almost a week with him. Ted seemed to be in excellent spirits and enjoyed driving his friends around the Salt Lake City area. He took them swimming and horseback riding. He and Callie took them one night to a homosexual nightclub. Alice Thissen was somewhat surprised that, although Ted said he had been there before, he seemed ill at ease in the gay club.

The trio from Washington found Ted's apartment very pleasant; he'd cut pictures out of magazines and tried to duplicate the decor he favored. He still had the bicycle tire, hung from the meat hook in his kitchen, and he used that to store knives and other kitchen utensils in a mobile effect. He had a color television set, a good stereo, and he played Mozart for them to accompany the gourmet meals he prepared.

During the first week in June, 1975, Ted came back to Seattle to put a garden in for the Rogers at his old rooming house, and he spent most of his time with Meg. She still made no mention of the fact that she'd talked with both the King County Police and the Salt Lake County Sheriff's Office about him. The cases of the missing women in Washington were no longer being played up in local papers.

Because neither King County nor the Seattle Police Department could spare the detectives detailed to the Task Force during the summer when so many of their investigators were on vacation, the Task Force was to be disbanded until September.

Meg and Ted decided to marry the following Christmas and, although they had only five days together in June, they made plans for her to visit him in Utah in August. Meg was almost convinced that she had been wrong, that she had allowed Lynn Banks to cloud her mind with suspicions that couldn't have any basis in fact.

But time was growing short, far shorter than either Meg or Ted realized.

If anything was bothering Ted Bundy's conscience during that summer of 1975, he didn't show it. He was working as a security guard, still managing the building he lived in, and, if he drank more and more, drinking was a part of college life. But his grades in law school had continued to drop; he wasn't beginning to live up to the potential of a man with his I.Q., his boundless ambition.

It was close to 2:30 A.M. on August 16th, when Sergeant Bob Hayward, a stocky, balding twenty-two-year veteran of the Utah Highway Patrol pulled up in front of his home in suburban Granger, Utah. Bob Hayward is the brother of Captain "Pete" Hayward, the homicide detective Chief in the Salt Lake County Sheriff's Office, but his duties are quite different. Like Washington state, Utah's Highway Patrol deals only with traffic control, but Hayward has the kind of sixth sense that most long-time cops have, the ability to note something that seems just a hair off center.

In the balmy August predawn, Hayward noticed a light-colored Volkswagen bug driving by his home. The neighborhood was strictly residential, and he knew almost everyone who lived along his street, knew the cars that usually visited them. There was rarely any traffic at this time, and he wondered what the Volkswagen was doing there.

Hayward threw on his brights so that he could catch the license plate on the bug. Suddenly the Volkswagen's lights went out, and it took off at high speed. Hayward pulled out, giving chase. The pursuit continued through two stop signs and out onto the main thoroughfare, 3500 South.

Hayward soon was just behind the slower car, and the Volkswagen pulled into an abandoned gas station parking lot and stopped. The driver got out and walked to the rear of his car, smiling. "I guess I'm lost," he said ruefully.

Bob Hayward is a gruff man, not the sort of highway patrolman that a speeder or reckless driver would choose to meet. He looked closely at the man before him, a man who appeared to be about twenty-five, who wore blue jeans, a black turtleneck pullover, tennis shoes, and longish, wild hair.

"You ran two stop signs. Can I see your license and registration?"

"Sure." The man produced his I.D.

Hayward looked at the license. It had been issued to Theodore Robert Bundy, at an address on First Avenue in Salt Lake City.

"What are you doing out here at this time of the morning?"

Bundy answered that he had been to see *The Towering Inferno* at the Redwood drive-in and was on his way home when he'd become lost in the subdivision.

It was the wrong answer; the drive-in Bundy mentioned was in Hayward's patrol area, and he'd driven by earlier that night. *The Towering Inferno* was not the picture playing there.

As the burly sergeant and Bundy talked, two troopers from the Highway Patrol pulled up in back of Hayward's car, but remained inside, watching. Hayward seemed to be in no danger.

Hayward glanced at the Volkswagen, and noticed that, for some reason, the passenger seat had been removed and placed on its side in the back seat.

He turned back to Bundy. "Mind if I look in your can?"

"Go ahead."

The highway patrol sergeant saw a small crowbar resting on the floor in back of the driver's seat, and an open satchel sitting on the floor in front. He played his flashlight over the open satchel, and saw some of the items inside: a ski mask, a crowbar, an ice pick, some rope, wire.

They looked to Hayward like the tools of a burglar.

Hayward placed Ted Bundy under arrest for evading an officer, frisked him, and handcuffed him. Then he called Salt Lake County for back-up from a detective on duty.

Deputy Darrell Ondrak had the third watch that night, and responded to 2725 W. 3500 South. He found troopers Hayward, Fife, and Twitehell waiting with Ted Bundy.

Bundy maintains today that he gave no permission to search his car; Ondrak and Hayward say that he did.

"I never said, 'Yes, you have my permission to search,' " Ted says, "but I was surrounded by a number of uniformed men: Sergeant Hayward, two highway patrolmen, two uniformed deputies. I wasn't exactly quaking in my boots, but . . . but I felt I couldn't stop them. They were intent and hostile and they'd do what they damn well pleased."

Ondrak looked in the canvas satchel. He saw the ice pick, a flashlight, gloves, torn strips of sheeting, the knit ski mask, and another mask—a grotesque object made from a pair of pantyhose. Eye holes had been cut in the panty portion and the legs were tied together on top. There was a pair of handcuffs, too.

Ondrak checked the trunk and found some large green plastic garbage bags.

"Where'd you get all this stuff?" he asked Ted.

"It's just junk I picked up around my house."

"They look like burglar tools to me," Ondrak said flatly. "I'm going to take these items, and I suspect the D.A. will be issuing a charge of possession of burglary tools."

According to Ondrak, Ted simply replied "Fine."

Detective Jerry Thompson met Ted Bundy face to face on that early morning of August 16, 1975. Thompson, tall, good-looking, perhaps five years older than Bundy, was later to become an important adversary, but now they barely glanced at each other. Thompson had other things to do, and Bundy was intent on bailing out and going home. He was released on P.R. (personal recognizance).

It was the first time in his adult life that Ted Bundy had ever been arrested, and it had been such a chance thing. Had he not driven by the home of Sergeant Bob Hayward, had he not tried to run from the pursuing policeman, he would have been home safe.

Why had he run?

On August 18th, Thompson glanced over the arrest reports for the weekend. The name "Bundy" caught his eye. He'd heard it someplace before, but he couldn't quite place it. He hadn't even known the name of the man brought in early Saturday morning. And then he remembered. Ted Bundy was the man that the girl from Seattle had reported in December of 1974.

Thompson read over the arrest report carefully. Bundy's car was a light-colored Volkswagen bug. The list of items found in the car now struck him as much more unusual. He pulled out the DaRonch report, and the Debby Kent file.

The handcuffs found in Bundy's car were Jana brand; the handcuffs on Carol DaRonch's wrist were Gerocal, but he wondered just how many men routinely carried handcuffs with them. There was the crowbar, similar to the iron bar that DaRonch had been threatened with.

Ted Bundy was listed as being five feet, 11 inches tall, weighing 170 pounds. He was a law student at the University of Utah . . . yes, that's what his girlfriend from Seattle had said too. He'd been arrested in Granger, which was only a few miles from Midvale where Melissa Smith had last been seen alive.

There were more similarities, more common threads in front of Thompson than he'd yet had in his ten months of trying to find the man with the Volkswagen—"Officer Roseland."

On August 21, Ted was arrested on the added charges: possession of burglary tools. He did not appear to be visibly upset by the arrest and had deft explanations for the items found in his car. The handcuffs? He'd found them in a garbage dumpster. He'd used the pantyhose mask as protection under his ski mask against the icy winds of ski slopes. And didn't everyone own crowbars, ice picks, garbage bags? He seemed amused that the detectives would consider any of these things burglary tools.

It was a posture that Ted Bundy would assume over and over again as the years passed. He was an innocent man, accused of things that were unthinkable for him.

The arrest by Sergeant Hayward on August 16th was the catalyst to a flurry of intense activity in the Salt Lake County Sheriff's Office during late August and September of 1975. Captain Pete Hayward and Detective Jerry Thompson felt they had their man in the DaRonch kidnapping, and suspected that Ted Bundy might well be the man who had taken Melissa, Laura, and Debby away.

Ted readily signed a permission-to-search form on his First Avenue apartment, and accompanied Thompson and Sergeant John Bernardo as they scrutinized the neat rooms. It was not a forced search; there was no search warrant listing specific items. In essence, this meant that the detectives had no authority to remove anything from Ted's apartment—even if they should come across something they felt might be evidence. If they did, they would have to go to a judge and obtain a search warrant listing those items.

Thompson glanced up at the bicycle wheel suspended from the meat hook, at the assortment of knives hanging from it. Then he glanced at a chopping block.

Following Thompson's glance, Ted said mildly, "I like to cook."

The detectives saw the rows of law text books. A few months later, a Washington detective would comment to me that the Utah investigators had found a "weird sex book" in Ted's library. When I asked Ted about it later, he told me that he had Alex Comfort's *Joy of Sex*, and I laughed. I had a copy too, as did thousands of other people. It was hardly Krafft-Ebing.

There were other items in the apartment, seemingly innocuous, but meaningful in the probe going on. There was a map of ski regions in Colorado, with the Wildwood Inn in Aspen marked, a brochure from the Bountiful Recreation Center. Questioned, Ted said he'd never been to Colorado, that a friend must have left the map. He thought he must have driven through Bountiful, Utah, but felt someone else had dropped the brochure in his apartment.

Thompson insists today that he found patent leather shoes in Bundy's closet on that first visit, but, when he returned later with a search warrant, they were gone. A television set and a stereo he had seen were also absent.

If the two detectives had expected to find something solid to tie Ted with the murdered Utah victims, they were to be disappointed. There were no women's clothes, jewelry, or purses.

When they had searched the whole place, Ted agreed to allow them to photograph his Volkswagen bug, parked in the rear of the building. It had dents and rust spots, a tear at the top of the rear seat.

Bernardo and Thompson left; they felt they were closer to unraveling the truth, but were somewhat disconcerted by Ted Bundy's casual attitude. He certainly didn't appear concerned.

One of Ted's women friends in Salt Lake City was Sharon Auer. She put him in touch with attorney John O'Connell, a tall, bearded man who affected a cowboy hat and boots. A respected criminal defense attorney in the Mormon city, O'Connell immediately put a lid on Ted's conversations with detectives. The lawyer called Thompson and said that Bundy would not come to their offices as scheduled, on August 22nd.

Although Ted would not talk to detectives any longer, his mug shot, along with several others, was shown to Carol DaRonch and the drama teacher, Jean Graham, who had seen the stranger just before Debby Kent vanished forever.

It had been ten months, but Mrs. Graham chose Bundy from the stack of photos almost immediately. His mug shot showed him clean shaven; she said that Ted Bundy was a ringer for the man she'd seen, and all that was missing was a moustache.

Carol DaRonch was not as definite. The first time she thumbed through the packet of photos, she set Ted's picture aside, but did not comment on it. When Thompson asked her why she had separated that photo from the others, she seemed reticent.

"Why did you pull that one out?" Thompson asked.

"I'm not sure. It looks something like him . . . but I really couldn't say for sure."

The next day, Bountiful detective Ira Beal showed her a laydown of drivers' license photos. In this group, Ted was depicted as he had looked in December, 1974, and appeared quite different than the man in the mug shot taken in August of 1975. Ted was—and is—a man with a chameleonlike quality, his appearance changing dramatically in almost every picture taken of him, apparently through no conscious effort on his part.

Carol looked at the second set of pictures. This time, she chose Ted Bundy's picture almost at once. Like the teacher, she remarked that he had had a moustache when she encountered him on November 8th, 1974.

The kidnap victim's identification of Bundy's Volkswagen was less clear. She had seen the pictures taken of it several times, and, by the time she was taken to view it, it had been sanded, the rust spots painted over, and the tear in the back of the seat mended. It had also been scrubbed and hosed down inside and out.

Ted Bundy would never again be out of the constant attention of law enforcement agencies. He was not in jail, but he might as well have been. Surveillance units watched him continually during September of 1975, and wheels were turning behind the scenes. His gasoline credit card records had been requested, his school records were subpoenaed, and, probably the most disastrous move as far as his future freedom was concerned, Utah detectives had contacted his fiancée, Meg Anders.

16

I had neither seen nor heard from Ted Bundy since the Crisis Clinic Christmas party in December, 1973. And then, my phone rang on an afternoon in late September, 1975.

It was Ted, calling from Salt Lake City. I was surprised, but glad to hear his voice. I felt a sharp twinge of guilt when he began, "Ann, you're one of the few people I can really trust in Seattle."

Great. I remembered turning his name in to Dick Reed in August of 1974, and wondered just how trustworthy he would find me if he knew that. But that had been a long time ago, and I hadn't heard a word about him since. I wanted to ask him what he was doing in Salt Lake City, but he had something on his mind.

"Listen, you have contacts with the police. Could you find out why they're subpoenaing my law school records down here?"

A dozen thoughts raced through my mind. Why now? Why after thirteen months? Was Ted being investigated because of what I had done so long before? Had I implicated him in something that apparently had him very concerned? I had never heard of Carol DaRonch, Melissa Smith, Laura Aime, or Debby Kent. I was completely unaware of the Utah investigation, and it didn't seem possible that the Task Force would wait more than a year to follow up on a lead I had given.

I answered slowly. "Ted, I probably could find out, but I wouldn't do anything underhanded. I'd have to tell them who wanted to know."

"No problem. I'm just curious. Go ahead and tell them that Ted Bundy wants to know. Call me back, collect, at 801-531-7733 if you find out anything."

I stared at the phone in my hand. I truly couldn't believe the conversation just finished. Ted had sounded exactly as he always had: cheerful and confident. I debated calling King County Police.

I'd never interfered in their investigations, and I hesitated now. It was almost four o'clock, and the detectives would be going off shift within a few minutes.

I called the county's Major Crimes Unit, and Kathy McChesney answered. I explained that Ted Bundy was an old friend of mine, and that he had just called me requesting information about the subpoena. There was a long pause, and the receiver was covered while she conferred with someone in the office. Finally, she was back on the line.

"Tell him . . . tell him, that he's just one of 1,200 people being checked out, that it's just a routine inquiry."

They were stalling—not me—but Ted. I'd been around police homicide units long enough to know that they wouldn't be requesting records from that many suspects, that something was definitely up. I didn't argue; Kathy was clearly uncomfortable. "O.K. I'll tell him that."

Subpoenas are not issued without probable cause; obviously, something was happening, something big. I felt a chill. Not even a television script could make it believable that a crime writer could sign a contract to write a book about a killer, and then have the suspect turn out to be her close friend. It wouldn't wash.

I called Ted back that night, waited as the phone rang six, seven, eight times. Finally, he answered, panting. "I had to run up the stairs. I was down on the front porch," he told me.

"I called them," I began, "and they said to tell you that you're only one of about 1,200 guys they're checking out."

"Oh . . . O.K., great."

He didn't seem worried, but I wondered how somebody as sharp as Ted was could believe that.

"If you have any more questions, they said you could just call them direct."

"Right."

"Ted . . . what's happening down there?"

"Nothing much. Oh, I got picked up on a Mickey Mouse thing in August by the state patrol. They're claiming I had burglary tools in my car, but the charge won't stand up."

Ted Bundy with burglary tools? Impossible.

But he continued. "I think they have some kind of a wild idea that I'm connected with some cases up in Washington. Do you remember something about some missing girls up there?"

Of course, I remembered. I'd been living with it since January of 1974. He claimed to have almost no knowledge of the cases, and he'd almost thrown away his last statement. It was as if he'd said he was wanted for a traffic violation in Washington. I didn't know what to say. I knew that whatever was coming down, it had to be based on more than my suggesting his name.

"I'm going to be in a line-up tomorrow," he said. "Everything's going to turn out all right. But if it doesn't, you'll be reading about me in the papers."

I couldn't understand how a line-up in Utah could have anything to do with the cases in Washington. He hadn't mentioned Carol DaRonch or the kidnapping case at all. If he was a suspect in Washington, he would be in a line-up in Seattle; the only people who could conceivably identify the "Ted" from Washington were the witnesses from Lake Sammamish. But something kept me from asking him more.

"Hey, thanks. I'll keep in touch," he said, and we said goodbye.

On October 2nd, a brilliant gold and blue autumn day, I attended a junior high school football game. My son, Andy, was starting at right end. He broke his thumb on the first play, but his team won, and we were in a good mood as we stopped at McDonald's for hamburgers on the way home.

Back in the car, I switched on the radio. A bulletin interrupted the record playing, "Theodore Robert Bundy, a former Tacoma resident, was arrested today in Salt Lake City and charged with aggravated kidnapping and attempted criminal assault."

I must have gasped. My son looked at me, "Mom, what's *wrong?*"

"It's Ted," I managed to stammer.

"Isn't that your friend from the Crisis Clinic?"

"Yes. He told me I might be reading about him in the papers."

This time, there was to be no quick release on P.R. Ted's bail was set at $100,000 and he was locked in the county jail.

Detective Dick Reed called me that night. "You were right!" he said.

I didn't want to be right. I didn't want to be right at all.

I slept little that night. Even when I'd suggested Ted's name to Reed, I hadn't really visualized him as a man capable of violence; I hadn't allowed my thinking to go that far. I kept seeing Ted as I remembered him, picturing him hunched over the Crisis Clinic phones, hearing his warm, sympathetic voice. I tried to picture him now behind bars, and I couldn't.

Early the next morning, I received a phone call from the Associated Press. "We have a message for Ann Rule, transmitted over our wires from Salt Lake City."

"This is Ann."

"Ted Bundy wants you to know that he is all right, that things will work out."

I thanked them, hung up the phone and it rang almost at once. First, a reporter from the *Seattle Times* wondering what my connection was with Ted Bundy. Was I a secret girlfriend? What could I say about Ted? I explained who I was—a writer like the reporter calling. "I've done several pieces for the *Sunday Times Magazine*. Don't you know the name?"

"Oh, yeah—Rule. So why did he send you that message over A.P.?"

"He's a friend. He wanted me to know he was all right."

I didn't want to be quoted by name. I was still too confused by what had happened. "Just say that the man I know couldn't be responsible for any of the things he's accused of."

The next call followed immediately. It was the *Seattle Post-Intelligencer* who had also picked up the A.P. message. I repeated what I'd told the *Times* reporter.

It was as if someone had died suddenly. People who had known Ted from fee Crisis Clinic—Bob Vaughn, Bruce Cummins, John Eshelman—all calling to talk about it. And none of us believed Ted capable of what he'd been charged with. It was unthinkable. We kept recalling anecdotes about Ted, trying to convince each other that what we were reading in blaring headlines could not be happening.

I didn't know then that Carol DaRonch, Jean Graham, and Debby Kent's girlfriend, Jolynne Beck, who had seen the man in the auditorium on November 8th, had all picked Ted out of the Utah line-up on October 2nd. Ted had been one suspect, standing in a seven man line-up, surrounded by detectives, all of them a little older, a little heavier than he was. The question would arise: was this a fair line-up?

I wrote to Ted on October 4th, telling him of support from Seattle, of the calls from his friends, of the favorable statements being published in the Seattle papers, promising him that I would continue to write. I ended that letter, "There is nothing in this life that is a complete tragedy—nothing—try to remember that."

Looking back, I wonder at my naiveté. Some things in this life *are* complete tragedies. Ted Bundy's story may well be one of them.

I was about to become a part of Ted's life again. To this day, I do not know what tied us together. It was more than my zeal as a writer; it was more than his tendency to manipulate women who might be able to help him. There is a vast, gray area somewhere in between that I have never been able to clearly define.

His attorney, John O'Connell, called me during Ted's first week in jail, seeking information on the investigation in Washington. I could tell him nothing; that would have meant a betrayal of my responsibility to detectives in Seattle. All I *could* do was keep writing to Ted. Whatever his crimes might have been, whatever hidden things might someday be revealed, he seemed to need someone.

I was beginning to be torn apart.

And Ted began to write to me, long scrawled letters on yellow legal pad sheets. His first correspondence was full of his sense of displacement—letters from a young man who had never been in jail. He could not quite believe it; he was both astonished by his plight and outraged, but he was quickly learning the ropes of survival inside. Much of his prose was turgid and overly dramatic, but he *was* caught in a situation that seemed impossible for Ted Bundy, and he could certainly be forgiven his tendency toward pathos.

"My world is a cage," he wrote on October 8, 1975. "How many men before me have written these same words? How many have struggled vainly to describe the cruel metamorphosis that occurs in captivity? And how many have concluded that there are no satisfactory words to communicate their feelings except to cry, 'My God!' I want my freedom!"

His cellmate was a fiftyish old-timer whom Ted saw as a "star-crossed alcoholic;" the man quickly set about teaching the "kid" the ropes. Ted had learned to hide his cigarettes and, when they were gone, to roll his own. He learned to tear matches in half—because matches didn't last long. He saved oranges, styrofoam cups, toilet paper, realizing he was dependent on the whim of the trustees for all the small things that made jail life a little more bearable. He learned to say "please" and "sir" when he wanted to make a phone call or needed an extra blanket or soap.

He wrote that he was growing personally, however, that he was discovering new things about himself and through his quiet observation of his fellow prisoners. He praised his friends' loyalty and agonized over what the publicity surrounding him might be doing to those close to him. Still, he never lost sight of a happy ending. "The nighttime hours are the hard hours. I make them easier by dwelling on the building which must be done when the storm is past. I will be free. And, someday, Ann, you and I will look upon this letter as a note from a nightmare."

It *was* a note from a nightmare. The flowery, often trite, phrases could not take away from the fact that being locked up was a kind of hell for Ted.

I continued to write to him, and to send whatever small checks I could manage for cigarette and canteen money. I didn't know what I believed, and all my letters were couched in terms that were deliberately ambiguous. They contained information on what was appearing in the local press, details about what I was writing, and on calls from mutual friends. I tried to block the pictures that occasionally seized my mind and shook it. I tried to think back to the old days; it was the only way I could respond to Ted as I always had.

The second letter from the Salt Lake County Jail came on October 23rd, and much of it was a poem, countless stanzas on life in jail. He was still only an observer—not a participant. The poem rambled over both sides of sixteen pages of the yellow legal paper.

He called it "Nights of Days," and it began:

> This is no way to be
> Man ought to be free
> That man should be me.

The meter often faltered, but the words all rhymed as he again bemoaned his lack of privacy and the cuisine in the jail, the omnipresent game shows and soap operas on the television set in the day room, programs which he termed "visual brain cancer."

He wrote—as he often would—of his belief in God. We had never talked about religion, but now Ted was apparently spending a lot of his time reading the Bible.

> Sleep comes on slowly
> Read the words of the wholly (sic)
> The scriptures bring peace
> They talk of release
> They bring us to God
> In here that seems odd
> But His gift is so clear
> I find that He's near
> Mercy and redemption
> Without an exception
> He puts me at ease
> Jailer, do what you please
> No harm can befall me
> When the Savior does call me.

The endless poem talked of another release: sleep. He could forget the nightmare he was living, the bars, and the screams of other prisoners, when he slept, so he napped whenever possible. He was trapped in a "caged human sea."

Moving easily from the Bible to the menu in jail, a bit of his old humor surfaced:

> It makes me feel blue
> Taking food from the animals in the zoo
> Porkchops tonight
> Jews are uptight
> I gave mine away
> It still has a tail
> And as for dessert
> The cook, that old flirt
> Surprised us with mellow
> Peach jello.

For all his days in jail to come, he would decry jello.

As for the other residents of the jail, Ted found them childlike—
"Overgrown kids."

> Some really believe
> They were born to deceive
> To make a bank roll
> From money they stole
> They do not relate
> To going it straight
> Except when in court
> They sometimes resort
> To making a plea
> For a new life and leniency.

His own inner ordeal emerged at the end of the poem; the fear
of the "cage" was there.

> Days of days
> Self-control pays
> Don't lose your mind
> Panic's not kind . . .
> Days of days
> My integrity stays.

Was this poem contrived? Something to play on my sympathies
which really needed no stimulus at all? Or was it the true outpouring
of Ted's anguish? In the fall of 1975, I was terribly confused, besieged
on one side by detectives who felt sure that Ted was as guilty as hell,
and, on the other, by the man himself who insisted again and again
that he was innocent and being persecuted. It was a dichotomy of
emotions that would stay with me for a long, long time.

At the time, I still felt that I might have caused Ted's arrest; it would
be years before I learned that my information had been checked
out and cleared early in the game, and then buried in the thousands of slips of paper with names on them. It had not been my
doubts, but Meg's, which had pinned him to the wall.

My mixed loyalties threatened to cost me a vital portion of my income. I heard via the grapevine that the King County Police wanted those two letters Ted was known to have sent me, and that, if I didn't turn them over, I could forget about getting any more stories from that department. It would mean that a quarter of my work would be cut off, and I simply couldn't afford it.

I went directly to Nick Mackie. "I have heard rumors that if I don't turn over Ted's letters to the Task Force, your doors will be closed to me. I think I should tell you frankly how I feel, and what is happening in my life."

I told Nick that I had learned that my children's father was dying, that it would only be a matter of weeks or a few months at most. "I've just had to explain that to my sons, and they don't want to believe it. They hate me because I had to put it into words to prepare them. He is so ill that I no longer have any financial support from him, and I'm trying to make it alone. If I can't write up county cases, I don't think I can hack it."

Mackie is an infinitely fair man. More than that, he could empathize with me. He was raising two sons alone; he had lost his wife a few years earlier. What I was telling him struck a nerve. And we had been friends for years.

"No one has ever said you would be barred from this department. I wouldn't allow it. You know you can believe me; you've always been fair to us and we respect you for it. Of course, we'd like to see those letters, but whether you turn them over or not, things will be like they always were here."

"Nick," I said honestly. "I have read those letters over and over, and I can't find anything in them that makes Ted sound guilty, even unconscious slips. If you'll let me ask him if you can see them, and if he agrees, I'll bring them to you immediately. That's the only fair way I can do it."

Nick Mackie agreed. I called Ted, and explained my problem, and he responded that, of course, I must let the county detectives see his letters. He had nothing to fear from them, nothing to hide.

I met with Mackie and with Dr. John Berberich, the psychologist for the Seattle Police Department, and they studied the first letter and the second long poem. There seemed to be nothing inherent there that would be a subconscious or overt admission of guilt.

Berberich, who is built like a basketball player, talked with me and Mackie over lunch. Was there anything I could remember about Ted's personality that made me suspicious? Anything at all? I searched back through the years and could find nothing. There was not the slightest incident that I could enlarge upon. "He seemed to me to be a particularly fine young man," I responded. "I want to help. I want to help the investigation, and I want to help Ted, but there just isn't anything weird about him—nothing that I ever saw. Ted is illegitimate, but he seems to have come to terms with that."

I had thought that Ted might stop contacting me after I'd shown his letters to the detectives. He knew that I moved constantly in the circle of the very investigators who were trying to catch him in a slip. But his correspondence continued, and my ambivalence rose to a level where I was laboring under more stress than I could stand.

In an attempt to sort out my feelings, to deal with that stress, I consulted a psychiatrist. I handed him the letters.

"I don't know what to do. I don't even know what my motivations really are. Part of me wonders if Ted Bundy is guilty, not only of the cases in Utah, but of the cases here in Washington. If that is true, then I can write the book I've contracted for and write it from a position that any author would envy. I want that, selfishly for my own career, and because it would mean financial independence. I could send my children to college, and we could move to a house that isn't falling down around our ears."

He looked at me. "And?"

"And, on the other side of it, the man is my friend. But am I supporting him emotionally, writing to him, because I just want to solve all those murders, because I owe something to my detective friends too? Am I, in essence, trying to trap him? Am I being unfair? Do I have the right to correspond with Ted when I have a niggling feeling that he might be guilty? Am I playing straight with him?"

"Let me ask you a question," he countered. "If Ted Bundy proves to be a murderer, if he is sent to prison for the rest of his life, what would you do? Would you stop writing to him? Would you drop him?"

That answer was easy. "No! No, I would always write to him. If what the detectives believe is true, if he is guilty, then he needs someone. If he had that on his conscience. No, I would keep writing, keep in touch."

"Then that's your answer. You're not being unfair."

"There's another thing. I can't understand why Ted is reaching out to me now. I haven't seen or heard from him in almost two years. I didn't even know he'd moved away from Seattle until he called me just before his arrest. Why me?"

The psychiatrist tapped the letters. "From these, I get that he apparently looks upon you as a friend, perhaps as a kind of mother figure. He needs to communicate with someone he feels is on his intellectual level, and he admires you as a writer. There is the possibility of a more manipulative side. He knows you are close to the police and he may want to use you as a conduit to them, without his actually having to talk to them himself. If he has committed these crimes, he is probably an exhibitionist, and one day he'll want his story told. He senses that you would do that in a manner that would portray the whole man."

I felt somewhat better after that visit. I would try not to look ahead, but I would keep up my contacts with Ted. He knew about my book contract; I hadn't lied. If he chose to stay close to me, then I would let him call the shots.

17

If I was feeling guilty and somewhat disloyal to Ted during fall, 1975, Meg Anders was going through sheer hell. The information she had given to the Salt Lake County Sheriff's office had been discounted until Ted's first arrest on August 16th. Now, detectives in Utah, Colorado, and Washington were anxious to know everything Meg remembered about Ted, all the bits and pieces of information that had made her suspect her lover. They were trying to find the man responsible for the most brutal series of killings in their memories, and it looked very much indeed as if Ted Bundy was that man. Ted's privacy, Meg's privacy, did not matter any longer.

Meg had adored Ted from the moment she met him in the Sandpiper Tavern. She never had been able to understand what it was that made him stay with her; she'd had an overwhelming sense of failure for most of her life. She'd always felt she was the one member of her immediate family who hadn't lived up to their expectations. Everyone but Meg worked in a prestigious profession, and she considered herself "only a secretary." The love of a brilliant man like Ted had helped to assuage her feelings of inferiority, and she was about to see that relationship exposed to merciless probing.

Neither the Salt Lake County investigators nor the Seattle Task Force detectives liked what they had to subject Meg Anders to, the questioning that would delve into the most intimate details of her life, the slow tearing down of all that she had built up in the six years before. But one thing was apparent; Meg Anders knew more about the hidden Ted Bundy than anyone alive, with the possible exception of Ted himself.

On September 16th, Jerry Thompson and Dennis Couch from the Salt Lake County Sheriff's Office and Ira Beal from the

Bountiful, Utah Police Department had flown to Seattle to talk with Meg. They had first spoken with her father in Utah who suggested that it might be of inestimable value to the investigation if they would speak directly with Meg.

Thompson was aware that Meg's doubts about Ted had predated the murders in Utah, had gone all the way back to the disappearance of Janice Ott and Denise Naslund in July of 1974.

The three Utah detectives met Meg in an interview room in the King County Police Major Crime Unit's offices. They noted her nervousness, the terrible emotional strain she was under. But they also saw that she was determined to lay out all the information that had led her, finally, to the police.

Meg lit the first of a whole pack of cigarettes that she would smoke during the long interview. She stated firmly that she did not want the proceedings recorded on tape.

"Ted went out a lot in the middle of the night," she began. "And I didn't know where he went. Then he napped during the day. And I found things, things that I couldn't understand."

"What sort of things?"

"A lug wrench, taped halfway up, under the seat of my car. He said it was for my protection. Plaster of paris in his room. Crutches. He had an oriental knife in a kind of wooden case that he kept in the glove compartment of my car. Sometimes, it was there; sometimes it was gone. He had a meat cleaver. I saw him pack it when he moved to Utah."

Meg related that Ted had never been with her on the nights the girls in Washington had vanished. "After I saw the composite pictures of 'Ted' in the paper in July of 1974, I checked back through the papers in the library to get the dates the girls disappeared, and I checked my calendar and my cancelled checks, and he just . . . well, he just was never around then."

Meg said she had been more afraid after her friend, Lynn Banks, returned from Utah in November of 1974. "She pointed out that the cases down there were just like the ones up here, and she said, 'Ted's in *Utah* now.' That's when I called my father and asked him to get in touch with you down there.

"Will you tell Ted that I've told you all this?" Meg asked Thompson, as she lit another cigarette.

"No, we won't," the detective promised. "What about you? Will you tell him?"

"I really don't think I will. I keep praying about it, and I keep praying you'll find out. And I guess I keep hoping that you'll find out it's not Ted, that it's someone else . . . but deep down, I'm just not sure."

Asked to explain her doubts in detail, Meg talked about the plaster of paris she'd seen in Ted's room at the Rogers's. "I confronted him about it, and he told me he'd stolen it from that medical supply place where he was working. He said he didn't know why. 'Just for the hell of it,' he said. He said the crutches were for his landlord."

Meg said that she'd once found a paper sack full of women's clothing in Ted's room. "The top item was a bra, a large size bra. The rest was just clothing, girls' clothes. I never asked him about it. I was afraid, and kind of embarrassed."

The detectives asked Meg if Ted had changed in any way in the last year or so, and she told them that his sexual drive had diminished to almost nothing during the summer of 1974, of his explanations about work pressures. "He said there was no other woman."

The questions were excruciatingly embarrassing for Meg.

"Had he changed in any other way, in his sexual interests?"

She looked down. "He got this book, this *Joy of Sex* book, sometime in December, 1973. He read about anal intercourse, and he insisted on trying it. I didn't like it, but I went along with him. Then there was something in that book about bondage. He went right to the drawer where I kept my nylons. He seemed to know which drawer they were in."

Meg said she had allowed herself to be tied to the four bedposts with the nylon stockings before having sex. The whole thing had been distasteful to her. She had acquiesced three times, but, during the third occasion, Ted had started to choke her, and she'd panicked. "I wouldn't do that anymore. He didn't say much, but he was unhappy with me when I said, "'No more.' "

"Anything else?"

Meg was mortified, but she continued. "Sometimes, after I was asleep at night, I'd wake up and find him under the covers. He was looking at . . . at my body . . . with a flashlight."

"Does Ted like your hair the way it is now?" Ira Beal asked. Meg's hair was long and straight, parted in the center.

"Yes. Whenever I talk about cutting it, he gets very upset. He really likes long hair. The only girl I've seen—for sure—that he dated besides me has hair just like mine."

The three detectives exchanged glances.

"Does Ted always tell you the truth?" Thompson asked.

Meg shook her head. "I've caught him in several lies. He told me that he was arrested down there for a traffic violation, and I told him I knew that wasn't the truth, that there'd been items in the car that looked like burglary tools. He just said they didn't mean too much, that it was an illegal search."

Meg told them that she knew Ted had stolen in the past. "I know he stole a television in Seattle and some other things. One time, just one time, he told me if I ever told anyone about it, that he'd . . . break my fucking neck."

Meg said that she was in constant touch with Ted, that she had spoken to him only the night before, and that he'd been his old, tender self again, telling her how much he loved her, planning their marriage. "He needs money: $700 for his attorney, $500 for tuition. He still owes Freda Rogers $500."

Meg knew too that Ted's cousin had told him that he was illegitimate when Ted was eighteen or nineteen. "It really upset him. Nobody had ever told him before."

"Does Ted ever wear a moustache?" Beal asked her suddenly.

"No, sometimes a full beard. Oh, he had a fake moustache. He used to keep it in his drawer. Sometimes he stuck it on and asked me how he looked in it."

The interview ended. Meg had smoked an entire pack of cigarettes. She had pleaded with the Utah investigators to tell her that Ted could not be involved, but they couldn't.

The picture of Ted Bundy that was emerging was far different than that of the perfect son, the modern day prototype of an Horatio Alger hero.

Meg Anders was living a dual existence, something that was intolerable for her, something that was standard for her lover. She talked often to Ted on the phone, and he played down the police interest in him, even though, as he talked, he was under constant surveillance by the Utah lawmen. And she continued to answer questions put to her by the detectives who were trying to place him during all those essential time periods, some of them now a year and a half before.

July 14, 1974 was an infamous day in Washington—the day that Janice Ott and Denise Naslund had vanished from Lake Sammamish State Park.

Meg remembered that Sunday. "We'd had an argument the night before. I was surprised to see him that morning. He came over, and I told him I was going to church and then planned to lie out in the sun. We quarreled again that morning. We just weren't getting along. I was really surprised to see him later."

Ted had called Meg sometime after six that evening and asked her to go out to eat.

"Was there anything unusual about him that night?"

"He looked exhausted, really wiped out. He was getting a bad cold. I asked him what he'd done that day because he was so tired out, and he said he'd just lain around all day."

Ted had removed a ski rack from his car—a rack that belonged to Meg—and placed it back on her car that night. After they'd gone out to eat, he'd fallen asleep on her floor, and gone home at 9:15.

Beal and Thompson wondered if it was possible. Could a man leave his girlfriend on a Sunday morning, abduct, rape, and kill two women, and then return casually to his friend's home and take her out to dinner? They questioned Meg again about Bundy's sex drive. Was he—they tried to phrase it tactfully—was he the kind of man who normally had several orgasms in a period of lovemaking?

"Oh, a long time ago, when we first started going together. But no, not lately. He was just normal."

Thompson made a decision. He pulled out a picture of all the items found in Ted's car when he'd been arrested by Sergeant Bob Hayward on August 16th. Meg studied them.

"Have you ever seen any of these things?"

"I haven't seen that crowbar. I've seen the gloves, and the gym bag. Usually, it's empty. He carries his athletic supplies in it."

"Did you ever confront him about the taped lug wrench that you found in your car?"

"Yeah, he said you never know when you can get caught in the middle of a student riot."

"Where was it kept?" Thompson asked.

"Usually in the trunk of my car. He borrowed my car a lot. It was a Volkswagen bug too, a tan one. Once, I saw the wrench under the seat in front."

Meg recalled that Ted had often slept in his car in front of her house. "I don't know why. He was just there. This was a long time ago, and there was a crowbar or a tire iron or something that he left in my house one night. I heard him come back in, and I opened the door to see what he wanted. He looked really sick, like he was hiding something, and I said, 'What have you got in your pocket?' He wouldn't show me. I reached in and pulled out a pair of surgical gloves. Weird. He didn't say anything. It seems incredible now that I didn't just say, 'Go away.'"

It *was* weird. But, until the events of 1974 and 1975, Meg had never connected Ted's nocturnal habits to anything definite. Like so many other women in love, she had simply put it all out of her mind.

18

Ted wrote me in October, 1975 that he felt as if he were "in the eye of a hurricane," and, indeed, he had been in the center of some manner of storm ever since his arrest in August. I hadn't known of this arrest until he phoned me at the end of September, and he had passed it off with a shrug to me just as he had with Meg and his other Washington friends. It would be a long time before I learned of the investigation that went on throughout the entire autumn. Once in a great while in the years ahead, a detective would let something slip, and then say hastily, "Forget I said that." I didn't forget, but I didn't tell anyone what I'd heard, and I most assuredly didn't write anything about it. Occasionally, odd bits and pieces would leak to the press, but the entire story would never be known to me until after the Miami trial, four years hence. As it was, having only fragments of the story, I tried to withhold judgment. Had Ted been a complete stranger to me—as all the other suspects I'd written about had been—resolution of my feelings might have come sooner. I don't believe it was because I was dense; better minds than mine continued to support him.

In each case that I researched after the "Ted" murders, each young woman's murder where a suspect was arrested, I traced back to see where that man had been on the days of crimes where Ted was a suspect. And, for the "Ted" crimes, the men had solid alibis.

By the fall of 1975, there were more than a dozen detectives in Washington, Utah, and Colorado working full-time on Ted Bundy: Captain Pete Hayward and Detective Jerry Thompson from the Salt Lake County Sheriff's Office; Detective Mike Fisher from the Pitkin County District Attorney's Office in Aspen, Colorado; Detective Sergeant Bill Baldridge from the Pitkin County Sheriff's Office; Detective Milo Vig from the Mesa County Sheriff's Office in Grand Junction, Colorado; Detective Lieutenant Ron Ballantyne and Detective Ira Beal from the Bountiful, Utah Police Department; Captain Nick Mackie, and Detectives Bob Keppel, Roger Dunn, and Kathy McChesney from the King County, Washington Sheriff's Office; Detective Sergeant Ivan Beeson, and Detectives Ted Fonis and Wayne Dorman from the Seattle Police Homicide Unit.

Ted had stated to Jerry Thompson and John Bernardo that he had *never* been to Colorado, had explained away the maps and brochures of the ski areas by saying "Somebody must have left them in my apartment." Mike Fisher, in checking Bundy's credit card slips, found that that was not true. Moreover he was able to place Bundy's car—the VW bug, bearing two separate sets of plates—in Colorado on the very days that the victims in that state had vanished, and within a few miles of the sites of the disappearances.

The Chevron Oil Company duplicate records noted that Ted had purchased gas as follows: on January 12, 1975 (the day Caryn Campbell disappeared from the Wildwood Inn) in Glenwood Springs, Colorado; on March 15, 1975 (the day Julie Cunningham walked away from her apartment forever) in Golden, Dillon, and Silverthorne, Colorado; on April 4, 1975 in Golden, Colorado; on April 5, in Silverthorne; and on April 6 (the day Denise Oliverson vanished) in Grand Junction, Colorado.

But only once had "Ted" ever been seen, and that was in Lake Sammamish State Park on July 14, 1974. The King County detectives began to chart as much of Ted Bundy's life as they could ferret out. That was why his law school records had been subpoenaed. Because their probe into Ted had been carried out with a minimum of fanfare, Detective Kathy McChesney had been very startled when I had called her at Ted's behest. The investigators had not known that Ted was even aware that he was under suspicion in Washington.

At the same time that Ted's Utah law school records were subpoenaed, his telephone records were requested from Mountain Bell in Salt Lake City, records going back to September, 1974 when he'd first moved to Utah.

Kathy McChesney asked if I would come in for an interview in early November, 1975; she had been given the assignment of interviewing the women Ted had known in Seattle, however peripherally.

Again, I repeated—this time for the record—the circumstances under which I'd met Ted, our work at the Crisis Clinic, our close, but sporadic, friendship over the intervening years.

"Why do you think he called you just before his arrest in Salt Lake City?" she asked.

"I think it was because he knew that I worked with you all the time, and I don't think he wanted to talk to detectives directly."

Kathy thumbed through a stack of papers, pulled one out, and said suddenly, "What did Ted say to you when he called you on November 20, 1974?"

I looked at her blankly. *"When?"*

"Last year on November 20th."

"Ted didn't call me," I answered truthfully. "I hadn't talked to Ted since sometime in 1973."

"Yes, we have his telephone records. There's a call to your number a little before midnight on Wednesday, November 20th. What did he say?"

I had known Kathy McChesney since we had both been in the King County Police Basic Homicide School in 1971 (she as a deputy sheriff and myself as an invited "auditor"). She had been promoted to detective, although she looked more like a high school girl, and she was sharp. I'd interviewed her countless times when she worked in the sex crimes unit. I wasn't trying to evade her question, but I was puzzled. It's difficult to remember what you were doing on a particular date a whole year before.

And then it dawned on me. "Kathy, I wasn't home that night. I was in the hospital because I'd had an operation the day before. But my mother told me about a funny call. It was a call from a man who wouldn't leave his name, and . . . yeah, it was on November 20th."

That mystery was solved, but I have often wondered since if the events to follow might have somehow been different if I had been home to take that call. In the years ahead, I would receive dozens of phone calls from Ted—calls from Utah, Colorado, Florida—as well as scores of letters, and we would have several face-to-face meetings. I would be caught up in his life again, torn between belief in him completely and the doubts that grew stronger and stronger.

Kathy McChesney believed me; I'd never lied to her and I never would. If I'd known who the man was who'd called me, I would have told her.

Ted also made two other calls on the night of November 20th—two calls between eleven and midnight. Although he had broken his "secret" engagement to Stephanie Brooks in January of that year, sent her away without any apologies or explanations, he had placed a call to her parents' home in California at 11:03 P.M. Stephanie hadn't been there. A woman friend of the family recalls that she talked to a friendly sounding man who asked for Stephanie. "I told him that Stephanie was engaged, and living in San Francisco . . . and he hung up."

Ted had next dialed an Oakland residence where none of the occupants had ever heard of Ted Bundy or Stephanie Brooks. The couple who lived there had no contacts in Seattle or Utah, and the man who answered figured it had been a wrong number.

By the time Ted reached my number in Seattle, he'd been very upset, according to my mother. In wondering who that call might have been from, Ted's name had never entered my mind. Now, as Kathy asked me about it, I knew that the timing of the midnight call might be imperative; Ted had called me twelve days after Carol DaRonch had escaped her kidnaper, and after Debby Kent had vanished, twenty days after Laura Aime disappeared, a month after someone spirited Melissa Smith away.

"I wish I'd been home that night," I told Kathy.

"So do I."

Kathy's assignments took her to the elder Bundys' residence in Tacoma. They believed none of the charges against their son. There would be no permission to search their home or the area around their cabin on Crescent Lake. What was unthinkable would not be helped along by the Bundys. And there was no probable cause to obtain search warrants.

Freda Rogers, Ted Bundy's landlady for five years, was also fiercely protective of him. From the day he had located his room at 4143 12th N.E., by knocking on doors, Freda had liked him. He had been a good tenant, more like a son than a roomer, often putting himself out to help them. His room in the southwest corner of the old house had rarely been locked, and it was cleaned every

Friday by Freda herself. Surely, if he had something to hide, she reasoned, she would have sensed it. "His things are all gone; he moved everything out in September of 1974. Look around, if you like, but you won't find anything."

Detectives Roger Dunn and Bob Keppel checked the Rogers's house from top to bottom, even climbing up into the attic. If anything had been hidden up there, the insulation would have been disturbed, and it had not been. They moved over the grounds with metal detectors, looked for spots where something might have been buried. Clothes? Jewelry? Parts of a bicycle? There was nothing.

Kathy McChesney talked with Meg Anders. Meg produced checks that Ted had written in 1974. They were not incriminating in the least; simply small checks written for groceries. Meg's own checks helped her to isolate what *she* had done on particularly important days and to determine whether she had seen her fiancé on those days.

Asked about the plaster of paris she had seen in Ted's room, Meg said she'd seen it first a long time ago, perhaps in 1970. "But I saw a hatchet under the front seat of his car, a hatchet with a pinkish leather cover, in the summer of 1974, and the crutches. I saw them in May or June of 1974. He said they belonged to Ernst Rogers."

"We'd been to Green Lake one day. I asked him about the hatchet, because it bothered me. I can't remember what his explanation was, but it made sense at the time. It was in August of 1974; I'd just come back from a trip to Utah. He was talking about getting a rifle that day. The cleaver, and the meat tenderizer . . . I saw those when he was packing. And the oriental knife. He said someone gave him the knife as a present."

"Can you think of anything else that bothered you?" McChesney asked.

"Well, it didn't then, but he always kept two pair of mechanic's overalls and a tool box in the trunk of his car."

"Did Ted have any friends at Evergreen College in Olympia?"

"Just Rex Stark, the man he worked with on the Crime Commission. Rex was on the campus in 1973 and 1974, and Ted stayed some nights with him when he worked in Olympia. Rex had a place on a lake there."

Ted Bundy with Stephanie, the woman to whom he was secretly engaged September 2, 1973.

Lynda Ann Healey, the first victim, who disappeared one month after Ted's final break-up with Stephanie.

Georgeann Hawkins.

Janice Ott.

Captain Herb Swindler of the Seattle Police Department, with photographs of some of the missing women. Lynda Ann Healy (top and bottom left), Donna Manson (top middle), Susan Rancourt (top right), Roberta Kathleen Parks (bottom middle), and Georgeann Hawkins (bottom right).

The detective who took this picture was standing next to Brenda Ball's skull on Taylor Mountain near Seattle. In this dense underbrush on the lonely mountain foothill were found the skulls of Brenda, Roberta Kathleen Parks, Lynda Ann Healy, and Susan Rancourt.

Police sketch of "Ted" as seen in Lake Sammamish State Park on July 14, 1974.

Roger Dunn, King County Police. Dunn was the only member of the task force who actually met Ted face-to-face and talked to him.

Bob Keppel, King County Police, who bore the brunt of the Bundy investigation in the county for six years.

"Did he have friends in Ellensburg?"

"Jim Paulus; he knew him from high school. And his wife. We visited them once."

Meg knew of no one Ted might know at Oregon State University. No, there had never been any pornography in his room. No, he didn't own a sailboat, but he had rented one once. Ted often liked to search out lonely country roads when they went on drives.

"Did he ever go to taverns alone?"

"Only O'Bannion's and Dante's."

Meg consulted her diary. There were so many dates to remember.

"Ted called me from Salt Lake City, on October 18th last year, three times. He was going hunting with my father the next morning. He called me on November 8th after 11:00. (Salt Lake City time zone would make it after midnight there.) There was a lot of noise in the background when he called."

Melissa Smith vanished on October 18th. On November 8th, Carol DaRonch was abducted at 7:30, and Debby Kent vanished forever at 10:30.

Recalling July, 1974, Meg remembered that Ted had gone to Lake Sammamish State Park on July 7th—the week before Denise and Janice disappeared. "He told me he was invited to a water skiing party. When he came over later, he said he hadn't had a very good time."

In fact, there had been no party, although the King County detectives learned later that two couples who knew Ted from Republican Party functions had been at Lake Sammamish water-skiing, and they'd seen Ted walking along the beach alone. "We were surprised to see him there because he was supposed to be at a political meeting in Tacoma that weekend." Asked what he was doing, Ted had responded "Just walking around." They had invited him to join them skiing, but he'd demurred because he had no shorts with him. Ted had had a windbreaker slung around his shoulders. They had seen no cast.

On the next Sunday, the 14th, Meg, of course, had seen Ted only early in the morning and then again sometime after six when he came to her home to exchange the ski rack and to take her out for hamburgers.

"My mother always keeps a diary," Meg said. "My folks came up to visit me on May 23, 1974. On Memorial Day, the 27th, Ted went with us for a picnic on Dungeness Spit."

"What about May 31st?" Kathy McChesney asked. That was the night Brenda Ball had vanished from the Flame Tavern.

"That was the night before my daughter was to be baptized. My parents were still in Seattle and Ted took us all out for pizza, and then dropped us off before nine." (Brenda had disappeared some time after 2 A.M., twelve miles south of Meg's apartment five hours later.) Liane had been baptized at 5 P.M. the next day and Ted had arrived to attend the ceremony. Afterward, he stayed at Meg's place until 11 P.M. "He was very tired, and he fell asleep on the rug that night too," she told McChesney.

Meg furnished the name of a woman that Ted had dated during the summer of 1972, a woman who had caused her to break up with her lover briefly. This woman, Claire Forest, was slender, brunette, with her long straight hair parted in the middle. When she was contacted by detectives, Claire Forest remembered Ted well. Although she had never been seriously interested in him, she said, they had dated often in 1972.

"He didn't feel that he fit in with my . . . my 'class.' I guess that's the only way to describe it. He wouldn't come to my parents' home because he said he just didn't fit in."

Claire recalled that she had once taken a drive with Ted, a drive over country roads in the Lake Sammamish area. "He told me that someone, an older woman—I think he said his grandmother— lived around there, but he couldn't find the house. I finally got fed up with it and asked him what the address was, but he didn't know."

Ted, of course, had no grandmother near Lake Sammamish.

Claire Forest said that she had had intercourse with Bundy on only one occasion, and although he had always been tender and affectionate with her before, that sex act itself had been harsh.

"We went on a picnic in April on the Humptulips River, and I had quite a lot of wine. I was dizzy, and he kept dunking my head under. He was trying to untie the top of my bikini. He couldn't manage it, and he suddenly pulled my bikini bottom off and had intercourse with me. He didn't say anything, and he had his fore-arm pressed under my chin so hard that I couldn't breathe. I kept telling him I couldn't breathe but he didn't let up the pressure until he was finished. There was no affection at all.

"Afterward, it was like it had never happened. We drove home and he talked about his family . . . everyone but his father.

"I broke up with him because of his other girlfriend. She was almost hysterical when she found me with him once."

Claire Forest was not the only woman who would recall that Ted Bundy's manner could change suddenly from one of warmth and affection to cold fury. On June 23, 1974, Ted had shown up at the home of a young woman, a woman who had known him on a platonic basis since 1973. She introduced him to a friend of hers, Lisa Temple. Ted didn't seem particularly interested in Lisa, but, later, he invited the two women and another male friend to go on a raft trip with him on June 29th. The two couples had dinner with friends in Bellevue on June 28th, spent the night, and set out the next morning for Thorpe, Washington. The man who accompanied them was later to recall that, while searching for matches, he had found a pair of panty hose in the glove box of Ted's Volkswagen. He had grinned and thought nothing of it.

The raft trip had started out with great hilarity, but, halfway down river, Ted's attitude had changed suddenly and he seemed to delight in tormenting Lisa. He insisted that she ride through the white water on an innertube tied behind the raft. Lisa had been terrified, but Ted had only stared at her coldly. The other couple were ill at ease too. Ted had put the raft into the water at Diversion Dam, a dangerous stretch where rafts were rarely launched.

They had made it, finally, through the rough water with both girls thoroughly frightened. Ted had had no money so Lisa bought dinner in North Bend for the quartet.

"He drove me home," she remembers, "and he was nice again. He said he would be back about midnight. He did come back, and we made love. That's the last time I ever saw him. I just couldn't understand the way he kept changing. One minute, he was nice, and the next he acted like he hated me."

Kathy McChesney located Beatrice Sloane, the elderly woman who'd befriended Ted when he worked at a Seattle yacht club.

"Oh, he was a schemer," the old woman recalled. "He could talk me out of anything."

Mrs. Sloane's recollections of Ted and Stephanie corresponded with what Kathy had already learned about that early romance. There was no question that the woman had known Ted, and known him quite well. Kathy drove her around the University District and she pointed out addresses where Ted had lived when she knew him. She recounted the things she'd loaned him: the china, silver, money. She recalled rides she'd given him when he had no car. He seemed to have been like a grandson to her, a highly manipulative grandson.

"When was the last time you saw him" McChesney asked.

"Well, I saw him twice, actually, in 1974. I saw him in the Albertson's store at Green Lake in July, and he had a broken arm then. Then I saw him on the 'Ave' about a month later and he told me he was leaving soon to go to law school in Salt Lake City."

The King County detectives contacted Stephanie Brooks, happily married now, and living in California. She recalled her two romances with Ted Bundy—their college days, and their "engagement" in 1973. She had never known about Meg Anders; she had simply come to the conclusion that Ted had courted her a second time solely to get revenge. She felt lucky to be free of him.

There seemed to be two Ted Bundys emerging. One, the perfect son, the University of Washington student who had graduated "with distinction," the fledgling lawyer and politician, and, the other, a charming schemer, a man who could manipulate women with ease, whether it be sex or money he desired, and it made no difference if the women were eighteen or sixty-five. And there was, perhaps, a third Ted Bundy, a man who turned cold and hostile toward women with very little provocation.

He had juggled his concurrent engagements with Meg and Stephanie so skillfully that neither of them knew of the other's existence. Now, it seemed that he had lost them both. Stephanie was married, and Meg declared that she no longer wanted to marry Ted. She was deathly afraid of him. Yet, within a matter of weeks, she would take him back and blame herself for ever doubting him.

As far as women went, Ted always had a back-up. Even as he sat in the Salt Lake County Jail, unaware that Meg had talked volubly about him to detectives, he had the emotional support of Sharon Auer. Sharon seemed to have fallen in love with him. I would soon realize that it was not prudent to mention Sharon's name to Meg, or to speak of Meg to Sharon.

It is interesting to note that through all the trials, through all the years of black headlines that would label Ted a monster, and worse, he would always have at least one woman entranced with him, living for the few moments she could visit him in jail, running errands, proclaiming his innocence. The women would change as time passed; apparently, the emotions he provoked in them would not.

19

Ted had his detractors as he languished in jail in Salt Lake City during the fall of 1975, but he had his staunch supporters, too; one of them was Alan Scott, the cousin he'd grown up with since he'd moved to Tacoma when he was four years old. Scott, himself a teacher of disturbed youngsters, insisted that he had never detected the slightest signs of deviant behavior in Ted. He, his sister Jane, and Ted had always been close, closer than Ted had ever been with his half-brothers and -sisters. His cousins were not Bundys, and Ted had never really felt part of the Bundy clan.

It is ironic then that Jane and Alan Scott would prove to be further links in the chain of circumstantial evidence tying Ted with the missing Washington girls. They did not do so willingly. Indeed, they believed in his innocence completely. They worked to solicit funds for Ted's defense, and many of his old friends contributed.

Dr. Patricia Lunneborg of the psychology department at the University of Washington stated flatly that Ted Bundy could not possibly be a killer, and said that there was absolutely no reason to believe that he had ever known Lynda Ann Healy, despite the fact that they had both taken abnormal psychology (Psych. 499) in the winter and spring quarters of 1972. "There are hundreds of students, in many different sections of 499," she said scornfully. "There's no way to prove they were in the same sections."

Lunneborg said she intended to do everything she could to support Bundy against the ridiculous charges and innuendos about him.

But there was another link between Bundy and Lynda Ann Healy, and that link was through his cousin Jane. When Lynda had lived in McMahon Hall, her roommate was the woman who would later be Jane Scott's roommate. Detective Bob Keppel located Jane on a fishing boat in Alaska and interviewed her in a phone call to Dutch Harbor.

Jane was not a willing witness; she too said her cousin had been normal, kind, not the kind of boy or man who would kill. She had seen him, she said, three or four times during the first half of 1974. Jane had met Lynda Healy; she could never recall that Ted had. Yes, there had been some parties over the years but she didn't know for sure Ted had ever attended the same parties that Lynda had.

"Did you ever speak of Lynda's disappearance to Ted?" Keppel asked.

"Yes," she said reluctantly. "But I can't remember anything specific. We just talked about what a terrible thing it was."

Alan Scott was even less cooperative, an understandable position. Alan had lived at Freda Rogers's home from September 1971 to February 1972. He and Ted had remained in close contact, and Alan had talked to Ted within days of the disappearances of Roberta Parks, Brenda Ball, Georgeann Hawkins, Denise Naslund, and Janice Ott. "He was relaxed, happy, excited about going to law school in Utah, and looking forward to marrying Meg."

Scott didn't add that a man who had abducted and killed young women couldn't have acted so calm, but that was his implication. Scott had gone sailing with his cousin on Lake Washington, and they often hiked together.

"Where?" Keppel asked.

"In the Carbonado area. And off Highway 18 near North Bend."

Taylor Mountain, the resting place of four of the Washington victims' skulls, was off Highway 18 near North Bend.

Keppel said quietly, "When did you hike up there?"

"July, 1972, through the summer of 1973."

Scott did not want to show the King County detectives just where they had hiked. He was reluctant to incriminate his cousin and, in the end, it would take the threat of a subpoena to make him lead them over the trails that had become familiar to Bundy.

On November 26, 1975, a subpoena was served on Alan Scott and he accompanied Bob Keppel to the area where he had hiked with Ted. They drove toward Taylor Mountain, and Scott pointed out rough fields and woods along the Fall City-Duvall Road, the Issaquah-Hobart Road. "Ted knew the roads around here, and we drove around in my car, looking at old farms and barns. There was one place with a great footbridge along the Fall City-Preston Road. That's the only time we really got out and hiked." He pointed out the road, three-quarters of a mile north of Preston. "We hiked about two hours up the hillside."

The area was only a few miles from Taylor Mountain.

Apparently, the region between Issaquah and North Bend had been a favorite haunt of Ted's. He had driven Meg there, and Claire Forest, mentioned it to his elderly woman friend, and taken his cousin there. He had gone to Lake Sammamish State Park, alone, only a week before July 14th. Was it merely coincidence or was it meaningful to the investigation?

Contrary to published reports, there *were* some eye-witness identifications of Ted Bundy. One witness was "contaminated," however, by the zeal of a newswoman. When Ted was arrested in the DaRonch kidnapping case, the television reporter rushed to the home of one of the women who had been approached by the stranger at Lake Sammamish on July 14th. The anchorwoman held out a photo of Ted Bundy, and asked, "Is this the man who asked you to help him?" The woman could not identify him; the man in the picture shown to her looked older than the handsome, tanned man she had seen. When King County detectives later showed her a mug lay-down of eight pictures—including one of Ted Bundy—she admitted that it was too late; she'd already been shown a picture and, now, she was confused. It was a major blow to the investigation.

The tearing hurry of the news media to show Ted to the public continued to get in the way of the probe. Two other women who had seen the "Ted" at the park recognized him at once—but they recognized him from the pictures they saw in the paper and on television. They were convinced that Ted Bundy and the other Ted were one and the same—but any defense lawyer would contend that they had been subconsciously swayed by glimpsing Ted's picture in the media.

A male witness who was present at Lake Sammamish on July 14 was out of the state when the news of the Utah arrest broke, and he'd seen no pictures of Ted at all—yet he picked Ted Bundy's picture from a mug lay-down without hesitation. So did the Oregon district attorney's son who had been in Ellensburg on April 17th when Susan Rancourt vanished. He was "seventy percent" sure, far from being as valuable in court as one hundred percent would have been. "I drove back to Seattle from Ellensburg late that night," he recalled. "When I was about ten miles east of Issaquah, I noticed a small foreign car pulled off on a Side road. The tail lights were small and round, like a VW's."

The spot he mentioned was close to Taylor Mountain. Another tiny link?

For a fiction writer, it would have been enough. For an actual criminal investigation, it was circumstantial evidence, block upon block piled up until there was no doubt in the Washington detectives' minds that Theodore Robert Bundy was the "Ted" they had sought for so long. But enough to bring charges? No. They didn't have so much as a single hair, a button or an earring, nothing that locked Ted Bundy tightly to any of the victims. No prosecutor in his right mind would touch it. They would count over forty "coincidences," and, even taken all together, it wasn't enough.

The final "coincidence" was a case that Seattle Morals Detective Joyce Johnson had investigated, a rape case that occurred on March 2, 1974, at 4220 12th Avenue N.E., only a few houses from Freda Rogers's rooming house.

The victim, an attractive twenty-year-old woman, had gone to bed around 1 A.M. on that Saturday morning. "My shades were drawn, but there's a place where one of the curtains doesn't meet the sill and someone could look in and see that I was alone. About three-quarters of the time, I have someone with me. That morning, I'd forgotten to put the wooden slat in the window to lock it. The man took off the screen, and, when I woke up about four, I saw him standing in the doorway. I saw his profile. There was a light shining through from the living room where he'd left his flashlight on. He came over and sat on my bed and told me to relax, that he wouldn't hurt me."

The woman had asked him how he'd gotten in and answered, "It is none of your business."

The man had worn a tee shirt, jeans, and had a dark navy watchcap pulled over his face to below his chin. "It wasn't a ski mask, but I think he had made slits in it for his eyes because he could see. His voice was well-educated. He'd been drinking; I could smell it. He had a knife with a carved handle, but he said he wouldn't use it if I didn't fight."

The man had taped her eyes, and then he had raped her. She didn't fight him. When he was finished, he'd taped her hands and feet, telling her it was just to "slow her down."

She heard him go into the living room and crawl through a window, then the sound of footsteps running toward the alley.

She heard no car.

She told Detective Johnson, "He was so calm and sure of himself. I think he's done it before."

The Seattle Police detectives, and Captain Nick Mackie and his detectives—Bob Keppel, Roger Dunn, Kathy McChesney—were convinced that they had found "Ted." They listed the tie-ins in the missing girls' cases:

* Ted Bundy matched the physical description—so much so that four people had connected him to the composite drawing of the man seen at Lake Sammamish.
* He often wore white tennis outfits.
* He had lived within a mile of Lynda Ann Healy, Georgeann Hawkins, and Joni Lenz.
* He drove a light tan Volkswagen.
* He often affected a British accent.
* He played racquet ball.
* He had had a knife, a cleaver, a taped wrench, a crowbar, a hatchet, crutches, plaster of Paris, surgical gloves, and unexplained women's clothing in his possession.
* His whereabouts on the vital days could not be accounted for.
* He had missed work for three days before and two days after the Lake Sammamish disappearances.
* He regularly traveled 1–5 between Seattle and Olympia.
* He had a friend on the Evergreen State Campus, often stayed with him.
* He had a friend in Ellensburg—a friend who recalled Ted's visiting in the spring of 1974.
* He'd had panty hose in the glove compartment of his car.
* His cousin knew Lynda Healy; he had taken the same classes Lynda had.

* He'd been seen at Lake Sammamish State Park a week before Janice and Denise vanished.
* He had hiked in the Taylor Mountain area.
* He liked to sneak up behind women; he liked to frighten women.
* He preferred women with long dark hair, parted in the middle.
* He had tried to choke at least two women while making love to them.
* He frequented Dante's Tavern, the tavern Lynda had gone to the night she vanished.
* His manner toward women could change in an instant—from tenderness to hostility.
* He often wore a false moustache.
* He liked to sail, had rented sailboats.
* In the Colorado cases, his credit cards had been used in the same areas and towns, on the same days the women vanished.
* He had lied and he had stolen.
* He appeared to be fascinated with bondage and sodomy.
* He'd been arrested with a ski mask, panty hose mask, handcuffs, gloves, garbage bags, strips of cloth, and a crowbar in his possession.
* He'd reported his license plates missing in Utah, but kept them and used them interchangeably with the new plates issued to him.
* His blood type was O, the type found on kidnap victim's Carol DaRonch's coat.
* He'd been identified by DaRonch, Graham, Beck, the young man in Ellensburg, and by three witnesses at Lake Sammamish State Park on July 14th.
* He'd been seen by his elderly benefactress in July, 1974 with his arm in a cast.
* During 1974 he'd slept during the days and was gone—somewhere—late at nights.
* A woman was raped by a man answering his description only three doors from the Rogers's rooming house.
* One of his high school friends was acquainted with Georgeann Hawkins's family.

* He was intelligent, charming, and could approach women easily and successfully.
* He habitually wore corduroy trousers (the ribbed pattern in the blood of Lynda Healy's bed?).

The list went on and on, and the investigators always came back to the fact that wherever Ted Bundy went, there was soon a lovely young woman, or two, or three, missing . . .

On the other hand, there were dozens of people who were willing to swear that Ted Bundy was a perfect citizen, a man who worked to wipe out violence, to bring about order and peace through the "system," that Ted Bundy was a lover, not a destroyer, of mankind. If he was what detectives believed, a mass killer, he had been cast from an entirely new mold.

On November 13, 1975, while Ted remained in the Salt Lake County jail and his friends and relatives sought to raise the $15,000 needed to bail him out, what came to be known as the Aspen Summit Meeting was held. Mackie, Keppel, and Dunn were there, Jerry Thompson and Ira Beal from Utah, Mike Fisher from Aspen, and dozens of other detectives who had unsolved cases of missing and murdered girls. Inside the Holiday Inn, the details of all those investigations were exchanged, and the name Theodore Robert Bundy was heard often. A tremendous amount of information was exchanged, only making each department involved more certain that they now had their killer in jail. In jail, but with not enough physical evidence to bring further charges. Newspapers were full of suppositions, but few facts.

If the mysterious, unknown "Ted" had frustrated them before, the known Ted Bundy still eluded them.

On November 20th, Ted was freed on bail—$15,000 raised by Johnnie and Louise Bundy. When, and if, he returned to face trial on the kidnaping charges involving Carol DaRonch, that money would be returned and then given to John O'Connell to pay for Ted's defense.

In Seattle, Meg Anders was so frightened of her ex-lover that she made detectives promise that she be notified the minute he crossed into the state of Washington. It is indicative of his persuasive powers to note that, within a day or so of his return to

Washington, he was back with her, living in her apartment. All her doubts had been erased, and she was completely in love with him again. She did not deny published reports that they were engaged to be married. She berated herself for having betrayed him and would, for years, stand by him.

Ted was free, but not truly free; wherever he went, he was under constant surveillance by officers recruited from both the King County and Seattle Police departments. Mackie explained it to me, "We can't charge him, but we can't risk letting him out of our sight. If anything should happen while he's up here, if another girl should disappear, there'd be hell to pay."

And so, from the moment Ted's plane landed at Seattle-Tacoma airport, he was tailed. He seemed, at first, to ignore the sneaker cars that followed him as he spent his days with Meg and her daughter, or stayed in a friend's apartment.

I didn't know if I'd hear from Ted when he was in Seattle, but several detectives took me aside and said, "If he calls you, we don't want you going anywhere alone with him—not unless you tell us where you're going to be first."

"Oh, come on," I said. "I'm not afraid of Ted. Besides, you're following him everyplace anyway; if I'm with him, you'll see me."

"Just be careful," a Seattle homicide detective warned. "Maybe we'd better know where to find your dental records in case we need to identify you."

I laughed, but the words were jarring; the black humor that would surround Ted Bundy evermore had begun.

20

Ted called me shortly after Thanksgiving, and we made arrangements to meet for lunch at the Brasserie Pittsbourg, a French restaurant in the basement of an old building in Pioneer Square, a restaurant only two blocks from both the Seattle and King County Police headquarters.

I hadn't seen him for two years, yet he seemed hardly changed, except that his beard was fuller. He was a little thinner perhaps, I thought, as he walked toward me through the rain, grinning. He wore corduroy slacks, a beige and brown coat sweater.

It was strange; his picture had been on the front page of Seattle's papers so often that he should have been easily recognizable, but no one even glanced at him as we spent three hours together. With all the "sightings" there had been of the phantom "Ted," no one noticed this real Ted at all. We stood in line, ordered the daily special, a carafe of Chablis, and I paid for it. "When this is all over," he promised, "I'll take *you* out to lunch."

We carried our plates into the back room and sat at one of the old tables with its butcher paper cloth. It was good to see him, good to know that he was out of the jail that he'd hated so. It was almost as if nothing had happened at all. I knew that he was a prime suspect, but that was all I knew at the time; I had no knowledge at all beyond the few innuendoes I'd read in the papers. Now, it didn't seem that any of the charges could be possible. I didn't know that Meg had told detectives so much, didn't know a single detail of the day-and-night investigations that had gone on since August.

I was a little nervous, and I glanced around, half-expecting to see several detectives I would recognize sitting at other tables. In fact, I had had lunch with Nick Mackie and Dr. Berberich at the same restaurant a few weeks before, and the Brasserie Pittsbourg was a popular eating spot for detectives. The food was excellent, and it was convenient.

"I wouldn't be surprised to see Mackie here," I told Ted. "He eats here about three days a week. He wants to talk to you. Maybe you should do it. He's not a bad guy."

"I have nothing to talk to him about. I'm sure he's a nice enough guy, but there's no point in our meeting. If they were alert, they could have seen me yesterday. I walked right through the first floor of the courthouse, right by their offices, and nobody spotted me."

The surveillance had become a game to him. He found the men tailing him clumsy and awkward and was taking delight in losing them. "A few turns down alleys, around a few corners, and they can't find me. Or sometimes, I go back and talk to them, and that really throws them. What do they expect? I've got nothing to hide."

He took particular pride in having lost Roger Dunn in the library at the University of Washington. "I went in the front door of the men's room and out the back. He didn't know there was another door. For all I know, he's still standing out there, waiting for me to come out."

He was not amused, however, at the prevailing attitude about his guilt in the minds of the public. He was particularly incensed because he had planned an afternoon of fun for Meg's twelve-year-old daughter and the girl's best friend. "Her mother wouldn't even let her child go to a hamburger stand with me. It's ridiculous. What did she think I was going to do? Attack her daughter?"

Yes, I thought to myself, she probably did. I had certainly not made up my mind about Ted's guilt at that fall meeting in 1975, but I wouldn't have gambled my daughters' safety on my own feelings.

Ted's stance was that of an innocent man; he was hurt by the accusations, and he'd just spent eight weeks in jail. I tried to put myself in his place, to deal with his outrage. And still, I was consumed with curiosity. But there was no way I could come right out and ask, "Ted, did you do it? Did you do any of it?" There are no rules of social etiquette for questioning an old friend accused of crimes that were so awful.

He continued to toss away the Utah charges as if they were no more important than a slight misunderstanding. He was supremely confident that he would win in court in the DaRonch case; the burglary tools charges were too ridiculous to discuss. Things were fine with Meg. If only the police would leave them alone, allow them to enjoy this time together. She was a wonderful woman, supportive, sensitive.

We sipped wine, ordered another carafe, and watched the rain run down the windows, windows in the basement restaurant that were at sidewalk level so that we could see only the lower legs and feet of those who passed by outside. He seldom met my eyes. Instead, he sat sideways in his chair, his gaze fixed on the wall opposite.

I toyed with the fresh red carnation in the vase between us, smoked too many cigarettes, as did he. I offered him some from my pack when his ran out. The tables around us were vacated, and we were finally the only people left in the room.

How could I phrase it? I had to ask *something*. I studied Ted's profile. He looked as young as he ever had, and, somehow, more vulnerable.

"Ted . . ." I said at last. "Were you aware of all the girls up here who were missing last year? Had you read about it in the papers?"

There was a long pause.

Finally, he said, "That's the kind of question that bothers me."

Bothers how? I couldn't read his face; he still looked away from me. Did he think I was accusing him? Was I? Or did he find it all a deadly bore?

"No," he continued. "I was so busy going to law school at U.P.S. I didn't have time to read the papers. I wasn't even aware of it. I don't read that kind of news."

Why wouldn't he look at me?

"I don't know any of the details," he said. "Just things my lawyer is checking out."

Of course he was lying to me. He had been teased by a lot of people about his resemblance to the "Ted" in the park. His own cousin, Jane Scott, had talked to him about her friend, Lynda Ann Healy. Carole Ann Boone Anderson had kidded him incessantly in their offices at the Department of Emergency Services. Even if he had no personal knowledge or guilt in the cases, he did know about them.

He simply didn't want to talk about them at all. He wasn't angry with me for asking; he just didn't want to discuss it. We talked of other things, old friends, the Crisis Clinic days, and promised to meet again before he had to go back to Utah to stand trial. When we stood outside in the rain, Ted reached out impulsively and hugged me. Then he was dashing off down First Avenue, calling back, "I'll be in touch!"

As I walked up the hill toward my car, I felt the same emotions that would tear me up so many times. Looking at the *man*, listening to the *man*, I could not believe he was guilty. Listening to the detectives whom I also liked and trusted, I could not believe he was not. I had the distinct advantage of not being physically attracted to Ted. Any tender feelings I had for him were those of a sister for a younger brother, perhaps more compelling because I had lost my younger brother.

I didn't see Ted again until Saturday, January 17, 1976. My ex-husband died, suddenly but not unexpectedly, on December 5th, and, once again, family concern had blocked thoughts of Ted from my mind. I talked to him on the phone once or twice in December, and he was up, confident, anxious for the court battle that lay ahead.

When he called and asked me to meet him on January 17th, I was surprised to hear from him. He said he'd suddenly wanted to see me, that he was leaving soon to go back to Salt Lake City to stand trial, and asked if I minded driving out to the Magnolia District of Seattle to meet him in a tavern there.

As I drove the twenty-five miles, I realized that no one knew I was meeting Ted. I also knew somehow that he had lost his ever-present surveillance team. When he walked up to meet me a little after noon at the tavern that was a popular watering hole for soldiers from nearby Fort Lawton, I looked up and down the street for the sneaker cars that I had long since learned to recognize. There were none.

He grinned. "I lost 'em. They aren't as clever as they think they are."

We found a table on the other side of the tavern from the shouting soldiers. I had a package under my arm, a dozen copies of magazines with my stories in them that I'd picked up from the post office. It wasn't until Ted had glanced at it several times that I realized he suspected I might have a tape recorder. I ripped open the package and handed him a magazine.

He seemed to relax.

We talked for five hours. My memory of that long conversation is just that; it is indicative of my belief at that time in his innocence that I didn't bother to jot down notes when I got home. In many ways, it was a much more relaxed meeting than the earlier lunch. Again, we drank white wine, so much white wine for Ted at least, that, by the end of the afternoon, he was unsteady on his feet.

Because of the wine, or perhaps because we'd gotten our first meeting since his arrest over with, Ted seemed less edgy than he had been before. Considering the turns that our conversation took, this was remarkable, and yet I felt able to bring things up that might well have angered him.

The din on the other side of the tavern seemed far away; no one could overhear us. A fake gas log blazed merrily in the fireplace next to our table. And, as always, rain droned steadily down outside.

I asked Ted at one point, "Ted, do you *like* women?"

He considered the question and said slowly, "Yes . . . I think I do."

"You seem to care for your mother. I guess it all goes back to that. Remember, when you told me how you found out for sure that you were illegitimate and I reminded you that your mother had always kept you with her, no matter how difficult it might have been for her?"

He nodded. "Yes, she did. I remember when we talked about that."

He volunteered information. He told me that it had been Meg who had turned him in to the police. I felt the old tug of guilt because he didn't know that I had given them his name too. He evidently thought I was privy to more information than I really was. "Those crutches in my room—the crutches she told them about. Those were for my landlord. I used to work for a medical supply house, and I got them and the plaster of Paris there."

I didn't show it, but I was surprised. I hadn't heard about the crutches or the plaster of Paris, and I certainly didn't know before this that Meg had gone to the police.

Ted seemed to have no rancor at all toward Meg, who had plunged him into about as much trouble as a man can be in. His mild, forgiving stance seemed inappropriate. I wondered what Meg had told detectives about him. I wondered how he could forgive her so easily. Here, he was telling me that he loved her more than he ever had, and yet, if it were not for Meg, he would not be on his way back to Utah in a few days to stand trial for kidnapping; the most he would have had to worry about were the charges of evading an officer, and possession of burglary tools.

I would have thought most men would have despised a woman who had done that to them, but Ted talked of the wonderful times they had had together while he was home during Christmas, their closeness—even though they were constantly followed by police.

It was too mystifying for me to even question him about; it was something I would have to ponder on. I nodded agreement when he asked me to look after Meg, to see that she had someone to talk to. "She's shy. You call her, will you? Talk to her."

Ted was still confident. It seemed as though the trial in Salt Lake City was more of a challenge than a threat; he was like an athlete about to enter the Olympics. He would show them.

At one point during that long afternoon, I got up to go to the ladies' room, walked past tables full of half-drunk soldiers, past a couple of dozen people who hadn't seemed to recognize Ted as the infamous Ted Bundy. As I walked back to our table, suddenly someone was behind me, his hands lightly gripping my waist. I jumped, and then I heard a laugh. Ted had come up behind me, so quietly that I hadn't even realized he'd left the table. Later, I learned that Ted enjoyed sneaking up on women (according to Meg and Lynn Banks), that he delighted in leaping out at them from behind bushes and hearing them scream. And I remembered how he had startled me that day in the tavern.

As the afternoon lengthened and it grew dark outside, the impenetrable murkiness of a January night in Seattle, I decided to tell Ted where I stood. I chose my words as carefully as possible. I was probably more honest with him about my feelings than I would ever be again. I told him about my visit to the psychiatrist, about my dilemma in being fair to him, while I knew I had a book contract on the story of the missing girls.

He seemed to understand completely. His manner with me was the same as it had been five years before when I'd talked about my problems in the Crisis Clinic offices. He assured me he could relate to my ambivalence.

"And, you know . . . I have to tell you this," I continued. "I cannot be completely convinced of your innocence."

He smiled. The same flat response I was to grow used to.

"That's O.K. I can understand that. There are . . . things I'd like to tell you, but I can't."

"Why?"

"I just can't."

I asked him why he didn't just take a polygraph examination and get it over with.

"My lawyer, John Henry Browne, feels that it's best."

It was a paradox in itself that Browne should be advising Ted. Ted hadn't been charged with anything in Washington, although he certainly was under continued surveillance, and he'd been accused by the press and most of the public. But Browne worked for the Public Defender's Office, an agency funded to defend suspects actually *charged* with crimes.

It seemed to be a game with no rules. It wasn't usual either for a man to be convicted by the media. Ted had been asked not to use the University of Washington's Law School library any more; it frightened women students to see him there.

"Ted," I said suddenly. "What did you want when you called me from Salt Lake City that night in November in 1974?"

"What night?" He seemed puzzled.

"It was November 20th, when I was in the hospital. You talked to my mother."

"I never called you then."

"I saw the phone records from your apartment phone in Salt Lake City. You called just before midnight."

He didn't seem upset, just stubbornly resistant.

"The King County Police are lying to you."

"But I *saw* the records."

"I *never* called you."

I let it go. Maybe he didn't remember.

Ted bragged more about how clever he'd become at losing the men tailing him, of how he taunted them.

"I know. Billy Baughman says you walked back to his car and asked him if he was with the Mafia or the police, that you just wanted to be sure."

"Who's he?"

"He's a Seattle homicide detective. He's a nice guy."

"I'm sure they're all princes."

Ted had talked in any depth to only one of the detectives who dogged his tracks. John Henry Browne had told him not to talk with police, that he was under no obligation to do so, but Roger Dunn had come face to face with Ted as he parked his car near a friend's apartment on December 3rd.

The two men, hunter and hunted, had stared at each other, and Ted had asked Dunn if he had a warrant.

"No. I just want to talk to you."

"Come on in. I'll see what I can do."

If Dunn had expected any voluntary give and take, he was disappointed. Ted had immediately gone to the phone and called Browne's office, informing an aide that Dunn was with him.

Before Dunn had finished reading Ted the Miranda warning, Browne called, asked to speak to him, and told him to leave the apartment as soon as possible; he didn't want Ted talking to any Washington state officers.

Ted had been more sympathetic. "I'd really like to help you out. I know the pressure on you from the press is heavy. I personally feel no pressure, but I won't talk to you now. Maybe later, John and I might get in touch with you."

"We'd like to eliminate you as a suspect if we could. So far, we haven't been able to."

"I know there are things I know that you don't know, but I'm not at liberty to discuss them."

Roger Dunn had heard much the same sentiment that Ted would repeat to me often, had also noted that Ted would not meet his eyes. And then the interview had quickly ended. Ted had held out his hand and they shook.

They had taken each other's measure; they were never to meet again.

Sitting in the smoky tavern, I felt that there was more Ted wanted to say to me. It was nearing six, and I had promised my son I'd take him to a movie that night for his birthday. Ted didn't want the visit to end. He asked me if I would go with him someplace to smoke marijuana. I demurred. I didn't use marijuana, and I had promised my son I'd be home early. And too, although I was not frightened, I may have been a little ill at ease.

Ted was quite intoxicated as he hugged me outside the tavern, and then disappeared into the misty rain. I would see him again, twice, after we said good-bye, but I would never see him again as a free man.

21

It is my belief that Ted's trial in Salt Lake City on the aggravated kidnapping charge involving Carol DaRonch was the only legal proceeding where he had everything going for him. He had chosen to leave his fate up to a judge alone and to dispense with a jury. On Monday, February 23, 1976, the trial opened in Judge Stewart Hanson's courtroom. Ted was enthusiastic about Hanson's reputation as a fair-minded jurist; he truly believed that he would walk away a free man. He had John O'Connell on his side, a veteran of twenty-nine murder trials, and considered to be one of the top attorneys in Utah. He had friends in the courtroom: Louise and Johnnie Bundy, Meg, others who had flown in from Seattle, those who still believed in him from Utah: Sharon Auer and the friends who had convinced him to join the Mormon Church shortly before his first arrest.

But Midvale Chief of Police Louis Smith, Melissa's father, was also there, and the parents and friends of Debby Kent and Laura Aime. There could be no charges involving their daughters, but they wanted to see what they felt to be only token justice done.

In the end, the verdict would depend on the reliability of the eye witness, Carol DaRonch, and on Ted Bundy's own testimony. O'Connell had attempted to have Sergeant Bob Hayward's testimony about Bundy's arrest on August 16th suppressed, but Hanson refused to do so.

There was, of course, no mention during that first trial of the other crimes in which Ted Bundy was a prime suspect, no mention of the fact that the Volkswagen he'd sold to a teenage boy (coincidentally an ex-classmate of Melissa Smith's) on September 17, 1975 had been seized by the police and systematically ripped apart as criminalists looked for physical evidence that would tie in to other cases in which Ted was suspected.

Carol DaRonch was not a confident witness; she appeared to be upset by the way Ted stared steadily at her. She sobbed during her testimony, recalling her terror of sixteen months before. But she pointed to Ted as he sat impassively at the defense table, identifying him positively as the man who had told her he was "Officer Roseland."

Ted sitting there, clean shaven, wearing a light gray suit, white shirt, and tie, looked anything but a kidnapper; the accusing witness was plainly hysterical, buckling again and again under O'Connell's questions, questions intimating that Carol DaRonch had been led to her identification of Ted by the subtle and not-so-subtle persuasion of the detectives under Captain Pete Hayward's command. For two hours, the defense lawyer cross-examined the weeping girl.

"You identified pretty much what law enforcement officers wanted you to, didn't you?"

"No . . . no," she replied softly.

Ted continued to stare at her implacably.

When Ted himself took the stand, he admitted that he had lied to Sergeant Bob Hayward at the time of his arrest for evading an officer, that he had lied to O'Connell. He explained that he had "rabbited" when Hayward chased him in the patrol car on August 16th—but only because he'd been smoking marijuana. He'd wanted time to get the "joint" out of the car, to let the smoke clear. He admitted that he had not been to a drive-in movie, but had told Hayward that. He had not admitted the real story to John O'Connell at first.

Bundy had no firm alibi for the night of November 8th, but he denied that he had ever seen Carol DaRonch before he saw her in court.

The handcuffs? Only something he'd picked up at a dump and kept for a curio. He had no key for them.

Assistant County Attorney David Yocum questioned Bundy under cross-examination.

"Have you ever worn a false moustache? Didn't you wear one when you were a spy in the Dan Evans campaign?"

"I wasn't 'spying' for anyone, and I never wore a fake moustache during that period," Ted answered.

"Didn't you brag to a woman acquaintance that you like virgins and you can have them any time"

"No."

"Didn't you tell that same woman that you saw no difference between right and wrong?"

"I don't remember that statement; if I made it, it was taken out of context and does not represent my views."

"Did you ever use an old license place on your car, after you'd received new plates from the state of Utah?"

"No sir."

Yocum then produced two gasoline credit slips.

"You notified the state that you had lost plates bearing the numbers LJE-379 on April 11, 1975. These slips show that you were still using those 'lost' plates in the summer of 1975. Why was that?"

"I cannot remember the incidents. The attendant probably asked for my plate numbers and I may have inadvertently given him the old numbers from memory."

Ted had lied, not big lies, but lies, and it tainted all the rest of his testimony. He admitted that he had lied to O'Connell about the marijuana until two weeks before trial. A jury might have believed him; Judge Hanson did not.

Hanson had retired to ponder his decision after final arguments on Friday, February 27th. On Monday, March 1, the principals were summoned into the courtroom at 1:35 P.M.

The thirty-seven-year-old judge by his own statement had spent an "agonizing" weekend. And he had found Ted Bundy guilty of aggravated kidnapping beyond a reasonable doubt. Ted, who had been free on bail, was remanded to the custody of the Salt Lake County Sheriff's Office to await sentencing.

Ted was stunned; Louise Bundy's sobs were the only sound in the courtroom on that snowy afternoon. Convicted, Ted said nothing until he was handcuffed by Captain Hayward and Jerry Thompson, and then he said scornfully, "You don't need these handcuffs. I'm not going anywhere."

Meg Anders watched as Ted was led out of the courtroom, seeing it all happen. It had been what she thought she wanted when she called police with her suspicions. Now she was sorry; she wanted Ted back.

Sentencing was set for March 22nd. There would, of course, be an appeal.

Ted was behind bars again, in a world that he hated. I wrote to him, vapid letters full of what was happening in my life, trivia. I sent him small checks through John O'Connell's office for use in the jail commissary, stationery, stamps. And, still, I suspended judgment.

Until *I* had proof that Ted was guilty of this, and perhaps of other crimes, I would wait.

The frequency of his letters to me increased. They were more telling of his state of mind than what someone else could paraphrase. Some of them are misdated, as if time itself had no meaning for him any longer.

22

His first postconviction letter was mailed on March 14, 1976, although he had mistakenly dated it February 14th.

"Dear Ann,

Thanks for the letters and the commissary contribution. I've been slow in returning letters since this most recent setback. Probably a function of my need to mentally rearrange my life; to prepare for the living hell of prison; to comprehend what the future holds for me."

He said he was writing to me as a "pump priming venture," to help him begin to assess what lay ahead. He was confounded by the guilty verdict and scornful of Judge Hanson, intimating that the jurist had been influenced by public opinion rather than by the evidence presented. He expected to receive a five-to-life sentence, and felt that the Department of Adult Probation and Parole were doing their presentence report with bias.

"The report seems to be focusing on the Jekel (sic) and Hyde theory, a thing disputed by all the psychologists who have examined me."

Ted said he had heard that the probation investigator seemed to believe that Ted had made some damaging admission to me in letters. Of course, he had not. I had had only those two letters from him before the trial, and, with his permission, had turned them over to King County Police detectives.

On March 22nd, Judge Hanson announced that he would delay sentencing for ninety days, pending a psychological evaluation. Ted wrote to me that night as he crouched on the floor with his back against the steel wall of his cell, trying to glean enough light from the hall fixture so that he could see to write. He did not seem to be particularly upset about the diagnostic evaluation which would take place at the Utah State Prison at Point-of-the-Mountain.

"If jail life is any indication, prison should be rich in the material that human suffering breeds, full of the startling tales which prisoners tell. For several reasons, I must take advantage of this opportunity and begin to draw upon this valuable reservoir of ideas. I will start writing."

What Ted wanted from me was my editorial advice and for me to serve as his agent to help him sell the books he wanted to write about his case. He was anxious that we move rapidly in establishing our roles as collaborators and to agree on a percentage agreement on the distribution of the profits that would surely be forthcoming. He asked that I keep his proposal confidential until the time was right and that I correspond with him through his attorney's office.

I didn't know just what it was that he intended to write, but I responded with a long letter detailing the various avenues of publishing, and explaining the correct manuscript form for submission. I also repeated again the information about the book contract I already had with W.W. Norton on the missing girls cases, and stressed my belief that his story would have to be a part of my book, just how much I couldn't know. I offered to share my profits with him, gauged by the number of chapters he might write in his own words.

And I urged him to wait a bit with his attempts to publish—for his own protection. His legal entanglements is Utah and Colorado were not over. Colorado was moving rapidly in their investigation, although the public—of which I was a part—knew few of the details. The discovery of the credit card purchases had leaked out, however.

And I had news. I was about to take a trip to Salt Lake City as part of the preparation for a travelogue book I was editing for an Oregon publishing house; I would try to get clearance to visit him in prison.

That clearance would not be easy to come by. I was not a relative, and I was not on the approved list of visitors for Theodore Robert Bundy. When I called Warden Sam Smith's office in the old prison in Draper, Utah, I was told that, if I called again when I arrived in Salt Lake City, they would make a decision. I was quite certain that the answer would be "no."

On April 1, 1976, I flew to Utah. I had never flown in a jet, hadn't flown at all since 1954, and the speed of the flight, the knowledge that I could leave Seattle's rain and be in a comparatively balmy Salt Lake City within a few hours only added to my sense of unreality.

The sun was shining, and a dusty wind blew puffs of tumble weed over the brown landscape as I drove my rented car from the airport. I felt disoriented, much as I would three years later as I arrived in Miami—again because of Ted.

I called the prison and learned that visitors were not usually allowed on days other than Sundays and Wednesdays. It was Thursday, and already 4 P.M. I talked to Warden Smith who said "I'll have someone from the diagnostic staff call you back."

The call came. What was my purpose in wanting to visit Bundy? "I'm an old friend." "How long would I be in Utah?" "Only today and tomorrow morning." How old was I? "Forty." That answer seemed right; I was too old to be a "Ted Groupie."

"O.K. We're granting you a special visit. Be at the prison at 5:15. You'll have one hour."

The Utah State Prison at Point-of-the-Mountain was about twenty-five miles south of my motel, and I had barely enough time to find the right freeway, going in the right direction, and reach Draper, the post office stop, population 700. I looked to my right and saw the twin towers with guards armed with shotguns. The old prison and the landscape around it seemed to be all the same gray brown color. A feeling of hopelessness seized me; I could empathize with Ted's despair at being locked up.

I'd spent a summer working as a student intern at the Oregon State Training School for Girls when I was nineteen and I'd carried a heavy ring of flat keys wherever I went, but that was a long time before; I'd forgotten the security needed to keep human beings behind walls and bars. The guard at the door told me I couldn't take my purse inside.

"What can I do with it?" I asked. "I can't lock it in my car because my keys are in it. May I bring my keys in?"

"Sorry. Nothing inside."

He finally relented and opened up a glassed-in office where I could leave my car keys after I'd locked my purse in the rental car. I carried my cigarettes in my hand.

"Sorry. No cigarettes. No matches."

I put them on a counter, and waited for Ted to be brought down. I was feeling the claustrophobia I always feel in jails, even though my work may take me into almost every jail in Washington sooner or later. I felt my chest tighten, my breath catch.

To get my mind off my cloistered feelings, I glanced around the waiting room. It was, of course, empty; it was not regular visiting hours. The dull walls, sagging chairs, seemed not to have changed in fifty years. There was a candy machine, a bulletin board, pictures of the staff, a left-over religious Christmas card. To whom? From whom? Disciplinary notations on prisoners. For Sale notices. An application to sign up for self-defense classes. Who? The staff? The visitors? The inmates?

Where would we talk? Through a glass wall via phones? Through steel mesh? Some people hate the smell of hospitals. I hate the smell of jails and prisons, all the same: stale cigarette smoke, Pine-Sol, urine, sweat, and dust. I didn't want to see Ted in a cage. It would be too humiliating for him.

A smiling man walks toward me—Lieutenant Tanner of the prison staff—and asks me to sign in. But first, we move through as electric gate that clangs shut behind us heavily. I sign my name, and Lieutenant Tanner sees me through a second electric gate. "You can talk here. You'll have an hour. They'll bring Mr. Bundy down in a few minutes."

It is a hallway! A tiny segment of space between two automatic gates on either side. There are two chairs shoved against a rack of hanging coats, and, for some reason, buckets of varnish beneath them. A guard sits in a glass enclosure four feet away. I wonder if he will be able to hear what we say? Beyond me is the prison proper, and I can hear footsteps approaching. I look away, the way one averts his eyes from someone crippled or malformed. I cannot stare at Ted in his cage.

The third electric door slides open and he is there, accompanied by two guards. They search him, pat him down. I was not searched. Had they checked me out? How did they know I had no contra-band, no razor up my sleeve?

"Your I.D. Ma'am?" Someone is talking to me.

"It's in the car. I had to leave everything in the car."

The doors open again as I run back to retrieve my driver's license, something to prove who I am. I hand it to a guard and he studies it, hands it back. I have not looked directly at Ted. We both wait.

And now he stands in front of me. For a crazy instant, I wonder why prisoners wear tee shirts proclaiming their religious preferences. His is orange and says "Agnostic" on the front. I look again. No, it reads "Diagnostic."

He is very thin, wears glasses, and his hair is cut shorter than I have ever seen it. He smells of acrid sweat as he hugs me.

They leave us alone to talk in this funny coatroom-hall. The guard behind the glass across from us appears to be disinterested, and we are interrupted only by a steady stream of people—guards, psychologists, prisoners' wives headed for an Al-Anon meeting. One of the psychologists recognizes Ted and speaks to him, shakes hands.

"That's a doctor who did a psychological profile on me for John [O'Connell]. He told John, off the record, that he couldn't see how I could have done it."

Many of the people moving past us, wearing civilian clothes, nod and speak to Ted. It is all very civilized.

"I'm in the 'fish tank,'" he explains. "There are forty of us in the diagnostic center. The Judge ordered that I be held in protective custody, but I turned it down. I don't want to be isolated."

Still, he admits to a good deal of trepidation on his arrival at Point-of-the-Mountain. He is aware that men convicted of crimes against women have a high mortality rate inside the walls. "They were lined up to see me when I arrived. I had to walk the gauntlet."

But he has found prison much better than jail. He is rapidly becoming a "jailhouse lawyer." "I'll survive inside—if I do—because of my brain, my knowledge of the law. They seek me out for legal advice, and they're all in awe of John. I only had one really bad moment. This one guy—a killer who literally ripped out the throat of the man he killed—walked over to me and I thought I'd had it. He was only interested in knowing about John, in finding out how he could get John to represent him. I get along fine with all of them."

He glances at the locked gate behind me. "They left it open when you went for your I.D. I saw the coats here, the door open, and the thought of escaping flashed through my mind, but only for a minute."

The trial just finished rankles Ted and he wants to discuss it. He insists that Carol DaRonch was talked into her identification of him by the Salt Lake County detectives. "Her original description of the man said he had dark brown eyes. Mine are blue. She couldn't make up her mind about the moustache and she said his hair was dark, greased back. She I.D.'d my car from a polaroid and the film was over-exposed; it made the car look blue and it's really tan. They showed her my picture so many times. *Of course*, she recognized it. But, in court, she couldn't even identify the man who picked her up and drove her to the police station.

"Jerry Thompson said he saw three pair of patent leather shoes in my closet. Why didn't he take a picture of them? Why didn't he pick them up for evidence? I've never owned patent leather shoes. Somebody said I wore black patent leather boots to church. Would I wear a *maniac's* costume to *church*?

"She never saw the crowbar. All she said she felt was a many sided steel or iron tool when she grasped it from behind. She said it was over her head."

Ted is as scornful of the psychologist, Al Carlisle, who is administering the tests to him as he is of the Utah detectives. Most of the tests are the standard ones that any psychology student is familiar with: the MMPI (Minnesota Multiphasic Personality Index) consisting of hundreds of questions that can be answered "yes" or "no" with some deliberate "lie" questions repeated at intervals. I spotted the lie questions when I was a freshman in college, particularly, "Do you ever think about things too bad to talk about?" The "correct" answer is "yes"—everybody does, but many people write "no." For Ted Bundy, that test was kindergarten stuff. The TAT (Thematic Apperception Test): look at a picture and tell a story from it. The Rorshach or "ink blot" test. Ted had administered these tests himself to patients. The Utah State Prison had its own psychological test, a series of adjectives where the subject underlines those that apply to his personality.

"He wants to know about my childhood, my family, my sex life, and I tell him what I can. He's happy and he says do I want to see him again? So I tell him 'O.K.' Why not?"

We pause as another group moves through the hallway.

"The next time I meet him, he's smiling. He has a diagnosis. I am a passive-aggressive personality. The man is so pleased with himself, Ann, and he sits back waiting. He expects more from me. What does he want? A full confession?"

I say little during our visit; he has so much to get off his chest, and, with the exception of visits from Sharon Auer and occasionally from O'Connell and Bruce Lubeck, his associate, Ted feels he has had no one to talk to who can communicate on his level.

"John thinks I should have gotten angry in court. He went to law school with Judge Hanson, and he knows the man. I was sitting there just trying to understand the motivations behind the prosecutors, and it was just too ridiculous to show emotion about. But John thinks I should have gotten mad!"

We talk about Sharon and Meg. He has known Sharon for more than a year, and she visits him faithfully every Wednesday and Sunday. "Don't mention Sharon to Meg. Sharon's jealous of Meg, and Meg doesn't really know about Sharon."

I promise that I won't involve myself in his complicated romantic life, and I marvel that he can keep two intense relationships going while he's locked up with a possible life sentence hanging over him.

"My mother's upset with Meg for telling the King County Police that I was illegitimate." The legitimacy of Ted's birth will eventually become the least of Louise Bundy's worries.

"This place . . . they've got everything they want in here: drugs, speed. I won't do drugs. I'm not going to do the usual prison trip. I'm adjusting, and I want to work for prison reform. I'm innocent, but I can work from the inside."

Ted still wants to write, and he feels that he can get writing out to me through Sharon. Sharon regularly carries papers, legal briefs, in with her when she visits. She could carry his writing out and send it to me.

"I need $15,000 to hire private detectives; I think Carol DaRonch, or someone close to her, knew the man who attacked her. I need money to hire a team of independent psychologists to submit a report to the sentencing board. Everybody makes decisions about me and I'm not even allowed to sit in on the meetings . . ."

"I don't think you should try to publish anything before the first of June," I said. "And Colorado. There's still Colorado."

"I talked to Colorado; they have no claim on me."

"What about those credit card slips in Colorado?"

He smiles. "It's not against the law to be in Colorado. Sure, I was there, but a lot of people go to Colorado."

I ask him if, when he writes, he will include a description of the murder cases, and he tells me that he believes those "sensational cases" will be essential to selling his book. "Sam Shepard was found innocent after years in prison," he recalls, "and his book on an innocent man's ordeal sold."

Sitting there in that airless cubicle, I am once again on his side. He seems too frail, so beleaguered by forces over which he has no control. And yet the charisma is still there. I *believe* his position as a man who is, as he has been most of his life, in a situation that has no relevance to the real Ted inside.

He remembers my world, and politely asks how my house sale is going, how my children are. He begs me to stand by Meg, tells me how much he loves her and misses her.

And then the guards are back. They tap him on the shoulder. They have given us an extra fifteen minutes. He rises, hugs me again, kisses me on the cheek. They pat him down again. That's why they didn't search me; if I'd given him anything, they would find it before I left.

The door slides open for me, and I pause for a minute, watching him as he is led back into the belly of the prison, dwarfed by the two guards.

"Hey lady . . . Goddammit! Watch out!"

The door is automatically closing, and I leap forward just in time to escape being caught in its metal jaws. The guard stares at me as if I'm retarded. Lieutenant Tanner thanks me politely for coming, walks me to the prison's front door.

And then I am outside again, past the twin towers, in my car and on the road back toward Salt Lake City. The wind has kicked up a dust storm and the prison behind me is almost obliterated from view. Suddenly, there are red lights whirling atop a van in back of me. I have become paranoid in that hour and a half at Point-of-the-Mountain, and I wonder why they are chasing me. What did I *do?* The van pulls up, closer, closer, and I prepare to pull over, and then it turns off on a side road, its wail fading in the wind.

I realize I am talking to myself. No, no . . . he couldn't have done it. He's been railroaded in there by public opinion. That man I just talked to is the same man I've always known. He has to be innocent.

Driving toward the city, I pass the turn-offs for Midvale, for Murray, names that had never been anything before but places on a map, now the sites of two of the abductions. I pass commuters, bored with their daily routine, and I am so thankful to be free. I can go to my motel, have dinner with a friend, get on a plane and go back to Seattle. Ted can't. He is locked up with the rest of the "fish." How could this happen to a young man with such a future ahead of him? I am so caught up in my reverie that I miss the turn to my motel, and wander, lost, in the wide, clean, but confusing streets of Salt Lake City.

It was that night—April 1, 1976—when I had the dream. It was very frightening, jarring me awake in a strange room in a strange city.

I found myself in a large parking lot, with cars backing out and racing away. One of the cars ran over an infant, injuring it terribly, and I grabbed it up, knowing it was up to me to save it. I had to get to a hospital, but no one would help. I carried the baby, wrapped almost completely in a gray blanket, into a car rental agency. They had plenty of cars, but they looked at the baby in my arms and refused to rent me one. I tried to get an ambulance, but the attendants turned away. Finally, in desperation, I found a wagon—a child's wagon—and I put the injured infant in it, pulling it behind me for miles until I found an emergency room.

I carried the baby, running, up to the desk. The admitting nurse glanced at the bundle in my arms. "No, we will not treat it."

"But it's still alive! It's going to die if you don't do something."

"It's better. Let it die. It will do no one any good to treat it."

The nurse, the doctors, everyone, turned and moved away from me and the bleeding baby.

And then I looked down at it. It was not an innocent baby; it was a demon. Even as I held it, it sunk its teeth into my hand and bit me.

I did not have to be a Freudian scholar to understand my dream; it was all too clear. Had I been trying to save a monster, trying to protect something or someone who was too dangerous and evil to survive?

23

Something deep in my unconscious mind had surfaced, had told me forcefully that I perhaps believed that Ted Bundy was a killer. But I had made my commitment to keep in contact with him, no matter what the future would hold. I suspected that he did not feel things the way I did, but I could not believe that he was not laboring under a terrible weight. I felt that perhaps I might one day be the vehicle through which he could rid himself of that weight. If he would talk to me about what had happened, could reveal the facts still hidden, it would not only help him to receive the redemption he had alluded to in his poem, it could give some measure of relief, of finality, to the parents and relatives who still waited to learn what had happened to their daughters. Oddly, I could never picture Ted as a murderer, never visualize what had happened. It was probably best that I couldn't. When I wrote to him, my letters had to be to the man I remembered, or I couldn't do it.

Once before, Ted had called me when he was in the grip of some emotional anxiety. Although he had denied making that call to me on November 20, 1974, I had seen the phone records. He *had* called that night, and I sensed that there would come a day when he would need me again. Something seemed to have gone so terribly wrong with Ted's mind and I now suspected the "sick" part of him was capable of murder. If that was true, then he would need someone who could listen, who would not judge, but who might help to make his confessions easier. I felt that Ted might be able to expiate his guilt through his writing, and I continued to encourage him to write.

He had asked me to call Meg. In our prison visit, he had told me "I love Meg spiritually," and I wondered if that did not mean that Meg was caught up with a man who, even if he were not in prison, would never marry her. For her sake, I wrote to him: "My gut reaction to discussions we have had about Meg recently—and years ago—is that you do not ultimately see your future with her as much as you love her and as much history as you share with her. There is something missing, something essential to a forever-after relationship. This, of course, is not something I would discuss with her, but I will encourage any effort she puts forth to become a complete person in her own right, so that she does not need any man quite as much as she needs you now."

He seemed to agree, but there would be letters where he was terrified that he would lose her. Even so, there was Sharon, and I kept my promise not to discuss either woman with the other.

I did call Meg, and she remembered me from that long-ago Christmas party. She seemed anxious to meet me again and we set up an appointment to have dinner together.

On April 7th (although he misdated the letter again as March 7, 1976), I had a letter from Ted, the first since I'd returned from Utah.

The small white envelopes furnished by the prison all had a preprinted return address giving a post office box in Draper, Utah, and above that, Ted wrote "T.R. Bundy."

Ted had pulled himself together now, an effort that would never fail to make me pause and consider the ability he had to do that. He could somehow manage to recoup and recover under such tremendous stress and adjust to each new situation.

His letter was an apology, in part, because he had usurped much of the conversation in our visit in prison. "I have developed a typical prisoner's syndrome: the obsession with my legal case . . . the trial and the verdict live in me like some cerebral ulcer."

He was writing many letters and observations in his cell, and commented that his left hand (he is left-handed) had become so strong that he broke his shoe laces without even trying.

Ted commented on the link between us, a link that seemed to be growing stronger: "You've called it Karma. It may be. Yet, whatever supernatural force guides our destinies, it has brought us together in some mind-expanding situations. I must believe this invisible hand will pour more chilled Chablis for us in less treacherous, more tranquil times to come."

Again, he urged me to take care of Meg for him, and he asked that I suggest to Meg that she read me some of the love poems he had sent to her. He enclosed one of those poems, a poem he had printed on blue paper in the prison's printing facility. It ended,

> I send you this kiss
> deliver this body to hold.
> I sleep with you tonight
> with words of love untold.
> I would love you, if I might
> with words that unfold
> these arms to press you tight.

When I met Meg for dinner on April 30, 1976, she carried with her a dozen or more poems, love poems from Ted. She had typed them carefully, with copies for herself and for Ted. They were romantic sonnets, something any woman in love would have clung to. And Meg was certainly a woman in love. Yet, even as I read them, I was struck with the incongruity of the situation. This was the woman who had placed Ted in his present jeopardy, and *I* knew that Sharon Auer was also in love with him—Sharon who thought Ted loved her.

Meg wept as she read over the poems, pointing out particularly tender phrases to me. "I can't understand how he can forgive me after what I did to him, how he can write me poems like this."

Meg slipped the poems back into the large manilla envelope and glanced around the room. No one had noticed her tears; the heavy-weight championship fight was on the television set above the bar and everyone was staring at it.

"You know," she said softly. "I don't make friends easily. I had one boyfriend and one woman friend. And now, I've really lost them both. I don't see Lynn any more. I can't forgive her for making me doubt Ted, and I don't know when I'll ever see him again."

"What was there, Meg," I asked. "What was there that made you go to the police? Was there anything besides Lynn's suspicions?"

She shook her head. "I can't tell you. I know you're writing a book. I hope you understand, but I just can't talk about it."

I didn't press her. I wasn't with her to try to squeeze information out of her. I was with her because Ted had asked me to stand by her. Pushing her would be too much like poking a creature with a stick, a creature already hurt.

And yet, Meg wanted information from me. She was jealous of Ted, even when he was locked up in the Utah State Prison. She wanted to know about Sharon. I told her, truth-fully, that I really didn't know much about Sharon Auer. I didn't mention that I had talked to Sharon on the phone when I was in Salt Lake City, and that I'd heard Sharon's voice turn icy when I mentioned Meg. That was my first realization that Sharon was seemingly as unsure of Ted, as possessive, as Meg was.

Meg struck me as terribly vulnerable, and I wondered why Ted could not let her go. She was thirty-one, and she wanted—needed— a marriage, a chance to have the children she longed for before there was too great a gap between them and Liane, before Meg was too old. Ted must have known that he would not be free for years, and yet he bound her to him through his poems, letters, calls. If anything, she loved him more than she ever had, and she was trying to cope with more guilt than she could bear.

It was odd; even as I mused about how Meg would survive with her complete dependence on Ted, I received a letter from him—on May 17th—wherein he seemed terrified of losing *her!* He was sweating out his last two weeks before the June sentencing date, and that may have contributed to his anxiety. He seemed to feel that Meg was pulling away from him, and he asked me to go to her and plead his case. He had no real reason to doubt Meg's loyalty, but he "sensed vibrations."

"You are the only person whom I trust," he wrote, "who is both sensitive and in a position to approach Meg for me. I think it would be easier for Meg to express herself to you than to me."

The letter ended with his opinions on the psychiatrists and psychologists who had spent three months examining him:

... after conducting numerous tests and extensive examinations, (they) have found me normal and are deeply perplexed.
Both of us know that none of us is 'normal.' Perhaps what I
should say is that they find no explanation to substantiate the

verdict or other allegations. No seizures, no psychosis, no disassociative reaction, no unusual habits, opinions, emotions or fears. Controlled, intelligent, but, in no way, crazy. The working theory is now that I have completely forgotten everything, a theory which is disproved by their own results. 'Very interesting,' they keep mumbling. I may have convinced one or two of them that I am innocent.

I did call Meg on Ted's behalf and found that she was completely unchanged in her devotion to him. She had managed to tell him that in a two-minute phone call to the prison, and urged me to assure him that she wasn't dating anyone else. He did not want to let her go, and Meg apparently did not want to leave him.

On June 5th, Meg came to my home to spend the evening. She had just seen her parents off after a week-long visit and was tense because they were not sympathetic about her continued allegiance to Ted. She was also apprehensive about Sharon, more aware of Sharon's relationship with Ted than he realized. I was in the middle of a situation that made me uneasy; I didn't want to cover for Ted if he was deluding Meg, but I didn't want to tell her about Sharon's twice weekly visits to the Utah State Prison either. I suspected that I was being subtly manipulated in keeping Meg bound to Ted.

I wrote to him about Meg on June 6th: "I think that she is aware of Sharon's relationship to you, but I stressed that I really know nothing about it, and I don't know, and I don't *want* to know. When the time comes to thinking of everyday conflicts, you will have to get your act together."

Ted's future was still in limbo. The sentencing on the DaRonch kidnapping conviction, set for June 1st, had been postponed for thirty more days. It was conceivable—but not likely—that he would receive probation. Or he could receive life in prison. Psychologists were still wrestling with his personality. I had received a phone call from Al Carlisle, the psychologist in charge of the report on Ted, one Sunday evening. He began abruptly, "Do you know Ted Bundy?"

"Who wants to know?" I'd responded; knowing Ted Bundy was becoming something that one did not brag about.

He had then identified himself, sounded a shy, diffident man. I told him only what I had seen—there was no point in my getting my dreams and fears into what was allegedly a rational psychological study. I explained that, in all my contacts with Ted, I had found him normal, empathetic, friendly, gentle. And that was true.

"Well," he said. "I've talked to a lot of people about him and I've been surprised at the widely divergent opinions about him."

I wanted to ask what they were, but it didn't seem the proper response. I waited.

"I like him myself. I've spent about twelve hours with him, and I like him." Carlisle wanted copies of the two "Ted letters" which had accrued such undeserved fame, and I said I would send them—but only with Ted's permission. Ted gave that, and I mailed them to the prison psychologist.

Ted wrote again on June 9th. With sentencing just around the corner, he had geared up for a fight. "The prospects are exciting!"

Ted found the psychological examinations "malicious, slanted, and infernal." Harking back to his own psychology training, he felt prepared to deal with the questions that the doctors asked him and his friends—questions which suggested that he might be strange, homosexual, or deviant in his demands during sexual intercourse. He was angry because his examiners had told him that some of his friends had had negative things to say about him, but would not reveal the content of interviews or the names of friends.

"I was aghast! Is this America? Am I to be attacked anonymously? I listed the names of several close friends, people who know me well. None had been contacted. Who are my detractors? No response . . ."

He *had* received some answers. The testing team had reported to him that the nameless interviewees had indicated that he was changeable.

"Well, sometimes you would appear happy, pleasant. Other times you would seem like a different person and unresponsive," they had told him.

"They are trying so desperately to create a split personality," he wrote angrily. "I'll tear them apart."

He was, indeed, looking forward to the hearing on his mental capabilities, positive that he could tear down all that the diagnostic team had constructed in the three months just past.

Ted had begun to enter into the legal fight for his own freedom, and his participation would escalate over the years ahead. He was "up," confident that his mind, his intelligence, could surpass whatever the psychiatric examination purported to reveal. I think he truly believed that, through his own rhetoric, he would be free. Ted did make his statements to Judge Hanson. As he made his plea, he was the cocky, witty Ted, the man so removed from the facts that the whole situation was ridiculous. It was a posture that would irritate several judges and juries in his future court wranglings, but it was seemingly an attitude necessary for the survival of his ego. I have always felt that Ted would, literally, rather *die* than be humiliated—would face life in prison or the electric chair before humbling himself in any way.

At the hearing, Ted was scornful as he attacked the arrests in August and October of 1975. He admitted to a certain "strangeness" of behavior when he'd been confronted by Sergeant Bob Hayward, but could see no connection with his actions, with the contents of his car, and the DaRonch kidnapping. He had had no alibi for the night of November 8, 1974, and he argued, "If I cannot remember precisely what occurred on a date which is now eighteen and one half months prior to my arrest for kidnapping, it is because my memory does not improve with time. It is safe to say what I was not doing, however. I was not having heart surgery, nor was I taking ballet lessons, nor was I in Mexico, nor was I abducting a complete stranger at gunpoint. There are just some things a person does not forget and just some things a person is not inclined to do under any circumstances."

Then Ted was sentenced on June 30th, despite his tearful plea that his being in prison would serve no purpose. "Some-day, who knows when, five or ten or more years in the future, when the time comes when I can leave, I suggest you ask yourself where we are, what's been accomplished, was the sacrifice of my life worth it all? Yes, I will be a candidate for rehabilitation. But not for what I have done, but for what the system has done to me."

He drew a comparatively light sentence. One to fifteen years. Because no other charges of such magnitude had been brought against him, he was sentenced under provisions for a lesser second-degree felony. All things being equal, he could hope to be paroled as quickly as eighteen months hence.

But, of course, all things were not equal. The investigation into the murder of Caryn Campbell in Aspen, Colorado was accelerating. Investigator Mike Fisher had the credit card slips, and he had received word from the FBI lab's criminalist, Bob Neill, that, among the hairs found when Ted's Volkswagen was processed and vacuumed, were hairs that were microscopically alike in class and characteristic to not one—but three—of Bundy's suspected victims: Caryn Campbell, Melissa Smith, and Carol DaRonch.

Hairs are not as individual as fingerprints, yet Bob Neill, a FBI crime lab expert for two decades, stated he had never found three victims' purported hairs in one spot before. "The chances of three different hair samples being so microscopically alike and *not* belonging to the victims are one in 20,000. I've never seen anything like it."

One Washington detective mentioned to me that the crow-bar found in Ted's car matched the depression in Caryn Campbell's skull. There was said to be an eye witness, the woman who had seen the strange young man in a second floor corridor of the Wildwood Inn minutes before Caryn vanished. The word among law enforcement networks was that the Colorado case was much stronger than the Utah kidnapping case had been.

If Ted was aware of the burgeoning Colorado case, and I suspect he was, he was still more caught up in the emotions that lingered after the sentencing in Utah when he wrote to me on July 2, 1976. That letter was classic in that it was the evaluation by the subject himself—an honors psychology graduate—of the psychiatric evaluation done on him.

The letter was typed, typed on an ancient machine with letters clotted with ink, but Ted's pride in his hour-and-a-half dissection of the psychiatric evaluation transcended the blurred pages.

I was whistling in the wind, yet in a curious sort of way, I felt a deep sense of fulfillment. I felt relaxed but emphatic; controlled, but sincere and filled with emotion. It didn't matter who was listening, although I desired each word to strike the Judge as forcefully as possible. Briefly, all too briefly, I was myself again, amongst free people, using all the skill I could muster, fighting the only way I know how: with words and logic. And all too briefly, I was testing the dream of being an attorney.

He knew he had lost, but he blamed that loss on the police, the prosecutors, the judge, on what he termed "the weaknesses of men who were too timid, too blind, too frightened, to accept the cruel deception of the state's case."

The psychiatric diagnoses had concluded that Ted Bundy was not psychotic, neurotic, the victim of organic brain disease, alcoholic, addicted to drugs, suffering from a character disorder or amnesia, and was not a sexual deviate.

Ted quoted Dr. Austin the psychiatrist, the one member of the team whom he had thought most forthright: "I feel that Mr. Bundy is either a man who has no problems or is smart enough and clever enough to appear close to the edge of 'normal.' . . . Since it has been determined by the Court that he is not telling the truth regarding the present crime, I seriously question if he can be expected to tell the truth regarding participation in any program or probation agreement."

Ted's conclusion was that Judge Hanson had swayed the entire evaluation by his original verdict, and that the diagnostic team had merely groomed their report to match the verdict.

Carlisle had evidently concluded that Ted was a "private person," one not known intimately by others. "When one tries to know him, he becomes evasive."

"Ann, think of me as you know me," Ted wrote. "Yes, I am a private person but so what . . . and the part about being someone incapable of being intimate . . . is absurd."

Ted had been given the California Life Goals Evaluation Schedules test. His answers had shown that he had six goals:

To have freedom from want.
To control the actions of others.
To guide other with their consent.
To avoid boredom.
To be self-fulfilled.
To live one's life one's own way.

None of these goals could be considered abnormal, and Ted was quick to point that out to me in his letter. He admitted readily that he was insecure, as Dr. Carlisle had suggested, and that perhaps he tried to structure his relationships with other people.

"Again, think of me, our Crisis Clinic days and more recently our conversations during our meetings in Seattle. It is entirely possible that I do structure my relationships with other people, maybe not consciously, but there must be some order in my life."

One of the conclusions that galled Ted the most was that Dr. Carlisle had found Ted to have a strong dependency on women, and deduced that that dependency was suspect.

"That I am dependent on you women has got to mean something. What though? I am undeniably dependent on women. Given birth by a woman, taught in school by women, and deeply, deeply in love with one woman. I ask any woman with whom I have been involved, socially, professionally, or intimately, to look at our relationship. Was I some twisted mass of nerves . . . subjugating myself to superior womanhood?"

Carlisle had found that Ted had a fear of being humiliated in his relationships with women, and Ted sardonically confessed a: "personal distaste for being put down and humiliated . . . Draw whatever inferences you must, but, like Brer Rabbit, throw me in that briar patch [female companionship] any time you want. We are still a long way from running about scooping up teenage girls."

For every conclusion that Dr. Carlisle asserted, Ted had a comeback. He denied that he "ran from his problems," or that he was unstable, pointing out his amazing strength under the rigors of the DaRonch trial, and his ability to function under stress. No one could fault him there.

Ted continued in his incisive critique. Citing Carlisle's report, he could not agree that the profile emerging was, as the psychologist noted, "consistent with the nature of the crime for which he was convicted."

"If this is true, (Ted wrote) there are a lot of potential kidnappers running around loose out there . . . The conclusion is preposterous and indicative of the strenuous attempt to satisfy the presumptions underlying the verdict. The report was a despicable fraud."

Ted's pain and hopelessness came through in the last paragraphs of that long, long letter.

"I am exhausted. The bitter reality has dawned, but the full impact of my fate has not been fully understood. Since the sentence was handed down, the first flashes of intense anger and despair have grown out of the knowledge that Meg and I shall never have a life together. The most beautiful force in my life has been separated from me."

He asked me to share the letter with Meg, explaining that it was the first he had written since being sentenced, and asked me to confort her. "There can never be any goodbyes for Meg and I, but I weep bitterly to think that there can be no more hellos."

I was mightily impressed by Ted's ability to think like a lawyer, in the polished order of his evaluation. His I.Q. had been tested at the Utah State Prison and found to be 124—not on the genius level, about what a student in a four-year college needs to graduate—but he was clearly superior to the test results. My loyalties wavered once again. It would always be so.

And yet, even as I read Ted's declaration of his great love for Meg, I was aware that he seemed to be able to dismiss his concurrent relationships with other women. If he could not be faithful to Meg, how could I fully believe in his steadfast love for her? It was so hard for me to *know*. Despite my dream, despite the bombardment of opinions from lawmen, there were still so many facets of his story that were hidden from me, and still that chance that Ted was being railroaded.

If he was manipulating me, he was doing an excellent job of it.

24

While Ted had been sentenced in the DaRonch kidnapping, it had been the most minor of the crimes he was suspected of, and, although Colorado authorities seemed to be putting a case together in the Campbell slaying, Washington State detectives were supremely frustrated.

In the fall of 1975, Captain Herb Swindler had been transferred out of the Seattle Police Crimes Against Persons Unit and became commander of the Georgetown Precinct in the South End of Seattle. There were rumors that Herb's preoccupation with psychics and astrologers, in all the occult possibilities in the mass killings, had begun to annoy the brass. With the reassignment to Georgetown, Herb would be out of the missing girls' cases for all intents and purposes; his duties would involve supervising the uniformed contingent of patrolmen in his precinct now. It was still a position calling for a high ranking officer and one with uncommon good sense, but Herb's contact with detectives would be minimal. And the hierarchy upstairs in the Public Safety Building would no longer hear tales of Swindler's bizarre investigative techniques.

It was not a slap in the face, it was more the gentle rapping of knuckles. Swindler had been the only detective who had believed that Kathy Parks of Oregon was part of the Seattle pattern—and he'd been right. It was September, 1975 when he'd been transferred out of the probe, ironically only a few weeks before Ted's arrest.

Swindler's replacement, Captain John Leitch, is a tall, blond veteran cop—a man my age, and a man of some brilliance. Herb had liked to talk over everything that was happening; Leitch was as close-mouthed as a Sphinx, and leery of me. In time, he would come to regard me with a certain grudging trust and took delight in teasing me about my "boyfriend, Ted." But, in 1976, John Leitch and I circled each other somewhat warily. I found him a solid administrator, who left the detectives in his unit alone to do their work, a cerebral kind of policeman. I don't know what he thought of me, although he tended to view me as part of the media rather than an ex-cop myself. I liked him, but he intimidated me.

He, on the other hand, was very concerned that I might be regarded as a "police agent" in the Ted Bundy transactions. He needn't have worried; it was a role I most assuredly did not want to play. I was still walking the tightrope between Ted and the detectives, a rope that seemed to wend over higher and higher precipices. It was imperative that I continue to write fact-detective stories, and any breach of faith with a police agency would mean the end of that. Neither did I want to be disloyal to Ted, although it was becoming more and more difficult not to believe that Ted was the man the police sought.

Nick Mackie, over in the county offices, had known me for so long that I wasn't much of a threat. During most of the spring and summer of 1976, we met sporadically to talk about Ted. Ted knew it, because I continued to forward messages from Mackie. At times, he grew churlish about my suggestion that he talk to the King County commander, but he never seemed truly angry about it.

Although Mackie never revealed to me exactly what the detectives had on Ted, he tried continually to convince me that they were right. I don't know how many times he asked me with some exasperation, "Come on. Admit it. You really think he's guilty, don't you?"

And I would always answer, "I don't know. I just don't know. Sometimes I'm sure he's guilty, and then, again, sometimes I wonder."

On two or three occasions my discussions with Mackie continued through lunch and far into the afternoon. Both of us were searching for answers that seemed always just beyond reach.

I was quite sure of one thing; after writing up at least a dozen cases in the Northwest dealing with "mass" killers of young women in the eight years preceding, I felt that *the* "Ted" had "souvenirs" hidden someplace, that he had kept a trophy from each killing.

"Nick, I think that somewhere, he's hidden earrings, clothing, possibly even polaroids, something from each girl. I've never found a case similar where the suspect didn't keep momentoes."

"I agree—but where? We've been through the Rogers's rooming house—the attic, the garage, and we've dug up the garden. We didn't find anything."

Of course, the elder Bundys had absolutely refused to allow their Tacoma home to be searched, nor would they permit a search of the grounds of their A-frame cabin vacation home on Crescent Lake. Senior Deputy Prosecutor Phil Killien had advised Mackie that there was not sufficient probable cause to obtain a search warrant for those properties. His inability to search for physical evidence to tie Ted in with the Washington cases—particularly at the Crescent Lake location—tormented Mackie. I didn't blame him, but without a search warrant anything detectives found would be considered "fruit of the poisoned tree," that is, inadmissible as evidence in a court of law because it would have been obtained illegally. If Keppel or Dunn—or McChesney—were to go to the A-frame cottage and find something like Georgeann Hawkins's purse, or Janice Ott's bike, or Lynda Healy's turquoise rings, it would be absolutely useless. Tainted evidence. I had had that concept hammered into my head when I'd taken a course entitled, "Arrest, Search, and Seizure."

Mackie mused. "We can't go—but I wish someone could, that someone could just bring us in one piece of physical evidence."

And, indeed, that was the only way it would be admissible. If I, myself, were to search any private property Ted was known to frequent—*after* this conversation with Nick—anything I found would be "fruit of the poisoned tree;" I would be an extension of the arm of the police department, because I had never considered searching on my own.

The detectives' hands were tied. The rules of the justice system in criminal investigations are so intricate, and most of them seem to be weighted heavily on the side of the suspect.

It was unlikely that Ted Bundy would ever be charged or tried in the Washington homicide cases. There was nothing more than the dozens of circumstances that seemed to defy probability.

Months later, when Captain John Leitch felt free to talk to me with cautious candor, he concurred that he felt the same way. It was his opinion that the only way Ted might be tried for the Washington cases would be if the eight cases were combined. "If all the known facts came out, on all the girls up here, I think there would be a conviction. But that seems to be the only way."

And no defense attorney would allow the Northwest cases to be lumped together. John Henry Browne would fight like a tiger if such a suggestion arose.

25

Caught in the Utah State Prison, Ted's ego seemingly remained intact. Our letters continued, in that odd intimacy that is sometimes maintained through the written word, an intimacy, and, occasionally, an honesty that is more difficult to keep alive in a face-to-face situation. If I could manage to suspend disbelief, I could continue to support him—if not wholeheartedly, then through my letters. The truth was caught somewhere, suspended, in a intricate cobweb of suspicion, denial, and continuing investigation.

I kept in touch with Meg too, and found her to be gathering new resolve; she signed up for some evening classes, started looking for a home to buy. And she was becoming increasingly suspicious of Ted's ties to Sharon Auer. When Louise Bundy returned from Ted's sentencing, she had made the tactical error of repeating over and over to Meg her feelings that Sharon was a "lovely person." Meg had finally deduced that Sharon was much more to Ted than an errand girl. When I spoke to her in August, 1976, Meg was vacillating between saying good-bye to Ted forever—not because of the charges against him, but because he had lied to her about Sharon—and continuing to support him with her love. She mailed him one letter to pave the way for a break, and then was instantly sorry, "I've been rethinking it . . . maybe I was too hasty."

Ted spent that summer in prison, becoming more acclimated to confinement; I didn't hear from him again until August 25th. I had suggested to him that I pass his letter on his feelings about the psychiatric report on to Nick Mackie, a suggestion that was not met with glee. Yet, this letter, arriving eight weeks after the outraged "evaluation" letter, seemed to reflect the emotions of a man who was getting it together again.

He was pleased to note that he had a new typewriter, earned, he said, when he wrote his first writ after being moved into the general population of the prison.

"General Population is the faceless mass of real prisoners we fish are always afraid were trying to rape us, and worse, steal our commissary. They were greatly overrated; they never steal commissary," Ted wrote.

Indeed, he was doing well among the general population. He had been afraid to move among these cons—cons for whom any man convicted of crimes against women or children is anathema, the lowest rung in prison hierarchy. Such men are often beaten, raped, or killed. But no one had threatened Ted, and he said he could move about the entire prison without fear because he had something of value to give the inmates of Point-of-the-Mountain: legal advice. He was often stopped and asked to help other prisoners prepare their appeals for new trials. Just as he had told me during my visit when he was still a "fish," he would survive because of his brain.

Further, he was something of a celebrity, and his out-spoken defense in his own legal encounters had impressed prison leaders. The old-timers made a point of being seen with Ted, of putting their stamp of approval on him.

"I think they also enjoy seeing a once-Republican, once-law student, one-time white-middle-class member attack the system as vigorously as they think it deserves," he commented. "I keep in close tough with the blacks and the Chicanos and my work for men in these groups has helped my image. One thing I have successfully avoided is the 'Wholly (sic)-than-thou; I'm so smart—I shouldn't be here with you criminals' image."

His days were spent working in the prison printshop, listening to other prisoners' grievances, and "wishing I were not here." He seemed happy to report that Meg was becoming more independent, even though it meant she didn't write to him as often as before, but he was looking forward to a visit from her on August 28th.

However, Ted had not become completely mellow; he launched into an harangue directed at Nick Mackie and other members of the law enforcement field. He did not want Mackie to read his letter on the psychiatric evaluation, although he forgave me for suggesting it.

I think you should know where I stand on the subject of policemen in general and Mackie in particular. Policemen have a job, a difficult job, to do, but I am sorry because I don't care one bit for the "job" they did on me no matter how genuine the devotion to duty. I have a standing policy from this point forward never to talk to a law enforcement officer about anything except the time of day and the location of the toilet. Mackie has earned my particular disrespect. True, he may be a good cop, feeds his dog Alpo, and doesn't eat his young alive, but my empathy for him ends there.

Someday, Ted said he would be interested to hear the "monstrous theory" held by the King County Police Department, but he was not presently interested in "story book fiction." He asked me to continue to stay in touch with Meg, and to "tell Mackie only that he has earned a special place in my heart, as I have probably earned one in his."

Ted's letters that summer and fall of 1976 ranged from the anger and humor of this one, to requests for information, to the blackest lines of depression. The mood swings, given his circumstances, were to be expected. His bid to remain free pending his appeal had been denied, and the Colorado murder charge hovered just ahead.

There were several letters where he asked me to check out the credentials of Northwest reporters who were attempting to interview him. I tracked most of them to their sources and reported that they seemed to be essentially innocuous writers from small publications.

Something happened to Ted's stability during the first week of September, something that seemed to make him despair completely. Reconstructing the time sequence later, I deduced that Meg had said something to him during their August 28th visit that made him think he had lost her forever.

The letter Ted sent me on *September* 5th was typed on the cover from a pad of typewriter paper, and its contents seemed steeped in the bleakest loss of hope. It could not be interpreted as anything other than a suicide note, and it frightened me.

Ted explained that the letter was like a call to the Crisis Clinic, but that there could be no reply. "I am not asking for help, I am saying goodbye."

He wrote that he could no longer straggle for justice, that he was not having just a bad day, but that he had reached "the end of all hope, the darkening of all dreams."

The letter as a whole—each sentence in it—could only mean one thing. Ted planned to kill himself: "What I am experiencing now is an entirely new dimension of loneliness mixed with resignation and calm. Unlike times of low morale I have survived in the past, I know I will not wake up in the morning refreshed and revived. I will wake up knowing only what has to be done—if I have the courage."

As my eyes raced down the page, I felt the hairs on the back of my neck stand up; it might, already be too late. He'd written this three days before.

The last sentences were a plea to the world who believed him guilty of any number of terrible crimes against women: "Lastly, and most important, I want you to know, I want the whole world to know that I am innocent. I have never hurt another human being in my life. God, please believe me."

Although he had said the letter could have no answer, I remembered that Ted and I had both had been taught at the Crisis Clinic that any contact made by someone in emotional distress—any reaching out—must be regarded as a cry for help. Ted *had* written to me, and I had to assume that meant he wanted me to stop him from destroying himself. I called Bruce Cummins, our long-ago mentor at the Clinic, and read him the letter. He agreed that I had to take some action.

I called John O'Connell's office in Salt Lake City. It was either that or notify Warden Sam Smith's office in the prison, and Ted had better friends in his lawyer's office. I reached Bruce Lubeck and told him that I feared Ted was about to kill himself. He promised to go out to Point-of-the-Mountain and see Ted.

I don't know if he went or not. I wrote a special delivery letter, a letter full of "Hang in there's" and sent it, holding my breath for days, expecting to hear a news bulletin.

It never came.

Instead, on September 26th, Ted wrote me a letter that was a partial explanation. He referred obliquely to hanging himself, but assured me that he was "hanging in there with nothing but my soul, I will add to your relief."

Apparently, it was not my letter that had turned him around, but a session of handball which he'd found to be an effective method of catharsis.

"It (handball) has a curious way of draining the bitterness away. Or perhaps it's the body's way of asserting itself over the destructive impulses of the mind, temporarily mindless of the body's uncompromising, unquestioning, eternal desire to survive. The body may only appear as host to the brain, but the intellect, fragile and selfish, is no match for the imperative of life itself. Hanging around, intangibly, is better than being tangibly nothing at all."

Ted apologized for alarming me; I wonder if he realized how very upset I had been to receive that suicide note, if he remembered how guilty I'd felt because I hadn't been able to save my own brother's life when he'd reached the point of suicidal thoughts.

Ted had decided to live, and, with his decision, his anger and bravado burst forth in his ensuing letters.

Again and again, he castigated the police. "Police detectives are a curious breed, but one learns quickly that when they have something they act first and talk later . . . I never underestimate the inventiveness and dangerousness of such men. Like wild animals, when cornered they can become very unstable."

Ted had reason to fear the "dangerousness" of police detectives. On October 22, almost exactly a year since he had been charged in the DaRonch kidnapping case in Utah, he was formally charged with the murder of Caryn Campbell in Pitkin County, Colorado. I suspect that he *was* as eager to confront his accusers as he told me he was. His strength in the face of attack seemed to be real, as it would always be. The overt challenges he could face; he was best on his feet, scornfully denying charges against him.

However, it is possible that Ted had not planned to be around when those charges finally came down. On October 19th, Ted had not returned to his cell from the yard. Warden Sam Smith announced that Ted had been discovered behind a bush, and that he'd had an "escape kit" on his person: a social security card, a sketch of a driver's license, road maps, and notes on airplane schedules.

Ted had written that his "pristine" behavior had allowed him more freedom around the prison, and now there was speculation that, with his job in the printshop, he might have intended to print up phony identification papers. He was immediately placed in solitary confinement. In retrospect, viewing Ted's propensity for escape that was to surface in the months ahead, it *is* likely that he had planned an escape from Point-of-the-Mountain, an escape that was aborted.

On October 26th I received a letter from Sharon Auer, who enclosed a brief note that Ted had sent her to send to me. Sharon was still very much a part of his life, even though his letters to me extolled no one but Meg. Sharon was horrified at the maximum security cell where Ted was being held, although her impressions of the "hole" were based on Ted's description of it as he was allowed no visitors.

Ted had written to her that he envisioned his cell as something resembling a Mexican prison. "Eight feet high, ten feet long, six feet wide. Two feet in from the front are steel bars running from floor to ceiling. A solid steel door—with only a peephole for the guard to look in—closes off the front of the cell. The walls have graffiti, vomit and urine coating them."

Ted's bed was a concrete slab with a thin mattress, and the only item of hope in the cell was a crucifix hanging over the wash basin. He could have nothing to read, but was allowed to receive letters. He would be there fifteen days, and Sharon was angry that he had received this harshest punishment possible for such a minor infraction as having a social security card on his person. She wrote that she was trying to write him three or four letters a day. "The bastards may not let me visit, but they're sure going to tire of carrying mail to him ..."

Reading her letter, I was again bemused and somewhat dismayed at what the denouement might one day be when those two women who loved Ted realized they had been deluded into believing that each was the *only* one. And I? I made up the third corner of the three-woman network giving Ted emotional support. I had managed to remain relatively unscathed. Torn by conflicting feelings and doubts still—but *I* was not in love with Ted. Sharon and Meg were.

Ted wrote to me from solitary confinement on Halloween. He said he had had only a woman's social security card, and not the kind used for identification, and blamed Warden Smith for blowing the circumstances out of proportion. I never found out what woman's name was on that card. Ted was angry, but he was not chastened.

> Adversity of this kind only serves to make me stronger, especially when it is clear to me that it is designed to create the pressure some believe will shatter my "normal facade." How absurd. Said one prisoner, when he heard of the decision to place me in isolation, "They're trying to break ya, Bundy. Yeah, they're just tryin' to break ya." I couldn't have agreed with him more, but since there is nothing to "break," I'll have to suffer instead. The fact that some persons continue to misjudge me has become almost humorous.

Ted commented on the Colorado case only to the extent that he insisted he was innocent of any involvement. He hinted that he had documents that would destroy Colorado's case. "The Colorado trial will mark the beginning of the end of a myth."

He said he had sent me a note via Meg—which was a slip because it had not been Meg who forwarded it, but Sharon. And he chided me gently for living in luxury in my new house, for writing to him on my new personalized stationery. "Personalized stationery is one of the small but truly necessary luxuries of life."

Ted was attempting to push my guilt buttons. I was free, and living in splendor, and he was in the "hole." I refused to take the bait, and wrote back,

> You said you'd given the message for me to Meg—but it was Sharon who sent me one. You probably just mis-spoke yourself. Don't go getting the two of them confused or you'll be in hot water! While you're envying my security, *remember* you have two members of the opposite sex in love with you, and I haven't got any. Fortunately, I've been so busy lately with work, housing, and the kid's problems, there hasn't been much time to ponder this glaring lack. I am still sleeping with my typewriter and it's still cold, lumpy and unresponsive.

Ted's reply came after his extradition arraignment on the Colorado murder charge, an arraignment that took place on his thirtieth birthday. I had sent him two humorous birthday cards (explaining that Hallmark didn't put out a card specifically for his predicament: "Hi there . . . Happy Thirtieth Birthday and Happy Arraignment.") He had chosen to view his situation with wry, angry humor and I geared my responses to that.

Ted wrote after the extradition hearing that he had drawn the largest crowd of reporters he'd seen in once place since his ordeal began, and he denigrated the press's sense of fair play and justice "—since it has none." He assured me that the "eye witness" in Aspen was of no consequence since she had picked out his picture a full year after the Campbell disappearance.

Although Ted's extradition arraignment on November 24, 1976 had drawn a flock of reporters, he was not the most famous prisoner in the Utah State Prison that week. It was a fellow convict—Gary Gilmore—a convicted murderer with a death wish, who made the cover of *Newsweek* on November 29th. Compared to Gary Gilmore, Ted was decidedly second string news. It would not always be so.

Gilmore was an habitual criminal who had shot two young men during robberies, and he had a kind of bitter mystique about him. He too was involved in a doomed romance with a woman who seemed as bedazzled and driven as Ted's Meg was. The tragic child-woman, Nicole Barrett, who had entered into an abortive suicide pact with Gary Gilmore, reminded me of Meg in her obsession with her lover—but Ted apparently saw no correlation at all between his romance and Gilmore's and detested the other man for his manipulation of Nicole. He had studied Gary and Nicole when they met in the visitors' area.

"The Gilmore situation grows curiouser and curiouser. Have seen him on occasion in the visiting room with Nicole. I'll never forget the deep love and anguish in her eyes. Gilmore, however, is misguided, unstable, and selfish . . . The media preys on this Romeo and Juliet saga. Tragic. Irreconcilable."

Nor did Ted have anything good to say about Gilmore's legal advisors.

Ted had little time to ruminate on the "saga" of Gary and Nicole; he was busy reviewing and indexing 700 pages of testimony from the DaRonch trial, and, at the same time, studying Colorado criminal law. After reviewing the Utah trial, he could not see how the judge could have found him guilty, and he was sure that there would be no guilty verdict in Colorado.

"I feel like a general conducting a battle, *not* General Custer either," he wrote enthusiastically. "Legally, I am on very solid ground!"

Ted never failed to comment on what was happening back in my world, even if it meant only a sentence or two at the end of his letters. This time, he wrote:

> I am anxious that Cosmopolitan et al return payment so you'll be able to rent a helicopter and get me out of here. The prison maintains, falsely, that I had airline schedules. Can you imagine! If I were foolish enough to go to an airport, I certainly wouldn't give a damn which flight I jumped on as long as I was assured the plane could take off and land. Doing well, battling like hell. You know what it takes for the tough to get going.
>
> love, ted.

The talk of escape, however flippant, had begun to flash a warning light on and off like a subliminal message on a television screen, hidden among Ted's discussions of legal battles. But then, all prisoners dream of escape, and all of them talk about it—the possibilities, the odds. A minuscule number actually try.

Ted had mentioned that he would be "having a change of scenery" and that meant that one day he would stop fighting extradition to Colorado, but he would do it in his own good time; he had much research to do first. There was no more money for lawyers, nothing more to be counted on from family and friends in Washington, and that meant he would be in the hands of public defenders. More and more, he was seizing his own legal destiny; like the Little Red Hen, he would do it himself.

Almost from the moment I moved into my new home, leaving the sea and the wind to take over the little beach house we'd vacated, my writing fortunes took an upward turn. I had assignment from *Cosmopolitan*, *Good House-keeping*, and *Ladies Home Journal*. After years with the pulps, I'd finally broken into the "slicks." Interestingly enough, all my assignments had to do with victims of violent crimes; the American public, in 1976, had finally begun to show concern for the fate of crime victims. Too many people had become victims or knew victims. Because I'd been busy moving and meeting publishing deadlines, I had not written to Ted for three or four weeks, and I got a rather plaintively hostile letter from him in mid-December.

Dear Ann,

I surrender. Did I say something offensive? Worse, yet, is my breath offensive? Have my letters been stolen by the C.I.A. and you think I don't write you anymore so you don't write to me? Am I too hopeless a case? (Don't answer that.) I can take it. Yessiree, never let it be said that I lost my cool just because my friends have forgotten me.

It was not a happy season for Ted. For the first time, he was behind bars at Christmas time. Only a year before, we had sat together at the Brasserie Pittshbourg; it seemed that twenty years had passed.

Ted's letter was his Christmas message, poems scrawled on the lined paper.

This note must do as my Christmas card to you; a way of thanking you for the merriment you have brought into my life, not to mention the life-sustaining support. Now all I need is one of those quaint verses that all the store-bought cards have:

> May Santa's reindeer be so kind
> Not to leave their droppings
> On your roof.
> . . .
> It's here!
> Don't pretend you couldn't tell.
> If you're not into Christmas
> Catch the first train to hell.
> So just tack up those house lights
> And mummify the tree
> Don't forget, without Christmas cards
> You'd never hear from me.

The final poem was a departure from the bitterness of the first two—a religious poem. Ted often referred to God in his letters, although he had never mentioned Him in any of our conversations outside prison walls.

I wrote immediately, and then called Meg to learn that she was on her way to Utah for Christmas and yet another reunion with Ted. I hoped that this visit would not be the catalyst for a renewed spate of dark depression for Ted as her last trip to Utah had been. His days at Point-of-the-Mountain were growing short; he would have to make the decision about going to Colorado soon. His name was still not well known in Aspen—except to policemen. Claudine Longet's murder trial was set in Aspen in January, and she was reaping the big headlines.

Evidently Meg's Christmas visit was more successful than their meeting in August had been. Ted wrote me two days before Christmas, describing their visit. "She came to me yesterday. In a visit so short and sweet, I am reunited with the missing element in my life. Seeing her is a glimpse of heaven. Touching her gave me a belief in miracles. So often I had dreamed of her that seeing her form real was a dazzling experience. She is gone again, and, again, I feel her absence in each unconscious moment."

He recalled the fight that he and Meg had had after I'd driven him to the Crisis Clinic Christmas party in 1972. After I had dumped him in his inebriated state at the Rogers's rooming house, he had gone to his room and fallen fast asleep.

"Meg and I had had an argument and she was scheduled to fly out early the next morning. She decided to stop by before the flight, kiss and make up . . . she threw rocks at my window and called me . . . Believing that I would have awoken if I was there, she rushed away heartbroken because she thought I was 'sleeping' with someone else, She has never fully believed my fervent assurances that I was in a deep, intoxicated sleep. I have never told her that I went with *you* to a party."

But, of course, *I* had told Meg on the night we met in December, 1973. Perhaps Ted hadn't heard me explain, or perhaps he had forgotten.

Ted wrote that he was trying to bring the Christmas spirit into his cell, putting all his Christmas cards on his desk. He had even bought and wrapped presents for his "neighbors." The presents were tins of smoked oysters and Snickers bars. "Now I am attempting the impossible: suggesting all us hardened cons sing carols on Christmas Eve. Thus far, I have been designated a sicko degenerate for such a perverse idea."

As far as I can determine, this Christmas of 1976 would be the last such holiday that Ted and Meg would share, even separated by mesh screens in a visitors' room. And yet, she seemed to be more than a love to him; she seemed to be a life force itself.

"What I feel for Meg is the ultimate omnipresent emotion. I feel her living inside me. I feel her giving me life when there is no other reason for it than appreciating the gift of life itself."

Ted enclosed a witness list for the Campbell trial in Colorado, pointing out that many names were misspelled. And he ended his Christmas letter:

> As for the New Year, it is going to start out so bad that it will have to get better. Perhaps if you put some Chablis in Hawaiian Punch cans and send me a case for the New Year, I can forget the ominous beginnings. But what the hell—
> Happy New Year.
>
> love, ted.

Ted would be leaving Utah for the last time on January 28th, headed for Colorado. He sent me a brief note on the 25th, telling me not to write again until he contacted me from his "new address."

The year ahead—1977—would bring tremendous upheavals in Ted's life, and in mine. I doubt that either of us could have possibly envisioned what lay ahead.

26

On January 28, 1977, Ted was removed from the Utah State Prison, spirited by car to Aspen, Colorado, and placed in a cell in the antique Pitkin County Jail. He had a new judicial adversary: District Judge George H. Lhor. Lohr didn't appear all that tough. After all, he had just sentenced Claudine Longet to a modest thirty days in jail for shooting "Spider" Sabich. Claudine would begin her sentence in April in the same jail, although her cell would be freshly painted for her and friends would cater in noninstitutional food.

Sheriff Dick Keinast was leery of Bundy and argued that he was an escape risk, because of the escape kit that had been allegedly discovered on him in the Utah prison. He wanted Ted to be handcuffed during his court appearances, but Lohr overruled him and declared that Ted could wear civilian clothing and appear unfettered.

The ancient courthouse which housed the jail had been built in 1887, and offered spartan accommodations, but Ted liked the change from the looming walls of the Utah prison.

When I phoned him in February, I was pleased and surprised to find that the Pitkin County Jail was operated much like the jail under my grandfather's jurisdiction so many years before in Michigan. It was a "Mom and Pop" jail where I called, heard a deputy yell down the hall, and then Ted's voice on the line. He sounded happy, relaxed, and confident.

Throughout his eleven-month stay in Colorado, I would speak with Ted frequently by phone. When he would assume more and more of his own defense, he would be allowed free phone privileges to help in preparing his case. Many of these calls, however, would be to me and other friends, and there was seemingly no limit put on the time he spent on long distance calls.

I can remember Bob Keppel and Roger Dunn shaking their heads at Ted's nerve combined with his easy access to a phone. "You aren't gonna believe this," Keppel told me one day when I was in the King County Major Crimes offices. "Guess who called us up?"

Of course, it had been Ted, brazenly phoning two of his most dedicated trackers to get information that he wanted for his Colorado defense.

"What did you tell him?" I asked Keppel.

"I told him that I'd be glad to trade information. If he wanted to talk with us, to ask questions, well, we had a couple of questions we'd been wanting to ask him for a long time. He didn't want to discuss our questions though. He was just calling us up as if he were a defense lawyer gathering facts. I can't believe his gall."

Ted called me often too. I was awakened many mornings around eight to hear the sound of Ted's voice, calling from Colorado.

There were not many letters, but I did get one mailed on February 24th. It was a happy letter. He was enjoying the vacation-like atmosphere of Aspen, even though he was in a jail cell. "I feel super. . . . Feel no pressure from the case. I mean *no* pressure. . . . They are beaten."

Ted deemed Pitkin County a "Mickey Mouse operation," and he was particularly scornful of Pitkin County District Attorney, Frank Tucker. Tucker was attempting, he wrote, to find areas of commonality between the Colorado killing and the Utah cases, and trying to gain insight into Ted's personality. Ted felt he could see completely through Tucker's case, and that he, the defendant, was a threat to the D.A. because of his self-confidence. "This man should never play poker. And from what I saw of him the other day, this man should never enter a courtroom."

Ted quoted from an interview D.A. Tucker had given about him.

"He (Ted) is the most cocky person I have ever faced. He tells his lawyer what to do. He arrives carrying armloads of books, as if he were an attorney himself. He sends notes to the judge and calls him at night. He refuses to talk to me or any other prosecutor."

It was, of course, exactly the image Ted wished to promulgate. "Flattery will get him nowhere. His story touches my heart but someone should tell him I didn't ask to come to Colorado. Imagine, the nerve of me telling my attorneys what to do! Never called a judge at night in my life."

Ted expected that he would get a fair trial in Aspen, and that it would not be difficult to pick an impartial jury in Pitkin County. He encouraged me to come for that trial if I could, and thought that the trial date would be set for sometime in early summer.

As I read this letter, this letter where Ted seemed so in control, I remembered the young man who had cried "I want my freedom!" from that first jail cell in Salt Lake County. He was no longer afraid; he had acclimated to his incarceration and he was reveling in the prospect of the fight ahead. The letter closed with, "We are looking at a trial date in late June or early July—God willing and the D.A. doesn't shit in his expensive trousers."

Yes, Ted had changed radically from the outraged, desperate man who wrote to me from jail in Salt Lake City eighteen months before. There was an asperity, a caustic bitterness now. I detected it in his phone calls to me. He hated policemen, prosecutors, the press. It was, perhaps, a natural progression for a man so long behind bars, for a man still proclaiming his innocence. He no longer talked or wrote to me about writing anything himself.

Although he hated the food in the Pitkin County Jail, he rather liked his cellmates and fellow prisoners, mostly drunks and small-time crooks brought in for short stays. He was working hard on his case, and by March he had plans to serve as his own defense lawyer. He was unhappy with the public defender, Chuck Leidner. Having been used to the skill of John O'Connell, he expected more, and public defenders are generally young lawyers, untried, without he experience of the big-time pros, the criminal defense attorneys who charge huge fees.

In March, the Colorado Health Department declared that the Pitkin County Jail was a short-term facility, and that no prisoner should be held there for more than thirty days. That produced a problem; Ted would have to be moved.

He told me he was reading a good deal, the only respite he had from television soap operas and game shows. His favorite book was *Papillon*, the story of an impossible prison escape from Devil's Island. "I've read it four times."

Again there was a subtle hint, but it seemed incredible to think that Ted could escape from the Pitkin County Jail, deep in the bowels of the old courthouse. And if the case against him was so full of holes—as he proclaimed—why should be escape? The Utah sentence had not been that severe, and it was doubtful that any charges would be forthcoming from Washington State. He could well be free before his thirty-fifth birthday.

Chuck Leidner was still representing Ted as they went into the preliminary hearing on the Caryn Campbell case on April 4th. Aspenites, who'd cut their courtroom gallery teeth on the Longet-Sabich case, jammed the courtroom. Rumor was that the Ted Bundy case might transcend even the histrionics seen earlier in the year.

Ted and his attorneys wanted the trial, if there was to be one, held in Aspen; they liked the laid-back atmosphere and, as Ted had told me in his letter, they felt that Aspenites had not yet made up their minds about his guilt or innocence.

Furthermore, D.A. Frank Tucker was under the gun. He had lost Claudine Longet's diary, a diary said to be of utmost importance to the prosecution in her murder case, an intimate journal that had somehow made its way to his home only to be strangely misplaced. Potential jurors in Aspen would remember that. Aware perhaps of his diminishing credibility, Tucker had brought in some manpower from Colorado Springs, two pros: District Attorneys Milton Blakely and Bob Russell.

In a preliminary hearing the prosecution lays out its case before the judge to establish cause to go to trial. Pitkin County's case was hinged—as were Salt Lake County's before it and the Florida cases after it—on an eye witness identification. This time, the eye witness was the woman tourist who had seen the stranger in the corridor of the Wildwood Inn on the night of January 12, 1975.

Aspen Investigator Mike Fisher had shown her a lay-down of mug shots a year after that night—and she'd picked Ted Bundy's. Now, during the preliminary hearing in April of 1977, she was asked to look around the courtroom and point out anyone who resembled the man she'd seen.

Ted suppressed a smile as she pointed—not to him—but to Pitkin County Undersheriff Ben Meyers.

The steam had gone out of the state's case. Judge Lohr listened as Tucker pointed out other evidence: Bundy's credit card slips, the brochure on Colorado ski areas found in Ted's Salt Lake City apartment with the Wildwood Inn marked, two hairs taken from the old

Volkswagen which microscopically matched Caryn Campbell's, the match between Bundy's crowbar and the wounds on the victim's skull.

It was a chance gamble for the prosecution, unless they could tie in some of the Utah cases. Judge Lohr ruled that Ted Bundy would stand trial for the murder of Caryn Campbell, adding that it was not his job to consider the probability of conviction, or the credibility of the evidence, only its existence.

After the preliminary hearing, Ted summarily "fired" his public defenders, Chuck Leidner and Jim Dumas. He wanted to get involved in his own defense. He was beginning a pattern that he would repeat again and again, a kind of arrogance toward those designated by the state to defend him; if he could not have what he considered the best, then he would go it alone. Judge Lohr was forced to acquiesce to his decision to defend himself, although he assigned Leidner and Dumas to remain on the defense team as legal advisors.

Although Ted opposed it, he was transferred on April 13, 1977 from the Pitkin County Jail to the Garfield County Jail in Glenwood Springs forty-five miles away, in accordance with the order sent down from the state Health Department.

The Garfield County Jail was only ten years old, and considerably more pleasant than his old basement cell in Aspen. We talked often on the phone, and he commented that he liked Garfield County Sheriff Ed Hogue and his wife, but that the food was still lousy. Despite the modern facilities, it was another "Mom and Pop" jail.

It wasn't long before Ted began to inundate Judge Lohr with requests for special treatment. Since he was serving as his own attorney, he needed a typewriter, a desk, access to the law library in Aspen, the free and uncensored use of a phone, help from forensic laboratories, investigators. He wanted three meals a day, and said neither he nor the other prisoners could survive without lunch. He pointed out his own weight loss. He wanted an order rescinded forbidding other prisoners to talk to him. (Hogue had issued this order soon after Ted arrived, after jailers intercepted a diagram of the jail, a chart outlining exits and the ventilation system.)

"Ed's a good guy," he told me on the phone. "I don't want to get him into trouble but we have to have more to eat."

His requests were granted. Somehow, Ted Bundy had managed to elevate the status of a county jail prisoner to that of visiting royalty. He not only had all the paraphernalia he wanted, but he was allowed several trips weekly, accompanied by deputies, to the law library in the Pitkin County Courthouse in Aspen.

He grew friendly with the deputies, learned about their families, and they liked him. He told me, "They're O.K. They even let me take a stroll along the river because it was such a nice day. Of course, they went with me."

I did not hear from Ted during the first four weeks of May, and I wondered what had happened. Although he seemed to be growing constantly more bitter, more sarcastic—as if he'd developed an impervious outer shell—he had written or called me regularly up until May. I finally got a letter written May 27th.

Dear Ann,

Just returned from Brazil and found your letters piled up in my post office box here in Glenwood. Jesus, you must have thought I got lost in the jungles down there. I actually went down there to find out where the sons of bitches are hiding the 11 billion tons of coffee they say the bad weather destroyed. Didn't find any coffee but brought back 400 pounds of cocaine.

Ted was still in contact with Meg, at least by phone, and she had passed on my concern about not hearing from him. No, he was not angry with me, he assured me. However, someone had told him that I had "developed an opinion relative to my innocence, which opinion was not in any way consistent with my innocence." Now, he wanted me to write to him and make a "frank statement" about how I felt regarding his guilt or innocence. He said he understood that I was very close to the police and that he knew they had convinced many people of his guilt, but he wanted a letter from me spelling out my feelings.

And he had yet another message for Nick Mackie, "Tell Mackie, if he doesn't stop thinking about me that *he* will end up at Western State [Washington's State Mental Hospital.] Deals indeed. I have got them up against the wall down here, and there (sic) are eternal optimists talking about deals."

The trial date had been put ahead to November 14, 1977, and Ted was proceeding without counsel. He was most enthusiastic about his new role, and felt he had the instincts of an investigator. "But most important, I will persist, and persist, and work and act until I succeed. No one can outwork me, because I have more at stake than anyone else."

He was also elated because he was costing the county a great deal of money. A local reporter had complained in print about the escalating costs of investigators, expert witnesses, extra personnel needed to guard Ted during his library trips, dental costs, supplies, the phone calls; Ted found this criticism "Goddam outrageous. No one asks the prosecutor or the police how much of the people's money they piss away. Dismiss the case, send me home and save all that money is my response."

He had used the $20 I'd sent him to pay for a haircut, his first since December 1976, and Judge Lohr had ordered that he be taken to a doctor to see if his loss of weight—which he blamed on the paucity of food in the Garfield County Jail—was as profound as Ted said. The day after the order, the jail had begun to serve lunch for the first time in its history, and Ted claimed a moral victory for that.

Ted suspected that the sheriff was trying to fatten him up before he went to the doctor, but he still termed Hogue a "good man." The sheriff had also consented to having Ted's friends and family send food in from outside. Packages of raisins, nuts, and beef jerky would be appreciated.

Although Ted had begun the letter with a touch of suspicious hostility, a request for a declaration of loyalty from me, his mood mellowed as he wrote.

Thank you very much for the money and the stamps. I know your recent successes have by no means put you on easy street, so donations to me no doubt represent sacrifices.

I will not take so long to write again. Promise.

Love, ted.

But he did. He took a long, long time to write, because Ted Bundy had gone away. Very suddenly.

27

That letter troubled me; Ted was, in essence, asking me to tell him that I believed wholeheartedly in his innocence, something that I could not do. It was something he had never asked of me before, and I wondered what had happened to make him wary of me. I had not betrayed his confidence. I had continued to keep the letters and calls rolling into Colorado and I had not shown Ted's replies to anyone. If I could not tell Ted that I believed he was innocent of all the charges and suspicions against him, I was maintaining my emotional support as always.

It had been the first week in June when I received Ted's questioning letter, and I was wrestling with how I could reply as Ted prepared for a hearing on whether the death penalty would be considered in his trial; it was a decision that was being made individually in each homicide case in Colorado. The hearing was set for June 7th.

As usual, Ted was chauffeured to Aspen from Glenwood Springs on the morning of June 7th, leaving a little before eight. He was wearing the same outfit he had worn when we had lunch at the Brasserie Pittsbourg in Seattle in December, 1975: the tan corduroy slacks, a long-sleeved turtleneck shirt, and the heavy, variegated brown coat-sweater. Instead of his usually preferred loafers, however, he wore his heavy prison-issue boots. His hair was short and neat, thanks, somewhat ironically, to the twenty dollar check I had sent him.

Pitkin County deputies Rick Kralicek and Peter Murphy, his regular guards, picked him up that morning for the forty-five-mile ride back to Aspen. Ted talked easily with the two deputies he'd come to know well, asking again about their families.

Kralicek drove with Bundy sitting beside him, and Peter Murphy sat in the back seat. Later Murphy would recall that as they left the outskirts of Glenwood Springs Ted had suddenly turned around and stared at him, making several quick movements with his cuffed hands. "I unsnapped the leather strap holding my .38, and it made a loud unmistakable 'snap!' Ted turned around and stared straight ahead at the road all the way into Aspen."

When they reached the courthouse, Ted was handed into the custody of Deputy David Westerlund, a lawman who had been his guard for only one day and was not familiar with him.

Court convened at 9:00 A.M., and Jim Dumas—one of the public defenders fired by Ted earlier but still serving him—argued against the death penalty for an hour or so. At 10:30 Judge Lohr ordered a break, saying that the prosecution could give its arguments when they reconvened. Ted moved, as he often did, to the law library, its tall stacks hiding him from Deputy Westerlund's view.

The deputy stayed at his post at the courtroom door. They were on the second floor, twenty-five feet above the street. Everything was normal, or seemed so. Ted was apparently doing some research back in the stacks, while waiting for court to begin again.

On the street outside, a woman passing by was startled to see a figure dressed in tans and browns suddenly leap from a window above her. She watched as the man fell, got to his feet and ran, limping, off down the street. Puzzled, she stared after him for a few moments before entering the courthouse and heading for the sheriff's office. Her first question galvanized the officers on duty into action, "Is it normal for people to jump out of windows around here?"

Kralicek heard her, swore, and headed for the stairs.

Ted Bundy had escaped.

He wore no handcuffs, and the leg irons he usually wore when he was outside the courtroom had been removed. He was free, and he'd had ample time to observe the area around the Pitkin County Courthouse when the deputies had kindly allowed him to walk near the river during exercise periods.

Chagrined, Sheriff Dick Keinast would admit later, "We screwed up. I feel shitty about it."

Roadblocks were set up, tracking dogs were called in, and posses on horseback fanned out around Aspen looking for the man who had telegraphed in so many ways that he was going to run for it. Whitney Wulff, Sheriff Keinast's secretary, recalled that Ted had often walked over to the windows during hearings, glanced down, and then looked at the sheriff's men to see if they were watching.

"I thought he was always testing us. Once he walked up close behind a girl court aide, and looked at us. I got worried about the possibility of a hostage and alerted the officer escort to stay closer to the prisoner."

But Westerlund had been a new man on the job, unaware of others' suspicions that Bundy was perhaps planning a break.

Ted had "double-dressed"—in the lingo of the con—wearing extra clothing beneath his standard courtroom outfit. His plan was so audacious that it went off like clockwork at the beginning. He had hit the ground on the front courthouse lawn, hit it so hard in fact that he'd left a four-inch-deep gouge in the turf with his right foot. Officials suspected that he might have injured that ankle—but evidently not enough to slow him down much.

Then Ted had headed immediately for the banks of the Roaring Fork River, the spot four blocks from the courthouse where he'd walked often before. There, hidden in the brush, he quickly removed his outer layer of clothing. He now wore a dress shirt; he looked like any other Aspen resident as he strolled with controlled casualness back through town. It was the safest place he could have been; all his pursuers had scattered to set up roadblocks.

The word of Ted's escape was a news flash on every radio station between Denver and Seattle, down into Utah. In Aspen, residents were told to lock their doors, hide their children, garage their cars.

Frank Tucker, the District Attorney who was the chief object of Ted's derision that summer, commented in I-told-you-so terms, "I am not surprised. I kept telling them."

Apparently everyone had been expecting Ted to run, but no one had done anything about it, and now *they* ran in circles trying to get him back. The roadblocks on the two roads leading out of town took forty-five minutes to set up; the dogs were delayed for almost four hours on their flight from Denver because carriers could not be located and the airlines refused to fly them without carriers. If there is a patron saint of escapees, he was looking down favorably on Ted Bundy.

Back in Seattle, I began to receive phone calls from friends and law officers, warning me that Ted was loose. It was their feeling that he might head toward me, thinking that I would hide him or give him money to get across the Canadian border. It was a confrontation that I didn't relish. I doubted that he would head back toward Washington; there were just too many people who would recognize him. If he got out of the mountains around Aspen, he would do better to head for Denver, or some other big city. Nevertheless, Nick Mackie gave me his home phone number, and my sons were instructed that they must get to their phone and call for help if Ted appeared at our front door.

My phone rang three times on the evening of June 7th. Each time I answered, there was no one there . . . or no one who spoke. I could hear sounds in the background as if the calls were coming from a phone booth on a highway, cars racing by.

I finally said, "Ted . . . Ted, is that you?" and the connection was broken.

When Ted made his desperate jump for freedom, it had been a beautiful sunny warm day in Aspen; but nightfall brought the temperature drops common to mountain towns even in summer. Wherever Ted was, he was undoubtedly cold. I slept restlessly, dreaming that *I* had gone camping and discovered that I'd forgotten to bring blankets or a sleeping bag.

Where *was* he? The tracking dogs had stopped, confused, as they'd reached the Roaring Fork River. He must have planned that. They couldn't pick up his trail beyond his first four block run to the river shores.

It began to rain in Aspen late in the afternoon of that Monday in June, and anyone unlucky enough to be without shelter would have quickly been soaked to the skin. Ted wore only a light shirt and slacks. He was possibly suffering from a badly sprained or broken ankle . . . but he was still free.

He must have felt like the protagonist of *Papillon*, the book he'd almost committed to memory during his long months in jail. Beyond the cleverness of escape, *Papillon* had dealt with mind control, man's ability to think himself past despair, to control his environment by sheer force of will. Was Ted doing that now?

The men who tracked Ted Bundy looked like something out of a Charles Russell or Frederick Remington painting, garbed in Stetsons, deerskin vests, jeans, cowboy boots, and carrying sidearms. They could have been possemen of a century earlier, looking for Billy the Kid or the James boys; I wondered if they would shoot first and ask questions later when—and if—they found Ted.

Aspenites vacillated between utter fear and black humor. While deputies and volunteers made a house-by-house search in the resort city, entrepreneurs hastened to capitalize on this new folk hero who was capturing the imagination of a town where ennui can set in quickly. Ted Bundy had thumbed his nose at the system, had beaten the "dumb cops," and hardly anyone stopped to think about the broken body of Caryn Campbell that had been found in the snowbank way back in 1975. Bundy was news, and good for laughs.

Tee-shirts began to appear on well-endowed young women, reading: "Ted Bundy is a One Night Stand"; "Bundy's Free—You can bet your Aspen on it!"; "Bundy lives on a Rocky Mountain High!"; "Bundy's in Booth D." (This last slogan referred to a national magazine article which stated that, if one sat in Booth D in a local restaurant, one could purchase cocaine.)

One restaurant put "Bundy Burgers" on its menu . . . open the bun and the meat has fled. A "Bundy Cocktail" served locally was made of tequila, rum, and two Mexican jumping beans.

Hitchhikers, wanting to be assured of a ride out of Aspen, wore signs reading, "I am not Bundy."

Paranoia reigned along with the high-jinks. One young male reporter, after interviewing three young women in a café about their reactions to Bundy's escape, was promptly turned in as suspect; his identification and press card had meant little.

Everywhere, fingers of blame were being pointed. Sheriff Keinast blamed Judge Lohr for allowing Ted to represent himself, and for letting him appear in court without his leg irons and handcuffs. Tucker blamed everyone, and Keinast admitted to one reporter wearily that he wished he'd never heard of Ted Bundy.

By Friday, June 10th, Ted had been missing three days and the FBI joined the manhunt. Louise Bundy appeared on television and begged Ted to come back. She was worried about Ted being out in the mountains. "But most of all I'm worried about the people who are looking for him not using good common sense and pulling the trigger first and asking questions later. People will think, 'Oh, he must be guilty; that's why he's running.' But I think just all the frustrations piled up and he saw an open window and decided to go. I'm sure by now he's probably sorry he did."

The number of searchers had dropped from 150 to 70 by Friday. The feeling was that Ted had made his way out of the search area, and possibly had had an accomplice. Sid Morley, thirty, serving a year for possession of stolen property, had become friendly with Ted in the Pitkin County Jail and transferred with him to the Garfield County Jail. Morley had failed to return from a work release job on the Friday before Ted's jump from the courthouse and the searchers felt he might have been waiting to help Ted.

However, Morley was taken into custody on June 10th near a tunnel on Interstate 70, fifty miles west of Denver. Questioned, he insisted that he'd known nothing about Ted's escape plans and he did not, indeed, seem to be involved. Morley's own opinion was that Ted was still in Pitkin County, but outside of Aspen.

Nationwide, it was a big week for escapes. Even as Ted Bundy was being tracked in Colorado, James Earl Ray, along with three other inmates, escaped from Brushy Mountain State Prison in Tennessee on June 11th. For one day, the story of that escape would take western headline precedence over Bundy's.

Ted Bundy *was* still in Pitkin County. He had made his way through town on June 7th to the foot of Aspen Mountain, and then hiked easily up the grassy slope; it had been a bad year for snow, but the warm winter was lucky for Ted. By the time the sun set that first night, he was up and over Aspen Mountain and walking along Castle Creek, headed south. Ted had maps with him of the mountain area around Aspen, maps which were being used by the prosecution to show the location of Caryn Campbell's body. As his own defense attorney, he had rights of discovery!

If he could have kept going south until he came to the hamlet of Crested Butte, he might have been able to catch a ride to freedom. But the winds and rain had driven him back to a cabin he'd passed along the way, a well-stocked and temporarily unoccupied mountain cabin.

Ted rested there after breaking in. There was a little food in the cabin, some warm clothing, a rifle. On Thursday morning, June 9th, better equipped and carrying the rifle, he headed south again. He might have made it to Crested Butte, but he didn't keep going straight south. Instead, he cut west over another ridge that wasn't so choked with lingering snow, and found himself along the East Maroon Creek.

He was going in circles now, and soon found himself again on the outskirts of Aspen. He headed back up Castle Creek for the cabin where he'd found shelter days earlier. He was too late. Searchers had found that he'd been there; in fact searchers were fanning out around the cabin as he watched behind vegetation a couple hundred yards away.

The posse members found scraps of dried food in the cabin and learned that the gun and ammunition were missing. They identified one fingerprint found in the cabin as being Ted's. Then they learned that someone had broken into a Volkswagen camper in a resort area on Maroon Lake—apparently on Friday, June 10th—and had taken food and a ski parka.

Despite the stolen bits of food, Ted had lost a lot of weight, his injured ankle was swelling, and he was close to exhaustion. He headed back north, toward Aspen. On Saturday night, June 11th, he slept in the wild, and Sunday found him skirting the edges of town. On Sunday night, he had been gone almost a full week; he was still free, but he was right back where he'd started and he needed a miracle to get out of town. Huddled, exhausted and shivering, in the tall bushes at the edge of the Aspen Golf Course, he saw an old Cadillac parked nearby. He checked and keys were in it. Ted seemingly had his miracle—wheels.

Crouching low in the seat, he steered first toward Smuggler's Mountain and the propitiously named Independence Pass route that headed east away from Aspen. Then he changed his mind; he would go west, instead, toward Glenwood Springs, back toward the jail where he'd been incarcerated, but further than that, beyond that, west to complete freedom.

It was now 2:00 A.M. on Monday, June 13th.

Pitkin County Deputies Gene Flatt and Maureen Higgins were patrolling the streets of Aspen, headed in an easterly direction that early morning when their attention was drawn to a Cadillac coming toward them. The driver appeared to be drunk; the car was wavering all over the road. They weren't even thinking of Ted Bundy as they turned around and followed the Cadillac. They expected to find a drunk driver inside. Actually, Ted was cold sober, but his reflexes were dulled by exhaustion; he couldn't control the Cadillac.

The patrol car pulled up alongside the fishtailing Cadillac and signaled it to pull over. Gene Flatt walked over to the driver's side of the car and looked in. The man inside wore glasses and had a band-aid plastered over his nose. But Flatt recognized him; it was Ted Bundy, who was about to be captured only blocks from where he had escaped.

Ted shrugged and smiled thinly as Flatt said, "Hello, Ted."

The mountain maps were found in the stolen car, indicating that Ted's leap from the courthouse had not been a spur of the moment impulse. He had planned the abortive escape attempt. Now, he was in more trouble than he'd been in before; he was lodged temporarily in the Pitkin County Jail until June 16th when he was arraigned on charges of escape, burglary, and theft. Judge Lohr handed down an order that Ted would henceforth wear handcuffs and leg irons when he was being moved from place to place. But he would still be allowed to have most of the privileges he'd been granted before so that he could participate in his own defense: the law library access, the free long distance calls, all the other investigative tools.

A week after Ted was recaptured, my phone rang a little before 8 A.M. Awakened from a sound sleep, I was startled to hear Ted's voice.

"Where are you?" I mumbled.

"Can you come and pick me up?" he asked, and then laughed.

He had not escaped again, but for a moment, I'd believed that he had somehow gotten out of jail once more.

He told me he was fine, a little tired, and suffering from the loss of about twenty pounds, but fine.

"Why did you do it?" I asked.

"Would you believe I just looked out the window and saw all that lovely green grass and blue sky out there and I couldn't resist?"

No, I wouldn't, but I didn't have to say so; it was a rhetorical question.

It was a short conversation, and when I wrote to him I couldn't help starting with, "Tried to answer your last letter but you'd moved and left no forwarding address."

I had not yet expressed my answer to his question in the letter written just before his escape. He wanted to know my feelings about his guilt or innocence. What I told him was that I felt the same way I had felt on the Saturday afternoon in January, 1976, our last meeting before he was returned to Utah for trial in the DaRonch kidnapping case. I had told him then that I could not fully believe in his innocence. I don't know if he recalled what I'd said or not, but my reference to that afternoon in the tavern seemed to be enough. I also reminded him that I had never written one line about him for publication. Although he was big news, and getting bigger, I had managed to keep that promise. It seemed to satisfy him.

His first letter after his capture was not as bitter or scathing as those just before had been; perhaps his taste of freedom had softened him somewhat.

Ted said he was recuperating from the effects of the failed escape, and that he thought very little of his few days of freedom. He was trying to forget being free, but he didn't regret taking the chance. "I learned much about myself, my weaknesses, my capacity to survive, and the relationship of freedom to pain."

Everything about this letter was muted; he had tried and he had failed, and it was as if he'd turned down the energy in his emotions. After he was recaptured, he had learned from Meg that she was involved with another man. A year before, he would have been beating his breast in agony; now he viewed Meg's final defection rationally and soberly. "Accepting the loss of her will never be easy. In fact, I doubt that I could ever truly say I accept her loving and living with another man. I will always love her so I could never say that I do not dream of our life together. But this new development, like my capture, must be taken calmly. My survival is at stake."

Perhaps that was the essential word: "survival." If he allowed himself to grieve for Meg, he would not be up to the fight ahead. He wrote that he could only hope for a belief in a life to come. "I would dream of loving Meg again in another time."

In retrospect, there is evidence that Carole Ann Boone (who had dropped the "Anderson" from her name) was in constant touch with Ted during this period, that Ted was not without a woman to stand beside him. He did not mention it to me at that point.

If survival was all, then Ted had to build up his body. He felt he had lost about thirty pounds during his days in the mountains, and he had been twenty pounds underweight to begin with. Jail food wouldn't do it. Every day there was a new cook—a trusty, a hired cook "who quits two days later," a secretary from the front desk, a jailer, a jailer's wife. Ted asked again for help from friends. He was healing much too slowly, and he needed healthy food. My assignment was to locate some powdered protein supplement. He told me I could probably find it in a health food store and that he preferred the two-pound can containing about 15 grams of protein per ounce. "Maybe some dried figs . . . maybe some canned nuts too, if you can afford it."

It seemed, from that letter, that Meg had gone out of Ted's life. Yet I wondered at her telling him she was involved with someone else. I had talked to her on the phone only a few days before and she had said there was no one, but that for *her* own survival she had to pull away from Ted. Perhaps she had made up a fictitious man, knowing that that was the only way Ted would release her. It must have been that; Meg and I had commiserated with one another over the seeming impossibility of finding a single man who met our qualifications and would also even consider accepting a woman with a child, or—in my case—with four children. No, I didn't think Meg had found anyone, not yet.

I felt sorry for Ted, picturing him all alone at last, and yet he had been largely responsible for his own plight. He'd lied to Stephanie, Meg, Sharon, and even to his casual romantic partners. I needn't have worried about him; Carole Ann visited him in jail whenever she could, worked as an "investigator" to refute the allegations against him. When she finally surfaced as his female defender, I was startled. Who was this woman who was giving countless anonymous interviews in support of Ted? I could never have guessed that it was the same woman who had teased him years before about being the infamous "Ted."

In response to Ted's requests, I sent him a large package containing ten pounds of protein supplement, vitamins, fruit, and nuts. When I carried it into my local post office, the clerk raised his eyebrows a bit as he looked at the addressee, but he said nothing. Postal clerks are like priests, doctors, and lawyers; they feel ethically bound to protect privileged information, and they respect their client's privacy.

28

I had no doubt that Ted had planned his escape; he had alluded to escape to me so many times. Although he hadn't wanted to discuss it in his first phone call to me or in his letters, he did tell Pitkin County Sheriff Sergeant Don Davis about his adventures during his week in the mountains. Yes, he had taken the rifle from the cabin, but he had thrown it away in the woods. A man with a rifle in June might have looked too suspicious. He had met few people out there in the wilderness, and when he did bump into some campers, he had pretended to be a man looking for his wife and children, just part of a happy family camp-out.

Later, he would tell me how he'd felt when he returned to the cabin. "They were there, so close I could hear them talking about me. They didn't even know I was watching them from behind some trees."

All in all, it had been an adventure for him, albeit a desperate adventure, and had only honed his will to be free. He *was* the prisoner in *Papillon*.

I didn't think that his escape necessarily marked him as a guilty man; an innocent man, seeing himself railroaded into a lifetime behind bars would have been as likely to run. He had felt trapped by the inexorable grinding of the wheels of justice and, despite his protestations that he felt no pressure, he felt tremendous pressure—not only from Colorado but from Utah and Washington.

Now he was in a hell of a mess. The murder trial in the Campbell case still loomed ahead. Now he was charged with escape, burglary, misdemeanor theft, and felony theft. Charges connected with his escape carried with them a possible ninety more years in sentences.

Lawmen had a higher opinion of Chuck Leidner and Jim Dumas as attorneys than Ted did. "They're damned good—almost awesome," one detective commented. Dumas, who had just finished his arguments against the death penalty when Ted made his two-story leap for freedom, also had a sense of humor. When he learned that his client had escaped, he said wryly, "That's the poorest show of faith in this argument that I've seen yet."

Ted hadn't wanted the public defenders however, and, with recent events, it was impossible for them to continue; Leidner was named as a potential witness for the prosecution on the escape charges.

Ted's longtime supporter and advisor, John Henry Browne from the Public Defender's Office in Seattle, had flown to Aspen as soon as Ted was captured. Browne, who could not officially represent Ted since he had never been charged in Washington State, had always been offended by the way the "Ted" case was handled and felt Bundy was being convicted in the public's eye through suspicion and innuendo. He spent his own funds to fly to confer with Ted in various states where he was being held.

In mid-June, 1977, it was Browne's mission to serve as an arbitrator between Ted and Leidner and Dumas. Browne was delighted when a new attorney was appointed to defend Ted: Stephen "Buzzy" Ware.

On June 16th, Judge Lohr appointed Ware as the new counsel for the defense. Ware looked anything but a winning defense attorney as he stood beside Ted, dressed in jeans and a sports coat. Buzzy Ware's hair was tousled, he wore glasses, and had a luxuriant moustache. Indeed, he looked more like a ski bum from the Aspen après-ski bars than he did a potential F. Lee Bailey. But Ware had made a name for himself; he had never lost a jury trial in Aspen. He flew his own plane and rode a motorcycle and he was known as the man to have on your side in narcotics cases. After being appointed to Ted's case, Ware flew off to Texas as defense counsel in a major federal racketeering case.

Ware was a winner, and Ted sensed that. At last, he again had someone beside him whom he could respect. In a phone call to me Ted was ebullient as he talked about his attorney. Any residual effects of his failed escape were forgotten by August as he filed a motion for a retrial in Utah in the DaRonch case (based largely on what he felt were Detective Jerry Thompson's suggestions to DaRonch that she pick Ted's picture).

The prosecution team in Colorado was attempting to beef up its case against Bundy by bringing in "similar transactions," trying to introduce testimony about the kidnapping conviction, the murders and disappearances of Melissa Smith, Laura Aime, and Debby Kent in Utah, perhaps even the eight Washington cases. Taken in toto, the crimes attributed to Ted Bundy bore a familiar pattern, a commonality; taken separately, each case was lacking in clout.

One can only speculate what might have happened if Ted had had the continued support from Buzzy Ware that fed new energy into the defense. On the night of August 11th, Ware and his wife were involved in a motorcycle crash, an accident that killed Mrs. Ware instantly and left the brilliant young attorney with skull and facial fractures, internal injuries, and a broken leg. Ware was in a coma, and there was some question about whether he would be permanently paralyzed, but no question at all about whether he could continue assisting Ted.

Ted was desolate; he had counted on Buzzy Ware to extricate him from his Colorado difficulties and now, once again, he was alone. He also felt that he was aging rapidly, that recent newspaper photos of him made him look years older than his true thirty years.

I wrote to him in mid-August, commiserating with him about the loss of Ware, and assuring him that the photos in the paper were only revealing the residual effects of his ordeal in the mountains, and that they were also the result of harsh lighting.

His answer was the last letter I would receive from Colorado.

Fate does have a way of taking me by surprise, but the past two years have been so filled with surprises and shocking occurrences that my 'down periods' have become progressively shorter. Am I becoming shock proof? Not exactly. There was a definite moistness in my eyes when news of Buzzy's accident arrived. However, they were genuinely tears for him and not for me. He is such a beautiful person. As for my case, my confidence in it could not be diminished if every defense attorney in the country expired.

He wrote that he felt it was almost a sacrilege to continue on with his case without pause, that he should stop for a time in respect for Ware, but that he had to continue. He seemed to see some light far ahead of him, and he was heading directly toward it.

> In many ways the dark, far corner has been turned. I sense it now. The escape episode was at the end of a stretch, and the movement made now is toward a return. The media even seems to be humanizing me a little. More important, the DaRonch case has been broken. More later. My love,
>
> ted.

But, by September, Ted was screaming "injustice" and "political manoeuvering" when EI Paso County D.A. Bob Russell sought to include the Utah cases in the Campbell trial by introducing the hairs found in Ted's old Volkswagen—hairs that matched the public hair of Melissa Smith in Midvale, and head hairs from Caryn Campbell and Carol DaRonch. Ted countered by saying that his understanding after reading the autopsy reports on Laura Aime and Melissa Smith was that the young murder victims might have been held captive for up to a week before they died. His argument was that this showed a clear lack of commonality since Caryn Campbell was known to have succumbed within hours of her abduction. Further, the Utah women had been struck with a blunt instrument, according to the post mortem reports, and Caryn Campbell with a sharp instrument. Ted argued that these differences made the diverse cases ineligible as "similar transactions."

Despite the vigorous fight going on in his legal arena, despite Carole Ann Boone, Ted did not forget Meg that September. He called me on September 20th and asked that I send a single red rose to Meg, to arrive on the 26th. "It's the eighth anniversary of the night I met her. I want just one rose, and I want the card to read, 'My heart valves need adjusting.' Love, ted."

I sent Meg that last red rose, after arguing with the florist who insisted that I could get four red roses for the $9 minimum. Ted had stipulated it be only one. He never offered to pay for the rose. I don't know what Meg's reaction was. I never talked to her again.

Ted spent the fall of 1977 working feverishly on his defense for the trial ahead. He didn't write any longer, but called me when he had something to talk about. Security was tighter now; he was not allowed to dial the phone numbers himself and had to wait for a deputy to do it. On his daily trips to the law library, he wore both handcuffs and leg irons. But again, he began to be so familiar to his captors, so affable, that the cuffs and irons were removed. He seemed to have nothing on his mind but winning in court; the escape several months behind him was dimming in everyone's memory.

On November 2, 1977, a suppression hearing was held behind closed doors in Judge Lohr's courtroom. Ted was elated when Lohr refused to allow either the Debby Kent or the Laura Aime cases to be introduced at the Campbell trial.

Two weeks later, a similar hearing was held where pathologists testified pro and con on the similarities of the head wounds suffered by Melissa Smith and Caryn Campbell. For the prosecution, Dr. Donald M. Clark said that such fractures were "unusual—not in the common area," and that the fractures were "strikingly similar" both in the assumed weapon used and in the fractures themselves.

For the defense, Dr. John Wood, the Arapahoe County Coroner, testified that the only similarity in the two skull fractures was that they had occurred in the same spot on the skull. Wood first said that Melissa Smith's wound had been caused by a blunt instrument, while Caryn Campbell's had been dealt with a sharp object. Under cross-examination, however, Dr. Wood admitted that if Ms. Campbell's scalp had been bruised as well as cut (which it had been), then the same weapon could have caused the wounds on both victims' heads. Looking at the pry bar taken from Ted Bundy's Volkswagen, he agreed that it could have caused the injuries sustained by both women.

Lohr pondered on the pathologists' testimony, and finally ruled that the information on the Smith case would be inadmissible in the Campbell trial. Ted had won and won big, in keeping the three Utah cases hidden from jurors' ears, but he lost when Lohr ruled to admit Carol DaRonch's testimony, *and* the ski brochure found in Ted's Salt Lake City apartment with the Wildwood Inn marked.

In that November week, too, Ted learned that the higher court in Utah had rejected his appeal on the DaRonch kidnapping case.

He would try again one day on that. Now, Ted wanted a change of venue before the January 9th trial date. He had once approved the idea of being tried in Aspen—but that was before his escape, before he became a household word and a joke in the wealthy ski resort town. It was unlikely that there was anyone in Aspen now who didn't know exactly who Ted Bundy was, and who hadn't memorized the smallest details of the crime he was accused of. A trial in Aspen would be a circus; it was unthinkable.

Surprising circumstance removed me even further from Ted's world at the end of November; one of my magazine articles had sparked the interest of a Hollywood production company and, after two brief phone calls, I found myself on a plane headed for Los Angeles. After a day-long meeting, it was agreed that I would return for three weeks in December to write the screen "treatment" of the story. I was thrilled, terrified, and unable to believe what had happened. After six years of making an adequate—but somewhat precarious—living for us, I could glimpse an easier life ahead. Of course, I was naive, as unworldly as any Cinderella stepping into the Hollywood ball.

I phoned Ted and told him that I would be at the Ambassador Hotel in Los Angeles for most of December, and he wished me well. He was seeking funds to pay for an impartial public opinion survey to determine just where—if anyplace—in Colorado he might get an unbiased trial. He suspected that Denver would be the place, a city big enough so that the name "Ted Bundy" didn't ring a bell.

His arch enemy, D.A. Frank Tucker of Pitkin County, had been struck down but not through any machinations by Ted himself. Tucker had been indicted by a grand jury on thirteen count of unlawful use of public funds!

One of the charges against Tucker alleged that he had arranged for a seventeen-year-old girlfriend' abortion and billed the surgery to Garfield County. Others contended that he had made double billing to two separate counties for pleasure junkets he had taken with the young woman. The *Rocky Mountain News* quoted Tucker's ex-wife as saying she had confronted the beleaguered D.A. with questions about the purported abortion and "he admitted it."

If nothing else, Aspen could be counted on to make headlines. There were Tucker's problems, Claudine Longet—who had taken up with her defense attorney (after neatly separating him from *his* wife)—and Ted.

My trip to Hollywood paled in comparison. I spent my days working with writer-director Martin Davidson and my evenings wandering around the lobby of the Ambassador Hotel. I ate supper several times with Adela Rogers St. Johns who also lived in the hotel, and listened to her tales of Clark Gable, Carole Lombard, and William Randolph Hearst, and her shock at hearing that this was the first time I had ever left my children for more than an over-night trip. She found me an overprotective mother.

I could now identify more easily with some of Ted's cultural shock as he'd gone from the life of a law student to his existence as a prioner. I was homesick, wilted by the 90 degree heat, bemused by the pink Santa Clauses skipping past palm trees and roof-high poinsettias, and attempting to learn an entirely new form of writing: movie scripts. Everyone in Hollywood seemed to be under thirty, and I would never see forty again. Just as Ted had, I longed for the sight and sound of rainy Seattle.

A few days before Christmas, I turned in my treatment and the producers liked it. I signed a contract to write the whole movie. They told me it would take six weeks. Could I leave my children that long? I would have to; it was too big an opportunity to turn my back on. I had no way of knowing I would be away from home for seven months.

That Christmas was frantic; two days to shop, one day to cele-brate, and a week to find babysitters and pack up to return to California.

Ted's Christmas was bleak; he had learned on December 23rd that the change of venue he'd requested had been granted—not to Denver but to Colorado Springs, sixty miles south, the El Paso County bailiwick of D.A. Bob Russell who'd been brought in by Tucker to aid in prosecuting him. Three of the six inmates on death row had been sent there by juries in Colorado Springs. It was not a beneficent region for accused killers.

Ted faced Judge Lohr after hearing of the decision and said flatly, "You're sentencing me to death."

On December 27th, he got better news. Judge Lohr ruled on Bundy's motion to eliminate the death penalty as an alternative penalty in his trial. Lohr became the first judge in Colorado who would find the death penalty unconstitutional. Of course, Ted said he did not expect the final verdict to be guilty, but he felt this was a landmark decision for all who opposed the death penalty.

On December 30th, I received a phone call from Ted, a call to wish me Happy New Year. We talked for about twenty minutes. On the surface the only thing unusual about that call was that he seemingly had called only to visit; his calls before had invariably been initiated because he had something on his mind, or he needed a favor done. This call was low-key, companionable, as if he were a friend calling from across town instead of across several states.

He commented that the jail was empty and lonesome; all the short-time prisoners had been released to spend the Christmas holidays with their families, and he was the only prisoner left in the Garfield County Jail. And he complained, as always, about the food.

"The cook took off too—he left everything to be warmed up, and they even warm up the jello. The stuff that's supposed to be hot is cold, and vice versa."

I laughed at his standard lament about the omnipresence of jello—warm jello—in his life. There was so much more unsaid than said; he was less than two weeks away from his murder trial, but there was little I could say that might alleviate the stress connected with that event. It had all been said. I wished him luck and told him that even though I would be in Los Angeles, I would keep in touch. Inwardly I tried to block the picture of what it must be like to be all alone in jail while the rest of the world celebrated the new year.

"I need your address . . . where you'll be in Los Angeles," he said, and I gave it to him, waited while he wrote it down.

He wished me luck too, in *my* new venture, and then "Happy New Year."

Ted was saying "goodbye" to me, but there was nothing in his conversation that indicated that. I hung up, troubled, thinking of the holiday season six years before. So much had happened since then and so few of the events of the past half dozen years had been happy for either of us. I mused that it was fortunate that humans have not the power of second sight, that we don't know what lies ahead.

Ted made several other calls on that next-to-last day of 1977: to John Henry Browne, to a reporter in Seattle, a man whom he alternately liked and deprecated. To the reporter, he commented inscrutably that he intended to watch the Washington Huskies in the Rose Bowl game, "but not from my cell." I don't know if he called Meg, but I suspect that he called Carole Ann Boone. Carole Ann, who had visited him in his jail cell, who is rumored to have given him a lot of money, who had held his hand and gazed at him with love—just as so many other women had before her.

And then Ted reviewed his plan. He was no longer worried about the upcoming trial; he didn't intend to be there to attend it.

He knew the Garfield County Jail better than any jailer did. He knew the habits and peccadilloes of the four jailers better than they did themselves. He'd become adept at charting their movements. His ex-cellmate, Sid Morley, had given him the lay-out of the jail months before, and Ted had memorized every corner and cubbyhole in the building. He had a hacksaw, passed to him by someone whose name he would never reveal; he had long since adopted the prison code that one never "snitched."

There was a metal plate in the ceiling of his cell, a plate where a light fixture was to be installed. There had been a long delay in getting the electrical work done although electricians were scheduled to complete it within a few days. With his hacksaw, Ted had spent six or eight weeks tediously cutting a 12 × 12 inch square out of the ceiling. He'd cut it so precisely that he could replace it at will . . . and no one had noticed it. At times, he had been away from his cell for two days, and still his "trap door" hadn't been discovered.

He'd worked at night, when other prisoners were taking showers, the noise of the drumming water and their shouts drowning out his handiwork. The hole had been limited in diameter by steel reinforcing rods in the ceiling. To allow himself to crawl through that hole, he had dieted down to 140 pounds. His complaints about the jail food were only a cover.

During the last two weeks in December, Ted had often wriggled through the ceiling and crawled through the dusty space above him, crawled, in fact, all over the space between the jail's ceiling and the roof above. Each time he returned to his cell there would be the heart-stopping moment when he thought that he'd been discovered, fully expected to find deputies below him "waiting to blow me away."

Incredibly, there never were, even though Detective Mike Fisher had warned Sheriff Hogue that he felt in his bones that Ted was getting ready to run. The taciturn Fisher was not a man to cry "Wolf," but no one listened to his warnings.

Ted was packed, ready to go. All he needed was the right spot and the right time. The ceiling route was the only way. His cell door was made of solid steel, and there were two more locked doors between him and freedom. His knees ached from crawling around on the cinderblocks above his cell. He was looking for the easiest way down, and then, on December 30th, he had found it. A single shaft of light, filled with floating bits of dust, pierced the darkness from below. There was a hole in the plasterboard above a closet in jailer Bob Morrison's apartment.

The place was an echo chamber where a pin drop sounded like a crashing rock and Ted had waited, poised, over the hole in the plasterboard. Morrison and his wife were eating dinner; he had heard their conversation clearly. Could they hear him as well?

"Let's go to a movie tonight," Mrs. Morrison said.

"Sure, why not?" the jailer answered.

Ted was paranoid; he suspected it was all a plan to trap him. He knew Morrison had a muzzle loader, could well be waiting to shoot him as he lowered himself through the closet ceiling. He sat there, scarcely breathing for half an hour. He heard the Morrisons put on their coats, heard their front door slam.

It was perfect. All he had to do was drop into their apartment, changes clothes, and walk out the front door.

He knew he would have a head start when he went. For the past few weeks he had changed his pattern, telling the jailers he felt ill and couldn't face the thought of eating breakfast. He'd worked on his legal briefs all night and slept late, always leaving his breakfast tray outside his cell undisturbed.

No one ever checked his cell after supper was served. And no one would check it until lunch was served the next day.

Locked in his windowless cell, Ted had no idea what the weather was like outside; he couldn't know that six inches of fresh snow had fallen during the day, adding to the foot already on the ground, and temperatures were well below freezing. If he had, it wouldn't have mattered.

His decision made, Ted returned to his cell, stuffed the legal papers he would need no longer beneath the blanket on his bunk, and looked around his Garfield County jail cell for the last time.

Then he was up through the ceiling, replacing the square of ceiling-board, and crawling over to the opening above the closet. He climbed down, fell from a shelf, and found himself in Morrison's bedroom. He shed his jail garb for a pair of blue jeans and a gray turtleneck shirt, some blue tennis shoes. He put Morrison's two working replicas of antique guns—a rifle and a derringer, both muzzle loaders—in the attic, just in case Morrison came back before he left the apartment.

And then Ted Bundy walked out the front door into "the beautiful Colorado snowy night."

He found an MG Midget, saw it had studded radial tires. Even though it looked as though it wouldn't make the summit of the pass, it had keys in it.

Ted Bundy drove out of Glenwood Springs. The car blew up on the pass, as he'd expected, but the man who picked him up took him to the bus station in Vail. Ted caught the 4:00 A.M. bus to Denver, arriving at 8:30 A.M.

Back in the jail, a jailer knocked on the door of Ted's cell at 7 A.M. with the breakfast tray. There was no response. He peeked through the door's small window and saw what he assumed was Ted's figure asleep in the bunk.

Jailer Bob Morrison, off duty, went to his closet around 8:15 and took out some clothing; he noticed nothing unusual.

In Denver Ted took a cab to the airport and boarded a plane for Chicago; no one even knew he was gone. By 11:00 A.M. he was in downtown Chicago.

Lunchtime came in the Garfield County Jail; Ted's breakfast tray, untouched as usual, sat on the floor outside his cell. This time the jailer looked at the lump in the bed and called Ted's name. Still no response. The cell was unlocked, and the jailer let go an oath as he stripped the covers from the bunk. There was nothing underneath but Ted's law reference books and legal papers. They had, indeed, brought him freedom—but not in the accepted sense.

There was hell to pay around the Sheriff's office, with recriminations flying right and left. There were cries that the captors had been warned, and that they'd let this man, this man accused of almost a score of murders, walk away.

Undersheriff Robert Hart commented that he doubted that Ted had taken to the mountains this time. "He couldn't take the chill in the hills around Aspen in June, so I don't think he would try it around here in December. We're dealing with a highly intelligent person. He would have this escape worked out thoroughly. Bundy had unlimited use of the telephone. He had a credit card to place calls wherever he wanted. And the court ordered us not to listen in on his calls. Hell, he could have called President Carter over in Europe if he was of a mind to do it."

Roadblocks were set up, tracking dogs called in again, but the spirit had gone out of the chase; Ted had a seventeen-hour head-start on his pursuers.

He was sitting in the club car on the train from Chicago to Ann Arbor, sipping a drink in comfort as the men far behind him called each other names, and waded through snowbanks. How he would have relished the sight.

In Aspen Ted achieved the status of Billy the Kid at the very least. By God, Bundy had done it; he had made the police look like Keystone Kops! A poet took pen in hand and wrote:

> So, let's salute the mighty Bundy
> Here on Friday, gone on Monday
> All his roads lead out of town
> It's hard to keep a good man down.

The Aspen State Teacher's College humor magazine, *The Clean Sweep*, hastened into print with several articles on Bundy:

Bundy Bound for Berkeley: Apparently bored by seclusion in the Garfield County Jail, Theodore Bundy decided to leave on New Year's Eve in search of intellectual stimulation and some holiday cheer. Bound for Berkeley, California, he plans to participate in the University atmosphere by both teaching and studying. Called by some the Houdini of prisoners, Bundy will teach courses in escapism, disguise, and also will give an intricate study in what has become known as the Bundy Bread and

Water Diet. The intellectual and multitalented Bundy plans to study while attending the University at Berkeley. He will complete his law degree and also take courses in both criminology and theatre so that he can successfully pursue one of several career possibilities. Future avenues include Garfield County Sheriff and the television lead in an updated version of "The Fugitive" series. Rumors of Bundy working as the wine steward at the Bacchanal and opening a light fixture company in Utah have both been proven false.

Under the Student Forum Advice Column:

Dear Freddie—
I'd like to open a light fixture company in town. How should I go about it?

Bundy

Dear Ted—
Wait until the reward gets bigger. . . . then call me.

And, beneath a picture of an old car, the question in the Snap Quiz of the Month:

What celebrity drove this car to Aspen?
A. Marlon Brando
B. Jack Nicholson
C. Linda Ronstadt
D. John Denver
E. Theodore Bundy
Answer: Theodore Bundy.

It was all hilarious—and frustrating for law enforcement. There would be no trial in January now. Ted had tried the unthinkable, and won.

29

Back in Seattle, I read the newspaper accounts of Ted's second escape incredulously; I had detected no hints at all that he planned to bolt and run when we'd talked earlier on December 30th. But, of course, I would probably have been the last person he would telegraph his thoughts to. I was too close to the police. And yet, he'd wanted to say goodbye.

I studied a map of the United States. If I were Ted, where would *I* go? To a big city, certainly, and then where? Would he bury himself in a sea of faces in a metropolis, or would he try to cross national borders? He had asked for my address in Los Angeles. I felt a vague stirring of unease. Los Angeles was a big city indeed, and only 120 miles from the Mexican border.

The FBI came to the same conclusion. Ray Mathis, in charge of public information for the Seattle office of the FBI, and an old friend—a man I had once introduced Ted to at a Christmas party—called and asked for my address in Los Angeles. He wanted to know when I would be flying down to California.

I had planned to leave on January 4th, but my car had been struck from behind by a drunk driver. It had almost totaled the first new car I'd ever had and had left me with a severe whiplash. I put off my flight until January 6th.

Ray gave me the names of two agents in charge of the Fugitive Unit in the Los Angeles FBI office. "Call them the minute you get off the plane. They'll be in touch with you, watching you. We don't know where he is—but he may try to contact you there."

All of it was unreal. Only a few years before, I had been—if there is such a creature—a typical housewife, a Brownie leader. Now, I was off to Hollywood to write a movie, with the FBI waiting for me. I felt as if I belonged in an episode of "Mary Hartman, Mary Hartman."

The two FBI agents met me as I arrived at my new apartment in West Hollywood. They checked the double locks on the door and found them sound, satisfied themselves that my third floor apartment was not accessible from the ground; any intruder would have to shinny up reed-thin bamboo trees.

"Do you think he'll call you?"

"I don't know," I said. "He has my address and my phone number."

"If he does, don't let him come here. Arrange to meet him some place public, a restaurant. Then call us. We'll be in disguise at another table."

I had to smile. The ghost of J. Edgar Hoover still prevailed: I had always found that FBI agents looked *exactly* like FBI agents, and I commented on my impression. They were chagrinned and assured me that they were "masters of disguise." If I doubted their expertise at disguise, I *did* appreciate their concern, however.

I have often been grateful that Ted did not run in my direction. I was saved a scene I could only imagine. All writers have a sense of the dramatic, but I couldn't quite see Ann Rule from the little town of Des Moines, Washington in the midst of an arrest of one of the country's Ten-Most-Wanted criminals—that "criminal" an old friend.

Joyce Johnson, who was to be a faithful—if sometimes needling—correspondent during my sojourn in Hollywood wrote,

> Dear Ann,
> Just to let you know that I'm protecting your interests here in the police department. I told Captain Leitch that you are hiding Ted in your apartment, and is he mad! He says you'll never get another story, but he really likes the new guy who's writing crime stories, and lets him see all the files. If you and Ted go to Mexico, send me a postcard.
>
> Love, Joyce

The weeks ahead were uncomfortable, but not frightening. I had no fear of Ted Bundy. Even if he was what he was said to be—a mass murderer—I still felt he would never harm me, but neither could I help him in his escape. That was something I just couldn't do.

When I returned to my apartment complex each night, I parked my rental car in the dark underground garage, traversed its length, and emerged among the lush flowering shrubbery that threatened to overgrow the swimming pool. Shadows were everywhere, and the last stretch of sidewalk before I came to my building in the rear of the complex was pitch dark; the lights had burned out. I sprinted for the door, pushed the elevator button, made sure no one was inside the self-operated lift, and ran from there to the door of my apartment.

Actually, I was more leery of some of the peculiar occupants of my building than I was of bumping into Ted. *He* was a known quality to me; they were not. My only fear as far as Ted was concerned was that I didn't want to have to face turning him in.

I needn't have worried. On the night I arrived at the Los Angeles airport on January 6th, Ted was pulling out of Ann Arbor, Michigan, my girlhood home, in a stolen car, headed for Tallahassee. Florida. By the time Marty Davidson and I began work on our script in earnest, Ted was comfortably ensconced in the Oak in Tallahassee, calling himself Chris Hagen. If he thought of me at all, it was only in passing. I was part of the other world, the world left behind forever.

Living in his shabby room, Ted was as happy and contented as he'd been in years. Just to open his eyes in the morning and see the old wood door, paint peeling and scarred, instead of a solid steel door, was glorious. At first, simply freedom itself was enough. He was around people, part of a college group, a group he had always found healthy and exciting.

He had meant to be completely and utterly law abiding, to get by without a car, without even a bicycle. He had meant to get a job—construction work preferably, but maybe even as a janitor. He wasn't in as good physical shape as he'd been most of his life; the months in jail had caused his taut muscle tone to waste away, despite the pacing he'd done in his cell, despite the push-ups and sit-ups he'd made himself do faithfully. And then, he was drastically underweight; he'd had to starve himself so he could get through the hole in the ceiling. It would take awhile to build up again.

He had gone through the records of graduates of Florida State University and decided that a graduate student named Kenneth

Misner, a track star, would be the first man he'd be. He researched Misner's family, his home town. He had an I.D. card made up in Misner's name, but he didn't want to use it yet; he needed a driver's license, other I.D. After he had all the verification that he needed to prove he was Kenneth Misner, then he would develop two or three more sets of I.D.—American first, and then Canadian. But he mustn't hurry it; there was time now, all the time in the world.

His days were simple; he arose at six and bought a small breakfast at the cafeteria on campus, skipped lunch, and had a hamburger for supper. In the evening, he walked to the store and bought a quart of beer, took it back to his room and drank it slowly. God! Freedom was so sweet; there was such pleasure in the simplest things.

He thought a lot about jail as he sipped the beer, smiling to himself as he went over the escape again and again. It had worked far better than he himself could have imagined. They had *never* understood what he was capable of. They'd been so grim and self-righteous about those damnable leg irons, irons they'd chained to the floor of their police cars. Hell, he'd had keys for those leg irons all along, made for him by a cellmate. He could have unlocked them at any time, but what good would it have done? Why should he jump out of a moving police car in the winter mountains when he could go through the ceiling any time he chose and get a fourteen-to-sixteen-hour headstart on the bastards?

He knew he should be working harder at finding a job, but he'd never been much of a job hunter. The days melted into each other, and it was all so good.

He knew he was acquisitive—that "things" meant a lot to him. He'd had his apartment in Salt Lake City exactly as he wanted it, and the damned cops had taken it all away from him. Now he wanted some things to brighten up his world again. He'd passed the bicycle several times on his way to the store. It was a Raleigh; he'd always been partial to Raleighs. They had a good, strong frame, but whoever owned this one apparently didn't give a damn about it. The tires were flat, and the rims had rusted. He took it, fixed the tires, polished up the rims. Riding it felt great. He'd ride it to the store to buy milk, and nobody ever looked twice at him.

There were other things he took, things he needed, things anybody needed if they were going to live like human beings: towels, cologne, a television set, racquet-ball racquets, and balls. Now he could play on the courts at F.S.U.

In the evenings, he mostly stayed in his room, watching television, finishing off the beer. He tried to be in bed by 10:00 P.M.

Stealing those things he needed seemed O.K. It was like going to the supermarket and slipping a can of sardines into his pocket to have for supper. He *had* to steal if he wanted to have anything; the $60 left after he'd paid his deposit was melting away, no matter how spartan he tried to keep his meals.

Friends were one thing he really couldn't afford. There was an unemployed rock band living down the hall, and he chatted with them occasionally, but he couldn't get really close to anyone in the Oak. As far as a girlfriend, that was impossible. He had no past; he might only get attached to someone and then have to disappear. How could he approach a woman when he—Chris Hagen—Ken Misner—who-knows-who-else—had only been "born" a week before?

With each day that passed, he berated himself because he wasn't actively looking for work. If he didn't have a job, there'd be no paychecks, and how was he going to explain that to the landlord of the Oak on February 8th when the $320 came due?

Still, he couldn't seem to make himself move on the job. It was too great just to be able to play ball, ride his bike, go to the library, watch TV, feel part of the human race again.

His room was becoming better furnished all the time; it was to easy to pick things up. And then it was so easy to slip women-shoppers' wallets out of their purses left in shopping carts. Credit cards. Credit cards would buy anything; he just had to remember to keep changing them before they were reported as stolen.

The world owed Ted Bundy. It had taken everything he had away from him, and now he was just making up for those stolen years, those years of humiliation and deprivation.

He was trained to take short cuts. Maybe that's why he couldn't bring himself to take buses when it was so easy to steal a car. He never kept them long. Later, he wouldn't even be able to count how many cars he'd stolen during the six weeks he spent as a free man in Florida. There was one he'd picked up in the Mormon Church parking lot. He had only driven it a few blocks before he realized the thing didn't have any brakes. He'd kill himself if he tried to drive that one. He dumped it in another churchyard.

And thief that he was, he had ethics. There was one little Volkswagen that he picked up, and realized at once that it must belong to some young girl. It was old and had a couple hundred thousand miles on it, but she'd had it souped up and polished and reupholstered. It was clearly somebody's pride and joy and he couldn't steal it. He made it a point never to steal from someone who couldn't afford it. If the car was new, and loaded with fancy extras, that told him that the owner could afford to lose it. But the little Volkswagen, he couldn't steal that one; he parked it a few blocks from where he'd taken it.

And so the days passed in Tallahassee—warm, almost dreamy days, and chilly nights when he was safe in his room, watching television, planning for the future, a future he could not quite manage to get running smoothly.

With the Florida metamorphosis, his appearance changed once again. Where he had been gaunt and skinny, the milk, beer, and junk food now began to add pounds; his face took on a rounded look. There was a hint of jowls around his chin. His body, trapped for so long in the confines of a cell, built up muscle from the bikeriding and racquet ball. He kept his hair short, and combed flat to discourage waves and curls. He'd always had the pronounced dark mole on the left side of his neck—one reason he'd worn turtlenecks almost exclusively—but none of the wanted posters mentioned it; perhaps no one had noticed it. Now, he penciled in a fake mole on his left cheek, started a real moustache. Other than that, he made no effort to disguise himself. He knew that he had been blessed with features that seemed to change imperceptibly through no will of his own, always attractive, but somehow anonymous. He would capitalize on it.

The one thing that ate at him was that he had no one to talk to, no one at all, beyond and occasional "How ya doin?" exchanged with the band guys down the hall, a few meaningless words with a pretty girl who also lived in the Oak. Before, although he had never been in a position to and never really wanted to bare his soul, there had always been someone to talk to, even if it meant the rhetoric of the courtroom, jokes with his jailers. And there had been letters to write. Now, there was no one. He had to savor what he had accomplished inside his own head, and the loneliness took much of the joy out of it. Theodore Robert Bundy had achieved a measure of fame back in the West; in Florida, he was nobody. There were no reporters fighting for interviews, no news cameras trained on him. He had been "on stage"—admittedly in a negative way—but he had been someone to reckon with.

Ted Bundy had arrived on the Florida State University Campus on Sunday morning, January 8, 1978, and settled into his room at the Oak. Unheralded, unrecognized, he moved about the campus, sometimes even sitting in on-classes, eating in the cafeteria, playing racquet ball in the athletic complex south of the campus proper. He knew no one and no one knew him; to the rest of the inhabitants of the college society, he was only a shadowy figure—a nobody.

The Chi Omega sorority house, a sprawling L-shaped edifice of brick and frame, is located at 661 W. Jefferson only a few blocks away from the Oak, but it is a world apart—expensively constructed, clean decorated with impeccable taste, one of the top sororities on campus, and home for thirty-nine coeds and a housemother.

I had pledged Chi Omega—another in the string of coincidences that have seemed to bind me to Ted—pledged it, indeed, way back in 1950 in its Nu Delta chapter on the Willamette University campus in Salem, Oregon. I remember the white carnations, the treasured pin with the owl and the skull, and, through the odd computer indexes of the brain, remember even the secret password. But that was in the days when sentiment reigned, when we gathered breathlessly on the house balcony to hear serenades from fraternity boys, much as the first Chi O's did when the sorority was founded in the deep South. The girls who lived in the Chi O House in Tallahassee were young enough to be my daughters.

The Chi Omega House on West Jefferson was the college home for the most beautiful, the brightest, the most popular, and, as always, the "legacies," pledged because their mothers and grandmothers had been Chi O's before them. Where we had been honor bound to be safely home by 8:00 P.M. on week nights and 1:00 A.M. on weekends, there were no curfews in 1978. Each resident had memorized the combination lock to the back door, a door which opened into the rec room on the first floor. They could come and go at will, and, on Saturday night, January 14, 1978, most of the girls who lived in the sorority were out very late—into the wee hours of the morning. There were several "keggers" on campus that night, functions that we had referred to as "beer busts," and many of the Chi O's were slightly intoxicated when they arrived home. Perhaps that may explain in part how the horror could happen only thin walls away from the girls who were spared, without their hearing so much as a footfall.

The downstairs of the Chi Omega House contained the recroom, and, to the west of it, a formal living room, seldom used except to entertain visiting alumni and during rush week. Beyond that, there was the dining room and kitchen. There were two "back" staircases, one leading up to the sleeping rooms from the rec room—the route usually taken by girls returning home late—and one opening off the kitchen. The front staircase led up from the foyer just inside the double front doors. The foyer was papered in a bright metallic blue and was illuminated by a chandelier, illuminated quite brightly according to the witnesses who would testify later.

For parents, sending their cherished daughters off to college, there would seem no safer place than a sorority house, full of other girls, watched over by a housemother, doors always locked. The only male usually allowed upstairs was Ronnie Eng, the houseboy who'd been dubbed the "sorority sweetheart." All the Chi O's were fond of Ronnie, a dark, slender, shy young man.

On that Saturday, most of the girls who lived in the Chi Omega House had plans for the evening. Margaret Bowman, twenty-one, daughter of a wealthy and socially prominent family in St. Petersburg, Florida, was going out on a blind date at 9:30, a date arranged for her by her friend and sorority sister, Melanie Nelson. Lisa Levy, twenty, also from St. Petersburg, had worked all day at her parttime job, and she decided she'd like to go out for a little while. Lisa and Melanie went to a popular campus disco—Sherrod's—which is located right next door to the Chi Omega House, at 10:00 P.M.

Karen Chandler and Kathy Kleiner, who were roommates in number 8 in the sorority, went in opposite directions that evening.

Karen went home to cook dinner for her parents, and returned before midnight to work on a sewing project in her room. Kathy Kleiner attended a wedding with her fiancé, and then went out to dinner with friends. Both of them were in their beds and sound asleep before midnight. Nita Neary and Nancy Dowdy and dates too that night they would not return until late. "Mom" Crenshaw, the housekeeper, retired around 11:00 She was on call if her girls needed her.

Lisa Levy was tired from her day's work had stayed only about half an hour at Sherrod's. Then she left, alone, and walked next door to the Chi O House and went to bed in number 4: her roommate had gone home for the weekend.

Sherrod's many levels were crowded that night, as they always were on weekends. Melanie sat with another sorority sister, Leslie Waddell, and Leslie's boyfriend, a Sigma Chi.

Mary Ann Piccano was at Sherrod's that night too, accompanied by her apartment mate, Connie Hastings. Mary Ann had a somewhat disturbing encounter with a man she had never seen before. The slender, brown-haired man had stared at her until she grew uncomfortable. There was something about the way this eyes bore into her that made her skin crawl. At length, he had come over to her table, bringing her a drink, and asked her to dance. He was handsome enough, and there was no rational reason for her to feel so wary, no reason to refuse really; Sherrod's was a place where on often danced with strangers. But, as she rose to join him on the dance floor, she whispered to Connie, "I think I'm about to dance with an ex-con . . ."

During the dance, he did or said nothing to substantiate her gut feeling about him, but she found herself trembling. She couldn't look at him and when the music finally ended, she had returned gratefully to her table. When she looked for him later, he was gone.

Melanie, Leslie, and her friend left Sherrod's a little after 2:00 when it closed, and walked next door. When they reached the back door, Melanie commented to Leslie that the combination lock wasn't working. "This is strange," she murmured. "The door isn't locked."

Leslie only shrugged. They had been having trouble with the door's closing and locking tightly for the past few days.

The trio walked through the rec room, lighted now with only a few dim table lamps. Margaret Bowman was already home and was waiting in the rec room, anxious to talk to Melanie about her date. Leslie's boyfriend didn't have a ride home, and Margaret loaned Leslie the keys to her car.

Melanie and Margaret walked to Melanie's room, discussing the events of Margaret's date while Melanie got into her pajamas. Then they walked to Margaret's room, number 9, and continued talking as Margaret undressed.

Nancy Dowdy returned from her dinner date a few minutes after Melanie and Leslie did; she too found the door mechanism ineffective and tried to make sure the door was shut tight. She paused for a moment at the top of the front stairs to say "goodnight" to Melanie and Margaret, and then went to bed. She was asleep by 2:15.

It was 2:35 A.M. exactly on Margaret's clock when Melanie said "goodnight" to her. Margaret wore only her bra and panties at that time. Melanie shut the door to Margaret's room tightly, heard it click, and then walked down the hall to the bathroom where she chatted with another sorority sister, Terry Murphree, who had just gotten off work at Sherrod's.

The time sequence would become extremely important.

Melanie Nelson had a digital clock in her room, and she glanced at it as she turned out the light; it was 2:45 A.M. She was asleep almost at once.

It was 3:00 A.M. when Nita Neary arrived at the Chi Omega House, accompanied by her boyfriend. They had attended one of the beer parties on campus, but Nita had had only a few beers; she had a cold and wasn't feeling very well.

When Nita came to the back door, she found it standing open. This didn't particularly alarm her; she too was aware that it hadn't been working right. Nita stepped inside and moved through the rec room, turning off the lights. Suddenly, she heard a loud "thump!" Her first thought was that her date had tripped and fallen on his way to his car. She ran to the window, but saw that he was fine, just getting into his vehicle. A moment later, she heard running footsteps in the corridor above.

Nita moved to the doorway leading into the foyer, hidden there from anyone coming down the front stairs. She could see the foyer well; the chandelier was still lit. The double white front doors were about sixteen feet away.

The footsteps sounded on the front stairway now, running.

And then she saw him, a slender man, wearing a dark jacket. A navy blue knit cap (what she called a "Toboggan") something like a watch cap, was pulled down over the top half of his face. She saw him only in profile but she could make out a sharp nose.

The man was crouched over, his left hand on the doorknob. And, in his right hand, incredibly, he held a club, a club that seemed to be a long. She could see it was rough, as if covered with bark. At the base of the club, where he held it, there was some cloth wrapped around it.

One second. Two. Three . . . and the door was open and the man was gone.

Thoughts flashed through Nita Neary's mind. She hadn't had time to be frightened. She thought, "we've been burglarized . . . or maybe one of the girls had the nerve to sneak somebody upstairs."

The only man who she was used to seeing around the sorority house was Ronnie Eng, and for a moment, she wondered, "What was Ronnie doing here?"

She hadn't seen the man's eyes at all, only that glimpse, now frozen in her conscious mind, of the crouching figure with the club. She ran up the stairs and woke her roommate, Nancy Dowdy. "There's someone in the house, Nancy! I just saw a man leave."

Nancy grabbed the first thing at hand—her umbrella—and the two girls tiptoed downstairs. They checked the front door and found it locked; Nita had shut and locked the rear door when she came in. They debated what they should do. Call the police? Wake Mom Crenshaw? Nothing seemed to be missing. Nothing seemed to be wrong. Nita demonstrated to Nancy the way the man had crouched, described the club. "At first, I thought it was Ronnie, but this man was larger and taller than Ronnie."

They walked back up the stairs, still discussing what they should do. As they reached the top, they saw Karen Chandler come out of number 8 and begin to run down the hall. She was staggering and she held her head in both hands. They assumed she was ill, and Nancy ran after her.

Karen's head was covered with blood, blood that streamed down over her face, and she seemed to be delirious. Nancy led her into her own room and gave her a towel to help staunch the flow of blood.

Nita ran to wake Mom Crenshaw, and then went into number 8, the room Karen shared with Kathy Kleiner. Kathy sat in her bed, holding her head in her hands. She was moaning unintelligibly and blood gushed from her head too.

Nancy Dowdy dialed 911, almost hysterical herself, and said that help was needed at once at the Chi Omega House at 661 West Jefferson. The first call was garbled. The dispatcher understood that "two females were fighting over a boyfriend." That was the way Tallahassee Police officer Oscar Brannon received the call. "To my sadness," he would later remark, "I found out differently."

Brannon was a mile or two away from the Chi O House and arrived at 3:23 A.M. Within three minutes, he was joined by a fellow Tallahassee officer, Henry Newkirk, Florida State University police officers Ray Crew and Bill Taylor, and paramedics from Tallahassee Memorial Hospital.

Neither the officers nor the paramedics had any idea what lay ahead of them.

Brannon and Taylor remained downstairs and got a description of the man Nita had seen and broadcast it to all units working the area; Crew and Newkirk ran upstairs. Mrs. Crenshaw and eight or ten of the girls were milling around in the hall. They pointed to Karen and Kathy; both girls seemed to be terribly injured.

Paramedics Don Allen, Amelia Roberts, Lee Phinney, and Garry Matthews were directed to the second floor where the victims lay moaning. Allen and Roberts worked on Kathy Kleiner. Kathy was conscious, but she had lacerations and puncture wounds on her face, a broken jaw, broken teeth, possible skull fractures. Someone had given her a container to catch the blood that gushed from her mouth. She called for her boyfriend and for her pastor. She had no idea at all what had happened to her; she'd been sound asleep.

Allen's supervisor, Lee Phinney, moved to help Karen Chandler. She too had a broken jaw, broken teeth, possible fractures of the skull, and cuts. The paramedics fought to open an airway for both the injured girls to keep them from choking to death on their own blood.

The injured girls' room—number 8—looked like an abattoir, with blood sprayed on the light walls. Bits of bark—oak bark—covered their pillows and bedclothing.

Karen did not remember anything either. She too had been sleeping when the man had hammered blows on her head.

Pandemonium reigned. While the other policemen moved down the corridor, checking room by room, Officer Newkirk gathered the girls into number 2. No one could answer his questions; no one had heard a thing.

Officer Ray Crew came to number 4, Lisa Levy's room, with Mrs. Crenshaw trailing behind. Lisa had gone to bed around 11:00 and she apparently hadn't awakened, despite the chaos on the second floor. Crew opened Lisa's door. He saw her lying on her right side, the covers pulled up over her shoulders. The housemother told Crew her name.

"Lisa?"

There was no answer.

"Lisa! Wake up!" Crew called.

The figure on the bed didn't move at all.

Crew reached out to shake her shoulder gently, started to roll her over on her back. It was then that he observed a small blood stain on the sheet beneath her. He turned to Mrs. Crenshaw and said tightly, "Get the medics."

Don Allen grabbed his gear and ran to Lisa. The paramedic checked for a pulse, and found none. He pulled her onto the floor, and immediately began mouth-to-mouth resuscitation and cardiopulmonary massage. Lisa's complexion was pallid, her lips blue, her skin already cooling, and yet the paramedics could not see exactly what was wrong with her. She wore only a nightgown; her panties lay on the floor beside the bed.

Allen cut off her nightgown, searching for some injury that caused her condition. He saw pronounced swelling around her jaw, a condition usually produced by strangulation, and an injury on her right shoulder, an ugly purpling bruise. Her right nipple had been bitten almost off.

There was no time to dwell on the horror of what had happened; Allen and Roberts inserted an airway into the girl's trachea, forcing oxygen into her lungs so that, to the lay observer, it seemed that she was actually breathing on her own as her breasts rose and fell rhythmically. They inserted a catheter needle into her vein and started a solution of D_5W to keep the vein open preparatory to the administration of drugs. They were on standing orders to follow all these procedures in the case of a patient near death. Next, they called the emergency room doctor on standby via radio-telementry for drug orders. They administered drugs that might start her heart beating for ten to twenty minutes.

It was hopeless and they knew it, but the girl who lay motionless on the floor before them was so young. They never got a pulse; all they elicited was a slight, irregular pattern on their heart monitor. It was only electrical-mechanical-disassociation, the electrical impulses of a dying heart. Lisa Levy's heart itself never beat at all. Lisa Levy was dead.

Still, she was transported to the hospital with sirens wailing. She would be pronounced D.O.A.

Melanie Nelson was still asleep in her room. She wakened suddenly as she saw a man beside her bed, a man shaking her and calling her name. She heard him breathe, "My God! We have another one."

But Ray Crew was relieved to see that Melanie was not dead; she'd only been sleeping. She sat up and followed him out into the hall, grabbing a coat against the chill of the early morning.

Melanie didn't know what had happened. She saw her sorority sisters huddled together in one room, saw the policemen and paramedics milling about, and assumed that the house was on fire. She asked, "Is everyone home?"

And the answer came. "Everyone but Margaret."

Melanie shook her head. "No. Margaret's home. I talked to her." She grabbed Officer Newkirk's arm and said, "Come on, I'll show you."

The two walked down the hall to room number 9. The door was ajar now, although Melanie distinctly remembered shutting it when she'd left Margaret after saying goodnight forty-five minutes earlier. She pushed the door a little and could see Margaret's figure in the bed; there was just enough light from the streetlight outside the window so that she could recognize Margaret's long dark hair on the white pillow.

"See," Melanie said. "I told you she was home."

Newkirk stepped into the hall, turned on the light. What he saw made him push Melanie into the hall, and shut the door firmly. He felt as if he were walking through a nightmare.

Margaret Bowman lay on her face, the covers pulled up around her neck, but he'd seen the blood on her pillow. Moving closer, he could see the red liquid that had welled up on the right side of her head and clotted in her ear. Oh God, he could actually see into her brain; her skull had been shattered.

Newkirk pulled the bedspread down a little. A nylon stocking had been cinched so cruelly around her neck that the neck appeared to be half its normal size, and was probably broken.

Almost without thinking, he touched her right shoulder, lifted her a bit off the bed. But he knew she was dead, that nothing more could be done for her. He let go of her shoulder and placed her gently back in the position he'd found her in.

Newkirk looked around the room. There was bark everywhere—on the bed, caught in the girl's hair, glued to her face by blood. And yet, there seemed to have been no struggle at all. Margaret Bowman still wore a shortie yellow nightgown, and a gold necklace was caught up in the stocking around her neck. Her panties, however, lay on the floor at the end of the bed.

Newkirk sealed off the room after paramedic Garry Matthews confirmed that Margaret was dead, and had been for some time. The post mortem lividity that begins soon after death, the purplish red striations that mark a body's nether side, pooled blood no longer pumped by a living heart, was already apparent.

Newkirk notified Tallahassee Police headquarters that there was a confirmed "Signal 7," a dead body at the Chi Omega House.

The terrible toll now stood at two dead, two critically injured, but the rest of the sorority girls were safe, all gathered in number 2, shocked, weeping, unbelieving. How could they have slept through such mayhem? How was it possible that a killer could enter their sleeping area so easily without anyone knowing?

It had to have happened with such rapidity as to be unimaginable. Melanie Nelson had seen Margaret Bowman alive and happy at 2:35, and Nita Neary had seen the man with the club leaving at 3:00 A.M. Melanie had gone back and forth across the hall until 2:45 A.M.!

One of the coeds who huddled, shivering, in number 2 was Carol Johnston. Carol had come home about 2:55, parked her car behind the Chi O House, and entered through the back door. Like Nita would moments later, Carol found the door ajar. She went through the foyer and up the front stairs. When she reached the second floor hall, she was somewhat surprised to see that all the lights were off—a most unusual occurrence. The only light at all was from a desklamp her roommate always left on when Carol was out, and it made just a slice of light under her door.

Carol had changed into her pajamas and made her way down the black hall to the bathroom. The door to the bathroom is a swinging door. As Carol stood inside, brushing her teeth, the bathroom door creaked, something it invariably did when someone passed by in the hall just outside. Carol had thought nothing of it, assuming it was one of the other girls. A moment later, she emerged and walked down the hall, guided by the light from her room.

Carol Johnston had gone to bed, unaware that she had missed the killer by no more than a fraction of a second.

The man in the dark knitted cap may have entered the Chi Omega House earlier in the evening, may have waited until he thought all the girls were in and asleep, or he may have entered through the unlocked rear door after 2:00 A.M. Some investigators feel that Lisa Levy was attacked first, and her killer waited in her room for other victims to come home. It is more likely that Margaret Bowman was the first victim, Lisa the second, and Kathy and Karen almost afterthoughts. If that is true, the man, in the grip of compulsive, maniacal frenzy, moved through the Chi Omega House second floor with his oaken club, killing and bludgeoning his victims—all within a space of less than fifteen minutes! And all within earshot of almost three dozen witnesses, witnesses who didn't even hear him.

Lisa Levy and Margaret Bowman were now lying in the morgue of Tallahassee Memorial Memorial Hospital, awaiting post mortem examinations early Sunday morning. The area around the Chi Omega House, indeed the whole campus, was alive with patrol cars and detectives' cars from the Tallahassee Police Department, the Leon County Sheriff's Office, and the Florida State University Police Department, all looking for the man in the dark jacket and light trousers. They had no idea what he looked like—no hair color, no facial description beyond the fact that he'd had a large, sharp nose. It was unlikely that he still carried the bloodied oak club. It *was* likely that he might have bloodstains on his clothing; there had been so much blood let in that catastrophic fifteen minutes as he ravaged the four sleeping girls.

In the Chi O House itself, room numbers 4, 8 and 9 were littered with the debris left by both the killer and the paramedics, the walls sprayed with droplets of scarlet, the floors and beds full of blood and bits of bark from the death weapon. Officer Oscar Brannon went to the rec room, and, on his hands and knees, collected eight pieces of the same bark on the floor of that room; entry had obviously been made through the back door where the lock had been nonfunctional.

He found a pile of oak logs in the back yard of the sorority house. It appeared that the killer had picked up his weapon on the way in.

Brannon and Sergeant Howard Winkler dusted for latent prints in all the rooms—doorways, wall posters, around the combination lock that had failed. They took photographs. In Margaret Bowman's room, Brannon noticed a Hanes "Alive" stocking package lying across the wastepaper basket—empty—only the cardboard and cellophane remaining. A new pair of pantyhose lay on her roommate's bed. It seemed that the killer had brought his own garottes with him.

A BOLO (Be On the Look-Out) bulletin was quickly in the hands of every officer in Tallahassee and Leon County.

There had been no pictures taken of Lisa Levy in her room; she had been rushed to the hospital in the vain hope that some spark of life remained, but Tallahassee I.D. Officer Bruce Johnson had taken photographs of Margaret as she lay on her bed, her face pressed into her pillow, her right arm straight down beside her body, her left arm, hand palm up, bent over her back, her legs straight. No, Margaret had not fought her murderer at all. It had been the same with Lisa; she had been found with her right arm beneath her.

Sheriff Ken Katsaris of Leon County was there, Captain Jack Poitinger, Chief of Detectives, and Detective Don Patchen of the Tallahassee Police Department. In fact, there wasn't a lawman in all of Leon County who was not aware of what had happened within an hour after the mass slaughter. Not one of them had ever had to deal with anything like the savage violence they were faced with.

Patrol officers fanned out through the neighborhood in door-to-door canvass. Nothing. A surveillance van parked on the street stopped everyone who passed by. Nothing. The suspect was simply gone.

The paramedics had delivered the victims, alive and dead, to the hospital, and were back on the street shortly after 4:00 A.M.

Their night's work was far from over.

The old frame duplex at 431 Dunwoody Street was approximately eight blocks from the Chi Omega House, closer as the crow flies. Two-tenths of a mile. It was typical of many of the twenties vintage structures bordering the campus proper which had been turned into rental housing—nothing fancy, but adequate. There were two "shotgun" apartments at 431 Dunwoody. Debbie Ciccarelli and Nancy Young lived in A, and Cheryl Thomas lived in B. Each apartment opened onto a common screened front porch with a single door, but the duplexes had separate entries—entries leading into a living room, a bedroom, and, in the rear, a kitchen. They shared a central wall and when the place had been remodeled into two units, nobody had been much concerned with insulation against noise.

That didn't matter in the least to the three girls who lived at Dunwoody Street; they were close friends. Cheryl and Nancy were both dance majors and had once been dorm roommates on campus. The trio visited back and forth and often went out together socially.

On Saturday night, January 14th, the three girls—and Cheryl's date, a dance student—had gone dancing at Big Daddy's, another popular spot for young people in Tallahassee. Cheryl and her date had left before closing and as Cheryl had a car and her date didn't, she had driven him home, arriving about 1:00 A.M. He served her tea and cookies and they talked for about half an hour. Then she drove the two miles to the Dunwoody duplex and was in her apartment by two. She flipped on the television set, walked to the kitchen and made herself something to eat, fed her new kitten.

Within minutes of her arrival home, Nancy and Debbie drove up. They shouted at her, complaining good-naturedly that her TV was too loud; she laughed, and turned it down.

Cheryl Thomas is a tall, lithe girl with the body of a ballerina, dark-eyed, with long dark hair falling to the middle of her back, dimpled, pretty, somewhat shy. She glanced around the neat kitchen with its red-and-white print curtains and tablecloth, and turned out the overhead light, leaving just a nightlight on.

Cheryl waited for her kitten to follow her, and then closed the accordion-pleated divider separating the kitchen from her bedroom. She changed into panties and a sweater—it was a chilly night—and then pulled back the blue madras spread on her bed, a bed that was just on the other side of the wall from the bedroom of her friends next door. She was asleep almost as soon as her head hit the pillow.

Something roused her a short time later—a noise, something falling? She listened for a moment, and then decided it must have been the kitten. Her window sills were full of plants and the cat liked to play there. There were no more sounds, and she turned over and went back to sleep.

Next door, Debbie and Nancy had also settled down for the night. To the best of their recollection, they were asleep by 3:00 A.M.

Debbie woke from her sound sleep around 4:00. She sat up, listened. It sounded as though there was someone beneath the house with a hammer, banging again and again. Debbie slept on a mattress on the floor and felt it as the whole house seemed to reverberate from the thumping sound that came from some place just beneath her bed or the wall between her bed and Cheryl's.

Debbie shook Nancy awake. The sounds continued for about ten seconds, and then it was quiet again. The two girls in A waited, trying to identify the noises Debbie had heard. They were afraid.

Then they heard new sounds, sounds coming from Cheryl's apartment. She was moaning, whimpering, as if in the grip of a bad dream.

Debbie crept to the phone and called her boyfriend, asking him what they should do. He told her just to go back to sleep, that everything was probably fine. But Debbie had a gut feeling; something was terribly wrong.

The three girls had long since established a security check. They were *always* to answer their phone—no matter what time of day or night. Nancy and Debbie huddled together and dialed Cheryl's number. They could hear her phone ring once . . . twice . . . three times . . . four . . . five. . .

No one answered.

"O.K. That's it," Nancy said. "Call the police . . . *now!*"

Debbie reached the Tallahassee Police dispatcher at 4:37 A.M. and gave their address. As she was doing this, a terrible crashing noise came from Cheryl's apartment, a noise that seemed to emanate from her kitchen, as if someone was running, banging into the kitchen table, the cabinets. And then there was only silence.

Debbie and Nancy stood trembling in the middle of their bedroom, heard the sound of cars pulling up in front. It had been only three or four minutes since they had called for help. When they looked out their front door, they were astounded to see—not one squad car, but a dozen!

Debbie and Nancy stood in their doorway and pointed to Cheryl's door, told the first officers—Wilton Dozier, Jerry Payne, Mitch Miller, Willis Solomon—Cheryl's name. The patrolmen banged on Cheryl Thomas's door, calling her name. There was no answer. Dozier sent Miller and Solomon to the rear of the house to spot anyone who might be attempting to exit at the back.

Dozier found Cheryl's door would not open. Solomon shouted from behind the duplex that a screen was off a window to the kitchen, and that that window could be opened. Dozier attempted to crawl into Cheryl Thomas's apartment that way, but, at that moment, Nancy remembered that a spare key to Cheryl's apartment was usually hidden just above the screen door to the porch. No one knew it was there other than the three girls who lived at Dunwoody Street.

Dozier inserted the key, and the door finally gave. As their eyes adjusted to the dim light inside the duplex, Payne and Dozier could see the girl lying diagonally across the bed in the middle room, could see blood on the bed and the floor.

Next door, Nancy and Debbie heard a shout, "My God! She's still alive!" and they started to cry; they knew that something awful had happened to Cheryl. The next shout instructed Officer Solomon to call the paramedics, and then other officers came to the sobbing girls' duplex and told them gently to go inside and shut their door.

Dozier and Payne attempted to help the girl on the bed; Cheryl was semiconscious, whimpering, unresponsive to anything the policemen said to her. Her face was turning purple with bruises; it was swollen, and she seemed to have suffered severe head wounds. She lay on the bed, twisting with pain and groaning. Cheryl wore only panties; her breasts were exposed; the sweater she'd worn when she went to bed had been ripped off.

Paramedics Charles Norvell and Garry Matthews, who had just cleared the Tallahassee Memorial Hospital after transporting Karen Chandler and Kathy Kleiner to the Emergency Room, got the call to return to the Florida State Campus, and they arrived within minutes to treat this latest victim. Cheryl Thomas was carried out of her apartment and rushed to the hospital. Like the others, she had been bludgeoned about the head and was critically injured.

It seemed almost too incredible to believe, but it looked as though the Chi Omega assailant, his blood lust unsatiated, still in the grip of whatever compulsion drove him, had run from the sorority house to the little duplex on Dunwoody, run as if he'd known exactly where he was going, knew who lived inside . . . and there had attacked still another victim.

Dozier secured the scene of this latest attack until detectives arrived, and I.D. technicians: Mary Ann Kirkham from the Leon County Sheriff's Office and Bruce Johnson from the Tallahassee Police Department.

Johnson took photographs of the bedroom, the three-quarter bed pushed up against the white siding walls, the tumble of bedding pushed to the floor at the side of the bed, the piece of wood lath—red-stained—at the foot of the bed, the curtain ripped from its rod in the kitchen window, while Deputy Kirkham painstakingly bagged and marked the evidence.

As Kirkham prepared to pick up the bedding from the floor, she found something tangled in the sheets. At first, she thought it was only a pair of nylons. Then she looked again. It was a pair of pantyhose, pantyhose that had been fashioned into a mask with eyeholes cut out, the legs tied together. There were two wavy brown hairs caught up in the mask.

There were no keys in the apartment, and the deadbolt on the kitchen door was still locked, although the chain was off. It was likely that the suspect had enetered and left through the kitchen window.

As the Chi Omega bedding had been collected—folded carefully and slipped into large plastic bags so that nothing would be lost—Cheryl Thomas's sheets, blankets, and pillow-case were bagged into evidence.

Again, all likely surfaces were dusted for latent prints, all rooms vacuumed and the residue picked up, retained for evidence.

The piece of lath, possibly eight inches long and less than an inch thick, hardly seemed heavy enough to have inflicted the kind of damage Cheryl Thomas had suffered; it was more the type of stick used to prop windows open, and the red stuff staining one end was long dried. It would prove to be only paint.

This time, the investigators found no bark. Whatever weapon the intruder had used, he had apparently taken it with him in his flight.

Karen Chandler, Kathy Kleiner, and Cheryl Thomas had been lucky—although they would always bear the physical and emotional scars of that long night. When they would appear eighteen months later in a Miami courtroom, when they would face the man accused of injuring them—Ted Bundy—they bore few outward signs of the damage done to them. Only Cheryl would walk with a hesitancy, a distinct limp; she, of course, had once dreamed of a career as a dancer.

Physicians at Tallahassee Memorial found that Karen Chandler had a concussion, a broken jaw, had lost teeth, suffered facial bone fractures and cuts, and had one finger crushed. Kathy Kleiner's injuries were similar: she had a broken jaw in three places, a whip-lash injury to her neck, deep lacerations on her shoulder. All of Kathy's lower teeth were loosened, permanently, and it was neces-sary to place a pin in her jaw.

Cheryl Thomas's injuries were the worst. Her skull was fractured in five places, causing her permanent hearing loss in her left ear. Her jaw was broken, her left shoulder dislocated. Her eighth cranial nerve was damaged to such an extent that not only was she deaf-ened, but the young dancer would never have normal equilibrium.

Karen and Kathy would be in the hospital for a week; Cheryl would not be released for a month.

Not one of the three girls had any memory at all of being attacked; not one could describe the man who had beaten them with such frenzy.

Lisa Levy and Margaret Bowman would, of course, never have their day in court, never face the man accused of their murders. For them, there would be a kind of silent testimony: the terrible pictures taken of their bodies, the almost expressionless reading of their autopsy reports.

Dr. Thomas P. Wood, a pathologist on staff at Tallahassee Memorial Hospital, performed the post mortem examinations on the dead girls on Sunday, January 15th—one week to the day since Ted Bundy had gotten off the bus at the Trailways Station in Tallahassee.

He began the autopsy on Lisa's body at 10:00 A.M. Lisa had been strangled, leaving the characteristic petechial hemorrages in the strap muscles of her neck, a ligature mark on her throat. She had a bruise on her forehead, scratches on her face. X-rays showed that her right collarbone had been broken by a tremendous blow. It was Wood's opinion that she had been rendered unconscious by the blows to the head. If she was, it was a small blessing.

Her right nipple was attached by only a thread of tissue. But this mutilation was not the worst; there was a double bite mark on her left buttock. Her killer had literally torn at her buttock with his teeth, leaving four distinct rows of marks where those teeth had sunk in.

Lisa had been sexually assaulted—but not in the usual sense; an unyielding object had been jammed into her body, tearing and bruising the rectal orifice and the vaginal vault, causing hemorrhage in the lining of the womb and other internal organs.

The weapon which had inflicted this damage was later found in the room. It was a Clairol hair mist bottle with a nozzle-top. The bottle was stained with blood, fecal matter, and hair.

The man who attacked Lisa Levy as she had lain asleep had struck her, strangled her, torn at her like a rabid animal, and then ravished her with the bottle. And then, apparently, he had covered her up and left her lying quietly on her side, the covers pulled up almost tenderly around her shoulders.

The post mortem on Margaret Bowman began at 1:00 P.M. that gray Sunday. The blows dealt to the right side of the girl's head had caused depressed fractures, driving the broken pieces of skull into her brain itself. The area of trauma was "complicated," meaning, to the layman, that there was such extensive splintering of the skull that it was hard to tell where one fracture ended and the next began. The ugly wounds began above the right eye, and continued to behind the right ear, crushing and pulverizing the delicate brain tissue beneath. One fracture was two-and-a-half inches in diameter, and the damage behind the ear was four inches in diameter. Oddly, it would seem at first, there was more damage to the left side of the brain than the right. But there was an explanation: the force dealt to Margaret Bowman's head was so tremendous that her brain had been slammed against the left side of the skull when she was struck with the oak club on the right.

The pantyhose ligature was cut from Margaret's neck, buried so deep that it could hardly be seen in the flesh. It was a Hanes "Alive" Support brand, a fabric of great tensile strength. One leg had been cut off by the killer, but the legs had been knotted above the panty portion—just as the pantyhose mask found in Cheryl Thomas's apartment had been. The delicate gold chain the dead girl had worn was still entangled in the garotte.

In Dr. Wood's opinion, Margaret, like Lisa, had been unconscious from the head blows when the ligature was tightened around her neck, killing her by strangulation.

Unlike Lisa, Margaret Bowman bore no evidence of a sexual assault, but she had "rope burn" abrasions to her left thigh where her panties had been pulled off with force.

Neither girl had broken nails, no damage at all to their hands that would indicate they had had a chance to fight for their lives.

Pathologist Wood had been in practice for sixteen years; he had never seen anything like what he was seeing before him.

Rage, hate, animalistic mutilation. And why?

30

Almost anyone living in the vicinity of the Florida State University campus on that terrible weekened would have heard the sirens of the medic units, been aware that police activity was profound, realized that something more than an accident or a usual investigation was the cause.

Henry Polumbo and Rusty Gage, two of the musicians who lived in the Oak, returned to their rooms at 4:45 on Sunday, January 15th, even as the paramedics were carrying Cheryl Thomas to the aid unit a few blocks away. They heard the sirens, but they didn't know what had happened.

As Polumbo and Gage walked up on the front porch, they saw the man who'd moved into number 12 a week before: Chris Hagen. He was standing at the front door. They spoke to him and he said "Hi." He was staring out in the direction of the campus; they don't remember what he was wearing exactly, but Gage recalled a windbreaker, a shirt, possibly jeans—dark in color all of it. They don't remember that he seemed nervous or upset. They went upstairs to bed and assumed Hagen had too.

By the next morning, as the post mortems began on Lisa Levy and Margaret Bowman, the radio news broadcasts were full of information about the killer in the Chi Omega House, about the attack on Dunwoody Street. There was a shocked gathering of residents in Polumbo's room; they were horrified, and they were discussing what kind of man could have done such a thing.

As they talked, Chris Hagen walked in. Chris had never come right out and said what he was doing in Tallahassee. He'd told them that he'd been a law student at Stanford University in Palo Alto, and they'd assumed he was continuing his studies at Florida State but he hadn't said it in so many words. He *had* boasted to them that he knew law very well, and that he was a lot smarter than any policeman. He'd said, "I can get out of anything because I know my way around."

They'd put it down to bull-shitting.

Henry Polumbo remarked that he felt the killer was a lunatic, and was probably lying low as the police investigation accelerated.

The other started to agree, but Hagen argued with them. "No . . . this was a professional job; the man has done it before. He's probably long-gone by now."

Maybe he was right; Hagen had said he knew about such things, knew the law, and felt cops were stupid.

While the students at Florida State tentatively began their regular routines, moving—especially the coeds—in a kind of quiet dread, the search for the killer went on. The Leon County Sheriff's Office, the Tallahassee Police Department, the Florida State Police Department, the Florida Department of Law Enforcement all worked side by side. the streets in and around the campus were staked out constantly by officers sitting quietly in their vehicles, patrolling. After dark, those streets were almost deserted, and all doors were double-locked, blockaded. If it could happen the way it had in the Chi O House, in the duplex on Dunwoody, could there be safety for any woman in the region?

The evidence, handled through a tight chain-of-evidence so that its progress from the attack sites to the lab at the Florida State Department of Law Enforcement could be traced exactly, was tested, examined, placed under lock and key.

There was a lot of evidence; it would one day take eight hours to log it into the trial, and, yet, there was so little that could help in the probe as far as leading the investigators to the man they sought.

Blood samples—not of the killer—but of the victims. Dr. Wood had deeply excised the section of flesh bearing the teeth marks in Lisa's buttock and refrigerated it in normal saline solution to preserve it. He personally saw Sergeant Howard Winkler, head of the Crime Scene Unit of the Tallahassee Police Department, take possession of it.

In trial, there would be defense arguments that the tissue sample had been improperly preserved—that it had shrunk. It had been taken from the saline solution and placed in formalin.

Yet Winkler had photographed the bite marks, to scale, with a standard morgue ruler beside them; whatever shrinking occurred, the scale photos would never change, and a forensic odontologist would be able to match those bite marks to a suspect's teeth almost as precisely as a fingerprint expert could identify the loops and whorls of a suspect's fingers.

If a suspect was ever found.

There was the Clairol hair mist bottle, stained with type O blood—Lisa's type.

There were the two hairs found of latent prints lifted, all of which would prove of no value; the killer apparently knew about fingerprints.

There was a wad of chewed gum found in Lisa's hair, gum that would inadvertently be destroyed in the lab and made useless for testing for secretion, or for teeth impressions.

There were all the sheets, pillows, blankets, nightgowns, panties.

There were the fragments of oak bark. But how could one piece of bark be traced to a certain source—even if the death weapon was ever found?

There were the pantyhose. The Hanes's garotte from Margaret's neck, stained deeply with her blood, the Sears-brand mask from Cheryl's apartment. That mask would be found to resemble almost exactly the mask taken from Ted Bundy's car when he'd been arrested in Utah in August of 1975.

There were tests on all the victims' sheets and bedding for the presence of semen. When acid phosphotase is applied to material, the presence of semen produces a purplish-red stain. There was no semen found on Lisa's, Margaret's, Karen's, or Kathy's sheets.

There was, however, a semen stain approximately three inches in diameter on Cheryl Thomas's bottom sheet. Richard Stephens, an expert in serology at the Florida Department of Law Enforcement's crime lab, did intensive testing on that semen stain.

Approximately eight-five percent of all human beings are "secretors." Enzymes are secreted in bodily fluids—saliva, mucous, semen, perspiration, urine, feces, and these enzymes will tell a serologist what blood type that person has. If a sample of cloth bearing a bodily fluid stain is dropped into a control sample with the same blood type, the sample will *not* agglutinate (the cells with not clump together). If it is dropped into a control sample of another blood type, there will be agglutination.

Stephens's agglutination tests for known blood types *all* showed cell clumping when the Thomas sheet samples were inserted. The test was inconclusive.

Next, he used a process known as electro-phoresis. A sample of the semen-stained sheet was placed in starch gel and heated until it took on a "jellolike" consistency. It was then put on a glass slide, and stimulated electrically, causing the proteins to move, and a small metabolite was added to show the rates of movement. There was no detectable PGM enzyme activity.

It would appear then that the man who'd ejaculated that semen was a non-secretor. Yet, to Stephens, the results were inconclusive; there were too many variables that could affect the tests: age of stain, condition, the material it was on, environmental factors such as humidity and heat. Also, the rate of secretion varies in individuals depending on the condition of their systems at any given time.

Ted Bundy has type O positive blood, and he is a secretor.

It was a puzzle. In his trial, the defense would claim that the enzyme tests, the agglutination tests, had proved that Ted could not have left the semen in Cheryl's bed. Perhaps. The prosecution would stress only that Cheryl Thomas could not remember if she had changed her sheets that Saturday, January 14th. Neither side would go a step further, would ask Cheryl if she had had sexual relations with *another* man in that bed earlier in the week, and the question was left suspended. If Cheryl had not changed her sheets, the inference left unspoken by the prosecution was that the semen stain, the stain where the blood type could not be determined, had been left there by someone else *before* the man who bludgeoned her entered her apartment. This stain of ejaculate was one piece of physical evidence that Ted's supporters would refer to again and again as proof, positive that he was innocent.

For a lay jury, it seemed to be a moot point anyway. The scientific testimony would appear to pass over their heads like so much gobbledy-gook.

What the case would come down to was Nita Neary's eyewitness identification of the man in the "Toboggan" cap, the man she saw leaving the Chi Omega House with a blood-stained club, the bite marks in Lisa Levy's flesh, the hairs in the pantyhose mask. The rest would all be circumstantial.

But, on January 15th, that was academic. The lawmen didn't even have a suspect, and none of them had ever heard of Theodore Robert Bundy—missing now for sixteen days from his jail cell in Colorado.

31

Ted still lived at the Oak, and he had stepped up his thefts. With the stolen credit cards, he could eat and drink luxuriously at expensive restaurants in Tallahassee, he could buy items that he needed, but he couldn't figure out a way to get the $320 he needed for his upcoming rent.

I was in Los Angeles, still half-expecting to see him step out of the shadows in the apartment complex in West Hollywood, still expecting to see his friendly grin.

Someone tried to steal my car, pried the whole ignition out of the battered Pinto my producers had rented for me from Rent-a-Wreck. When the deputy from the Los Angeles Country Sheriff's substation a block away came to take my report, he glanced around my apartment and asked me if I had chosen it myself, or if someone had rented it for me. I told him my producers had picked it out.

He grinned. "Do you know you have the only apartment on this floor that isn't a hooker's pad?"

No I didn't. But it explained why there were so many knocks on my door in the wee hours of the morning.

Like the FBI men before him, he double-checked my locks and warned me to be careful. I could be forgiven for a slight tinge of paranoia.

I got another car from Rent-a-Wreck and life went on. Florida was a long, long way away. I'd never been there, and had no plans to ever go there.

I received a letter from my mother in Oregon; in it, she enclosed a two-inch clipping giving the sparest of details of the Chi Omega murders. And she wrote, "It sounds a lot like the 'Ted' murders. I wonder . . ."

No, I didn't think so. *If* Ted had been guilty of the crimes he was accused of in Washington, Utah, and Colorado, and I'd always had great difficulty really believing that, he had made a clean escape. He was free. Why would he jeopardize that freedom which meant so much to him? The Chi Omega murders, the other attacks, had been different, the work of an almost clumsy, rampaging killer.

32

A young man named Randy Ragan lived in a house just behind the Dunwoody Street duplex. If he stood in the back door, he could look directly at Cheryl Thomas's back door. On January 13th, he'd found the license tag missing from his 1972 Volkswagen Camper. It couldn't have just dropped off; it had been firmly attached with nuts and bolts.

The license number was 13–D–11300.

Ragan reported the tag as lost, and then received a new tag.

Ragan lived so close to Cheryl's apartment, so close to the Chi Omega House, in fact, and so close to the Oak.

On February 5th, Freddie McGee, who worked for the Florida State Audio-Visual Department, reported that a white Dodge van owned by the department had been stolen, driven off by someone after he'd left it parked on campus. It had borne Florida plates which were bright yellow and read 7378; in addition, it had a Florida State University number, 343, painted on the back.

"Thirteen" is a state designation meaning that a vehicle has been licensed in Leon County. The "D" is for a small vehicle, and Ragan's camper would have fit in that category. If someone attempted to put Ragan's plate on a larger vehicle, he would ultimately be spotted by a trooper and pulled over. But no one spotted the Dodge van stolen from the Audio-Visual Department—no one in Tallahassee or its environs at any rate.

Tallahassee is in the northwestern portion of Florida; Jacksonville is 200 miles away in the northeast, along the St. Johns River which leads out into the Atlantic Ocean.

On Wednesday, February 8, 1978, fourteen-year-old Leslie Ann Parmenter left Jeb Stuart Junior High School on Wesconnett Boulevard in Jacksonville a little before 2:00 P.M. Leslie's father is James Lester Parmenter, Chief of Detectives for the Jacksonville

Police Department, an 18-year veteran on that force. She expected to be picked up by her twenty-one-year-old brother, Danny, and she crossed the street in front of the junior high school and entered the K-Mart parking lot, keeping an eye out for Danny.

Policemen's children tend to be a bit more careful than the average, are warned of dangers a bit more often. It had not saved Melissa Smith in Midvale, Utah almost four years earlier. It *would* save Leslie.

It was raining that day in Jacksonville, and Leslie Parmenter bent her head against the sprinkles that were gaining momentum. She was startled when a white van moved toward her and stopped suddenly.

A man, a man needing a shave, with dark-framed glasses, wavy dark hair, plaid slacks, and a dark navy-type jacket jumped out of the van and walked over to her, blocking her path.

The teenager saw that he had a plastic badge pinned to his jacket; it read "Richard Burton," and "Fire Department."

"I'm from the Fire Department and my name is Richard Burton," he began. "Do you go to that school over there? Someone told me you did. Are you going to the K-Mart?"

She stared at him, perplexed, and more than a little frightened. Why should it matter to him *who* she was? The man was nervous, seemed to be choosing his next words. Leslie didn't answer him; she looked around for the sight of her brother's truck, the truck that bore the name of the construction firm her father owned and Danny worked for.

The man didn't look like a fireman. He was too disheveled, and he had a strange look in his eye, a stare that made her shiver. She tried to side-step him, but he continued to block her path.

At that moment, Danny Parmenter drove into the lot. He'd stopped work early because of the rain, another factor that probably saved Leslie. He saw the white Dodge van, saw the door was open, and the driver was standing beside it talking to his sister. He didn't like the look of it.

Danny Parmenter pulled up beside the stranger and asked him what he wanted.

"Nothing," the man mumbled. He seemed agitated by the arrival of the girl's brother.

"Get in the truck," Danny said quietly to Leslie, and then he got out and walked toward the man in the plaid pants. The man backed away, and hurriedly climbed into the van. Again, Parmenter asked him what he wanted.

"Nothing . . . nothing . . . I just thought she was someone else. I was just asking her who she was."

And then the van's window was hastily rolled up, and the man drove out of the lot. Parmenter had noticed that he'd been so nervous that he was actually trembling, his voice quavering.

Danny Parmenter followed the van, then lost it in traffic, but not before he wrote down the license number: 13–D–11300.

Had Leslie not been a detective's daughter, the incident might have been forgotten, but Parmenter had a feeling in his bones when Danny and Leslie told him about what had happened that evening. The whole thing smelled bad, and he was grateful that his daughter was safe. But he didn't stop there; his whole orientation was to protect every man's daughter.

He knew that the "13" meant Leon Country way across the state. He would check it out with detectives in Tallahassee. His own duties kept him busy for most of February 9th; he would not have time to call the capital city until late afternoon.

Lake City, Florida lies about halfway between Jacksonville and Tallahassee. Pretty, dark-haired, twelve-year-old Kimberly Diane Leach lived in Lake City. She was a tiny girl, five feet tall, 100 pounds. On February 9th, she was very happy; she'd just been elected first runner-up to the Valentine Queen at Lake City Junior High School.

Thursday, February 9th was a gusty, rainy day in Lake City, but Kim was at school on time. She was there when her homeroom teacher took roll. Perhaps because she was so excited about being on the court for the Valentine's Dance, Kim forgot her purse when she left her homeroom and went to her first period P.E. class. When she *did* discover that she'd left it behind, her teacher gave her permission to go back and get it. It meant running through the rain to another building, but Kim and her friend, Priscilla Blakney, didn't mind. They ran from the back door which opens onto West St. Johns Street. They reached their homeroom without incident, and Priscilla started to follow Kim back out into the rain swept courtyard, then remembered something she had to get. When she ran after Kim, she was startled. She saw a stranger beckoning Kim toward a white car. Later, her recollections would be somewhat garbled—perhaps by her shock at Kim's fate. Had she seen Kim *in* the vehicle? Or had she only imagined it? But she had seen the man.

And Kim was gone.

Clinch Edenfield, an elderly school crossing guard, working that morning in the 35 degree chill, buffeted by winds that reached 25-miles-per-hour, had noticed a man in a white van. The van had been blocking traffic, and Edenfield saw that the driver was staring at the schoolyard. He forgot that van quickly; it was irritating—nothing more.

Clarence Lee "Andy" Anderson, a lieutenant and paramedic in the Lake City Fire Department, drove past the junior high school a few minutes later. Anderson had been working double shifts, and he had problems on his mind which distracted him. He too was annoyed that the white van was blocking traffic, and he braked behind it.

On his left, Anderson noticed a teenaged girl with long dark hair. The youngster seemed to be on the verge of tears. The girl was being led toward the van by a man who appeared to be in his early thirties, a man with a full head of wavy brown hair. The man was scowling, and Anderson had the impression that he was an angry father, retrieving a daughter who'd been sent home from school. He mused that somebody was going to get a spanking as the man pushed the girl into the passenger seat of the van, and then hurried to the driver's side, gunned the motor, and roared away.

Anderson said nothing to anyone. The incident hadn't seemed that unusual. A man called away from the job because his kid had gotten into trouble at school could be expected to be angry. The firefighter drove on to work, to the fire department which is housed in the same building as the Lake City Police Department.

Jackie Moore, the wife of a Lake City surgeon, was driving east on Highway 90 that morning, after picking her maid up. She saw a dirty white van approaching, and gasped as the van suddenly swerved into her lane, swung back, and then swerved toward her car again almost forcing her off the road. She caught a glimpse of the driver. It was a brown-haired man, a man who seemed angry, enraged. He was not looking at the road at all; he was looking down toward the passenger seat, and his mouth was open—as if he were shouting.

And then the van disappeared westbound, leaving Mrs. Moore and her maid trembling at how close they had come to a head-on collision.

Kim's parents, Thomas Leach, a landscaper, and Freda Leach, a hairdresser, went through their work day, unaware that their little girl was missing. It was late in the afternoon when the school's attendance office called Freda routinely to ask if Kim was ill. She wasn't in school.

"But Kim *is* in school," her mother answered. "I drove her there myself this morning."

"No," was the answer. "She left during first period."

The Leaches felt stark dread, something that only parents can know. They tried to hope that Kim had varied her usual dependable pattern, that she would come home after school with a good explanation. When she didn't, they hurried to Lake City Junior High School and searched the grounds. School authorities felt that Kim had run away, but her parents wouldn't believe that; she had been too excited about the Valentines's Day dance for one thing. But the most important element was that Kim simply wouldn't run away.

Kim didn't arrive home for supper, as the streets outside grew dark, and the wind whipped sheets of rain against their windows. Where *was* she?

Her parents called her best friend, all her other friends. None of them had seen Kim. Only Priscilla—who had seen her walk away toward the stranger.

The Leaches called the Lake City Police. Chief Paul Philpot tried to reassure them. The most dependable of youngsters sometimes runs away.

Even as he tried to believe what he told her frantic parents, he sent a call out to all patrolmen to watch for her. Kim was a straight A student, again, like all the others, superior in every way. She would not have run away.

The BOLO on Kimberly Leach listed the clothing she had been wearing when she was last seen: blue jeans, a football jersey with 83 on the back and chest, a long brown coat with a fake-fur collar.

Brown hair, brown eyes, pretty; she looked a few years older than her age, but she was really only a child.

Kimberly Leach was the same age that Meg Anders's daughter had been when Ted Bundy was first arrested in Utah, Meg's daughter who looked upon him as a father substitute. The same age that the little girl had been whose mother would not allow her to go out for hamburgers with Ted, the ruling that had so insulted him. "What did she think?" he'd asked me indignantly, "That I'd attack her daughter?"

That afternoon, Detective James "Lester" Parmenter in Jacksonville didn't know that Kim Leach was missing in Lake City, but he was still very concerned about the man in the white van who had approached *his* daughter. He called Detective Steve Bodiford at the Leon County Sheriff's Office.

"I need a little help. I'm trying to check out the ownership on a white Dodge van—license number 13-D-11300. The computer's got it listed to a Randall Ragan in Tallahassee. I'd like to have him checked out. Somebody with his license number frightened my daughter yesterday. I think he was trying to pick her up. She's only fourteen."

Paremeter told Bodiford of the incident in the K-Mart lot, and Bodiford agreed with it was worth following up.

He had no idea how valuable the tip was, with its far-reaching ramifications.

On Friday, February 10th, Bodiford tracked down Randy Ragan in the frame house behind Dunwoody Street, Sure, Ragan said, he'd lost his plate, on about January 12th. "I didn't report it stolen. I just got a new tag."

Bodiford noted the proximity to the Dunwoody crime scene, noted that a white Dodge van had been stolen on campus on February 5th, and put the two together.

And then he read the bulletin out of Lake City, and he felt cold; if there was a connection between the cases in Tallahassee and twelve-year-old Kimberly Leach's disappearance, he didn't want to think about the child's fate. She was alone, and the girls in Tallahassee hadn't had a chance, even surrounded by other people.

Parmenter, hearing how all the coincidences linked up, felt a chill too; his daughter had come so close. If it hadn't been for Danny's arriving just when he did. . . .

Parmenter knew that his children might hold the key to the missing stranger in the white van. He arranged for them both to be hypnotized by a fellow officer, Lieutenant Bryant Mickler. Perhaps there was something in their subconscious minds that they were blocking.

It proved to be an ordeal for Leslie Parmenter. She was a good subject for hypnosis; Leslie not only recalled the man who'd approached her—she actually relieved the experience, and she became hysterical. There was something about the man's face—this "Richard Burton, Fire Department"—that terrified her, as if she had sensed the evil there, the danger.

Parmenter explained, "When he got her to the point where she saw his face, she went hysterical. He had to stop right then and bring her out of it. She was fighting it, because she didn't want to see his face. And what happened to make her so fearful, I don't know."

A half hour after the session, still trembling and afraid, Leslie nevertheless cooperated, along with her brother, with Police Artist Donald Bryan. They worked up a composite sketch of the man with Danny and Leslie separated. First one, and then the other. Each of the young Parmenters came up with almost identical likenesses.

Later, a few days after Ted Bundy's arrest in Pensacola, Florida on February 15th, Parmenter would look at Ted's mug shots. "I thought, well, shucks. . . . you put glasses on that, and you've got a duplicate almost."

And, also a few days after Bundy's arrest, Tallahassee Investigator, W. D. "Dee" Phillips showed the Parmenter children a stack of mug shots, including one of Ted Bundy, and Danny Parmenter picked two photos. He chose Bundy's second.

Leslie Parmenter didn't hesitate at all. She picked Bundy's mug shot instantly.

"Are you sure?" Phillips asked.

"I'm positive," she answered.

But Kimberly Leach was gone. No one would find any trace of the child for eight weeks, despite a massive search that would cover four counties and nearly 2,000 square miles. Gone . . . like the others before her, young women that she had never even heard about, young women almost a continent away.

33

It was February 10, 1978, and things were closing in on Ted Bundy. Still, no one *knew* he was Ted Bundy, but the "dumb cops" whom he detested and reviled were beginning to pick up on him. He'd stalled his landlord, told him that he would have the money for the two months' rent in a day or so, and that was smoothed over for the moment, but he was planning to leave Tallahassee. He wouldn't have the money and couldn't see any way to get it.

Stake-outs by the Tallahassee Police Department and the Leon County Sheriff's Office were still beefing up the surveillance on the Florida State campus. Some of the cars were marked; some were not.

Roy Dickey, a six-and-a-half-year veteran of the Tallahassee force, sat in his patrol car near the intersection of Dunwoody Street and St. Augustine at 10:45 P.M. on the night of the 10th. He'd been there for two or three hours, and he was getting bored. Stake-outs are tiresome, muscle cramping, and often nonproductive. Occasionally, he talked by walkie-talkie with Officer Don Ford who eatched and waited on the corner of Pensacola and Woodward.

And then Dickey saw a man walking toward the intersection, a man who had come from the Florida State stadium and driving range area. The man was in hurry. He walked east on St. Augustine, and then cut north on Dunwoody, before disappearing between Cheryl Thomas's duplex and the house next to it.

The man wore blue jeans, a red quilted vest, a blue cap, and jogging shoes. As he passed under the street light on the corner, he looked over at the patrol car—briefly—and Dickey saw his face clearly.

Later, when he saw a picture of Ted Bundy, Dickey would recognize him as the man who'd passed him so casually.

Leon County Deputy Keith Daws was working surveillance on the next shift—midnight to 4:00 A.M.—in an unmarked Chevy Chevelle. It was now the early morning of February 11th—1:47 to be exact.

Daws turned onto West Jefferson near the Chi Omega House and saw a "white male fiddling with a car door" up ahead of him. Daws eased his car up to where the man was bending over the door of a Toyota. When he saw the deputy's car in the middle of the street, the man stood up and looked around.

Daws identified himself and asked, "What are you doing?"

"I came down to get my book."

Daws saw that the man had a key in his hand . . . but no book.

"Maybe I'm stupid or something," the deputy drawled. "But you say you've come to get your book, and you don't have no book."

"It's on the dash on the other side of the car," the man answered easily.

Daws studied him. He looked to be in his late twenties, wore blue jeans that looked brand new, an orange-red quilted "lining" vest. When he kept over with the key, the deputy could see there was no wallet in the back pocket of the jeans. The brown-haired man also looked "wasted. . . . completely exhausted."

There *was* a book on the passenger side dashboard, but the man said he had no I.D. He'd just come down from his room. He hadn't parked on West College Avenue where he lived because all the spots were filled.

That made sense; parking on campus was tight. First come, first serve.

Daws shined his flashlight into the green Toyota's interior, and saw that the seat and floorboards were covered with papers. He saw the tiny tip of a license tag under the papers on the floor.

"Whose tag is that?"

"What tag?" The man was fumbling with the papers and his hand hit the tag.

"That tag you've got your hand on."

The man in the vest handed the tag to Daws, explaining that he'd found it somewhere, and never thought that someone might miss it.

The tag read, 13–D–11300.

Daws didn't recognize the number, but he routinely walked over to his car radio to check it with "Wants and Warrants" for stolen. He left the man standing by the Toyota. Daws had one hand on his microphone and the tag in the other.

And then the man suddenly sprinted, running across the street, between two apartment houses, and leaping over a retaining wall.

Daws was caught by surprise. The man had seemed to be cooperative. He would later ruefully describe the scene to a Miami jury. "The last time I saw him, I could have hit him with a baseball. You're talking about the width of this courtroom."

The runner had leapt over the retaining wall, directly into the back yard of the Oak . . . and disappeared.

The tag, of course, was registered to Randy Ragan, but, when Daws went to Ragan's house, he was obviously not the same individual who had run from the deputy. The man who had "rabbited" was later picked out of a photo line-up by Daws; it was Ted Bundy.

Daws, whose frustration at the near-miss was still evident when he testified in court, was even more disgusted when he read the next morning of the search for a Dodge van. There had been a white Dodge van with a flat tire parked—illegally—just behind the Toyota that the suspect was unlocking. When the detectives returned to look for it, it was gone.

34

The man later identified as Ted Bundy had leapt over the retaining wall backing on the Oak and disappeared in those early morning hours of February 11th. His landlord, who knew him, of course, as Chris Hagen saw him on the 11th and noticed that he seemed "tired—like he'd really been through it . . ."

Ted's stay at the Oak—and in Tallahassee itself—was about to end, but first, on the evening of February 11th, he treated himself to one last meal at the Chez Pierre in the Adams Street Mall, a meal where the tab for the French cuisine and wine came to $18.50. He paid for it with one of the stolen credit cards, also charging a $2.00 tip.

The waitresses at the Chez Pièrre remember him because he had such "a cold air about him. He kept to himself. You couldn't make conversation with him. He ordered good wine. One night, he drank a full bottle and on another occasion he ordered a bottle of sparkling white wine and drank half of it."

Ted had always liked good wine.

On February 12th, he gathered up the possessions he'd accumulated; he had considerably more paraphernalia to carry with him than he'd had when he arrived in Tallahassee on January 8th—the television set, the bicycle, his racquet ball equipment. He gave a box of cookies to a girl down the hall, and he left.

He had wiped the room down completely. Later, detectives would find *no* fingerprints at all, no sign that anyone had spent a month in room number 12 at the Oak.

The white Dodge van, stolen from the Audio-Visual Department, was no longer useful; he abandoned it in front of 806 West Georgia Street in Tallahassee. On February 13th, it would be spotted and recognized by Chris Cochranne, an Audio-Visual employee, and would be taken in by police for meticulous processing. The van was covered with a thick layer of dust and dirt—except for the area around the door handles and on the passenger door. There, the technicians processing the vehicle found "wipe marks" as if someone had deliberately tried to remove fingerprints.

Doug Barrow, fingerprint expert for the Florida Department of Criminal Law Enforcement, also found wipe marks on some of the windows, and on the arm rests and in other spots inside the filthy van. In other parts of the van he was able to lift fifty-seven latent prints—prints which all proved to have been left by Audio-Visual employees.

There was so much dirt, so many leaves and particles of vegetable debris, in the back part of the van that it looked as if it had been placed there to obliterate whatever might be on the carpet beneath. And through this pile of soil and leaves, there remained the imprint of something heavy, something that had been dragged from the van.

Serologist Stephens found two large dried bloodstains smeared on the synthetic carpeting, an unusual carpeting made up of green, blue, turquoise, and black man-made fibers. The stains proved to be from a person with type B blood. Mary Lynn Hinson, a crime lab expert in cloth fibers, was able to isolate a great many fiber strands which were caught and twisted in the van's carpet. She also photographed some distinct footprints in the pile of dirt—footprints left by a pair of loafers and by a pair of running shoes.

The criminalists had weeks of work ahead of them, and most of that work would have to wait until they had some shoes, some blood, some fibers for comparison purposes. Police didn't know the man they sought, and they didn't have Kim Leach's body, or the clothes she had worn when she disappeared. Nor could they know the significance of two small bright orange price tags found caught under the front seat of the van. One read $24, and the other, stuck on top of it, read $26. The store name was Green Acre Sporting Goods, a sports equipment company with seventy-five outlets in Alabama, Georgia, and Florida. Detective J.D. Sewell was assigned to find *which* store used that reddish-orange type of price sticker, that marking pencil, and what item might have sold for $24 or $26.

Ted had always favored Volkswagen bugs; on that last day in Tallahassee, he spotted a little orange VW, a car belonging to a young man named Ricky Garzaniti, a construction worker for Sun

Trail Construction. Garzaniti would report to police that someone had stolen his car on February 12th from 529 East Georgia Street.

The keys had been in it; it was a sitting duck for Ted. He had a stolen tag, a tag he'd taken off another Volkswagen in Tallahassee: 13–D–0743. He stowed his Raleigh bike and the television set in the back, and left Florida's capital city for what he fully expected would be the last time.

This time, he headed not east, but west. At nine the next morning, a desk clerk, Betty Jean Barnhill, in the Holiday Inn in Crestview, 150 miles west of Tallahassee, had an argument with a man who'd arrived in an orange Volkswagen. When he'd finished his breakfast, he'd attempted to pay for it with a Gulf credit card, a card bearing a woman's name. When he started to sign the woman's name to the charge slip, she told him that he couldn't do that. He became so angered that he threw the card in her face and left hurriedly. Later, when she perused articles about the arrest of Ted Bundy, she recognized him as the man who'd been so furious.

There are no sightings reported of Ted Bundy and the orange car between 9:00 A.M. on February 13th and 1:30 A.M. on the morning of February 15th.

David Lee, a patrolman in the city of Pensacola, a city so far west that it is almost in Alabama, was working "third watch" on February 14–15th—8 P.M. to 4 A.M.—in West Pensacola. He knew his area well, knew the closing hours of most of the businesses in his sector.

Lee's attention was drawn to an orange Volkswagen bug emerging from an alley near the Oscar Warner's Restaurant. On that Tuesday evening, Lee knew that Warner's had closed at 10:00 P.M. He also knew what the vehicles of all the employees looked like. There was a driveway all around the building, with the alley leading up to the restaurant's rear door. When the officer first saw the bug, he thought it might have been the cook's—but then saw it was not.

Lee did a U-turn and came back; the Volkswagen cruised slowly as the squad car pulled in behind it. There had been no violations; at this point, Lee was simply curious to see who was driving, since the alley up to the restaurant was not a short cut.

He picked up his microphone and requested a "Wants and Warrants" check on the license plate. Then he flicked on his blue lights, signaling the Volkswagen to pull over; the tag came back: stolen.

As the lazy blue beam revolved atop Lee's cruiser, the orange car ahead picked up speed. The chase continued for a mile, over the line into Escambia County, with speeds up to sixty miles per hour. Just past the intersection of Cross and West Douglas Streets, the Volkswagen pulled over.

Lee drew his service revolver and walked up to the driver's side; he suspected there was someone else in the front seat. He was wary, and his back-ups were far behind him.

Ted Bundy's life has a way of running in circles. Once before, he had raced away from a policeman in a Volkswagen; once before, he had finally pulled over. That had been way back in August of 1975, way back in Utah. This was Pensacola, Florida and the officer ordering him out of the car had a deep southern drawl . Otherwise, it was almost a repeat. Only this time Ted was at the end of his rope. This time he would fight.

David Lee was a year younger, and about twenty pounds huskier than Ted, but his attention was divided between the man who sat in the driver's seat and the possibility that someone else was hidden in the car. He knew that was the way most cops got killed.

He ordered Ted out and told him to lie face down on the pavement. Ted refused, and Lee couldn't see his hands. Finally, Ted obeyed, but as Lee handcuffed his prone suspect's left wrist, Ted suddenly rolled over and kicked Lee's feet out from under him, and then hit the officer. Now, Ted was on top of the scramble of arms and legs.

Lee still had his revolver out; he fired one round—straight up— to get the suspect off him.

And then Ted was running south on West Douglas Street. Lee was right behind him, shouting "Halt! Halt or I'll shoot!"

Ted made the intersection and turned left on Cross Street. His only response to Lee's shouts was to turn to the left slightly. Lee saw something in his left hand; he'd forgotten about the handcuff in the excitement of the moment and thought the man he was chasing had a gun. He fired another round, this time directly at the suspect.

Ted hit the ground, and Lee thought he'd hit him. The officer ran up to see how badly the runner was injured, and his quarry came up fighting again. He hadn't been hit at all, and he was struggling to grab Lee's gun. The fight lasted for a long time, at least it seemed a long time to Lee.

Someone was yelling "Help!" over and over. Lee was startled to realize it was the suspect.

As he recalled the incident later in court, he would comment, "*I* was hoping there was help coming for *me*. Some guy came out of his house and asked me what *I* was doing to the man on the ground. I was in uniform, too."

Finally, Lee's strength prevailed and he managed to subdue the suspect and cuff his hands behind his back.

He had not the slightest idea in the world that he had just arrested one of the FBI's Ten-Most-Wanted criminals.

Lee took the man to his patrol car, read him his rights under Miranda, and headed for the station. The suspect, all the fight gone out of him, seemed strangely depressed. He kept repeating, "I wish you had killed me."

As they neared the jail, he turned to Lee and asked, "If I run from you at the jail, then will you kill me?"

Lee was puzzled; the man wasn't drunk, and he'd only been arrested for possession of a stolen vehicle. He couldn't understand the black, suicidal mood that had suddenly gripped his prisoner.

Detective Norman M. Chapman, Jr. was on call that night. Chapman is a man with a voice like warm maple syrup. If he weighed fifty pounds more, the dark-haired, moustachioed, detective would look like Oliver Hardy's twin; if he weighed fifty pounds less, he could double for Burt Reynolds. When he walked into Pensacola headquarters at 3:00 A.M. on February 15th, he saw the suspect lying on the floor asleep. He woke the prisoner and took him upstairs to an interview room, where he read him his rights again from a Miranda warning card.

The suspect nodded and gave his name: Kenneth Raymond Misner.

"Misner" had three complete sets of identification, all in the names of coeds, twenty-one stolen credit cards, a stolen television set, a stolen car, stolen tags, the bicycle. He gave his address as 509 West College Avenue, Tallahassee.

"Ken Misner" agreed to a recorded statement. He appeared somewhat the worse for wear; he had scratches and bruises on his lips and cheeks, blood on the back of his shirt. He signed his rights' waivers, and admitted that he had stolen the credit cards from women's pocket books, the car, and license tags. He'd stolen the ID's from taverns. Why had he attacked Officer Lee? That was simple enough: he'd wanted to get away.

At 6:30 A.M. on February 15th, the interrogation was stopped when "Misner" requested a physician. He was taken to a hospital for treatment of his injuries—injuries that were limited to the cuts and bruises. Then he slept through the morning back in jail.

In Tallahassee, 200 miles away, the *real* Ken Misner was astounded to learn of his "arrest." The F.S.U. track star had had no idea, of course, that someone had appropriated his name, his life.

Tallahassee Detective Don Patchen, and Leon County Detective Steve Bodiford drove to Pensacola on the afternoon of the 15th; they knew the prisoner was not Misner, but they didn't know who he really was, only that he had some connections in their jurisdiction. They talked briefly with the suspect, saw that he was in good condition, but exhausted. "We know you're not Ken Misner," they told him. "We'd like to know who you are."

He refused to tell them, but said he would talk to them the next morning. At 7:15 A.M. on February 16th, the still unidentified prisoner listened to his rights, and again signed the waivers, "Kenneth Misner." He was quite willing to discuss the thefts. He admitted stealing the credit cards: Master Charge, Exxon, Sunoco, Gulf, Bankamericard, Shell, Phillips 66, many copies of each with different names. He couldn't remember exactly where he'd gotten them, but most of them had come from purses and billfolds in shopping malls and taverns in Tallahassee. Some of the names were familiar; some were not. There had been so many.

The interview ended as Bodiford said, "State your name."

The suspect laughed. "Who *me*? Kenneth R. Misner. John R. Doe."

The still unknown prisoner asked to make some phone calls. He wanted to call an attorney in Atlanta, explaining that he wanted advice on just when he should reveal his true identity, and what plea he should make.

The attorney was Millard O. Farmer, a well-known criminal defense lawyer whose particular area of expertise is the defense of those indicated in homicide cases where the death penalty was involved. Farmer allegedly told Ted that an associate would fly down to Pensacola the next day and that he could give his name then, but not to admit to anything.

Until that unveiling, Ted requested that he be allowed to call friends, that no news of his arrest or his identity be released until the next morning, the 17th.

Ted placed a call sometime after 4:30 P.M. on February 16th—a call to John Henry Browne, his old lawyer-friend in Seattle. Browne learned that Ted was in Pensacola, that he'd been arrested, but that no one knew who he was yet. Browne found Ted's condition distraught, had difficulty in eliciting the facts. It took Ted three or four minutes to explain why he was in custody, and Ted didn't much want to talk about that; he wanted instead to talk about the old days in Seattle, to learn what was happening in his hometown.

Browne told him a dozen times not to talk to anyone without the advice of an attorney. Given Ted's rambling state of mind, he felt that Ted would jeopardize himself if he talked to detectives. Ted had always listened to Browne's advice before. That all changed on February 16th. Ted didn't seem to be listening any longer.

Pensacola Public Defender, Terry Turrell, went to Ted's cell at 5:00 P.M. and stayed with him until 9:45 P.M. He could see the man was caving in; his head was bowed, he was crying, smoking cigarettes one after another.

During the time Turrell spent with Ted, Ted made several long distance phone calls—to whom Ted wouldn't say.

And, strangely for a former Protestant, a somewhat-failed Mormon, Ted requested to see a Catholic priest. Father Michael Moody was closeted with him for awhile, and then left, carrying with him whatever privileged information Ted may or may not have given him.

Pensacola detectives say that they shared hamburgers and French fries with him that evening, that he ate. I don't know.

I only know that the carefully constructed facade was cracking apart, falling away in shards of despair. I know, because I talked to Ted Bundy several hours later; for the first time, he wanted to loosen a terrible burden from his soul.

35

On that Thursday night, February 16, 1978, I was in my apartment in Los Angeles. Somehow, the news of Ted's arrest had filtered out to the Northwest news sources—even before Pensacola and Tallahassee detectives knew for sure who they had. Ted was being interrogated in Pensacola when my father called me from Salem, Oregon about 11:00 P.M. (Pacific Coast Time) and told me, "They've caught Ted Bundy in Pensacola, Florida. It's on the news up here."

I was shocked, relieved, incredulous—and then, I remembered the single clipping I'd seen about the Chi Omega murders in Florida. I looked at my mother, who had just flown down that day to attend a premiere with me the next night, and said, "They've caught Ted . . . and he *was* in Florida."

That was all the information I had. The details—all the details of the Florida cases—would become known to me over the next eighteen months, but I had a terrible feeling that Ted Bundy was inextricably bound up with those murders on the campus of Florida State University. Until that point, I had always nourished a small hope that the police, the media, the public, might be wrong in their assumption that Ted was a killer. Now, knowing he was in Florida, that hope crumbled. I fell asleep, and dreamed—not dreams, but haunting nightmares.

I was awakened by the shrill ring of the phone just beside the couch where I slept in the one-room apartment. I fumbled for the phone in the dark.

A deep, distinctly southern voice asked if I was Ann Rule. I said I was, and he told me he was Detective Norman Chapman of the Pensacola Police Department.

"Will you speak to Theodore Bundy?"

"Of course. . . ." I looked at the clock. It was 3:14 A.M.

Ted's voice came on the line. He sounded weary, disturbed, confused.

"Ann . . . I don't know what to do. They've been talking to me. We've been talking a lot. I'm trying to decide what I should do."

"Are you all right? Are they treating you all right?"

"Oh yeah . . . we've got coffee, cigarettes . . . they're O.K. I just don't know what I should do."

Perhaps because I had been roused from a sound sleep, because *I* had no time to think, I responded with the honesty that can come with surprise; I decided the time had come to face whatever facts had to be faced.

"Ted," I began. "It's been a long time, and I think maybe now it's time to get it all out. I think maybe you should tell someone about it . . . all of it . . . someone who understands you, someone who's been your friend. Do you want to do that?"

"Yes . . . yes . . . can you come? I need help . . ."

In a sense, it was a call I had expected for years—ever since I'd learned that Ted had called me that midnight in November of 1974, when he had been obviously disturbed about something. That had been after the last victim—Debby Kent—had vanished in Utah. I had always felt since that Ted knew I knew that he could tell me the terrible things bottled up in his mind, and that I could take it. Was this the call?

I told him that I thought I could come, but that I didn't have enough money for a plane ticket, didn't even know when planes left Los Angeles for Florida. "I can find the money—someplace— and I'll get there as soon as I can."

"I think they'll pay for your plane ticket from here," he said. "I think they want you to come too."

"O.K. Let me have a cup of coffee and get my head together. I'll check with the airlines, and I'll call you back in a few minutes. Give me the number where you are."

He gave me the number, the number in the captain's office in the Pensacola Police Department, and then we hung up.

I immediately called the airlines, found I could get a plane out early in the morning, and would get to Pensacola, via Atlanta, the next afternoon. I felt Detective Chapman wanted me to be there; why else would he have called me? I later learned he had contacted my babysitter in Seattle on my home phone, and had had to put his captain on the line before my sitter would release my number. They had gone to a lot of trouble to find me.

Yet, when I tried to call back to the interrogation room only minutes later, I was told by the desk sergeant that no calls were being allowed in! I explained that I had just talked to Norm Chapman and Ted Bundy and that they were expecting my call, but the answer was still no.

I was completely mystified until I received a phone call 30 hours later from Ron Johnson, an Assistant Florida State Attorney. "I want you to come. I think you should come, but the detectives here want three days to get a confession from Ted Bundy. Then, if they don't get one, they will send for you."

They never did. I would never see any of those involved until I walked into Ted's Miami trial in July of 1979. And only then would I learn what had occurred during that long, long night of February 16–17, 1978, and in the days that followed. Some of the interrogation was on tape, an hours'-long tape played aloud in the Miami pretrial hearing. Some of it came out in preliminary hearings, testified to by the detectives themselves, these men who spent so many hours closeted with Ted: Norm Chapman, Steve Bodiford, Don Patchen, and Captain Jack Pointinger.

If I had been allowed to talk to Ted during those first days after his arrest in Pensacola, would things have been any different? Would there now be more answers? Or would I have flown to Florida only to be met with the same evasive, meandering statements that Ted gave to the detectives?

I will never know.

36

Detective Norm Chapman of the Pensacola Police Department is a most likable man. There is much evidence that Ted liked him; it would be hard not to. I think the man is sincere, that his earthy, "good-ole-boy" quality is genuine, and I think he wanted desperately to find out what had happened to Kimberly Leach, for her parents' sake. And he wanted to clear up the murders and beatings in Tallahassee. I think he also had self-aggrandizing motivations, just as we all do. For a cop with six years' experience on a department stuck way up in the panhandle of Florida to elicit a confession from one of the most infamous fugitives in America would be something to remember. The detectives' decision to block my phone call and my presence in Florida may have been the right one; it may have been tragically wrong.

In July, 1979, Norm Chapman sat on the witness stand in Judge Edward Cowart's Dade County courtroom, his shoulders and belly straining at his sports jacket, his white socks visible beneath his slacks. He was not a braggart. He was what he seemed to be, a smiling, garrulous man, a man who carried a tape that would electrify the courtroom.

Late on the evening of February 16th, Ted had sent word to Norm Chapman that he wanted to talk, and talk without counsel. The tape of that long conversation with Chapman, Bodiford, and Patchen began at 1:29 A.M. on February 17th. Ted's voice is strong, confident.

"O.K. Let's see: it's been a long day—but I had a good night's sleep last night and I'm coherent. I've seen a doctor, called a lawyer."

If Ted had expected a grand hurrah when he revealed that he was Theodore Robert Bundy, he was to be disappointed. The three detectives had never heard of him. It was anticlimatic. What good did it do a man to be one of the most hunted fugitives in America if there was such a blank response when he finally announced who he was? It wasn't until Officer Lee walked in with a copy of the FBI Ten-Most-Wanted flyer (to have Ted autograph it) that they really believed him.

Chapman offers, "We'll listen—whatever you want to talk about . . ."

Ted laughs. "It is a bit formal."

"Anytime you get tired of our worn-out faces, just say so," Chapman says.

"I'm in charge of entertainment . . ." Ted begins.

"You got plenty of cigarettes?"

"Yeah. . . . It was a big deal not to tell my name . . ."

"I think we all understand since you told us. We can see why you were reluctant. I must admit you kept your cool—standing before the judge and not telling your name. It's more than I could do."

"You know my background?"

"Only what you told me. I deal on a one-to-one basis. We'll listen."

"The name business is a good way to start. I just knew the kind of publicity—if I got arrested in Omaha, Nebraska . . . I knew it was inevitable you'd discover my I.D. picture. I'd gone through such an effort, so much to get free the first time, it seemed like such a waste to give up so easily."

Chapman says he's interested in hearing about Ted's escapes. And Ted is so anxious to tell about them. So clever, so well-thought-out, and then he'd been unable to tell anyone. It is ironic that it is to policemen—the "stupid cops" he's put down for so long—that he finally talks.

There is frequent laughter on the tape as he starts at the beginning with the leap for freedom from the Pitkin County Courthouse and continues through until he reaches Tallahassee. His voice drops and he takes deep breaths as he berates himself for not finding a job. He mentions how much he enjoyed playing racquet ball and offers to sign permission for his stolen car to be searched. And then his voice breaks.

"You start crying in certain areas, like when you're talking about racquet ball," Chapman comments.

"It was just so good to be around people, to be a part of people. I have a habit that makes me want to acquire things—little things. I had a nice apartment in law school, and it was all taken away from me. I told myself I could live without cars and bicycles and stuff—just being free was enough—but I wanted things."

More tears . . . his voice is choked as he describes stealing himself for being so stupid. "I never got a job. It was really stupid. I do like to work but I'm just reluctant to get a job. It was a terrible time not to get a job."

Chapman asks Ted if he's ever been to Sherrod's in Tallahassee.

"I never went there until a week and a half ago. The sound's unbearable in there; it's a disco."

"You ever crash fraternity or sorority parties for free beer or food?"

"No, I had a bad experience that way a long time ago. I walked in with a friend and there was a belligerent drunk. I was able to run fast enough."

"You remember Rush Week—the beer busts out on the lawns in January?"

"Yeah, I heard noise from some frats close to where I live."

"What did you do at night? Walk around?"

"I'd go to the library. I made a point of going to bed early. Once I had the TV, I'd stay in my room 'cause I had something to do."

Asked to describe his Saturday nights, Ted veers away. He does not remember stealing a license tag around January 12th or 13th, but he remembers one tag stolen six days after he got to Tallahassee, a tag from an orange and white van.

Asked if he'd ever wiped his prints off the cars he'd stolen, he replied with surprise, "Well . . . I wore gloves, just leather gloves."

Tears brim in his eyes, blur his words.

"Anything else in Tallahassee you can clear up for us?"

More tears . . . his voice is choked as he described stealing the neglected Raleigh bicycle. It seems to be an almost animate companion.

"I asked you about a white van—taken off campus . . ."

"I really can't talk about it."

"Why?"

"Just because I can't talk about it." Ted is crying.

"Because you didn't take it, or . . ."

Ted's voice is muffled by sobs. "I just can't . . . it's a situations—"

Chapman quickly shifts gears, changing the subject to Ted's arrest in Utah. Ted explains he got one to fifteen on a kidnapping charge.

"Man or woman?"

"Oh well . . . it's all so complicated. I thought you'd have all that background by now. I was in prison from March to late October, 1976, in Utah when the murder charge came down from Colorado."

The detectives take a picture, and someone asks, "What's your best profile? Hell, you made the top ten last week . . ."

"They'll take credit for my arrest."

"You don't like the FBI?"

They're overrated bastards."

Chapman asks Ted about happened in Colorado.

Standard Oil slips . . . I don't really understand how that came down. Oh yeah. . . . I had bought gas in Glenwood Springs the same day Caryn Campbell disappeared from Aspen about fifty miles away. If the bells rang before, they were *clanging*—especially since the Washington situation. I had a lot of connections in Washington—Governor's office, etc. The pressure was really on."

"What kind of homicide was it?"

"Well, I know because it was communicated to me—they were young women. The captain of King County Homicide was under pressure—but they never questioned me. They had no evidence."

"What kind of murders were they?"

"No one knows because the parts are scattered."

"How about Colorado?"

"I saw the autopsy pictures. Blunt trauma and strangulation . . ."

"In what way?"

"I don't know."

Chapman switches gears again, asking Ted if he ever went in sorority houses to take wallets.

"No . . . too much risk. Too much security. I'd assume they'd have locks, lock devices, sound systems . . ."

At this point, Ted requests that the tape recorder be turned off; he asks that no notes be taken.

According to Detective Chapman's courtroom testimony, a "bug" had been activated in the interrogation room—a bug that failed to record.

In Washington State, such surreptitious recording of an interview would have made the whole interrogation tainted; in Florida, no.

The interrogation went on throughout the night, and Bodiford, Patchen, and Chapman insist that Ted made statements that were far more damaging than those captured on any tape. Judge Cowart would eventually rule that *none* of the statements Ted Bundy made on the night of February 16–17, 1978, would be admitted into the Miami trial, but the conversation that is alleged to have taken place *after* the recorder was turned off is the most chilling.

The three detectives say that Ted told them he was a night person—"a vampire," and that he'd been a "voyeur—a peeping Tom." He said he had never "done anything" but that his voyeurism had to do with his fantasies.

He had apparently described one girl to them, a girl who had walked down a street in Seattle years before, when he was in law school in Tacoma. "I felt I had to have her at any cost. I didn't act on it though."

He had allegedly discussed a "problem," a problem that surfaced after he'd been drinking and driving around, a problem having to do with his fantasies.

"Listen," he said, after the tape was off. "I want to talk to you, but I've built up such a block so that I could never tell. You talk to me."

"Do you want to talk about the Chi Omega murders?"

"The evidence is there. Don't quit digging for it."

"Did you kill those girls?"

"I don't want to lie to you, but, if you force an answer, it would be a no."

"Did you ever act out your fantasies?"

"They were taking over my life . . ."

Bodiford asked again, "Did you ever carry out your fantasies?"

"The act itself was a downer . . ."

"Did you ever go to the Chi Omega House? Did you kill the girls?"

"I don't want to have to lie to you . . ."

There were more statements alleged to have been made by Ted that night and the next. One must decide whether to believe police detectives or Ted Bundy as to their authenticity.

According to the FBI information and several reporters who were deluging the Pensacola detectives with calls, they had caught a man suspected of thirty-six murders, a figure they found hard to believe.

When Chapman asked him about that during the post-taping conversation, Ted had reportedly replied, "Add one digit to that and you'll have it."

What had he meant? Was he being sarcastic? Did he mean *thirty-seven* murders? Or, no, it couldn't be ... did he mean a hundred or more murders?

The FBI figure had included several unsolved cases pulled in from left field, including some in northern California—cases that the detectives who'd dogged his trail didn't believe had strong links to Ted. But, off the record, Ted reputedly hinted to the Florida detectives that there were *six* states who would be very interested in him. *Six?* They say he talked of making a deal, of wanting to give information in return for his life, that he felt he had things in his mind that would be invaluable to psychiatric research. None of these statements is on tape, and, just as Ted seemed to approach specifics, the investigators say he backed off, teasing them, offering the "carrot," only to retreat.

When the statement "Add one digit to that and you'll have it," filtered down to Washington detectives, they immediately thought of two long-unsolved cases in their state.

In August of 1961, when Ted was fifteen, nine-year-old Ann Marie Burr vanished forever from her home in Tacoma, a home that was only ten blocks from the Bundy residence. Ann Marie had awakened during the night and told her parents that her little sister was ill. Then the freckled, blonde child had presumably gone back to bed. But, in the morning, Ann Marie was gone, and a window fronting the street was found wide open. She had been wearing only a nightgown when she disappeared.

Despite a tremendous investigation, headed by Tacoma Police Detective Tony Zatkovitch, no trace of Ann Marie was ever found. The former Tacoma detective remembers that the street in front of her home was torn up for repaving on the night she disappeared, and wonders if her small body was buried hastily in the deep ditches, to be covered over with tons of earth and asphalt in the days that followed. Now retired, Zatkovitch says that the name of Ted Bundy was never listed in the endless roster of suspects.

On June 23, 1966, Seattle homicide detectives had a case which matches the M.O. of the cases Ted is suspected of very, very closely. Lisa Wick and Lonnie Trumbull, both twenty, lived in a basement apartment on Queen Anne Hill with another girl. They were all United Airlines flight attendants, and all extremely attractive. The third girl was not at home on Wednesday, the 23rd, because she spent the night with another stewardess. Lonnie Trumbull was dating a King County deputy sheriff, and he saw her late in the afternoon, called her at ten that night. The pretty brunette, daughter of a Portland, Oregon Fire Department lieutenant, told her friend that everything was fine and that she and Lisa were about to retire.

When Lonnie's and Lisa's rommate returned the next morning at 9:30, she found the door unlocked—a very unusual circumstance—and a light on. When she walked into her friends' bedroom, she found them still lying in their twin beds, but they didn't respond to her greeting. Puzzled, she turned on the light.

"I looked at Lonnie and I didn't believe my eyes. Then I started to wake Lisa ... and she was in the same state," the girl told Detectives John Leitch, Dick Reed, and Wayne Dorman.

Lonnie Trumbull was dead, her head and face covered with blood. Her skull had been fractured with a blunt instrument. Lisa Wick was comatose. She too had been battered on the head, but physicians at Harborview Hospital speculated she had survived because the curlers she wore had absorbed some of the force of the blows. Neither girl had been sexually assaulted, and neither had struggled; they had been attacked as they slept. There were no signs of forced entry and nothing had been stolen.

Joyce Johnson sat beside Lisa Wick's hospital bed for days, listening for something the critically injured girl might say if and when she came out of her coma. Lisa did recover, but she had no memory of what had happened. She had gone to bed and awakened days later in the hospital.

The Seattle detectives found the death weapon in a vacant lot just south of the apartment building; it was a piece of wood eighteen inches long and three inches square and it was covered with blood and hair. The case remains today in the unsolved file of the Seattle Police Department.

Ted Bundy was twenty years old that summer, and, sometime in the summer of 1966, he had moved to Seattle to begin attending classes at the University of Washington. A year later, he worked in the Safeway store on Queen Anne Hill.

There are no other matches—nothing beyond proximity and M.O.—but both the Burr cases of the Wick-Trumbull cases came to investigators' minds when they heard of that throwaway remark Ted Bundy made on February 17, 1978.

Leon County Chief of Detectives, Jack Poitinger, would give a deposition to the defense team in which he recalled that Ted had told him a day later he had a desire to cause great bodily harm to females. Poitinger had asked him why he had such a proclivity for stealing Volkswagens, and he'd said it was because they got good gas mileage.

"Well, come on, Ted. What else is there about it?"

"Well, you can take out the front seat."

There was a hesitation on Ted's part, and Poitinger said, "It might be easy to carry someone in the car that way."

"I don't like to use that terminology."

The detectives and the suspect fished around for a word that would suit, and came up with "cargo."

"It's easier to carry cargo in them."

"Why is it easy to carry cargo?"

"You can control it better. . . ."

According to Poitinger's deposition, Ted had indicated that he preferred to end up in some sort of an institution in Washington State. An institution where he might be "studied."

"Studied for what?"

Poitinger, responding later to questioning by a Boundy defense attorney, Mike Minerva, said "I think the gist of the conversation was that his problem was that he had a desire to cause great bodily harm to females."

Chapman, whom Ted seemed to favor, asked, "Ted, if you will tell me where the body (of Kimberly Leach) is, I will go and get it and let the parents know that the child is dead."

"I cannot do that because the site (sight?) is too horrible to look at."

When Ted was subsequently transfered to the Leon Country Jail in Tallahassee in a tightly guarded caravan of cars, Detective Don Patchen asked him again, "Is the little girl dead?"

"Well, you gentlemen knew that you were getting involved with a pretty strange creature and you have known that for a few days."

"We need your help in finding Kim's body so that her parents can at least bury her and go on with their lives."

According to Patchen, Ted raised up in his chair, crumpled a pack of cigarettes and threw it on the floor, saying, "But I'm the most cold-hearted son-of-a-bitch you'll ever meet."

If all the off-the-record, and off-the-tape remarks made by Ted Bundy are to be given weight, there is, indeed, a side to the man never revealed to anyone but his alleged victims—and they cannot talk.

Norm Chapman swears that Ted did make those remarks, and that, at one point when Chapman accompanied him to the bathroom on February 17th, Ted had indicated he didn't *want* to talk to his Public Defenders, Terry Turrell and Elizabeth Nicholas.

"He said, 'Norman, you gotta get me away from those S.O.B.'s because they're trying to tell me not to tell you things I want to tell you.' He said he was wanting to tell us about him and his personality, his 'problem,' because the fantasies were taking over his life. He worked with people with emotional problems and he couldn't discuss *his* with anyone. He said to keep his fantasies going, he had to do acts against society. We presumed his 'problem' had to do with death. He said when he got into his 'lawyer' personality, he would talk to the Public Defenders and we should realize what a big concession it was for him to talk this way. He kept saying he didn't want to lie to us, but, if we forced him, he'd have to. He said this many times. I told him that I couldn't tell his P.D.'s to go away. He'd have to do that himself."

It was 6:15 A.M. (Florida time) when Ted called me on the morning of February 17th, telling me he wanted to get it all out, to talk. His Public Defenders waited outside the interrogation room and say that they were not allowed to see him until 10:00 A.M. At that time, they say they found him weeping, distraught, and rambling in his speech.

That evening Elizabeth Nicholas went to the Escambia Country Jail and demanded again to see Ted, telling the jailer she had an order for sleeping pills for Ted. The jailer blocked her way, and she called the judge. The jailer was furious and said he had the right to search her.

"I hope you have a woman to do it," she said.

"Listen, lady, there are naked men up there," the jailer hedged.

"Then I just won't look," she retorted.

She was allowed up into the jail area and saw that Ted was sleeping soundly.

In pretrial, eighteen months later, Ted Bundy testified that he had only fuzzy recall of that morning, and that he most certainly would have seen his attorneys if he'd known they were outside the interrogation room.

There had been a tug-of-war over the prisoner between detectives and Public Defenders. Just which group Ted really wanted to talk to—if either—is another area that remains clouded.

37

I had tried for most of that Friday, February 17, 1978, to get through to Ted, and, of course, I had met a brick wall in Pensacola, Florida. That Friday night should have been exciting for me; my first Hollywood premiere. I was guest of the director of the film—who was also my collaborator on a new movie script—and there were so many movie stars. It would have been grist for letter to send back to Seattle to my deluded friends who visualized my life in Los Angeles as something more exotic than it really was. Instead, it was all ashes. I kept hearing Ted's terrified voice, a call for help from 3,000 miles away.

I knew what he wanted, although he had not said it outright. He wanted to come home. He was ready, at that point, to confess it all, if only he could come back to Washington to be confined in a mental hospital. He had called me because he had no place else to go, because the running was over. There were no more corners in his mind where he could go to forget, and he was frightened.

I tried, literally, to save his life. I began to phone Washington state agencies to try to arrange something that would allow Ted to confess to me, and, through plea bargaining, to be returned to Washington for confinement in a mental hospital. All of Saturday, I was on the phone. First, I called Nick Mackie at home and asked if he could intervene, if he could call Chapman or Poitinger and explain that it was likely that Ted would talk to me, and that that as what the Washington contingent of investigators wanted. Mackie said he would contact Senior Trial Deputy Phil Killien, and get word back to me.

As far as funds available to pay for my plane fare to Florida and my housing there, he didn't know.

I called the Seattle Police Homicide Unit and talked to Lieutenant Ernie Bisset, assistant commander of the unit. Ernie felt that I should go to Pensacola if there was any way it could be managed. The Seattle Police had some money available for investigation, he said, and he would try to arrange for a plane ticket for me.

Bisset called back within half an hour. He had gotten an O.K. to pay for a trip to Florida for me, but it was up to me to see if authorities there would allow me to talk to Ted. The Seattle Police had no impact on what the Florida detectives wanted to do.

A short time later, Phil Killien called. I explained to him that Ted had seemed anxious to talk to me, but that I had been unable to get through to him by phone since Thursday night.

"Phil," I asked, "who has jurisdiction over Ted? Would it be Washington because the first of the crimes occurred in Seattle? Or would it be Florida?"

"Whoever has the body," he answered.

For a moment, I was confused. *Which* body? Washington had a half-dozen bodies, and Utah and Colorado had their share, but Florida had two too, with Kim Leach still missing. And so I asked Phil Killien "Which body?"

"His body. Ted Bundy's body. They have him, and that gives them primary jurisdiction. They can do what they want."

And so they could. If Florida didn't want me to talk to Ted, then I couldn't talk to Ted. It was clear that the detectives in that state did not want me, and what Ted wanted didn't matter in the least to them.

38

Although Ted was the prime suspect in the Chi Omega murders the Dunwoody Street attack, the abduction of Kimberly Leach, he was, for the moment, charged only with multiple counts of auto theft, auto burglary, credit card thefts, forgery and "uttering" (a somewhat archaic term meaning to declare or assert that a note, money, or a document is good or valid when it is actually counterfeit). Conviction on those charges alone could—like the charges after his first escape in Colorado—bring him more than a lifetime in prison: seventy-five years. But the State of Florida was looking for more, and they were taking no chances that the "Houdini of Jails" would bolt again. Whenever he was outside a cell, Ted wore handcuffs, chains, and a bulky orthopedic brace from his left foot to thigh, a brace that made him walk with a pronounced limp. When a reporter asked him at one hearing why he wore the brace, he grinned and said, "I have a problem with my leg—I run too fast." For the press, at least, he could summon up his old bravado.

While the processing of the orange bug and the white Dodge went on, so did the search for Kimberly; no one believed that they were looking for anything but a decomposing body. Detectives were also running down charge slips on the stolen credit cards in Ted's possession when he was arrested.

On February 18th, even as I had tried—naively—to work out plea bargaining for him, Ted had been taken from his cell in Pensacola and driven back to Tallahassee, the city he had never planned to visit again. Throughout his legal problems, there had always been certain lawmen and prosecutors who galled Ted: Nick Mackie, Bob Keppel, Pete Hayward, Jerry Thompson, Frank Tucker. He was about to run into another nemesis—Sheriff Ken Katsaris of the Leon County Sheriff's Office. Katsaris was a darkly handsome man of thirty five, a man who would jokingly tell a political meeting that "Ted Bundy is my favorite prisoner." Ted would come to despise Katsaris, and more and more would come to depend on Millard Farmer, the Atlanta attorney who is a founder of Team Defense, legal help for indigents who face the death penalty. Ted had talked by phone with Farmer even when he was incarcerated in Colorado, and now he wanted Farmer at his side. It would not please Florida judicial authorities who thought Farmer a disruptive force in a courtroom, given to grandstanding ploys.

Farmer gave an interview of the *Tallahassee Democrat* after Ted's arrest, an interview in which he characterized Ted as being "a person very disturbed mentally. He is emotionally disturbed. Attention being drawn [to him] is of interest to him. He enjoys playing the game. He appears to enjoy watching law enforcement people muddle in their ignorance."

But Farmer said that his defense team would volunteer to defend Bundy if he *was* charged with the Florida murders.

During the first week of March, 1978, Ted appeared in Judge John Rudd's courtroom twice: to hear the charges against him to date, and to fight a prosecution request that he be ordered to give samples of his hair, blood, and saliva. And he was, seemingly, back to his normal, joking self-confidence, despite the bulky brace on his leg, espite the fact he still wore a dirty ski sweater, rumpled slacks.

In view of his background, the thirty-four forgery counts and the uttering charges brought against him because he'd charged $290.82 worth of purchases on a credit card stolen from the wife of an F.S.U. criminology student were chicken feed. He appeared more rankled by Ken Katsaris's enjoyment of the limelight than he did by the innuendoes surrounding him.

I had written to Ted immediately after I learned that I would not be allowed to talk to him on the phone or to come to Florida, but I heard nothing from him until March 9th. The latter, mailed to Los Angeles, bears the date February 9, 1978. Again, he had lost track of time. It was not surprising. That latter was one of the most depressed communiqués I ever received from him, and, I believe, it includes key words explaining what had happened.

Ted began by saying it seemed as if his call to me in February had occurred many months before, although he could still remember it very clearly. He admitted to having been "in bad shape" at that time, but said he had been able to pull himself together within a day or two. He thanked me for my thoughtfulness and willingness to come to Florida to talk to him at that time, but said that unfortunate changes in circumstances had made such a journey "both impossible and unnecessary."

He wrote that each new phase of his existence seemed to be more unbearable than the last, and that he was finding it more and more difficult to express his emotions and observations in writing. Indeed, a great deal had happened to him since his December escape from the Garfield County Jail, but he said he was so bitterly disappointed that that opportunity had ended in failure that he was both unable and unwilling to discuss the events of the prior two months. "Two months, it feels like so much more time has gone by . . ."

His handwriting wavered on the page, and it was difficult to read; his writing had always varied with the intensity of his emotions at any given time.

> I try not to look forward. I try not to think back to the precious few days I had as a free person. I try to live in the present as I have on past occasions when I have been locked up. This approach worked in the past but is not working well now. I am tired and disappointed in myself. Two years I dreamt of freedom. I had it and lost it through a combination of compulsion and stupidity. It is a failure I find impossible to dismiss easily.
>
> > love,
> > ted.

P.S. Thanks for the $10.

How many times had he added that same P.S.? How many $10 checks had I sent over the years? Thirty . . . forty, maybe. And now, he was back inside again—far removed from the French restaurants, the sparkling wine, even the bottles of beer and milk he drank in his room at the Oak—with $10 to buy cigarettes.

Ted blamed his failure and capture on "compulsion," and he speaks of a "precious few days of freedom." Could forty-four-and-a-half days be called a "few," or was he speaking of the days between his escape and the first murders? Had he tried mightily to over-come his compulsion, only to find that he could not control it?

From that night of terror in the Chi Omega house—January 14th-15th—was Ted, in essence, not free at all, caught instead in a kind of mind-prison he himself could not escape? His failure to find honest work might be construed as stupidity, but I feel compulsion is the operative word in his letter.

After that one letter, I wouldn't hear from him again for four months, although I wrote to him several times. He was very busy, repeating and repeating patterns of behavior as if he were a squirrel on a treadmill.

On April 1, Ted asked for a judicial order that would permit him to defend himself on the credit card and auto theft charges. Just as he had done in Colorado, he wanted to be released from his cell three days a week to visit a law library, he wanted better lighting in his cell, a typewriter, paper, supplies, and he wanted jail personnel ordered to desist from interfering with or censoring legal corre-spondence going in or coming out. He wanted reduced bail too. A hearing was set for April 13th.

On April 7th, searches finally found what was left of twelve-year-old Kimberly Leach. When the Dodge van was processed, criminalists had taken samples of soil, leaves and bark found inside and caught in its undercarriage. Botanists and soil experts had identified the dirt as coming from somewhere close to a north Florida river. It had not been much of a clue to pinpoint exactly where Kim's body might be found—but it was a start.

Columbia County is bordered by the Suwannee River on the northwest and the Santa Fe on the south. Adjacent Suwannee County is bounded by the Suwannee on three of its four borders. The Withlaccoochee joins the Suwannee opposite Suwannee River State Park. The banks of these rivers seemed the most likely area in which to concentrate the search, although they had been searched before.

Late in February, searchers had found a huge tennis shoe, other debris, and strands of human hair along the Suwannee near Brandford, twenty-five miles from Lake City. They had gathered the possible evidence and retained it for testing, testing that did not reveal much.

There had been an "extraordinary find" rumored near the entrance to Suwannee State park in March, but no specifics had leaked out to the public and nothing official had come of it. The find had been a pile of dumped cigarette butts—the same brand as the contents of the ashtray in the VW bug Ted was driving when he was arrested: Winston's. Suwannee River State Park had the kind of soil, the kind of vegetation found inside the rear doors of the stolen van, and, on April 7, Florida Highway patrol Trooper Kenneth Robinson worked with a forty-man search team near the park, just off Interstate 10.

It was a baking hot day for April, with the temperatures heading toward the 90s, and the searchers fought off clouds of mosquitos as they broke through thickets, and probed into sinkholes with poles and into the deeper ones with scuba gear.

The morning's work produced nothing, and the crew stopped for a quick lunch in the shade. If their mission had not been so grotesque, they might have enjoyed the dogwood, the redbud blooming. But there was always the image in their minds, an image of the hidden body of the little girl gone now so long.

After lunch, Robinson's party organized searchlines radiating out from the sinkhole. Searchers on horseback had been through the region before, but it had not yet been searched on foot. Robinson, alone, walked through the underbrush for perhaps fifteen minutes. Ahead of him he saw a small shed made of sheet metal, an abandoned farrowing shed for a sow and her litter. A wire fence encircled the shed.

Robinson, a lanky man, hunkered down and peered into a hole on the open side of the shed. As his eyes adjusted to the dimness inside, he saw, first, the tennis shoe . . . and then what looked like a pull-over jersey, a jersey with the number 83 on it.

There was no leg or foot in the sneaker—only a bare bone. He felt sick. Sure, they had known what they might find, but the ignominy of the site, the thought that Kim Leach had been tossed away in a pigpen in this desolate area made him want to vomit.

Robinson stood up and backed away. He called for the men in his party, and they immediately roped off the pigpen that had become a tomb. It was 12:37 P.M.

Jacksonville Medical Examiner, Dr. Peter Lipkovic, arrived and the caved-in roof of the shed was carefully lifted off. There was little question that it was Kim. She was nude except for the tennis shoes and a white turtleneck shirt, but her long coat with the fake fur collar, her jeans, her jersey, her underclothing, and her purse were all there, piled in an incongruously neat pile beside the body.

Soon, dental records would verify absolutely that Kim Leach had been found.

Dr. Lipkovic performed an autopsy on the body, and found "about what you'd expect after eight weeks." Because the months of February, March and April had been unseasonably hot and dry, most of the body had virtually mummified, rather than decomposing. Internal organs were there, but desiccated. There were no bodily fluids; blood typing had to be done from tissue samples.

Cause of death was questionable, as it always is when bodies have lain undiscovered for so long. Lipkovic would say officially only, "She succumbed to homicidal violence to the neck region. There was a considerable amount of force applied to the neck that tore the skin, but I have no idea whether it was done with a blunt or a sharp instrument."

He did not know if she had been strangled, but he would not exclude the possibility. There were no broken bones, but something had definitely penetrated the neck. A penetrating injury is usually inflicted with a knife or a gun; there were absolutely no signs of bullet fragments or gunbarrel debris.

Unlike the girls in Tallahassee, Kim had suffered no skull fractures, apparently no bludgeon blows at all. There was evidence of sexual battery, but that too was impossible to confirm either at post mortem or with tests. Dr. Lipkovic said, somewhat inscrutably, that the injured areas of a body decompose more rapidly than those untraumatized. He meant that there was not enough vaginal tissue left to examine for signs of sexual assault.

Back at the state park, the searchers had continued to look for evidence: they found a man's khaki military-type jacket, blood-stained, about a hundred feet from the pigpen.

Kim had, in all likelihood, been dead when her body was driven to Suwannee State Park. There was very little blood at that site, and the deep indentation—the drag marks—through the soil in the Dodge van were consistent with a body's having been laboriously pulled out of the van.

Kim's parents accepted the news that she had, at last, been found with grief, but little shock; they had known she would never run away. They now had only one child, a younger son. "It's not much better now," Freda Leach said bitterly. "It's never going to be good."

When Ted was told that Kim had been found, he showed no emotion at all.

39

The Dodge van had already given up physical evidence. The soil and leaf samples had led searchers to the banks of the Suwannee. Its odometer showed that it had been driven 789 miles between the time it was stolen on February 5th and the time it was abandoned on February 12th. Now, Mary Lynn Hinson and Richard Stephens had some samples for comparison with the evidence they'd been holding Heretofore, it had been useless, only half of an intricate puzzle.

Kimberly Leach's blood type was B—the same type as the congealed blood pooled in the back of the van. However, the desiccated state of her body made it impossible to break the blood factors down to enzyme characteristics. Possible, but not probable or absolute, physical evidence. Semen stains on the child's underpants found next to the body had been made by a man with type O blood, a secretor. Ted Bundy's blood type. Again, a possible—not an absolute.

Ms. Hinson had a pair of loafers and a pair of running shoes which Ted had in his possession when he was stopped by Officer Lee. She compared the soles of both pairs of shoes—and found them identical to the footprints left in soil inside the Dodge van. More than possible, more than probable—but not absolute physical evidence.

The complex make-up of the van's carpeting with its four colors: green, blue, turquoise, and black would become very important in Hinson's testing of the hundreds of cloth fibers found in the van. Many of the fibers had been found intertwined. Shreds of one blue fiber—an unusual polyester weave with thirty-one strands to the yard—had come from Kimberly's football jersey. Identical fibers had been found clinging still to the navy blue blazer that Ted wore when arrested. Fibers from the bluejacket were identified microscopically with those caught in Kimberly's white socks. Again and again, Hinson found mute testimony that Kim's clothing had come into close contact with the carpet of the van (or with a carpet microscopically identical) and to the clothing worn by Ted (or clothing microscopically identical). The microanalist's conclusion was that it was very probably, "in fact extremely probable," that Kim's clothing had been in contact with the van's carpet and with Ted Bundy's blue blazer jacket.

Extremely probable—not absolute.

Hinson did not attempt to match any fibers vacuumed from the van except those that appeared to correspond to clothing worn by Ted or Kim or the carpeting. Patricia Lasko, a microanalyst from the Florida Department of Criminal Law Enforcement's crime lab, found no hair matches to either Kim's or Ted's hair among the one hundred samples found.

There were no Ted fingerprints; it was impossible to tell if Kim's prints had been there. Twelve-year-old children rarely have their fingerprints on file, and Kim's body had been too decomposed to lift complete prints from her fingertips.

Given the intermingling of the fibers from each subject's clothing, and the position in which Kim's body had been found, Medical Examiner Lipkovic surmised that the child had been killed during an act of sexual attack. Her body had apparently been left in that position as the process of rigor mortis began, and transported to the hogshed where it was found.

The price tags the Green Acres Sporting Goods Store, found in the van, were traced to Jacksonville. The store owner, John Farhat, recalled that he'd sold a large hunting knife sometime in early February. "I'd just marked it up from $24 to $26." It had been a cash sale. A brown-haired man in his thirties had purchased it. But Farhat had first picked a mug shot of another man—not Ted's. When he later saw a picture of Ted in a paper, he had called a state investigator and said he was now positive that the man who'd bought the ten-inch knife was Ted Bundy.

In the orange bug which Ted drove at his arrest in Pensacola, there was a pair of dark-framed eyeglasses—glasses with clear, nonprescription lenses. And there was a pair of plaid slacks. Were these the clothes and glasses of Richard Burton, Fire Department?

As always, Ted's credit card purchases would be worrisome for him, especially those where he purchased gas. Among the twenty-one cards found on him when he was arrested by Officer Lee were cards that had been stolen from Kathleen Laura Evans (Gulf), Thomas N. Evans III (Master Charge), and William R. Evans (Master Charge), cards that had all been in Ms. Evans's purse in Tallahassee when they vanished.

Over the years, detectives had found that Ted seemed to have a phobia about running out of gas, often purchasing gas in small amounts many times in one day. On February 7th and 8th, the Gulf and Master Charge cards had been used to buy gas in Jacksonville. One charge was for $9.67, and another was for $4.56. The license plate? 13–D–11300.

The desk clerk of the Holiday Inn in Lake City, Randy Jones, recalled registering a man he described as "Kind of ratty looking, with three days' growth of beard," on the evening of February 8th. Jones had noted that the man's eyes seemed "glassy," and another clerk had surmised that the man was either under the influence of alcohol or drugs. He had signed in under the name of "Evans," using one of the cards stolen in Tallahassee. He had charged a meal and several drinks in the lounge.

The next morning, "Evans" had checked out—but not officially. It would have cost him nothing to pay for his motel room, since he'd stolen the credit card in the first place, but he left directly from his room at 8:00 A.M.

Less than an hour later, Kimberly Leach was seen being led into a white Dodge van by an "angry parent." Firefighter Andy Anderson continued home to change clothing and said nothing about the incident. He was, he would later say, "half afraid of starting a turmoil . . . of seeing law enforcement sent on a wild goose chase;" he didn't really feel that the girl he'd seen with her "father" had any connection to the missing teenager. When Anderson did go to the police six months later, he willingly allowed himself to be hypnotized to bring back the scene in detail that he'd witnessed on the morning of February 9th, and he was able to describe Kimberly's clothing and the man who had taken her away.

"The man was clean shaven . . . 29–30–31, good looking, 160–65 pounds."

Jackie Moore, the surgeon's wife, *had* gone to the police, but she would not be able to identify Ted absolutely until she saw him erupt in anger in an Orlando courtroom two years later as she watched the television newscast of the trial. Only then, when she glimpsed the enraged profile of the defendant, could she superimpose it on the face that lingered in her memory.

Clinch Edenfield, the school crossing-guard, another eye witness, would prove to be an ineffective witness. Two years later, he would recall that February 9, 1978 had been a "warm, summery day." In face, it had been blustery, near freezing, and drenched with torrents of icy rain.

40

There would be few periods in the next eighteen months when Florida papers did not carry at least some story about Ted Bundy, but he would not be permitted the jail "press conferences" *he* wanted to hold. Once his anonymity had vanished, Ted wanted to tell the press his feelings about the spreading news coverage which pegged him as the number one suspect in both the Tallahassee and Lake City cases. He did manage to sneak out a few letters to newspapermen in Colorado and Washington denouncing the sweeping indictment of him by the Florida press.

The state of Florida was more interested in getting samples of his hair and blood—which were finally supplied. Ted refused to supply handwriting samples. Judge Charles Miner said that if Ted continued to refuse, he would be denied his right to be provided with information on the forgery cases.

On April 10, 1978, he was charged with two more forgery cases. One count alleged he had used a stolen Gulf Oil card in Lake City to buy gas on February 9th; the second was for the use of a stolen Master Charge in the same city. Lake City now had a legal hold on him. But Lake City would have a long wait; there were still sixty-two charges extant in Leon County. And, of course, he was still wanted in Colorado for murder and escape.

His legal troubles continued to pile up. On April 27, a warrant was issued to Ted in his Leon County jail cell, a warrant decreeing that he would be taken from that cell to a dentist's office where impressions of his teeth would be made. These impressions would be compared with the bite marks found on Lisa Levy's body.

Sheriff Katsaris was quoted as saying, "It's not an impossibility that someone will be charged in the Chi Omega killings in the near future . . ." At the same time, Judge Minor called off Ted's May 9th trial for auto theft and burglary, and said it would not be rescheduled until the suspect agreed to provide samples of his handwriting. The sudden trip to the dentist's office appeared to have been deliberately planned as a surprise for Ted; the word was that authorities did not want to give him a chance to "grind down his teeth" before the odontology impressions could be obtained.

There was much speculation that murder charges might be immediately forthcoming, but Katsaris scotched those rumors by saying, "They will probably be within the next couple of months . . . or not at all."

With the months creeping by—and no murder charges—it seemed that the Florida murders might culminate just as the earlier cases in Washington and Utah had; perhaps there was not enough physical evidence to risk going into trial.

In the meantime, Ted seemingly had once again acclimated to jail. The Leon County Jail is a white brick building four stories high, not new, but not a sweltering rathole as southern jails are often characterized in fiction.

He was being kept in isolation in a four-man security cell in the center of the jail on the second floor. He had no contact with the other 250 prisoners, and his only visitors were local public defenders. He seemed to like his jailers, particularly Art Golden, a lumbering, ruggedly good-looking man who was in charge of the jail. But then, Ted had never had much criticism for his jailers; it was the detectives and prosecutors who drew his diatribes.

His cell was clean, air-conditioned, and he was allowed a radio and newspapers. He knew that the Grand Jury seemed to be moving toward his indictment on murder charges.

Mindful of Ted's previous escapes, his captors were cautious. The light fixture in his cell was far too high for him to reach. The outer door had been beefed up with two extra locks, and only one jailer had a key that would open both. As usual, Ted decried his lack of exercise, the food, the lighting. He could not see the outside world. There were no windows in his cell, even barred ones.

Millard Farmer, still not officially Ted's attorney, hinted that he would file federal charges because the jail conditions violated Ted's rights. It was an all-too-familiar chant.

Although I had written to him several times during the spring of 1978, I didn't hear from Ted again until July. By that time, I had finally broken free of *my* sweatbox of a cell, the 8 × 10 room where I had been writing a movie script for seven months. That room hadn't had windows either, and it hadn't had air-conditioning. Only the worst smog in Los Angeles in twenty years had been able to creep through the cracks in the door, and the temperature in our "writers' room" had hit 105 degrees.

Ted's July 6th letter was an example of the sardonic humor he was often capable of, and a far cry from the desperate letter he'd mailed soon after his arrest. It was typed; along with what the jailers called his "stationery store" of legal supplies, he had been given a typewriter to prepare his defenses.

He apologized for failing to answer my last letter sent from California on May 21st, and, again, thanked me for the check I'd enclosed. Money was lasting him for quite awhile; he had stopped smoking. Ted had been surprised to find that I was still working away on the movie script in Hollywood into the later spring of 1978, and suggested that perhaps I had been naïve when I'd signed the contract and that I should ask for additional money for the four extra months I had worked.

At least they could give you 'mugger money' so the buggers don't have to go away empty handed. You said you lived in a 'trick pad?' Sorry, I can't interpret the L.A. dialect or whatever, oh there's the word: colloquialism. Does this mean that magicians hang out there; you know, rabbits out of hats and things. Or do you mean . . . do you suggest . . . a . . . ahmmmm . . . that persons get to know each other carnally for a negotiated price? If so, and if it pays better than writing—it would almost have to—you might consider getting into administration . . . You could apply for a small business loan to get started.

As far as his own life was going, Ted wrote that there was nothing happening to him that reincarnation wouldn't improve on. He didn't think about it; he viewed his world from the position of a "spectator, a captive audience."

He was due that afternoon to appear to stand trial for fourteen counts involving the use of credit cards. But, as he'd told me years before, he didn't sweat the small stuff and he had a "disposition made of duck feathers." He called the credit cards "damn pesky things," as well he might.

"Perfect time to use an insanity defense," he mused. "I saw them used on television, and, honest, I couldn't help myself."

Ted was not unaware of what was happening with other famous suspects, and he had followed the Son of Sam case, and concluded that if David Berkowitz could be found sane, it meant that no murder defendant in the country could be found legally insane.

"So I am pursuing a straight not guilty defense, since, for the record and the benefit of the censors reading this letter, I am innocent of those charges as a matter of law and fact. CYA*, my Dear.

"Bon chance, bon voyage, bon appetite, catch you later, don't talk to strangers unless they talk to you first, down some chablis for me, love, and so on . . . ted."

It had all become a grimly hopeless joke. I smiled a little at Ted's jest about his "defense." He had *stolen* the television set that he blamed for brainwashing him into stealing credit cards. His life was indeed a vicious circle. And his last admonition to me, "don't talk to strangers," was, under the circumstances, dark humor.

I answered in the same vein. "Sure, you can give up smoking . . . *you're* not under pressure they way *I* am."

I would write to Ted a few more times, but this was the last letter I ever got from Ted Bundy. There would be phone calls—hour-long collect phone calls—but never again a letter.

The net dropped over Ted with a dull thud on July 27th in what had been termed a "circus," and a "zoo." The latest episode in what Ted referred to as the "Ted and Ken Show" occurred on that steamy hot night in Tallahassee.

Sheriff Ken Katsaris had a sealed indictment, and he summoned reporters for a press conference at 9:30 that evening. Ted had been in Pensacola all day for a hearing and he was in that city when the Grand Jury handed down the indictment at 3:00 P.M.

Ted had been back in his cell an hour when he was taken downstairs where Katsaris waited. The sheriff was impeccable in a black suit, white shirt, diagonally striped tie. Ted wore baggy green jail coveralis as he emerged from the elevator under heavy guard. The

---

* CYA—"Cover Your Ass" in police and con lingo.

Nick Mackie, head of Task Force to investigate the case in Washington State.

Ted Bundy after his arrest in Utah. August, 1975.

Ted Bundy in 1977 after his first escape from jail in Colorado.

Ted Bundy in the Utah line-up where Carol DaRonch picked him as her kidnapper.

Carol DaRonch testifying in Florida as Judge Cowart listens. WIDE WORLD PHOTOS.

Ted Bundy with his lawyers at the first trial in Florida. June 25, 1979. UPI.

The last victim. Kimberly Leach disappeared from Lake City, Florida on February 9, 1978. She was 12 years old. WIDE WORLD PHOTOS.

Ted Bundy in court in Florida. WIDE WORLD PHOTOS.

Ted Bundy waving to reporters while the charges against him are being read. WIDE WORLD PHOTOS.

strobe lights for the cameras blinded him as he walked into the hallway and realized, instantly, what was happening. He quickly retreated into the elevator, mumbling that he would not "be paraded" for Katsaris's benefit.

Ted's face was the sick white of jail pallor, and his face was drawn, giving him as ascetic appearance. Finally, realizing there was no place for him to hide, he walked out of the elevator almost jauntily.

Katsaris opened the indictment and began to read: "In the name of, and by the authority of the state of Florida—"

Ted plainly hated his guts.

The prisoner approached the captor and asked sarcastically, "What do we have here, Ken? Let's see. Oh, an indictment! Why don't you read it to me? You're running for re-election."

And then, Ted turned his back on Katsaris, lifted his right arm to lean against the wall, and stared straight ahead, jaw set, head up. He was the persecuted man and he would play it that way. He seemed to rise above the nondescript coveralls, the jail slippers. His eyes blazed into the cameras.

The cameras were all on Bundy, but Katsaris went ahead through the indictment, ". . . the said Theodore Robert Bundy did make an assault upon Karen Chandler and/or Kathy Kleiner . . ."

Ted spoke to the press, "He said he was going to get me." And to the sheriff, "O.K. You got your indictment; that's all you're going to get."

Katsaris ignored him and continued to drone out the legalese which meant that Ted Bundy was being charged with murder. ". . . did then and there unlawfully kill a human being, to wit: Lisa Levy, by strangling and/or beating her until she was dead, and said killing was perpetrated by said Theodore Robert Bundy, and did then and there unlawfully kill a human being, to wit: Margaret Bowman, by strangling and/or beating her until she was dead . . . and that Theodore Robert Bundy, from or with a premeditated design or intent to effect the death of said Cheryl Thomas . . ."

It seemed to take hours, rather than minutes.

Ted made a mockery of it. He raised his hand at one point and said, "I'll plead not guilty right now."

Ted was gaining control of himself, grinning widely. He continued to interrupt Katsaris. "Can I speak to the press when you're done?"

Katsaris read on, many of his words lost behind Ted's banter.

"We've displayed the prisoner now," Ted said mockingly. "I think it's my turn. Listen, I've been kept in isolation for six months. You've been talking for six months. I'm gagged . . . you're not gagged."

When the indictment was finally completed, Ted was taken back to the elevator. He took his copy of the papers and held them up for the cameras . . . and then he methodically tore them in half.

For the first time, Ted Bundy would be on trial for his very life. He would not betray whatever emotions swept through him as he realized that.

Things grew gloomier the next day when Judge Charles McClure refused to allow Millard Farmer to defend Bundy. There had been enough "carnival," the state said, without allowing a man with Farmer's alleged reputation for courtroom histrionics into the case. Farmer was not licensed to practice law in Florida, and the state had the power to refuse such privileges.

Farmer argued vehemently that Ted was being deprived of his right to effective legal counsel, but Ted said nothing at all. He refused to answer any of the judge's remarks addressed to him, and McClure said implacably, "Let the record reflect that the defendant refuses to answer."

It was clearly a protest demonstration on Ted's part—a protest over his loss of Farmer. In all likelihood, he had expected the murder indictments; he probably did not expect that he would not have Farmer beside him, and that was a crushing disappointment. Like Buzzy Ware, Millard Farmer was the kind of lawyer Ted himself could respect. It was important to his sense of worth. To be an *important* defendant with a famous attorney could be dealt with; to be stuck with public defenders was more a blow to his ego than a threat to his life.

The net cinched more tightly. On July 31st, the sealed indictment that had been handed down in Columbia County (Lake City) lay waiting in Judge Wallace Jopling's courtroom in Lake City even as Ted pleaded not guilty in Tallahassee. Once again, Judge Rudd rejected Millard Farmer as defense attorney. Ted dismissed his public defenders. As before, he would go it alone.

No sooner were those proceedings ended than Judge Jopling opened the sealed indictment before him; Ted Bundy was now charged with first degree murder and kidnapping in the Kimberly Leach murder.

The Tallahassee cases were set to go to trial on October 3, 1978, and it was rumored that Ted would probably be facing back-to-back trials. Ted did not retreat. Instead, he attacked.

On August 4, 1978, Millard Farmer submitted a complaint charging the sheriff of Leon County, Ken Katsaris, and eight others (county commissioners, Art Golden, and Captain Jack Poitinger) with depriving Ted of his minimal rights as a prisoner. Ted sought $300,000 damages.

Ted was asking that he be allowed a minimum of one hour of daily outdoor exercise—without chains—adequate cell lighting, removal from isolation, and that Katsaris and the other defendants be stopped from "harassing" him. He also asked that he be awarded reasonable attorney fees. It was the audacious Ted Bundy back in action.

The state responded by again blocking Farmer from Ted's defense. Farmer suggested that Judge Rudd was "in the middle of a lynch mob" and called the state of Florida "the Buckle of the Death Belt" for prisoners. There were, at the time, some seventy to eighty prisoners on death row in Florida, convicted of first degree murder.

In considering a place to run to back in December of 1977, Ted might have done well to weigh other factors beyond the weather.

The headlines continued. Ted told an ABC reporter from Seattle that he had been cleared of suspicion in the 1974 cases in Seattle by an "inquiry judge." That was not true. Inquiry judges do not make such decisions in Washington State, and he was still regarded as the prime suspect in the eight Northwest cases.

Ted asked that Judge Rudd disqualify himself from the case, after Rudd refused Farmer's bid to defend him, calling Farmer's courtroom demeanor "disruptive." Rudd reacted to the motion that he step down succinctly, "Motion read, considered and denied. File it."

On August 14th, Ted appeared in Judge Jopling's Lake City courtroom and pleaded not guilty to the charges involving Kimberly Leach. "Because I am innocent."

Florida justice would not move swiftly. There were just too many murders, too many charges. The Chi Omega trial was put off until November, and there were indications that the Leach trial would also be delayed.

The indications were right. Ted would not go on trial for either the Tallahassee or the Lake City cases until mid-1979. In the meantime, he languished in isolation in the Leon County Jail, still overseen by his arch enemy: Sheriff Ken Katsaris.

I received a phone call from Ted on September 26, 1978—a collect call, but one which I accepted readily. I had heard nothing from him and had been following events in Florida only through the media since July. The connection was blurred; I was not sure that we were alone on the line.

He explained that a new order had come down, an order that allowed him to have outdoor exercise. "For the first time in seven months, they took me outside for something other than going back and forth to hearings. Two armed guards with walkie-talkies took me up on the roof and let me walk in circles. Down below, they had three patrol cars and three attack dogs."

I suggested that even he couldn't leap four stories.

"Who do they think I am?" he laughed. "The Bionic Man?"

He described his cell. "There's no natural light. It's an iron cell in the midst of other walls. There's one 150-watt recessed bulb in the ceiling with a plastic shield and a metal grating. By the time it flitters down to me, there's hardly *any* light. It's 1/60th of what it should be for humane purposes. I've got a bed, a combination sink-and-toilet, and a portable radio that gets two stations. It felt so good today to be out in the air without shackles, even to listen to the dogs bark—I haven't heard a dog bark in a long time."

Ted was adamant that "they" would never break him. "All the psychological evaluations they've done here . . . in the last one, they told the sheriff that, if he read the indictment to me the way he did, that it would break me, and I'd talk. Immediately after they took me back to my cell, two detectives came in and said, 'Now you see how much we've got on you? There's no place else to go—you might just as well make it easy on yourself and talk.' But they didn't break me then."

For the first time, Ted mentioned Carole Ann Boone to me, saying that he had become "very, very close" to her, and that he was listening to her advice on how to handle matters of interest to him.

He talked of his chagrin at losing Millard Farmer. "The man's about thirty-seven—looks fifty—and he handles about twenty capital cases a year. He runs himself into the ground. But now I'm prepared to defend myself in both cases."

He was angry that he was "being paraded" both in Tallahassee and Lake City, where he went three times a week for hearings on the Leach case. And yet, there was an undercurrent of pride that he was in the public eye again, and would be for a long time to come. "The Chi Omega case is very bizarre. I'm not going to go into it— but the combination of Ted Bundy and a case like that! I'll be in the limelight for a long time. The evidence has all been fabricated. The people here are absolutely determined to get convictions—even if they know they'll be overturned later. All they care about is shackling me and getting me up in front of a jury. And back-to-back trials to boot."

He'd said he was talking from the booking room in the jail, but he apparently had made his feelings about Florida lawmen vocal enough already so that he had no qualms about annoying them further.

It was September 26th—Ted's anniversary with Meg. A year before he'd asked me to send the rose. Now, he said that Meg had finally left him. "I guess she talked to some reporters . . . I don't know. I haven't heard from her in a long time. She told me she just couldn't take this anymore, that she didn't want to hear anymore about it. How long since you've seen her?"

A long time, I told him. It had been more than a year. I'm sure he realized what day it was. Perhaps that was why he had called me—to talk about Meg. He had Carole Ann Boone now, but he hadn't forgotten Meg.

I asked him what time it was in Florida, and he hesitated. "I don't know. Time doesn't mean anything any more."

Ted's voice drifted away, and I thought the line had been broken. "Ted? Ted . . ."

He came back on, and he sounded vague, disoriented. He apologized.

"Sometimes, in the middle of a conversation, I forget what I've said before . . . I have trouble remembering."

It was the first time I had ever heard him so unsure, almost slipping away from what was here and now. But then his voice became strong again. He was anxious for trial, anxious to face the challenge.

"Your voice sounds good," I remarked. "You sound like yourself."

His answer was a little strange. "I usually am . . ."

Ted had only one request. He asked me to send him the classified section of the *Seattle Sunday Times* . He didn't say why he wanted it. Nostalgia perhaps. Maybe reading the ads in his hometown paper would help to wipe out the sight of the iron walls with no windows.

I sent him the paper. I don't know if he got it. I wouldn't talk to him or hear from him again until just before his Miami trial in June, 1979.

41

It is extremely doubtful that Ted Bundy could ever have received an impartial trial in the state of Florida. He was becoming better known than Disney World, the Everglades, and the heretofore all-time media pleaser: Murph the Surf. Paradoxically, Ted himself both courted and demeaned publicity. His very attitude made him ripe for headlines.

On October 29, 1978, Dr. Richard Souviron, a forensic odontologist—an expert in matching teeth impressions to bite marks, in dental identification—put on a demonstration at a forensic seminar that seemed premature, at best. Souviron, from Coral Gables, presented slides, slides he said proved that "this suspect's" teeth matched the bite marks on the victim's buttock. Naturally, this information was disseminated throughout the state's media and everyone knew that Ted Bundy was the suspect referred to. Predictably, Ted screamed "Foul!"

Dr. Ronald Wright, chief deputy medical examiner for Dade County, equivocated when he tried to explain how such a gaffe could happen. "You have to balance the kinds of problems which might exist in regards to talking about a case in litigation against teaching the best possible method for correctly identifying murderers or clearing people of murder charges," he remarked.

The obvious question of course was why this could not have been done without hinting broadly at the identity of the principals involved. Beyond that, there were other cases which could have been offered as examples where identification had been made through teeth imprints. A Brattleboro, Vermont man had been convicted in 1976 of the rape murder of sixty-two-year-old Ruth Kastenbaum—convicted because the twenty-five bite marks on her body matched his teeth.

Souviron himself had another case where he had made bite mark matches: he had matched the teeth of a twenty-three-year-old man from Columbia, South Carolina to the body of seventy-seven-year-old Margaret Haizlip who lived in a rural area south of Miami.

But Ted was more newsworthy than an itinerant laborer from South Carolina, and Ted's teeth got the publicity. The publication of Souviron's findings seemed to go far beyond normal pretrial publicity. It seemed, for a time, that charges against Ted for murder might well be dismissed because of Souviron's statements.

They were not, however, and the state moved ahead, preparing for the two trials. Pretrial publicity is a two-edged sword; it can prejudice an innocent man so that he cannot obtain a fair trial, and it can, occasionally, result in a guilty man's going free when charges *are* dismissed. In other instance, such publicity can be tragic.

Two of Ted Bundy's most hated antagonists had dropped completely from the picture by late 1978, one through personal disgrace and the other when his health collapsed. I don't know if Ted knew about either of them, or if it would matter to him any longer.

Frank Tucker, the District Attorney from Pitkin County, Colorado was convicted—June, 1978, of two counts of embezzlement and acquitted of two counts. In December, 1978, he was convicted of one count of felony theft and two misdemeanor counts. Tucker cried—as Ted had about his own case—that the charges and convictions were all "politically motivated." He was disbarred, received five years probation, ninety days in jail (to be delayed,) and a thousand dollar fine. According to his attorney, Tucker planned to pursue a new career. He would go to morticians' school in San Francisco.

Now-Major Nick Mackie of the King County Police Major Crimes Unit in Seattle suffered a near-fatal heart attack in the spring of 1978, and paramedics had pronounced him clinically dead twice. Mackie survived but was forced to resign from the high-pressure job he'd handled so well for so long. The loss of Mackie would be a blow for the department.

Ted himself wasn't doing so well. As the Christmas season approached in 1978, he was again in jail, looking at a solid steel door—just as he had been a year before. But this year, there were no plans to escape; there was no *way* to escape. Again, he was faced with a murder trial—just as he had been in December, 1977. Indeed, he was faced with *two* murder trials.

Bundy had moved to have Judge John Rudd removed because of prejudice, and shortly before Christmas the Florida State Supreme Court acquiesced. There had been claims by the defense that Rudd had improperly communicated with the State Attorney's Office, and that he had evinced hostility toward the defense team. Rudd stepped down. A new judge would be appointed in the coming year. Larry Simpson, an assistant state's attorney, would be chief prosecutor in the Chi Omega case and announced that he was ready to go to trial at any time, but a trial before February seemed unlikely.

Ted had grudgingly accepted the aid of the Public Defender's Office and his defense team was headed by Mike Minerva. Ted apparently was aware finally that he would be a fool to attempt to defend himself in two murder trials.

In January, a new judge was appointed: Judge Edward D. Cowart of the Florida Circuit Court. Judge Cowart, fifty-four, is a great St. Bernard of a man, jowls bulging over his judicial robes, with a southern soothing voice. Cowart has been a navy bosun's mate and a policeman, before graduating from Stetson University Law School in St. Petersburg. His home court is in Miami, and he controls his courtroom with authority—authority that is often laced with sharp wit and homilies. He is given to saying, "Bless your heart" to attorneys and defendant alike. When an argument is not clear, he will say, "Cripple that and walk it by me slow." He is a man both benign and belligerent depending on the circumstance, and he knows his law inside out. In court, Cowart often seems to be giving instruction in law to the attorneys who appear before him.

Ted wasn't going to like him much.

On February 22nd, Coward announced that Ted would go on trial for the Chi Omega murders and the Tallahassee attacks, on May 21st. He also again denied Bundy's request for Millard Farmer. The judge said he would decide in April if a nonprejudiced jury could be empanelled in the capital city. He agreed with the defense that it was unlikely that back-to-back trials could be held without prejudicing the defendant.

Ted was still, officially, the lead defense attorney—Minerva was only there to advise him as far as he was concerned.

The defendant requested on April 11th that newspeople be barred from taking his picture when he was brought to the courthouse in chain and wearing his leg brace, and from attending the proceedings leading up to trial. He would be questioning witnesses himself, he said, and he didn't want the media listening in. Judge Cowart denied that request saying, "If you exclude the press, you exclude the public."

A month later, Ted had had enough of Judge Cowart and moved to have *him* step down just as Judge Rudd had, claiming that Rudd's prejudice had flowed to Cowart too. Cowart denied the motion, saying it was "legally insufficient." Anyone who has observed Judge Cowart over time would doubt that he could *ever* be swayed or prejudiced by other's opinions; he is a man who patently thinks for himself.

The Bundy hearings were now being recorded by a television camera and by one still camera—as had been agreed in a recent Florida Supreme Court edict. Cowart continued to deny Ted's request for the barring of all cameras. "We're conducting the public's business, gentlemen, and we're going to conduct it in the sunshine. We're sitting in Florida."

Cowart would rarely display any animosity toward the defendant who railed against him, although, as the months progressed, he would at times chastise Bundy's temper tantrums as he would a small child. He seemed to bear no particular ill will toward Ted. Even as Ted had asked to have him removed from the case, Cowart remarked on Ted's suit and tie, "You look nice today."

And Ted had responded, "I'm disguised as an attorney today."

The pretrial hearings began in May in Tallahassee. The defense wanted the bite-mark testimony out, claiming that there had been insufficient probable cause for the search warrant that brought Ted to a dentist to have his teeth impressions taken. The defense claimed that he had not been a true suspect in the Chi Omega killings at that time. Cowart delayed his ruling.

Ted Bundy's murder trial was to begin on June 11th, but, on the last day of May there were rampant rumors that he was going to change his plea—that he would plea bargain to a lesser charge than first degree murder, and thus save himself from the specter of the electric chair.

Florida's electric chair was a terribly real threat. Only five days before, Florida had proved that it *would* carry out its death sentences. On May 25th, John Spenkelink, convicted of the murder in 1973 of killing a fellow ex-con in a Tallahassee motel room, had been executed. It was the first execution in the United States since Gary Gilmore had gone before the firing squad in Utah on January 19, 1977, at his own request. It was the first where a condemned man had gone into the death chamber *against* his will in America since 1967.

Ted Bundy has been geographically close to both men; fully aware of the fate of both, and he must have realized that Spenkelink's fate might await him in the not-too-distant future.

Louise Bundy flew to Tallahassee, as did John Henry Browne. Carole Ann Boone joined his mother and Browne in urging him to plead guilty to lesser charges. There had been a great deal of negotiating back and forth between Tallahassee, Leon County, Lake City, the prosecution and the defense. It was rumored that, if Ted would plead guilty to second degree murder in the two Chi Omega cases and in Kimberly Leach's murder, he would avoid the chair. The state would agree that he serve instead three consecutive twenty-five-year terms.

On May 31, there was a private session in Judge Cowart's chambers with Ted and his attorneys present. Ted filed a secret motion— a motion believed to be the guilty pleas to second degree murder. It would mean that he might never walk free again, but he wouldn't die in the electric chair either.

According to Florida Deputy State Attorney Jerry Blair—who awaited his day in the courtroom with Ted in the Leach case—Ted acknowledged his guilt to everything he was charged with, in both cases. Blair alleged that Ted, in fact, carried in his hand a written confession. All of his legal advisors, including Millard Farmer and Mike Minerva, had urged him to accept the lifeline held out. But the plea bargaining broke down. Ted tore up the papers in his hand and told Cowart, "I'd like to withdraw that motion."

Ted moved to have his public defender, Minerva, removed from the case—claiming that Minerva was trying to coerce him into admitting guilt. The state attorneys could not enter into a plea bargain in such a case. With Ted intimating that his own attorney was pressuring him to confess, any plea bargaining would automatically be overturned by an appellate court. Blair vowed that "if he [Ted] wanted a trial, he was going to get it."

None of the specifics of Ted's "almost" guilty plea reached the press, but rumors were strong. And it had been Ted's last chance; Governor Bob Graham had predicted he would "sign more death warrants," and Ted's name seemed already to be written there in invisible ink.

Minerva wanted out. Ted wanted him out, calling his public defender "incompetent."

It looked like any trial would be postponed once again. Ted himself wanted a ninety-day delay, and the defense team wanted a psychiatric exam to see if he was sane in the legal sense—that is, that he had sufficient mental and psychological competence to participate in his own defense. This latter request angered him as much as anything had angered him before. Ted may have joked in his letter tome about an insanity defense, but he would not go that route seriously, now that he was up and confident again.

Judge Cowart was not about to stand for endless trial delays. He agreed to the psychiatric examinations and ordered that they be done forthwith. He had 132 prospective jurors on hold. It had already been eighteen months since the stranger crept into the Chi Omega mansion, since the man had beaten Cheryl Thomas at Dunwoody Street, and Cowart felt it was time for the trial to begin.

Two psychiatrists examined Ted during that first week of June, 1979: Dr. Herve Cleckly of Augusta, Georgia, and Dr. Emanuel Tanay, a professor at Wayne State University in Michigan. They agreed with Ted that he was not incompetent, but said he demonstrated certain antisocial behavior. Tanay said that Ted's personality disorder was such that it could affect his relationship with his attorneys and thus, in that way, hinder his ability to defend himself.

"He has an extensive history of self-defeating, unadaptable, antisocial behavior," Tanay said.

On June 11th, Judge Cowart ruled that Ted Bundy was competent to stand trial and said that he would delay his decision on granting a change of venue until he had seen some response from prospective veniremen in the Leon County area. He denied the defense request for an extension and refused to let Ted fire his attorneys. Temporarily, Bundy had a new attorney: Brian T. Hayes, a respected north Florida criminal defense attorney, but also a man who came with unsettling references at the time: he had been John Spenkelink's attorney.

I had written to Ted to tell him that I would be attending his trial, to see if I would be able to visit him, and to warn him that I would probably be wearing a press badge. It was the only way I could be sure of getting into the courtroom; the gallery would be jammed, and there would be long lines of curious court-goers. With Ted's growing hatred for reporters, I didn't want him to see me among a sea of media people and think I had defected completely to the fourth estate.

I had reservations to Tallahassee, but I would never see that city; Judge Cowart granted a change of venue on June 12th when four of the first five prospective jurors said they knew so much about the Chi Omega murders that they could not sit on the jury and be considered unbiased.

Cowart ordered the trial moved to Miami, and said jury selection would begin there on June 25th. Mike Minerva would not be joining the defense team; relations between himself and Bundy had become so abrasive that they probably could not hide their antagonism from a jury. Minerva also felt that he might bear Ted some unconscious resentment since Ted had cast so much doubt about his ability.

The defense team would be Leon County assistant public defenders, Lynn Thompson, Ed Harvey, and Margaret Good. They were all young, all determined to do their best, and all woefully inexperienced.

A Miami attorney, Robert Haggard, not much older than the rest of the team, volunteered to help. In my opinion, Haggard was the least apt of any of the team members. He seemed ill-prepared, and his manner—even his haircut—appeared to grate on Judge Cowart's nerves.

Peggy Good may have been the most effective of all Bundy's latest team of attorneys. Ms. Good, in her late twenties, impressed the jury simply because she was a woman standing beside a man accused of brutal attacks on other women. Slender, blonde, bespectacled, she chose loose, almost baggy, clothing that did nothing for her basic attractiveness. her voice would remain flat and serious. Only when she was tired, would she slip into the drawl of a true, down-home southern girl. Cowart liked her, and she would receive many of his "Bless your hearts."

Ted was pleased with her too. He was enthusiastic in his phone call to me on the evening of June 28th—a call placed from the Dade County Jail in Miami. Ted sounded confident. again and exhilarated. He admitted that he was exhausted, however. "They flew me down here in a single-engine plane, rushed me into jail, and we began jury selection the next morning. I lost a little of my momentum. Cowart's hurrying us through. We work 'til 10:30 every other night, and we're going to have Saturday sessions."

Breakfast in the Dade County Jail was, and God knows why, at 4:30 A.M., and Ted was tired, but elated over his defense team and his budget.

"The sky's the limit. The state has given us $100,000 for our defense. I'm glad I don't have Mike Minerva anymore. I like my defense team, especially the fact that I have a woman on my side. I have an expert on jury selection who's helping me pick my jury. He can tell by their eyes, their facial expression, their body language what they're thinking. For instance, one prospective juror today raised his hand to his heart, and that means something to my expert."

Even in Miami, however, most of those in the jury pool had heard of Ted Bundy. One juror selected, Estela Suarez, had never heard of him.

"She only reads Spanish language papers," Ted said enthusiastically. "She kept smiling at me . . . she didn't realize *I* was the defendant!"

There was one young woman Ted had felt ill at ease about, a girl he described as "a perfect candidate for a sorority . . . a nice, fresh-faced, rosy-cheeked, pretty young girl. I was afraid she'd identify with the victims."

Ted extolled Carole Ann Boone's loyalty. "She's thrown in her lot with me, moved down here, given up her job. She has all my files, and I've given her my permission to talk to the news media. In order for her to survive, I told her to ask for $100-a-day and board-and-room in payment for interviews."

Ted was eager to see me when I got to Miami. He suggested that I contact Sergeant Marty Kratz, the jailer on his floor, to arrange for a visit. "He's a pretty good guy."

He seemed to understand that I would have to be in the court-room sitting in the press section, and he assured me he would do everything he could to see I got into the trial, "If you have any trouble, you come to me. I'm the 'Golden Boy.' I'll see that you get in."

He was confident that we would be able to talk too during court recesses and before evening sessions. He was insistent that I try to get in to see him in jail as soon as I got to Miami. I fully expected that I would get to see him, but things would not work out that way.

Ted felt that he was going to have a fair trail; he even spoke well of Judge Cowart and said, "I'll never have an appeal based on the inadequacy of my defense team, because they're good."

"Are you able to sleep?" I asked.

"I sleep like a baby."

The only matter that was really rankling Ted at this point was Dr. Tanay's testimony. "I only agreed to talk to him because it was my understanding the session was to be tape-recorded for the benefit of the defense. Spenkelink's lawyer, Brain Hayes, told me to do that. I was appalled and shocked when Tanay got up in open court and said I was dangerous to myself and others, a sociopath, an antisocial personality, that I shouldn't be allowed to go free. That was when I realized, and only then, that the court had ordered the examination, not the defense."

"Are you still not smoking?" I asked.

"I wasn't, but I bought a pack just before that flight down here at night in that single-engine plane. I just finished it, and it's been several days, so that's not so bad."

He commented that the vast majority of the jurors picked at that point were black or blue collar workers and that seemed good. I asked if he didn't feel that the very intelligent potential juror—someone who might weight all sides of a question—might not also be the assiduous newspaper reader.

"No, that doesn't necessarily follow. A lot of the professionals are so caught up in their careers that they don't read anything but professional journals. Many of them don't seem to have heard about me."

"Are you at all afraid for your personal safety?"

"Not at all. I'm too well known—a cause célèbre. They won't let anything happen to me.They want to get me into court safely."

He sounded completely in control; there was none of the vagueness, the slipping-away, that I'd noticed in his phone call of nine months earlier. He explained how the trial would run, the pretrial period where all the 150 witness would give brief testimony to see if it could be allowed into trial itself or would be suppressed. He explained the trial phase, and the penalty phase, and said that the prosecution was allowing jurors to be seated who were against the death penalty. Ted was clearly a captain in charge of his own ship.

"What's on television in Seattle?" he asked. "Are they covering me very much back there?"

"Quite a bit. I watched you in Tallahassee when you introduced yourself to the prospective jurors there. You seemed very confident."

He was pleased.

I have no way of knowing if Ted truly felt the confidence which he projected, but going into his Miami trial, he seemed to believe that he could and would win. After an hour's conversation, conversation which he told me was being monitored by Dade County jailers, we hung up, promising to meet again, this time in Miami.

To newspapermen, Ted declined to predict the trial outcome. "If I was a football coach, I'd say when you're in your first game of the season, you don't start looking for the Super Bowl."

Dr. Emil Spillman, the Atlanta hypnotist who had been Ted's jury expert, told the press that Ted truly had chosen his own jury. They had had to go through seventy-seven potential jurors before they reached a final selection on June 30th. Spillman felt that Ted had passed over seventeen or eighteen choices whom he—Spillman— termed "emotionally perfect. But I told him, 'It's your life—not mine,'" Spillman shrugged. "He passed up some absolutely fantastic jurors."

The final twelve were largely middle-aged, largely black. Ted, and Ted alone, had chosen. It *was* his life.

The jurors were:

* Alan Smith, a clothing designer, who leaned away from the death penalty.
* Estela Suarez, a bookkeeper. It was Ms. Suarez who had sparked laughter in the courtroom during jury selection when she failed to recognize Ted as the defendant.
* Vernon Swindle, a worker in the mailroom of the *Miami Herald*, who said he didn't have time to read the papers he helped to put out.
* Rudolph Treml, a senior project engineer for Texaco, highly educated—a man with a scientifically oriented mind who would become the jury foreman, a man who said he only read technical journals.
* Bernest Donald, a high school teacher, a deacon in his church.
* Floy Mitchell, a housewife, devout, who watched soap operas more than she read the daily headlines.
* Ruth Hamilton, a maid, a church-goer too. Her nephew was a Tallahassee policeman.
* Robert Corbett, a sports enthusiast who rarely read the paper beyond the sports page. He knew Ted was accused of murdering "somebody."
* Mazie Edge, just retired as an elementary school principal. Her bout with the flu would soon delay the trial.
* Dave Brown, a maintenance engineer for a Miami hotel.
* Mary Russo, a supermarket clerk, who seemed in awe of her call to jury duty, and who did not favor the death penalty.
* James Bennett, a truck driver, father of five, who had never considered Ted's guilt "one way or another."

These, then, along with three alternates, would be the jury of Ted Bundy's peers, the citizens of Dade County, Florida who would decide whether the young man from Tacoma, Washington would live or die.

42

I flew out of Sea-Tac Airport in Seattle, headed for Miami, at one in the morning on July 3rd. I had been promised press credentials when I arrived at my destination: the Dade County Metro Justice Center. I understood there were three hundred reporters already there, ready to digest and disseminate every scrap of information on Ted Bundy via phone and wire to the rest of America.

Once again, I felt the sense of unreality of it all, more so when I found the in-flight movie was *Love at First Bite*. The rest of the passengers flying thousands of feet above a sleeping country laughed aloud at the high camp of George Hamilton's Dracula as he plunged his teeth into beautiful maidens. Under the circumstances, I found no humor in it.

It would be forty-two hours before I slept again. We crossed the Great Divide; to the left of the plane, I could see dawn beginning to break, but it was still pitch black to my right. Soon, I could see the historic rivers down below as they snaked their way to the sea, cities slumbering in the distance. We landed in Atlanta at 6 A.M., waited an hour or so, and then flew south in a smaller plane. The vast isolation of the Everglades seemed endless. And then there was Miami ahead. So flat, so spread out; it was the very antithesis of Seattle which is built on a succession of hills.

The July heat of southern Florida rose up and seemed to knock me backward as I emerged from the Miami airport. During the weeks I spent in Miami, I would never adjust to that palpable heat. It was constant; even the sudden late afternoon thunder storms wept only great drops of hot water and left the air as oppressive as it had been before. Nor did evening bring respite as it always did in the Northwest. The sight of palm trees assailed me with an attack of homesickness, reminded me of those long months in Los

Angeles, and reminded me also that Ted could probably *never* go home again.

I dumped my bags in my motel and took a cab to the Dade County Metro Justice Center, a lush, new complex which lies in the shadow of the Orange Bowl. As I entered the reception area of the Dade County Public Safety Department substation which housed the jail—connected by a sky bridge to the Metro Justice Building where Ted's trial was being held on the fourth floor—I was immediately aware of the intense security. No one was even allowed on the elevators to the upper floors without first being cleared and handed a badge.

I had to have that clearance badge before I could go upstairs to the Public Relations Office and get another clearance badge that would allow me into the trial! They were taking no chances of escape for Ted in Miami.

Henceforth, I would be "News Media, No. 15."

I went first to the ninth floor of the Metro Justice Building, and found that the entire top floor of the huge building had been given over to the press. I have never seen anything like it. The activity there was frantic; three dozen closed circuit television sets blaring out every word of the trial five floors below, anchormen, anchorwomen, technicians, reporters—scores of them—watching, broadcasting, editing, splicing. The cacophony seemed to bother no one. The rooms were thick with cigarette smoke, littered with coffee cups. The indoor-outdoor carpet was a squirming network of wires and cables.

Cables from a single TV camera in the courtroom had been strung from the fourth-floor courtroom, secured to the building exterior, and fed into this central control room. There a series of distribution amplifiers split the signal so that what was happening could be fed to all three networks at once. The segments chosen by the networks were relayed to the eighth floor where Southern Bell had installed a "microwave dish" to transmit the signals to downtown Miami for wire transmission to a special Florida TV system. The same signals went by wire to Atlanta where ABC transmitted them to New York via Telstar I satellite, and by Telstar II to California and the West Coast. CBS had provided the single courtroom camera, and it was being manned alternately by cameramen from all the networks.

Ted had told me he was the Golden Boy, and for the media he certainly appeared to be just that.

I looked around the room. Stations from Colorado, Utah, Washington, and Florida had tacked up handwritten signs as they established their "territory." The ninth floor of the Metro Justice Building would run around the clock throughout the trial. I, who have always bemoaned the loneliness of writing—trapped all alone in my basement office at home—wouldn't be lonely *here*. I was amazed at the discipline of my fellow reporters who seemed able to turn out finished copy in this boiler room of noise and scurrying activity.

I stashed my tape recorder upstairs; it would not be allowed in the courtroom. Later, I learned the trick of turning it on next to the closed circuit TV set in the backroom, and then racing down to the trial. That way, I would have both my notes from the "live" action, and the complete trial on tape.

I exited the elevators on the fourth floor and headed toward the courtroom. Quite frankly, I was terrified, venturing into totally uncharted territory, about to view the culmination of four years of ambivalence and worry.

If Judge Edward Cowart is a St. Bernard, then his bailiff, Dave Watson, is a feisty bulldog, protective, and fiercely so, of Cowart. We would all come to fear and respect Watson's authority as he bellowed "please be seated! Court will come to order!" and "Stay seated 'til the judge is out of the courtroom!" And woe be unto anyone who might have to visit the restroom during sessions. Watson would permit no aimless coming and going.

But now, bless him, he approached me as I stood tentatively outside the courtroom. In his seventies, white haired, he was wearing his "uniform" of sparking white shirt, dark trousers. I didn't know enough to realize this was the dreaded Bailiff Watson, and he smiled, put both his arms around me and said, "You go right on in, honey . . ."

Cowart's courtroom is a vast, octagonal room, the walls panelled with tropical wood and brass rectangles behind the bench of marble. Fake? Possibly. Light fixtures of white, aqua, red, and wine were suspended from the ceiling.

The thirty-three press seats were to the left as one entered; opposite them were seats reserved for law enforcement officers.

Beyond that were a hundred or more seats for the gallery. No windows, but it was air-conditioned.

I have always found a trial something of a temporary microcosm of life. The judge is the father, kindly, anthoritative, guiding us all—and Edward Cowart would fill that role well. The rest of us—jury, defense, prosecution, gallery, press—were to be thrown together in an intense communal experience. When it ends, it is somehow sad; we will never be this close again. Most of us will never meet again.

This trial would be, for me, akin to having all the characters in a long, long book finally come alive. I knew the names of almost everyone involved, had heard of them for years, though Ted was the only character I had actually seen in person before.

I took a seat in the press section, among strangers who would become friends: Gene Miller, two-time Pulitzer Prize winner from the *Miami Herald*, Tony Polk from the *Rocky Mountain News* in Denver, Linda Kleindienst and George McEvoy of the *Fort Lauderdale News* and *Sun-Sentinel*, George Thurston of the *Washington Post*, Pat McMahon of the *St. Petersburg Times*, Rick Barry of the *Tampa Tribune*, Bill Knowles, Southern Bureau Chief of ABC News—all scribbling notes in their own particular fashion.

Ted glanced over, recognized me, grinned, winked. He looked barely older than the last time I had seen him, but was perfectly attired in suit and tie, styled haircut. It was odd, somehow—as if time had stood still for him. *Dorian Gray* flashed through my mind. I was a grandmother now—twice over—and yet Ted was still the same outwardly as he had been in 1971, perhaps handsomer.

I looked around the courtroom. I saw faces that I have seen in dozens of trials, those whose whole life revolves around going to court; it is their only hobby, interest, avocation; neatly dressed old men, an old woman with garish make-up, her hair hidden by a wrapped stocking, a huge picture hat on top of it all. Housewives, playing hooky, a priest. Stolid rows of lawmen in uniform.

The front row—just behind Ted and the defense team—was jammed with pretty young women, as it would be each day. Did they *know* how much they resembled the defendant's purported victims? Their eyes never left Ted, and they blushed and giggled with delight when he turned to flash a blinding smile at them, as he often did. Outside the courtroom, some of them would admit to reporters that Ted frightened them, yet they couldn't stay away. It is a common syndrome, this fascination that an alleged mass killer has for some women, as if he was the ultimate macho figure.

By tacit agreement, that one front row was somehow reserved for the "Ted groupies," and indeed I would never see a trial with more attractive women present—the Chi Omegas, testifying about the night of January 14–15, 1978, the surviving victims, even the female detectives, deputies, and the court reporters.

The jury was not present those first days; we were still in pretrial, and Cowart had yet to rule on what the court would allow in. The jury remained sequestered in a plush resort on Bay Biscayne.

An uninformed observer would have difficulty distinguishing Ted from any of the young lawyers in the courtroom—Lynn Thompson, Ed Harvey, Bob Haggard, and for the prosecution, Larry Simpson and Danny McKeever, both from the State Attorney's Office.

The defense wanted many of the state's proposed witnesses out: Connie Hastings and Mary Ann Piccano, the girls who had seen the man in Sherrod's Disco earlier on that Saturday night; Nita Neary, the Chi O who had seen the man with the club; Dr. Souviron with his bite-mark testimony; Sergeant Bob Hayward on the Utah arrest; Carol DaRonch from Salt Lake City; Detective Norm Chapman and Don Patchen and their testimony about the conversations during the interrogation in mid-February in Pensacola.

Nita Jane Neary was on the witness stand as I entered the courtroom. She had been badgered by the defense and was almost tearful—but resolute. Asked if she saw the man in the courtroom that she'd seen that night, she said, "Yes, I believe I do." But she wanted a profile look.

Cowart ordered every man in the room to stand and turn sideways.

Nita Jane looked, but seemed reluctant to look directly at Ted. Then she raised her arm, somewhat mechanically and, still with eyes downcast, she pointed at the defendant.

Ted helped the court reporter by saying (about himself), "That's Mr. Bundy . . ."

The defense questioned Nita and her mother. Yes, her mother had shown her newspaper pictures of Ted Bundy taken after his arrest. But she had also picked him out of a mug lay-down later. She was positive.

Judge Cowart would subsequently rule to allow her eye-witness identification, possibly the worst blow that would be dealt the defense.

Ronnie Eng, "the sweetheart" of Chi Omega—the man Nita Neary had first thought she recognized—had been cleared by a polygraph, but he too appeared in pretrial. As he stood beside Bundy, there was little resemblance. Ronnie was dark-complex-ioned, shorter, with black hair. He made a shy, smiling witness.

Carole Ann Boone, Ted's staunchest ally, sat in the courtroom, her eyes meeting his often. A tall, big-boned woman of about thirty-two, she wore thick glasses, had short dark hair—*not* parted in the middle. She seldom smiled, and usually carried sheaves of reports. Her connection to the defendant seemed to be her only interest.

When court ended that first day, I approached Carole Boone and introduced myself. She glanced at me and said, "Yes, I've heard of you" and turned abruptly on her heel and walked away. Somewhat bemused, I stared after her. Did she dislike me so because I was wearing a press badge, or because I was an old friend of Ted's? I never found out; she never spoke to me again.

The next court session began with requests by Ted for more exercise, law library privileges, a typewriter.

Both the library and the exercise facilities were on the seventh floor of the jail building. Ted and his jail supervisor engaged in a little repartee.

"Can you have enough security for me?"

"We better have."

"How many? One? Two? Three?"

"We don't care to be specific. We'll have enough."

Cowart asked, "Can you read while you exercise, Mr. Bundy?"

Ted, wearing on this day a Seattle Mariner's tee-shirt, laughed faintly. He wanted an hour a day in the law library, an hour's exer-cise a day, unlimited visits with Carole Ann Boone who is "relaying my messages to me from my lawyers out west" and Cowart does not concur. Nor will there be a typewriter.

A few figure appears, another name from the book in my mind: Sergeant Bob Hayward of the Utah Highway Patrol, in Miami to describe Ted's arrest in August of 1975. When Hayward refers to a "panty hose mask," Judge Cowart objects for "Attorney" Bundy, saying, "You missed that, my friend—but we'll catch 'em together."

And now began one of the most bizarre sequences I have ever seen in a courtroom. Ted Bundy would be, at the same time, the defendant, the defense attorney, and then the witness.

Ted rose to cross-examine Hayward. He questioned the witness closely about the Utah arrest, the gear in his car, what was said, and tried to point out that he had never given permission to have his VW bug searched. Hayward, a bit put off by being questioned by the *defendant*, answered gruffly. "You told me to go ahead."

And then Ted questioned Deputy Darryl Ondrak of the Salt Lake County Sheriff's Office, arguing about whether the items found in his car *were* burglary tools, pointing out that, though he was charged, on that count, he was never tried on that count.

Cowart intervened: "You can argue that to the hills of Utah: *if* they were burglary tools. It's not relevant here. Quit when you're ahead . . . but I didn't say how far ahead."

Ted himself now became the witness and took the stand. He testified that Hayward's first words to him were, "Why didn't you get out of your car and run? I could have taken your head off."

He explained that he had been intimidated by the number of officers present and that the search was illegal in his estimation. He opened himself up to cross-examination by Danny McKeever and the admission that he had lied about going to the drive-in before being stopped.

Ted wanted the Utah arrest suppressed insisting its evidence was seized through an illegal search. Judge Cowart *would* suppress it—but not for that reason; he found that arrest too "remote" from this trial.

"You may step down, Mr. Bundy. But you may not be excused."

These transactions would result in a blow against the prosecution. They would not be able to compare the Utah pantyhose mask with the Dunwoody Street pantyhose mask in front of the jury.

The score now stood one-to-one.

Judge Cowart would rarely betray his own feelings during the trial, but he slipped a little as he glanced at a composite picture drawn by an artist from Nita Neary's description, a picture Peggy Good argued was meaningless.

"I may be blind," Cowart began, "but, looking at that last picture, I see a striking resemblance to . . . ah . . . whoever it was."

After hearing the tapes taken in Pensacola, and the testimony offered by Detectives Norm Chapman and Don Patchen of statements alleged to have been made by Ted—after the tape recorder was turned off—Judge Cowart made another ruling to suppress, a ruling that caused prosecutors Simpson and McKeever to sag in their chairs. The jury would not be allowed to hear or know of any of it. Nothing of the escape, the credit card thefts, the statements about "vampirism," "voyeurism," "fantasies." Cowart found that too much of the alleged conversations was missing, unrecorded. He would not allow the portions that *were* on tape. The credit card thefts were not part of the murder charges in Cowart's judgment.

The fantasy tape is out too.

The state is left with Nita Neary's eye-witness identification and Dr. Richard Souviron. The rest will be principally circumstantial. There are rumbles in the press section that Bundy *may* be back in the ball game.

43

Judge Cowart was ready to begin the actual trial; the defense was not. On July 7th, Ted and his attorneys argued that they had not had time to prepare the opening arguments.

"We need time between your rulings and our opening statement," Peggy Good argued. "We're exhausted; we've had only five hours sleep a night. You're turning this into a trial by endurance."

"You have four lawyers in Miami, one investigator, two law students helping you. As far as the court is concerned, I care about the entire system. I'm very satisfied that there is no reason to delay any further. In this circuit, it's not unusual to proceed until midnight. We vary the tune, but we've got the same fiddler, the same music. Every minute you've been here, I've been here; and I'm fresh as a daisy."

Ted tried another tack. "I'm concerned about Your Honor, how you're going to do this by one o'clock."

"You just watch us. I appreciate your concern."

And then, Ted was angry. It was Saturday noon, and he wanted to start Monday. Cowart did not.

"My attorneys are not ready!"

"We will begin, Mr. Bundy."

"Then you'll start without *me*, Your Honor!" Ted flared.

"As you like," Cowart said imperturbably, while Ted muttered, "I don't care *who* he is . . ."

But Ted was sitting at the defense table as the jury was brought in for the first time.

Larry Simpson made the opening statements for the prosecution, only after reporters had sent the youthful state attorney back out to comb his hair and re-enter for the benefit of the cameras.

He did a good job, diagramming the four Chi Omega cases, the Dunwoody Street case on a blackboard, listing the victims' names, the charges: Burglary (of the Chi Omega house); first degree murder, Lisa Levy; first degree murder, Margaret Bowman; attempted first degree murder, Kathy Kleiner; attempted first degree murder, Karen Chandler; attempted first degree murder, burglary, Cheryl Thomas. He was workmanlike and showed little emotion, but he was clear and concise.

Ted had picked Robert Haggard, the thirty-four-year-old Miami attorney who'd been on the case only two weeks, to make the opening statements for the defense. Judge Cowart had urged the defense to wait until their "half" of the trial to make the opening remarks, as was their option, but they forged ahead.

Haggard spoke for twenty-six minutes, rambled, and the prosecution objected twenty-nine times, an almost unheard-of number. Cowart *sustained* twenty-three of those objections.

Finally, Cowart threw up his hands and said to Haggard, "That's *argument*. Bless your heart. Come *aboard*."

I felt Ted himself could have done a better job of it.

Ted *did* choose to cross-examine Officer Ray Crew about his actions when he had gone to the Chi Omega House on the morning of the murders. I have no idea what was in the minds of the jury as Ted elicited information about the condition of the death rooms, the condition of Lisa Levy's body, but it seemed to me somewhat grotesque. If this calm, glib, young attorney might have been there to see Lisa's body himself, might have done that terrible damage to her, he was completely dispassionate as he questioned the officer.

"Describe the condition of Lisa Levy's room."

"Clothing strewn about, desk, books . . . some disarray."

"Any blood in any area in the room other than what you testified about earlier?"

"No sir."

"Describe the condition of Margaret Bowman's body."

"She was lying face down, mouth and eyes open. Nylon stocking knotted around her neck, head bloated and discolored."

Ted had been trying to show that the policeman had left his own prints in the room, that he had not proceeded carefully; instead he had only succeeded in impressing a horrible picture in the jury's minds.

And then the young women—victims, witnesses—were a steady parade through the courtroom doors. Melanie Nelson, Nancy Dowdy, Karen Chandler, Kathy Kleiner, Debbie Ciccarelli, Nancy Young, Cheryl Thomas. Dressed in bright cottons, they all had an innocence about them, a vulnerability.

There were no outward signs that Karen and Kathy had ever been injured; the pins in their jaws, the concussions, the bruises, had long-since healed. Only when they told of what had happened to them could one picture the horror.

They never glanced at Ted Bundy.

Cheryl Thomas had more difficulty. She limped as she made her way to the witness chair, sat with her right ear toward the prosecutor, so that she could hear him; she was still completely deaf in the other.

She did not testify about the struggle she had had to regain her health, of the moments of jogging, sit-ups. When she'd first started to walk, she had fallen to one side, but she'd learned to compensate by using her other senses—sight and feeling; she'd learned to develop a sense of balance with her mind. She did not mention how she had fallen again and again when she resumed ballet classes, that she'd had to start over from scratch. She testified very softly, often smiling shyly. The defense wisely chose not to question the victims.

Dr. Thomas Wood testified about the autopsies he had done on the dead victims, and then, over objections from Peggy Good, produced 11- by 14-inch color photos of the bodies, pointing out the damage to the jury.

It is standard for defense attorneys to protest autopsy pictures, declaring them "inflammatory and with no probative value," and it is standard too that the pictures are admitted.

I watched the faces of the jury as those terrible pictures were passed silently through their tiers of seats. The female jurors seemed to be managing better than the males, who paled and winced.

There were several shots of Lisa Levy's buttocks—with the teeth imprints clearly visible. There was one close-up of Margaret Bowman, called the "hole-in-the-head" picture by Judge Cowart, for want of a better term. There was a photograph of Lisa Levy's right breast, the nipple bitten through.

I had neither seen nor talked to Ted privately. He did not have the freedom to hold conversations with those in the courtroom that he had expected. At each recess, he was led, manacled, to a small room across the corridor. When court recessed for the day, that day when the post-mortem reports and the victims' pictures had been introduced into evidence, I stood outside in the hallway for a moment. Ted, carrying his usual pile of legal papers in his cuffed hands, emerged and walked within a few feet of me. He turned to me, smiled, shrugged, and disappeared.

In Florida reporters are allowed to view all the evidence that has been admitted. A group of us waited for Shirley Lewis, the court clerk, to trundle a huge cart full of physical evidence to her office, and there it was spread out on a table. A miasma, real or imagined, seemed to rise from the clutter there, and the laughter and black humor common among the press corps was silenced.

"We're not laughing now, are we?" Tony Polk of Denver said quietly.

We were not.

All the panty-hose masks were there—including the one Sergeant Bob Hayward had brought from Utah—strikingly similar to one another. The garotte from Margaret Bowman's neck, still bearing her dried blood, was there. And all the pictures . . .

I had long since managed to deal with the photographs that are part of homicide cases with a degree of detachment; they no longer upset me as they once did, although I make it a point not to dwell on them. By the time I stood in Shirley Lewis's office, I had seen thousands of body pictures.

I had seen pictures of Kathy Devine and Brenda Baker in Thurston County, but that was months before it was known there was a "Ted." Of course, there were no bodies to photograph in the other Washington cases and I had had no access to Colorado or Utah pictures. Now, I was staring down at huge color photographs of the damage done to girls young enough to be my daughters—at pictures of damage alleged to be the handiwork of a man I thought I knew. That man who only minutes before had smiled the same old grin at me, and shrugged as if to say, "I have no part of this."

It hit me with a terrible sickening wave. I ran to the ladies' room and threw up.

44

The cloyingly hot days in Miami's July took on a pattern. First, the mass exodus from the Civic Center Holiday Inn by most of the principals—barring the defendant—to the Justice Center three blocks away. Virtually all of the defense team, the prosecution team, the media people from out of town, Carole Ann Boone and her teenage son, the television cameramen and technicians were headquartered at the Holiday Inn, and some of the best quotes reporters elicited came in the evening when the little bar on the first floor was jammed with participants quaffing cold beers and gin and tonics. Here, the demarcation lines were not as pronounced as they were in the courtroom.

The dash to the Justice Center. "Get in there before Watson shuts the door!" The journey was not without its dangers. It was necessary to cross six lanes of rush-hour traffic, balancing on center islands as the commuters of Miami whooshed by, inches away. "Don't walk under the viaduct—a reporter from Utah got mugged the other evening by some guy on a bicycle with a six-inch blade."

But then, the motel itself was not exactly safe; Ruth Walsh, the ABC anchorwoman from Seattle, had lost her money, her jewelry—even her wedding rings—to a cat burglar who'd crept into her room from the balcony six floors up as she slept.

We were a long way from the beaches where the tourists frolicked.

A first cup of coffee of the day on the ninth floor in the communications center. Already, the phones were busy, reporters putting copy men on hold, waiting for a daily update. Here, the black humor mounted. Two television reporters mimicked a personal interview with Mrs. Bundy, one of them playing the defendant's mother in a high falsetto:

"And what was Ted like when he was a child, Mrs. Bundy?"

"Oh he was a good boy, a good, normal, All-American boy."

"What kind of toys did he like, Mrs. Bundy?"

"The usual things—guns, knives, panty hose—just like any boy."

"And did he have a job?"

"Oh, no. Teddy always had his credit cards."

Hoots of laughter.

Waiting for the proceedings to flash onto the closed circuit TV before them, the verse writers scribbled.

> Teddy came to Tallahassee,
> Looking for a pretty lassie,
> Creeping, sneaking through the dark,
> Lurking 'til he found his mark,
> Remember dear, remember well—
> His bite is much worse than his bark.

For some of the news people, the Bundy trial was only a story— and a great one at that; others seemed disturbed, too conscious of the waste of lives involved, not only the victims'—but the defendant's. We were watching a major tragedy unfold before us, and it meant far more than headlines.

Down on the fourth floor, the mood of the public was angry, vengeful. As I waited in line to pass through the metal detector, to submit to the search of my purse and papers that transpired everytime I entered the courtroom, I heard two men talking behind me.

"That Bundy . . . he ain't never gonna get out of Florida alive . . . he's gonna get what's comin' to him."

"They oughta take him out and nail his balls to the wall and leave him there 'til he dies. And that'd be too good for him."

I half-turned to look at them. Two nice, grandfatherly looking men. They echoed the feeling of the Florida public.

As the trial progressed, the crowds grew denser and more hostile. Could the jury feel it? Had they some suppressed anger of their own? You couldn't tell by looking at them. Their faces—like all jury faces—were bland, listening. One or two of them regularly nodded off to sleep during the long afternoon sessions. Upstairs, in the press room, reporters would spot that and yell at the television set, "Wake up! Wake up! Hey Bernest! Wake up! Floy! Wake up!"

Ted still glanced into the press section to see if I was there, still smiled faintly, but he seemed to be shrinking, his eyes a little more hollow each day, as if something inside him was drying up, leaving only an exhausted shell sitting at the defense table.

Despite the long procession of young women, the parade of police officers who began to blend into one another somehow, the word was that Bundy might win. There was so much about him that was being held back from the jury.

Danny McKeever, looking frazzled, gave short press interviews saying that he was worried—something a prosecutor rarely admits. The press began to lay odds that that "son of a bitch may pull it off."

We had missed a day in court because Mazie Edge had a virus; we would miss another when Ted himself came down with a high fever, a deep cough. On those days, with nothing else to do, we interviewed each other and side-bar stories of faint human interest were sent to home papers, stories describing how reporters from other areas felt—a kind of inbred journalism.

Ted was back then, looking paler, tired.

Robert Fulford, manager of the Oak, testified about his first contact with Chris Hagen, of renting a room with a bunk bed, a table, chest of drawers, and a desk to him. "He didn't have the rent when it came due. He said he could call his mother long-distance in Wisconsin and she'd send it down. I heard him make a call, and it seemed like he was talkin' to someone, but he never showed up with the rent. When I checked his room a couple of days later, he was gone."

The jury knew that Bundy had come to and left Tallahassee, but they would not know from whence—and why.

David Lee testified about his arrest of Bundy in Pensacola in the dark dawn of February 15th, told of how his prisoner had wanted to die.

The next day, July 17th, Ted did not come to court. At 9 A.M., he was not in his place at the defense table. The gallery muttered, and the press box wondered; Bundy was *always* in his seat, unmanacled, when court began, now he was not. Something was wrong.

The jury was kept sequestered as jailer Marty Kratz appeared. Kratz explained to Judge Cowart that there had been trouble with Ted in the jail.

At about 1:00 A.M., Ted had thrown an orange between the bars of Cell 406 and succeeded in smashing one of the lights installed outside to give him better illumination in that cell. Jailers had immediately moved him to Cell 405 and searched his first cell. Hidden far back in that cell, they had found shards of broken glass from the splintered lightbulb. What for? Suicide? Escape?

"When we went to get him for court this morning," Kratz continued, "we couldn't get the key in the lock. He'd jammed some toilet paper in there."

Reminded that he was due in court, Bundy had replied, "I'll be there when I feel like it."

Cowart did not take kindly to this information, and sent Ted's lawyers off to plead with their client to get himself to court in a hurry. He also found Ted in contempt of court for the delaying tactics.

At 9:30, Ted appeared—a Ted who was angry, arguing that his treatment in Dade County was not satisfactory to him. He again decried the lack of exercise, the withholding of files, the blocking of his access to the law library. His voice broke, on the verge of tears, as he talked to Cowart. "There comes a time when the only thing I can do is passively resist . . . I have potential . . . now . . . now . . . I've only used that part of my potential which is *nonviolent*. There comes a time when I have to say, 'Whoa . . .' "

"Whoa," Cowart answered. "If you say 'Whoa,' I'm going to have to use spurs."

Ted made a tactical error. He began to list the offenses against him, shaking his finger at Judge Cowart as he did so. Cowart took umbrage. "Don't shake your finger at me, young man . . . don't shake your finger at me!"

Bundy tilted his finger slightly toward the defense table.

"That's fine," Cowart said. "You can shake it at Mr. Haggard."

"He probably deserves it better than you do. In the three weeks I've been here, I've been taken to the law library three times."

"Yeah, and on at least three occasions you've just sat up there and talked to Sergeant Kratz. You never used the library itself."

"That's not true. It [the library] is a joke. But it's a better place to read than the interview room. There is no justification for the treatment I'm receiving. I am given a strip search after I see my attorney and that is unconscionable. Now, this railroad train is running, but if I'm going to get off, I'll get off if I need to demonstrate to this courtroom that they are influencing me and affecting me."

Cowart spoke as if to a spoiled child. "This court is going to proceed on schedule without your voluntary interruptions. We're not going to have it any more. Now I want you to discuss that with your counsel. I want you to know your rights, but I also want you to know that as forebearing as this court can be, it can also be that strong."

"I'm willing to accept the consequences of my actions, Your Honor, and anything I do I'm aware of what the court will do."

"Then we're together. Bless your heart, and I just hope you stay with us. If you don't, we'll miss you."

Bundy ended it with bitter humor. "And all these people won't pay their money to come see me."

Tempers were ragged for much of the day. When microanalyst Patricia Lasko testified that the two hairs found in the panty-hose mask at Dunwoody Street were "from Mr. Bundy or from someone whose hair is *exactly* like his," Haggard grilled her unmercifully.

The discussion of hair microanalysis became so esoteric that the jury appeared lost in the scientific terminology. Haggard badgered Ms. Lasko until the judge warned him.

When Haggard asked to examine Ms. Lasko's notes, she hung onto them stubbornly. Haggard wrenched them away, and Larry Simpson walked over and began a tug-of-war with the defense attorney over the notebook.

Judge Cowart chastised both attorneys and sent the jury out. Then he complimented the usually mild-mannered Simpson, "It's the first time I've seen you get your dander up."

It was true. There had been little fire in cross-examination from *either* side.

The state's case was coming to a close. Nita Neary had again raised her arm—this time in front of a jury—and pointed out Ted Bundy as the man she'd seen leaving the Chi Omega House just after the murders. The biggest gun of all—Dr. Richard Souviron, the dental odontologist—was about to begin.

Souviron, a handsome, dapper man with a flair for the theatrical, seemed to enjoy his time before the jury. He held a pointer and indicated the teeth on the huge color photo of Ted Bundy's mouth—the photo which had been taken after the search warrant was served in the Leon County Jail more than a year earlier.

The jury seemed fascinated; they had been confused, obviously, by the serology testimony on semen, and by the hair testimony, but they followed the dental testimony alertly.

The tissue from Lisa Levy's buttock had been destroyed for comparison purposes through improper preservation; only the bite mark, photographed to scale, was left. Would it be enough?

"These are laterals . . . bicuspids . . . incisors . . ."

Souviron explained that each individual's teeth had particular characteristics: alignment, irregularities, chips, size, sharpness—that these characteristics make them one of a kind. Souviron had found Ted's teeth particularly unique.

Dramatically, he tacked the enlarged picture of Lisa Levy's buttocks, bearing the purple rows of bite marks, on the display board in front of the jury. And then he placed a clear sheet on top of that—a sheet bearing an enlarged picture of the defendant's teeth.

"They line up exactly!"

Explaining the "double bite," Souviron continued: "The individual bit once, then turned sideways and bit a second time. The top teeth stayed in about the same position, but the lower teeth— biting harder—left 'two rings.'" The second bite made it even easier, Souviron said, to compare the teeth with the marks because he had twice as much to work with.

"Doctor," Prosecutor Simpson began. "Based upon your analysis and comparison of this particular bite mark, can you tell us within a reasonable degree of dental certainty whether or not the teeth represented in that photograph as being those of Theodore Robert Bundy and the teeth represented by the models that have been introduced as state's exhibits number 85, 86, made the bite marks reflected on your exhibit as marked and admitted into evidence?"

"Yes sir."

"And what is that opinion?"

"They made the marks."

It was the first time—the very first time in all the years since 1974—that a piece of physical evidence had been linked absolutely between a victim and Ted Bundy . . . and the courtroom erupted.

The defense, of course, wanted to show that "dental certainty" and forensic odontology is a primitive, and not widely accepted science. Ed Harvey rose for the defense on cross-examination.

He began, "Analyzing bite marks is part art and part science, isn't it?"

"I think that's a fair statement."

"And that really depends upon the experience and education of the examiner?"

"Yes."

"And your conclusions are really a matter of opinion. Is that correct?"

"That is correct."

"You've got a given set of teeth, or models, and a given area of skin, a thigh or a calf. Is there any way to test whether those teeth will make the same marks over and over?"

Souviron smiled. "Yes, because I did an experiment just like that. I took models and I went to the morgue and I pressed the models into the buttocks area on different individuals and photographed them. Yes, they can be standardized, and, yes, they do match."

Harvey feigned incredulity. "You said *cadavers?* Is that correct?"

"I couldn't find any live volunteers."

Harvey tried to find some areas of inconsistency, but his line of questioning failed.

Souviron explained further, and the jury leaned forward to listen. "If there's an area of inconsistency—out it goes. If there's a Vee'd-out central that wouldn't make this pattern, you'd say, 'Well, we'll have to exclude that person even though the arch size is the same, the cuspids are tucked down in behind the laterals and this type of thing. The centrals don't line up right.' [But] The odds of finding this would be a needle in a haystack—an *identical* set like Mr. Bundy's—with the wear on the centrals and everything, the chipped lateral incisor, everything identical. You'd have to be able to combine that with the three marks on the upper central incisors, and the odds against that are astronomical."

The state was closing its case with all flags flying. They called Dr. Lowell J. Levine, the chief consultant in forensic dentistry to the New York City Medical Examiner.

Levine testified that he believed Lisa Levy—or the person whose flesh appeared in the photograph he studied—had been "passive" when the bite marks were left on her body. "There is very little evidence of motion or swirling you'd normally get as tissue moves in various directions as the teeth move on the skin. It almost looks more like an animal which has bitten and kinda grabs. These things were left slowly, and the person was not moving. They [sic] were passive when they were left."

"Can you give us an opinion as to the uniqueness of teeth?"

"Everybody's teeth are unique to that particular person for a number of reasons. One, the shapes of the teeth are unique, in addition to the juxtaposition or the relationship of each tooth to the other is unique, the twisting or tipping or bending also adds to that uniqueness. Present and missing teeth . . . and those are basically gross characteristics. We also have other types of individual characteristics which are accidental characteristics such as breaking."

Mike Minerva, left behind in Tallahassee when Ted had grown disenchanted with him, was in the courtroom—apparently forgiven—to cross-examine Dr. Levine.

"When you say 'reasonable degree of dental certainty,' you are speaking of some kind of probability. Is that right?"

"A very high degree of probability. Yes sir."

Minerva was trying to make the "new science" suspect, to make it look simply "probable" and not "absolute," but Levine would not buckle under.

". . . in my mind it becomes a practical impossibility to come up with something with all the identical characteristics."

"Would you say that it is fair to say that odontology is a relatively new, newly recognized forensic science?"

"No. I do not think that is fair at all. Historically, you have a case of Paul Revere doing identifications. You have testimony admitted to the bar in Massachusetts in the late 1800s on identification, and you can find citations for bite-mark cases even in the legal justice system that go back twenty-five years. So what's new?"

The prosecution rested. Ted Bundy asked that Dr. Souviron be held in contempt of court for speaking out at the Orlando meeting prior to his trial on his case, and Cowart denied his request. In the empty courtroom, Ted studied the dental exhibits of his teeth and the pictures of Lisa Levy's bite marks.

I have no idea what his thoughts were.

45

Things were not good in the defense camp. Robert Haggard had resigned, hinting that the defendant's insistence on questioning Ray Crew, the police officer who was in the death rooms on the night of January 14–15, had been a mistake. The public defenders would not allow Ted to cross-examine witnesses any more.

On the first day of the defense, July 20th, Ted rose to address Judge Cowart. He was claiming that his attorneys were inadequate—the same attorneys that he had praised highly to me in his pretrial phone call. He blamed Mike Minerva for dropping out of the case without warning, the man he now said had "the most experienced courtroom presence in this case." He didn't mention that he himself had asked Minerva to leave.

"I did not have any choice in the selection of Bob Haggard to represent me here in Miami. In toto, I have not been asked at any time *my* opinion about who should be representing me within the public defender's office."

In fact, Ted did not like his whole defense team.

"I think it's also important to note that there are certain problems of communication between myself and my attorneys which have reduced my defense, the defense which is not my defense or sanctioned by me, nor one which I can say I agree with."

Ted complained that his lawyers ignored his input into the case, would not let him make decisions, and were stubbornly refusing him the right to cross-examine witnesses before the jury.

Cowart was aghast.

"I don't know of any case I've seen or experienced where an individual who is indigent has received the quality and quantity of counsel you have. There have been five separate counsel here representing you. It's unheard of. Who's minding the store for the public defender I can't tell you. And what's happening to all those other indigents they represent I can't tell you. This court has watched with a great deal of carefulness that, before witnesses are tendered, you are questioned, and this record will show hundreds of 'just a moment, pleases' where they [Ted's attorneys] go by and confer with you. I've never seen anything like it in the history of any case I've ever tried. Nor in twenty-seven years at the bar have I ever seen anything exactly like what has happened in the defense of this case."

But Ted was adamant; once again, he wanted to take over his own defense. Cowart said he would agree, but warned Ted that a lawyer who represents himself has a fool for a client. Ted responded, "I've always taken that particular axiom like someone who works on his own car has a fool for a mechanic. It all depends on how much you want to do by yourself."

It was an old, tired story. Cowart suggested that Ted's question was one of "submission of counsel."

"Imposition," Ted countered.

"No, it's submission, and this court has addressed that. If they don't do every little, single, solitary thing that you want 'em to, they're incompetent. And, bless your heart, if they *do* . . . *I'm* gonna fire 'em."

It is likely that Ted wanted to be sure the record showed that he had not had his attorney of choice. Millard Farmer's name wasn't mentioned, but the implication was clear.

Once again, Ted was at the helm, and his attorneys were only "advisors." Still, for the moment, Ed Harvey would question the defense witnesses. Harvey said—out of the hearing of the jury, a jury which did not seem to realize that the defense team was in a shambles—that he wanted out too.

The defense tactics were not to present any alibi for Ted Bundy, but to try to negate the state's evidence. Dr. Duane DeVore, an oral surgery professor from the University of Maryland, and an advisor in forensic dentistry to the chief medical examiner of the state of Maryland, testified that bite marks were *not* unique—though teeth themselves were.

". . . the material of skin is flexible, elastic, and, depending upon the bleeding structures underneath and the amount of blood, [a tooth] may not leave a unique mark."

DeVore produced four models of teeth from Maryland young-sters that he said could have caused the bite marks on the victim, but he admitted to Larry Simpson that Ted Bundy's teeth also could have made the same marks.

The defense produced a tape taken while Nita Neary was in a hypnotic trance where she said that the houseboy, Ronnie Eng, had resembled the intruder. Eng was brought into the courtroom and stood beside Ted. The jury looked on, and, of course, said nothing.

Serologist Michael J. Grubb, of the Institute of Forensic Sciences in Oakland, testified that the semen left on Cheryl Thomas's sheet could not have been deposited by Bundy—again in a long, highly technical discourse that seemed to confuse the jury.

Ed Harvey, trying one more time to save his client, asked for another competency hearing. "The man's life is at stake. He shouldn't be forced to take the services of public lawyers whom he has no confidence in. His conduct has revealed the debilitating effects of his mental disorder by reflecting a total lack of insight regarding the disorder and its effects on him, by reflecting a wholly inadequate ability to consult with lawyers about the case."

Danny McKeever opposed the competency motion. "The man is difficult to work with. He's almost cunning the way he works against his attorneys sometimes . . . but he's competent."

Ted smiled. Anything was better than being considered incompetent.

Cowart felt Ted was competent too, and a compromise was worked out as the trial approached its ending. Harvey would stay, Lynn Thompson would stay, and Peggy Good would make the final arguments. Bundy would comment later, "I feel, really, really, good . . ."

I had not seen Ted alone since I'd reached Miami, although I had left messages at the jail with my phone number. I don't know if he got them, or, if he had, if he was allowed to call out. Perhaps he no longer had anything he wished to say to me. So I cannot judge whether he was competent or not. It is a moot question whether his deliberate rocking of the defense team's already shaky platform was a move on his part to gain even more attention or whether it was an indication that he was, truly, no longer rational, a man in the grip of some kind of egomania that obliterated the issue of survival itself. I could only observe him in the courtroom, and he seemed hellbent for destruction.

Ted continued to denigrate his attorneys, still angry that they would not allow him more control.

"I've tried to be nice. We're speaking more to a problem attorneys have in giving up power. Maybe we're dealing with a problem of professional psychology. Where attorneys are so jealous of the power they exercise in the courtroom they're afraid to share it with the defendant. They are so insecure in their own skill and experience that they are afraid that anybody else might know as much as they do or can at least participate in the planning process."

Cowart commented mildly that Ted's attorneys had passed their bar exams, had graduated from law school. "I can't conceive of submitting myself, or I'm sure you wouldn't submit yourself, to brain surgery by somebody who had only a year and a half of medical school."

In actuality, of course, Ted's defense attorneys were not that experienced. Cowart had helped them often in phrasing questions, and much of their cross-examination was tedious, uninspired, and headed nowhere. But then Simpson and McKeever—for the state— did not rival Melvin Belli or F. Lee Bailey. The Bundy trial had been marked throughout with mediocrity; only the judge himself was a thoroughbred. However, if Ted could have worked with his attorneys instead of trying to tear them apart, he might have had an adequate defense. They had succeeded in barring the "fantasy tape," the Utah panty-hose mask, his former record, his escape. Despite any faltering on their parts, they might well have saved him *if* he had allowed it.

Moving into final arguments, the press was still wagering even odds on the outcome of the trial.

And yet, there seemed to be something happening, something that couldn't be stopped. Ted had spoken of "this railroad train running," and it struck a chord buried deep in the recesses of my memory. The outcome of the trial would not necessarily be the wrong verdict; that verdict was something that none of us had control over any longer. The truth had been lost somewhere among the games, the rituals, the motions, the petty arguments and the rational arguments, the quotes for the press, the notations for the record.

In all human endeavors that deal with what is unthinkable, too terrible to be dealt with squarely, we turn to what is familiar and regimented: funerals, wakes, and even wars. Now, in this trial, we had gone beyond our empathy with the pain of the victims, our niggling realization that the defendant was a fragmented personality. He knew the rules, he even knew a great deal about the law, but he did not seem to be cognizant of what was about to happen to him. He seemed to consider himself irrefrangible. And what was about to happen to him was vital for the good of society. I could not refute that. It had to be, but it seemed hollow that none of us understood that his ego, our egos, the rituals of the courtroom itself, the jokes and the nervous laughter were veiling the gut reactions that we should all be facing. We were all on "this railroad train running . . ."

I looked at the jury, and I *knew*. Never mind the odds. My God, they are going to kill Ted . . .

46

Ted himself had one "last hurrah" before final arguments. He had studied the blow-ups of his teeth carefully, listened stony-faced as Dr. Souviron testified that there was no question in *his* mind that it was Ted Bundy—and only Ted Bundy—who had sunk his teeth into Lisa Levy's buttock. In the emptied courtroom, he had even mugged a bit for the cameras, holding a model of his teeth against the picture of the dead girl's bruised flesh. And he had realized just how damning this forensic dentistry evidence was to his case.

In the absence of the jury, Bundy called his investigator, Joe Aloi, to the stand. Aloi is a hearty, husky man with Latin coloring, given to wearing flamboyant tropical shirts when he is not in the courtroom, a respected investigator who often joked with the press and the attorneys in the lounge of the Holiday Inn. Now Ted was trying, through him, to bring forth physical evidence that would dispute the accuracy of Souviron's testimony. The chip in one of his front teeth had not been there at the time of the Chi Omega murders, not according to Ted.

Aloi identified some photographs sent to him from Chuck Dowd, the managing editor of the *Tacoma News Tribune*, Ted's hometown paper—pictures that represented a chronological sequence since his first arrest in Utah.

Ted asked: "What was the purpose of enlarging certain portions of the photographs that you were attempting to obtain in chronological order?"

"I had received information from Mr. Gene Miller of the *Miami Herald* concerning a seminar Dr. Souviron had given. I was very concerned about when this characteristic occurred."

"And what characteristic is that?"

"This is concerning one of two front teeth—I don't know all the names—and I was concerned about this chip on the inside of the tooth, and whether it was or was not there and whatever specific times we could document some of the photographs in evidence to depict that this particular tooth was in very good condition at certain times. And, of course, at other times when Dr. Souviron had taken his samples from you if the tooth was in a different condition."

Ted asked what the photo blow-ups had revealed. An objection was sunstained. Judge Cowart coached the defendant-defense attorney.

"You might ask him if he was able to accomplish [discovery of the teeth in different conditions]. Try it that way and see if I object."

"The court is always right."

"No," Cowart demurred. "Not always."

"Did you accomplish what you set out to do?"

"No sir, I did not."

"And why not?"

Aloi responded, "The media, for legal reasons and perhaps for other reasons, would not be very cooperative."

The investigator explained that various newspapers would not release their negatives to him, negatives of pictures of Ted Bundy flashing his familiar wide smile. Aloi had been unable to lay his hands on pictures taken of Ted before his Pensacola arrest that would indicate positively that there was no chip in his front tooth at that time.

Ted changed places again, and, again, became the witness— questioned by Peggy Good. He testified that his tooth had been chipped in the middle of March, 1978—two months after the murders in Tallahassee.

"I recall I was eating dinner in my cell in the Leon County Jail and I bit down hard, just like you bite down on a rock or pebble, and I pulled it out and it was just a white piece of tooth, and it just chipped out of one of my central incisors."

Danny McKeever rose to cross-examine.

"You don't know what the Utah dental records look like, do you?"

"I've never seen the dental records themselves."

"Would you be surprised to know that those teeth appear to be chipped from the Utah dental records?" (Which, indeed, they did.)

"Yes, I would."

Now, for the first time, Ted called his friend, Carole Ann Boone, to the witness stand. Carole Ann answered Bundy's questions about her visits to him in the Garfield County Jail in late 1977.

"Did you visit me there? How many times?"

"I don't have my records with me, but I believe I visited with you on six or seven consecutive days—both in the morning and the afternoon. On a few afternoons, we visited in the law library in the courthouse and then we would walk back together to the jail, about half a block."

Ms. Boone testified that to the best of her memory, Ted had had no chip at all in his front tooth at that time.

Ted argued vehemently for a delay, for subpoenas that would force all newspapers to turn over their negatives of him. "I think you'd understand what I'm getting at. If that chip did not occur until March, 1978, a month or two after the Chi Omega crimes, and if the state's odontologists say that space between the two linear abrasions could only have been made by a tooth with a chip or a gap between the two central incisors then there's obviously something wrong with the observations made by the state's odontologists. Our contention all along, Your Honor, is that they have taken my teeth and twisted them every which way but loose to fit."

It was a vain plea. Cowart ruled that there would be no dash for new evidence on Ted's teeth, no subpoenas. As Ted moved to reopen, Cowart intoned:

"Mr. Bundy, you may jump up and down, hang from the chandelier, do anything you want to, but the court has ruled and the case is closed."

Ted muttered some derogatory statements under his breath.

"You impress me not, sir . . ." the judge replied.

"Well, I suppose the feeling is mutual, Your Honor."

"I'm sure it is, bless your heart."

Larry Simpson rose to give the closing arguments for the prosecution, speaking in his usual subdued manner; he talked for forty minutes.

"First degree murder can be committed in the state of Florida in two different ways. It can be done by a person who premeditates and thinks about what he's going to do and then goes out and does it. That's exactly what the evidence showed in this particular case, a premeditated, a brutal murder of two young girls sleeping in their beds. The second way is during the commission of a burglary. The state has proved a burglary in this case.

"I asked Nita Neary the question—on the witness stand—'Nita, do you recall the man you saw at the door of the Chi Omega sorority house the morning of January 15, 1978?' Her exact words were, 'Yes, sir. I do.' I asked her 'Nita, is that man in the courtroom today?' She said, 'Yes sir. He is.' And she pointed him out. That in and of itself is proof of this defendant's guilt, and it is sufficient to support a conviction in this case.

"In Sherrod's, Mary Ann Piccano also saw the man. He scared her so bad she can't even remember what he looked like. He came up to her and asked her to dance. What were the words Mary Ann Piccano used to her friend when she went to dance with the man? She said, 'I think I'm about to dance with an ex-con . . .' Ladies and gentlemen, this man was *next door* to the Chi Omega sorority house, the morning of the murders . . . *and there was something wrong with him!*"

Simpson continued to tote up the circumstantial evidence, the testimony of Rusty Gage and Henry Palumbo of the Oak that they had seen "Chris" standing at the front door of the rooming house just after the attacks, seen him looking back toward the campus. "They told you that the defendant in this case said to them that he thought this was a professional job—*a professional job*—done by somebody who had done it before and was probably long gone.

"Ladies and gentlemen, this man recognized from the morning of these murders that this was a professional job, that no clues had been left. He thought he'd gotten away scot free."

Simpson pointed out the links with the license tag stolen from Randy Ragan's van, the theft of the Volkswagen bug, the escape to Pensacola, the room left wiped clean of prints, empty of all possessions.

"He had loaded up and packed up everything he had and he was getting out of Dodge. That's what it amounts to. The heat was on and he was going."

Simpson spoke of Officer David Lee's arrest of Bundy in Pensacola. "Theodore Robert Bundy said to him, 'I wish you had killed me. If I run now, will you shoot me?' Why did he say those things to Officer Lee? Here is a man that has created, committed, the most horrible and brutal murders known to the Tallahasses area. That's why. He can't live with himself anymore and he wants Officer Lee to kill him right there."

Simpson built to a big finish. He had dealt with the eye witness, the circumstantial evidence, and now he brought in Patricia Lasko's testimony linking the two, curly-brown hairs in the pantyhose mask beside Cheryl Thomas's bed to their source: Ted Bundy's head. "That pantyhose mask came directly from the man that committed these crimes. The hairs from that pantyhose mask also came from that man."

Souviron's testimony was the clincher.

"What was his conclusion? With a reasonable degree of dental certainty, Theodore Robert Bundy made that bite mark in the body of Lisa Levy. Asked in cross-examination about the possibility of someone else in the world having teeth that could have left those marks, what did he say? He said it would be like finding a needle in a haystack. A needle in a haystack.

"When Dr. Levine was asked about the possibility of someone else leaving this bite mark, or someone else having teeth that could leave this bite mark, he told you it was a practical impossibility. A practical impossibility."

Simpson ended by decrying the defense's desperation.

"On cross examination, Dr. DeVore, the defense expert, had to tell you, and did, that the defendant, Theodore Robert Bundy, could have left that bite mark. Ladies and gentlemen, the defense was in a real problem situation. Anytime they've got to put a witness on [who will say] that their man *could* have committed this crime, they've got real problems. And it was a desperate move—a damned desperate move—that might have succeeded—but did not."

Final arguments, ideally, are filled with the kind of rhetoric that will keep listeners on the very edges of their seats. This is the stuff of which movies and television dramas are made. But the Bundy Miami trial had none of that fire, nothing to grip or compel, from the attorneys not even at the close.

Only the defendant and the judge filled their roles as if they'd been chosen by central casting.

Two jurors drowsed, incredibly, *drowsed* in their chairs as Ted Bundy's life hung in the balance.

Peggy Good, the last barrier between Ted and the electric chair, stood now to speak for the defense. She had little to work with—no alibis, no surprise witness to rise from the gallery and shout that there was, indeed, an alibi. She could only attempt to tear down the prosecution's case, to nibble away at the jury's consciences. Ms. Good had to overcome the testimony of forty-nine prosecution witnesses, the one hundred exhibits entered by the prosecution. She could only fall back on talk of "reasonable doubt."

"The defense is not denying there was a great and horrible tragedy that occurred in Tallahassee on January 15th. True, that these four unfortunate women were beaten while sleeping in their beds, injured . . . killed. But I ask you not to compound that tragedy by convicting the wrong man when the state's evidence is insufficient to prove beyond a reasonable doubt that Mr. Bundy, and no one else, is the person that committed these crimes. How tragic it would be if a man's life could be taken from him because twelve people thought he was probably guilty, but they were not sure. You must assure yourself that you will not wake up and doubt your decision and wonder if you convicted the wrong man here two weeks after he is dead and gone."

Ms. Good cast aspersions on the police investigation. "There are basically two ways for the police to investigate a crime. They can go to the crime scene, they can look for the clues, and they can follow the clues to their logical conclusions and find a suspect. Or they can find the suspect, decide on the suspect, and decide to make the evidence fit the suspect and work to make the evidence fit only him."

Good listed the areas she considered weak, condemning the introduction of the masses of bloodied sheets, bloody photographs, the lack of fingerprint matching, mishandling of evidence—even the eye-witness identification.

She found Nita Neary's identification faulty. "She wants to help if she can. And she can't let herself believe that the man who committed these crimes is still out on the street."

Good tried feebly to make Ted's retreat from Tallahassee seem reasonable. "There are lots of reasons a person might run from the cops. One reason is that you might be afraid you'd be railroaded. You might be afraid you'd be charged with something you didn't do. It's clear Mr. Bundy left town because he was out of money. He was running out on the rent."

Peggy Good was like the little boy with his finger in the dike, but there were too many new freshets erupting to hold back. In dealing with the testimony by Drs. Souviron and Levine, she suggested that the investigators had found Ted Bundy and matched his teeth to the bite, rather than searching for the person who had made the bite. "If you want to convict on the best shell in a confidence game, maybe you'll accept what Souviron and Levine have to say. It will be a sad day for our system of justice if a man can be convicted in our courts on the quality of the state's evidence, and you can put a man's life on the line because they say he has crooked teeth, without any proof that such are unique, without any scientific facts or data base to their conclusions."

Simpson came back with rebuttal. It was almost over.

"Ladies and gentlemen, the man who committed this crime was smart. This man premeditated this murder. He knew what he was going to do before he did it, and planned it, and prepared himself for it. If there is any question in your mind about that, just look at the pantyhose mask. That is a weapon that was prepared by the perpetrator of this crime. Now, ladies and gentlemen, somebody took the time to make this weapon right here, this instrument that could be used for both—a mask that could hide identity . . . or also for strangulation.

"Anybody who took the time to do that is not going to leave fingerprints at a crime scene. And there was not a *single* fingerprint in room 12 at the Oak; the room had been wiped clean!

"Ladies and gentlemen, this man *is* a professional, just as he told Rusty Gage at the Oak back in January, 1978. He's the kind of a man smart enough to stand in the courtroom and move to the end of the bannister and cross-examine witnesses in this case because he thinks he is smart enough to get away with any crime, just like he told Rusty Gage."

Ted himself had said nothing. He'd sat quietly at the defense table, sometimes staring at his hands, hands that did not appear particularly powerful, small hands with tapering fingers, knobbed at the joints as if with early arthritis.

It was 2:57 P.M. on July 23rd when the jurors retired to debate his guilt or innocence. Dave Watson, the old bailiff, guarded the door. An hour later, Ted was returned to his cell in the Dade County Jail to await the verdict.

All the life seemed to have gone out of the fourth-floor courtroom; it was, for the moment, an empty stage bereft of its players.

The ninth floor, however, had become a bee-hive of activity, alive with reporters, all the attorneys, anyone connected with the case—save the victims and the witnesses. The odds were still even. Fifty-fifty. Acquittal or conviction, and bets were being placed. It would surely be a long, long night—perhaps days before a verdict could be reached. There might even be a hung jury.

Louise Bundy was in Miami, waiting with Carole Ann Boone and her son—waiting to see if *Louise's* son would live or die. Although the penalty phase would be separate, no one doubted that, if Ted were convicted, he would also receive the death penalty. Spenkelink had only killed another ex-con; this case involved the deaths of innocent young women.

Ted gave a telephone interview as he waited to hear.

"Is it just being in the wrong place at the wrong time?" the reporter asked.

His voice came through, strong, almost surprised-sounding at finding himself in this predicament. "It's just being Ted Bundy in anyplace, I guess . . . anymore. It started out in Utah and it seemed like one set of circumstances seemed to bootstrap another, to feed on one another, and once you get people thinking in that vein . . . Police officers, they want to solve crimes, and I sometimes don't think they really think things through; they're willing to take the convenient alternative. The convenient alternative is me."

It was 3:50 P.M. The jurors sent out for legal pads, pencils.

4:12 P.M. Watson announces, "I'm going to the head. Hold 'em down if they knock."

5:12 P.M. Watson says the principals are spread out around Miami, that it will take half an hour to return them when the jury reaches a verdict.

6:31 P.M. Judge Cowart returns to the courtroom. The jury has a question. It will be their only inquiry. They want to know if the hairs were found *in* the panty-hose mask. The answer is that they were shaken from the mask.

The jury has stopped its deliberation to eat the sandwiches which were sent in. The feeling is that they will deliberate for a short time longer, and then retire for the night. There is such a massive amount of testimony and evidence to be got through.

And then, the word came. Electrifying. It is only 9:20 P.M. The jury has reached a verdict. As they file in, only Foreman Rudolph Treml glances at Ted. He silently hands seven slips of paper to Judge Cowart, who passes them to the court clerk.

Shirley Lewis reads them aloud. Guilty as charged . . . guilty as charged . . . guilty . . . guilty . . . guilty . . . guilty . . . guilty.

Ted betrays no emotion. Only a slight raising of the eyebrows, his right hand to his chin, rubbing gently. When it is all over, he sighs. Again, it his mother who cries.

It has taken the jury less than six hours of deliberation to decide his fate. All those kindly middle-aged women, the devout church-goers, the people who didn't read newspapers, this jury hand-picked by Ted himself. It appeared that they had been eager to debate the question of his guilt, almost as eager to find that he was, indeed, guilty.

Ted is lost to me. He has been lost since I looked at the pictures of the dead girls and knew what I knew . . . knew what I had never wanted to believe. There is no need to remain for the penalty phase. Whatever is to come after is already foretold in my mind. They are going to kill him . . . they are going to kill him . . . and he knew it all along.

47

I flew home, leaving Miami behind in the grip of a warm, pelting rain. I had to change planes in St. Louis, and there too, that city was criss-crossed with violent thunder storms. We sat on the ground for one hour, two hours, waiting for a break in the storm. At length, we were the last plane allowed off the ground as lightning seemed to split the air only feet from the wing-tips. The plane bucked and shook as if the pilot had no control, and we dropped, dropped, and then flew ahead. I was frightened; I had seen how very tenuous life can be.

When we finally left the storms of the Midwest behind us, I turned to the man beside me, a Boeing engineer, and asked him if he had been afraid.

"No. I've already been there."

It was a strange answer. He explained that he had been clinically dead as a youth, crushed beneath a car after he and several friends had hit a utility pole.

"I watched from somewhere up above and saw the troopers lift the car off someone. Then I saw that it was me lying there. I wasn't afraid, and I didn't feel any pain—not until I woke up in the hospital three days later. Since then, I've known that the soul doesn't die, only the body, and I've never been afraid."

I had seen nothing but death in Miami, heard nothing but death—and death seemed to lie ahead for Ted. Hearing the stranger's words was somewhat comforting. Ted had written in his last letter, "There's nothing wrong with my life that reincarnation couldn't improve upon."

It seemed to be his only option left.

I believed that the verdict had been the right verdict, but I wondered if it had been for the wrong reasons. It had been too swift, too vindictive. Was justice still justice when it manifested itself as it had in the less than six hours of jury deliberation? Was this the delayed justice that should have come before? Perhaps there was no way that it could have been done cleanly, concisely, in a textbook case.

The people had spoken. And Ted was guilty.

48

In Colorado, Ted Bundy had been a kind of lovable rogue, with many of the Aspenites delighting in his antics. Judge George Lohr had eliminated consideration of the death penalty in Colorado in Ted's murder trial there. Had he stayed in his Garfield County jail cell on that day before New Year's Eve, 1977, Ted might have won freedom (except for his still-uncompleted term in Utah) but he certainly would have had his life. By the summer of 1979, he would have been siting in one western prison or another, but he would not have found himself in the long shadow of the electric chair.

Florida—the "Buckle of the Death Belt"—was the worst possible state to which he could have run. No one in Florida had taken kindly to Ted Bundy's mocking superiority, his games. Not the police. Not the judges. And certainly not the public. In Florida, "killers" were killed themselves, and with as much dispatch as possible. An Oregon detective, returning from a seminar in Louisville, Kentucky in 1978, told me that he had talked with some of the Florida lawmen who had dealt with Ted. "They told me they would have killed him," the detective, recalled to me. "They said he would have had an 'accident,' while he was still in jail—but they didn't dare because he was too much in the public eye."

"Good ole boys"—policemen and laymen alike—didn't hold with women-killers, with despoilers and rapists. These were the men that Ted had scoffed at in his phone call from the Leon County Jail. These were the people who now would control his every move.

He had deliberately walked into the very jaws of death. Why?

Prosecutors Simpson and McKeever would ask for the death penalty, although, ironically, they stressed that they would not go for "overkill;" there was enough already without inundating the jury with the full background on the man they had convicted.

In the bifurcated trial, the second phase—the penalty phase—was slated to begin at 10:00 A.M. on Saturday, July 28th, despite the defense team's plea for a week's delay. The jury was taken back to their luxurious Sonesta Beach hotel to relax for the intervening days.

Ted had some new motions. Again, he wanted Millard Farmer. Arguing that Farmer had extensive experience with death penalty cases, he asked Judge Cowart if—now that he'd been found guilty—he could have the Atlanta attorney beside him.

"I've already ruled on that," Cowart said tersely. "I consider the making of the motion a second time an effrontery to the court."

Ted wanted to bring a Florida prison inmate in to testify about the woefully inadequate prison law library system in an attempt to point out how much good Ted could do in upgrading the library if he could work there as a law clerk.

Denied. But Cowart commented that Ted might have been a lawyer—if only he had not taken the path he had.

A motion to delay.

"That falls on totally deaf ears."

A motion to plea bargain after the fact, citing that jury trials are unfair because a guilty verdict invariably results in the death penalty. It was too late; Ted had been offered a plea bargain back in May, and he'd refused it.

Judge Cowart was annoyed when Peggy Good said that the penalty phase would rob Ted of "due process." As a Florida judge, he resented that state's being constantly referred to by defense lawyers in America as "notorious." (In actuality, _many_ states now have bifurcated trials—including Washington—and there are arguments just as cogent to show that they can tend to save a defendant from the death penalty.)

When the second phase of the trial began on Saturday morning, the state was remarkably restrained. Carol DaRonch Swenson, a young matron now, was called to the witness stand. The jurors looked on with interest as the tall woman in white satin slacks and blouse sat silently in the witness chair. She was, quite possibly, the most striking of all the women they had seen in the courtroom during the month-long trial with her great pansy eyes, her mane of long dark hair. But Carol DaRonch Swenson never spoke a word. A quick huddle between the opposing attorneys, a whispered word to the judge, and she stepped down. The defense would stipulate to Ted's conviction in February 1976 for the kidnapping in Utah in November 1974.

Jerry Thompson, the Salt Lake County detective who had run Ted to earth that first time, took the stand instead of Carol and told of that case, offered a certified copy of Ted's Utah conviction.

Michael Fisher, the slender, intense Pitkin County investigator from Aspen, Colorado, who had taken up the chase in his state, was just as succinct, and more inscrutable. He told of taking Ted from Point-of-the-Mountain prison to the Pitkin County Jail. He too read a stipulated statement: "On January 15, 1978, that you (Bundy) were under a sentence of imprisonment by the state of Utah and that you have not been paroled or otherwise released from that sentence."

The escape was never mentioned; it was left to the jury to surmise that a man never "paroled or released" from a sentence must have walked away from jail of his own accord.

There was so much that jury in Miami never heard. They knew nothing about all the dead and missing girls in Washington, nothing about the three dead girls in Utah, nothing about the five dead and missing girls in Colorado, nothing of the Pensacola fantasy tapes; presumably they did not know that the man before them was felt by many to be the most prolific mass killer in America.

The prosecution had, indeed, avoided any cries of overkill.

And yet, the specter of the electric chair hovered in that courtroom, as surely as if it had been brought in and placed before the bench. Ted expected it, his attorneys expected it, and the public demanded it.

Ted had a measure of forgiveness from one of the three women beaten into unconsciousness on the night of January 14–15, 1978. Kathy Kleiner DeShields said, "I feel sorry for him—he needs help—but what he did, there's no way to compensate for that."

Karen Chandler felt differently. "Two people dear to me are dead because of him and I really think he should be too."

Tiny Eleanor Louise Cowell Bundy, trembling with anxiety, would take the stand to plead for her son's life. This was her ideal child. This was the baby she had borne in shame, the little boy she had fought to keep with her, the young man in whom she had taken such overriding pride. He was to have been her vindication for everything; he was to have been perfect.

She made a pitiable figure on the stand, fighting as all mother will fight to save their young. Cowart was gentle with her, telling her, "Settle down, Mother. We haven't lost a mother in a long time so just don't be nervous."

Louise Bundy told the jury about Ted, the other four children. "We tried to be very conscientious parents, ones who did things with our children, gave them the best we could on a middle class income. But, mostly we wanted to give them lots of love."

Mrs. Bundy detailed Ted's schooling, his boyhood jobs, his Asian studies, his political activities, his jobs with the Seattle Crime Commission and the Governor Evans campaign. She might have been a proud mother at a church social function, bragging about her boy—instead of sitting in front of a jury begging for his life.

"I've always had a very special relationship with all my children. We tried to keep them all equal, but Ted, being the oldest, you might say was my pride and joy; our relationship was always very special. We'd talk a lot together, and his brothers and sisters thought of him as just the top person in their lives, as we all do."

"Have you considered the possibility that Ted might be executed?" Peggy Good asked quietly.

"Yes, I've considered that possibility. I had to—because of the existence of such in this state. I consider the death penalty itself to be the most primitive, barbaric thing that one human can impose on another. And I've always felt that way. It has nothing to do with what's happened here. My Christian upbringing tells me that to take another's life under any circumstances is wrong, and I don't believe the state in Florida is above the laws of God. Ted can be very useful, in many ways—to many people—living. Gone from us would be like taking a part of all of us and throwing it away."

"And if Ted were to be confined, to spend the rest of his life in prison?"

"Oh," his mother answered. "Of course . . . yes."

For the first time in the long trial, Ted Bundy cried.

There is little question that the jurors felt for Ted's mother; they were not to be swayed, however, about their opinion of Ted himself.

Larry Simpson voiced the unspoken thoughts in the courtroom as he finished his arguments for the death penalty.

"The whole four to five weeks that we've been here in this courtroom has been for one reason. And that is because Theodore Robert Bundy took it upon himself to act as the judge, jury, and everybody else involved in this case and took the lives of Lisa Levy and Margaret Bowman. That is what this case has been all about. They can stand before you and ask for mercy. How nice it would have been if Lisa Levy's and Margaret Bowman's mothers could have been there that morning of January 15, 1978 and asked for mercy for them."

Peggy Good argued that to kill Ted would be to admit that he could not be healed. Her argument that it was not a heinous crime was transparently specious. "One of the factors of the definition (of heinous crimes) is whether or not the victim suffered, whether there was torture or unnecessary cruelty to the victims. I believe you recall the testimony of Dr. Wood where he stated explicitly that both of these women were rendered unconscious by a blow to the head. They were sleeping; they felt no pain. They didn't even know what was happening to them. It was not heinous, atrocious, or cruel because of the fact that they were not aware of impending death, they did not suffer, and there was no element of torture involved whatsoever as to the victims who died."

No one, of course, would ever—could ever—know if Lisa or Margaret had suffered or the degree of that suffering.

The jury debated for one hour and forty minutes, and then returned with the expected verdict: the death penalty. Judge Cowart, who had already sentenced three murderers to the electric chair, could override that decision—should he choose to do so.

The jury would say later that they had been split at one point with a six-six deadlock, a deadlock that had been broken after ten minutes of "prayer and meditation."

It was Ted's own cold, nonemotional demeanor in court that had cost him his life. When he had risen to cross-examine Ray Crew, the police officer, he had turned off many of the jurors. One commented that the decision had seemed "a mockery of our system."

On July 31st, Ted had his day in court—unrestricted—speaking to Judge Cowart, making, not a plea for his life, but, instead, doing what he had told me he loved to do . . . "being a lawyer."

"I'm not asking for mercy. For I find it somewhat absurd to ask for mercy for something I did not do. In a way, this is *my* opening statement. What we've seen here is just the first round, second round, early round of a long battle, and I haven't given up by any means. I believe if I'd been able to develop fully the evidence which supports my innocence—which indeed I think created a reasonable doubt—been able to have quality representation, I'm confident that I would have been acquitted, and, in the event I get a new trial, will be acquitted.

"It wasn't easy sitting through this trial for a number of reasons. But the main reason it was not easy in the early part of the case was the presentation of the state case on what took place in the Chi Omega House, the blood, the pictures, the bloodstained sheets. And to note the state was trying to find me responsible was not easy. And it was not easy, nor did I ignore the families of these young women. I do not know them. And I do not think it's hypocritical of me, God knows, to say I sympathize with them, to the best I can. Nothing like this has ever happened to anyone close to me.

"But I'm telling the court, and I'm telling those people close to the victims in this case: I'm not the one responsible for the acts in the Chi Omega House or Dunwoody Street. And I'll tell the court I'm really not able to accept the verdict, because, although the verdict found in part that those crimes had been committed, they erred in finding who committed them.

"And as a consequence I cannot accept the sentence even though one will be imposed and even though I realize the lawful way the court will impose it—because it is not a sentence of *me*; it is a sentence of someone else who is not standing here today. So *I* will be tortured for and receive the pain for that act . . . but I will not share the burden or the guilt."

Ted continued with a diatribe against the press: "It is sad but true that the media thrives on sensation and they thrive on evil and they thrive on things taken out of context."

And Ted, as always, could see the drama of his legal battles: "And now the burden is on this court. And I don't envy you. The court is like a hydra right now. It's been asked to dispense no mercy as the maniac at the Chi Omega House dispensed no mercy. It's asked to consider this case as a man and a judge. And you're asked also to render the wisdom of a god. It's like some incredible Greek tragedy. It must have been written sometime and it must be one of those ancient Greek plays that portrays the three faces of man."

And so, at long last, there was no one left but Ted Bundy and Judge Edward Cowart. Antagonists, yes, but the two men had a kind of grudging admiration for one another. Another time, another place, and it might have all been so different. Never before had Cowart had such a literate, educated, wryly humorous defendant come before him. He too could see the waste, the roads not taken, and yet he had to do what he had to do. "It is ordered that you be put to death by a current of electricity, that that current be passed through your body until you are dead."

At that moment, it was clear that Cowart would have wished that things might have been different. He looked at Ted and said softly, "Take care of yourself, young man."

"Thank you."

"I say that to you sincerely; take care of yourself. It's a tragedy for this court to see such a total waste of humanity that I've experienced in this courtroom. You're a bright young man. You'd have made a good lawyer, and I'd have loved to have you practice in front of me—but you went another way, partner. Take care of yourself. I don't have any animosity to you. I want you to know that."

"Thank you."

"Take care of yourself."

"Thank you."

I watched that scene—not from my seat in the press section— but in front of my television set at home in Seattle, and I felt the chilling incongruity of it as keenly as if I had been there. Judge Cowart had just sentenced Ted to die in the electric chair; there was no way Ted could "take care of himself."

49

Peggy Good had pleaded in vain for Ted Bundy's life as the Miami trial neared its close, "The question and the choice is how to punish in this case. It is necessary that you consider the protection of society, but there are less drastic ways to consider the protection of society than taking another life. To recommend death in this case would be to admit failure with a human being. To recommend death is to confess the inability to heal, or to consider that there could be no healing."

I have been asked a hundred—a thousand—times what I truly believed about Ted Bundy's guilt or innocence, and until now I have always demurred. Now, I would like to attempt to express my thoughts on what made Ted run. It may be presumptuous on my part. I am neither a trained psychiatrist nor a criminologist. Yet, after almost ten years of knowing Ted through all the good times, the bad times, after researching the crimes he has been suspected of and those he has been convicted of, after agonizing reflection, I realize that I may know Ted as well as anyone has ever known him. And I can only conclude, with the most profound sense of regret, that he can never be healed.

I doubt that Ted will understand the depth of my feeling for him. The knowledge that he is undoubtedly guilty of the grotesque crimes attributed to him is as painful to me as if he were my son, the brother I lost, a man as close to me in many ways as anyone I have ever known. There will never be a time in my life when I will not think of him. I have felt friendship, love, respect, anxiety, sorrow, horror, deep anger, despair and, at the end, resigned acceptance of what has to be. Like John Henry Browne, and Peggy Good, like his mother and the women who loved him romantically, I have tried to save Ted's life . . . twice. Once he knew it, and once he didn't. He received the letter I mailed in 1976 when I begged him not to kill himself, but he never knew that I had tried to arrange a plea bargain in 1979 that might have meant confinement in a mental hospital instead of the trials that led him inexorably toward the electric chair. And, like all the others, I have been manipulated to suit Ted's needs. I don't feel particularly embarrassed or resentful about that; I was one of many, all of us intelligent, compassionate people who had no real comprehension of what possessed him, what drove him obsessively.

Ted came into my life, however peripherally, at a time when all the beliefs I had held smugly for many years had been shattered. True love, marriage, fidelity, selfless motherhood, blind trust—all those marvelous truths were suddenly only wisps of smoke blowing away in a totally unforeseen gust of wind.

But Ted seemed to embody what was young, idealistic, clean, sure, and empathetic. He seemed to ask nothing but friendship. He was, in 1971, a decisive factor in the verification that I was a person of worth, a woman who still had a great deal to give and to reap. He was most assuredly not a predatory male eager to "hit on" a newly divorced woman. He was simply *there*, listening, reassuring, giving credibility to what I was trying to become. Such a friend is not easy to turn one's back on.

I have no idea what I was to him, what I seemed to remain to him. Perhaps I only gave back to him what he had given to me. I saw him then as quite perfect, and he must have needed that. Perhaps he could sense an emotional strength in me, although I surely did not feel it myself at the time. He may have known that he could count on me when the going grew perilous for him. In times of deepest stress, he would turn to me, again and again. And I did attempt to help him, but I could never really assuage his pain because Ted could never bring himself to expose the soft underbelly of his anguish. He was a shadow man, fighting to survive in a world that was never made for him.

It must have taken incredible effort.

The parameters of that shadow man were constructed with such care; one misstep and they could all come apart.

The Ted Bundy the world was allowed to see was handsome, his body honed and cultivated meticulously, a barrier of strength against eyes that might catch a glimpse of the terror inside. He was brilliant, a student of distinction, witty, glib, and persuasive. He loved to ski, sail, and hike. He favored French cuisine, good white wine, and gourmet cooking. He loved Mozart and obscure foreign films. He knew exactly when to send flowers and sentimental cards. His poems of love were tender and romantic.

And yet, in reality, Ted loved *things* more than he loved people. He could find life in an abandoned bicycle or an old car, and feel a kind of compassion for these inanimate objects—more compassion than he could ever feel for another human being.

Ted could—and did—rub elbows with the governor, travel in circles that most young men could never hope to enter, but he could never feel good about himself. On the surface Ted Bundy was the very epitome of a successful man. Inside, it was all ashes.

For Ted has gone through life terribly crippled, like a man who is deaf, or blind, or paralyzed. Ted has no conscience.

"Conscience doth make cowards of us all," but conscience is what gives us our humanity, the factor that separates us from animals. It allows us to love, to feel another's pain, and to grow. Whatever the drawbacks are to being blessed with a conscience, the rewards are essential to living in a world with other human beings.

The individual with no conscience—with no superego at all— has long been a focal point for study by psychiatrists and psychologists. The terms used to describe such an individual have changed over the years, but the concept has not. Once it was called a "psychopathic personality," and then it became "sociopath." Today, the term in vogue is "antisocial personality."

To live in our world, with thoughts and actions always counter to the flow of your fellow men, must be an awesome handicap. There are no innate guidelines to follow: the psychopath might well be a visitor from another planet, struggling to mimic the feelings of those he encounters. It is almost impossible to pinpoint just when antisocial feelings begin, although most experts agree that emotional development has been arrested in early childhood— perhaps as early as three. Usually, the inward-turning of emotions results from a need for love or acceptance not filled, from deprivation and humiliation. Once begun, that little child will grow tall— but he will never mature emotionally.

He may experience pleasure on only a physical level, an excitable "high," and a sense of euphoria from the games he substitutes for real feelings.

He knows what he wants, and, because he is not hampered by guilt feelings or the needs of others, he can usually achieve instant gratification. But he can never fill up the lonesome void inside. He is insatiable, always hungry.

The antisocial personality *is* mentally ill, but not in the classic sense or within our legal framework. He is invariably highly intelligent and has long since learned the proper responses, the tricks and techniques that will please those from whom he wants something. He is subtle, calculating, clever, and dangerous. And he is lost.

Dr. Benjamin Spock, who worked in a veterans' hospital dealing with emotional illnesses during World War II, commented at the time that there was a pronounced cross-sex problem in dealing with psychopathic personalities. The male psychopaths had no difficulty in bewitching female staff members, while the male staff picked up on them rapidly. The female psychopaths could fool the male staff—but not the women.

Ted's retinue of friends and companions was always heavily weighted with women. Some loved him as a man. Some woman, like myself, were drawn to his courtly manners, his little boy quality, his seemingly genuine concern and thoughtfulness. Women were always Ted's comfort—and his curse.

Because he could control women, balance us carefully in the tightly structured world he had manufactured, we were important to him. We seemed to hold the solution to that dead hollow place inside him. He dangled us as puppets from a string, and when one of us did not react as he wanted, he was both outraged and confused.

I believe men, on the other hand, were a threat. The one man whom he felt he could emulate, the man whose genes and chromosomes dictated who he was, had been left behind. When Ted told me for the first time about his illegitimate birth, I sensed that he seemed to consider himself a changeling child, the progeny of royalty dumped by mistake on the doorstep of a blue-collar family. How he loved the thought of money and status, and how inadequate he felt when he found himself with women who were born to it.

Ted never really knew *who* he was supposed to be. He'd been taken away from his real father, and then taken away from his grandfather Cowell whom he loved and respected. He could not, would not, use Johnnie Culpepper Bundy as a role model.

I think his feelings toward his mother were marked with a raging ambivalence. She had lied to him. She had robbed him of his real father, although rational consideration shows that she had no choice. But half of Ted was gone, and he would spend the rest of his life trying to make up for that loss.

Still, he clung to his mother, tried to live up to her dreams that he must excel, that he was her special child who could do anything. Of all the women that Ted was involved with romantically, it was Meg Anders who lasted the longest—and it was Meg who was the most like Louise Bundy. Both of them are small, almost frail, women. And each was left alone with a child to raise. Each of them traveled far from their family homes to start a new life with that child. Meg Anders and Louise Bundy are the two women who, I believe, suffered the most agony when Ted's facade shattered.

The men that Ted was drawn to were all men of power, either through their accomplishments, their intellect, or their easy mantle of masculinity: his lawyer friend in Seattle; Ross Davis, head of the Washington State Republican Party; John Henry Browne, the dynamic public defender; John O'Connell, his Salt Lake City attorney; Buzzy Ware, the brilliant Colorado attorney he lost; Millard Farmer, denied to him by the Florida courts. Policemen had that same kind of power—especially Norm Chapman of Pensacola, who exuded strength, masculinity, and, yes, the ability to love.

Like a little boy who yearns to be important, to be noticed, Ted played perverse games with policemen. In many of his crimes, he would assume their mantle, their badges, and he would, for that time, be one of them. Although he often called policemen stupid, he needed to know that he was important to them, if only in a negative sense. If he could not please them, then he would *displease* them so much that he had to be noticed. He had to be so notorious that all other criminals would pale in comparison.

It is interesting to consider that when Ted confessed his escape and his intricate credit card thefts, when he discussed his terrible fantasies, it was to policemen. His voice on the tapes made in Pensacola is excited and full of pride. He is triumphant and in his element on those tapes, doing exactly what he wants to be doing as if he were laying a gift before them, expecting praise for his cunning. Those detectives were men who could *appreciate* his cleverness, and, as he said, "I'm in charge of entertainment . . ."

I have no doubt that Ted would have given anything in the world to have been able to change places with big, easy-going, Norm Chapman. Because that man—whatever his limitations— knew who he was . . . and Ted never had.

Women were easier to deal with. But women held the power to hurt and humiliate.

Stephanie Brooks was the first to hurt him badly. Although Ted had dated only infrequently in high school, he had longed for a relationship with a woman who was beautiful and wealthy. Stephanie did not make Ted an antisocial personality; she exacerbated what was already smouldering there. When she walked away from him after their first year together, he was ashamed and humiliated, and the rage he felt was out of all proportion. He was the little boy again, a boy who had had a toy wrenched away from him—and he wanted it back. True, he would smash it—and the relationship—when he got it back, but he had to have the opportunity to do that.

It took him years, but Ted did accomplish the seemingly impossible task of reworking the outer Ted until he was able to meet Stephanie's standards for a potential husband. Then . . . then, he could humiliate her just as she had humbled him—and he did. Once she had promised to marry him, he changed suddenly and sent her away. He put her on the airplane to California without so much as a kiss, saw her stunned face and turned his back on her.

But it didn't seem to be enough. His revenge brought no lessening of the void in his soul, and it must have been a terrible realization for him; he had worked, planned, schemed so that he could reject Stephanie, sure that he would feel whole and serene again, and yet he still felt empty.

He still had Meg, and Meg loved him devotedly, would have married him in a minute. But Meg was too much like Louise; any love he felt for either of them was tempered with scorn for their weakness. Somehow, he would have to punish Stephanie more.

It was, of course, only three days after Stephanie left Seattle in January of 1974 that Joni Lenz was bludgeoned and raped symbolically with the metal bed-rod as she lay sleeping in her basement room.

And so the answer to the question put to me so many times is yes. Yes, I believe Ted Bundy attacked Joni Lenz, just as I now am forced to believe that he is responsible for all the other crimes attributed to him. I have never said it out loud—or in print—but I believe it, as devoutly as I wish I did not.

The victims are all prototypes of Stephanie. The same long hair, parted in the middle, the same perfectly even features. None of them were random choices. I think some of them were chosen—watched for long periods before the attacks occurred—while others were picked rapidly because they were convenient targets during those times when Ted was in the grip of his maniacal compulsion.

But they all resembled Stephanie, that first woman who had pierced Ted's carefully constructed facade and revealed the yawning vulnerability beneath. That damage to Ted's ego could never be forgiven. None of the crimes filled the emptiness. He had to keep killing Stephanie over and over again, hoping that each time would be the time that would bring surcease. But the more there were, the worst it became.

Ted had said that "my fantasies are taking over my life," and I don't believe that he had any control over them. The compulsion that he excoriated in his first letter to me after his arrest in Pensacola dominated Ted; Ted did not dominate the compulsion. He could manipulate other people, but God help him, he could not stop himself.

He also said that acting out his fantasies was a "downer," and the depths of those downers can only be imagined by a rational mind. Since an antisocial personality has no empathy at all for others, it was not his victims' pain that tormented him; it was that there was no relief for him.

All of his victims were so lovely, so carefully chosen, that during the time they were living players in his obsessive rituals, he thought he cared for them. The rituals themselves left the chosen limp, bleeding, and ugly. Why did it have to be that way? He detested them for dying, for becoming ugly, for leaving him—again—alone. And, in the midst of the awful aftermath of the fantasies, he could not truly comprehend that it was *he* who had wrought the destruction.

Madness, yes, but madness is what I am trying to understand. Holding the reins of power was no fun when there was no one left to terrorize with that power.

I think the rest of the carefully regimented games came about accidentally, an extension of the killing games. Driven by rage, revenge, frustration, Ted killed. The sexual aspect of the murders was not a matter of satiating his drives, but rather the need to humiliate and demean his victims; he felt no true sexual release—only the blackest of depressions.

It was only after the killings that Ted realized just how newsworthy he was. He began to exalt in the thrill of the chase, and it became a part of the ritual, a part even more satisfying than the murders themselves. His power over the dead girls lasted such a short time, but his power over the police investigators went on and on. That he could do these things, take more and more chances, refine his disguises so that he could come out in the light of day—and still remain undetected—was the ultimate euphoria. He could do what no other man could do, and do it with impunity.

How often he would talk to me of being in the limelight, being the Golden Boy. It became life and breath to him.

And the games became more intricate. When Ted was finally arrested in Utah in 1975 by Sergeant Bob Hayward, he was outraged. One must understand that he actually felt this sense of indignation. As an antisocial personality, he could feel no guilt. He had only taken what *he* wanted, what *he* needed to feel whole. He was incapable of understanding that one cannot fulfill his own desires at the expense of others. He had not finished with the games, and the stupid police had ended them before he was ready.

When Ted complained throughout the years about jails, prisons, the courts, the judges, the district attorneys, the police, and the press, he was not aware that there was another side to it all. His reasoning was simplistic, but to him it made sense. What Ted wanted, Ted should have, and there was the blind spot in his superior intelligence. When he wept, he wept only for himself, but his tears were real tears. He *was* desperate, and afraid, and angry, and he believed that he was completely within his rights.

To convince him otherwise would be akin to explaining the theory of relativity to a kindergarten child. The mechanisms needed to understand the needs and rights of others are not integrated into his thinking processes.

Even today, I cannot hate him for that; I can only feel profound pity.

Ted has often bragged to me that psychiatrists and psychologists could find nothing abnormal about him. He had masked his responses, another red-flag indicator of the antisocial personality.

Dr. Herve Cleckley, the Augusta, Georgia psychiatrist who interviewed Ted prior to his Miami trial (the evaluation that Ted felt he was tricked into), is an expert on the antisocial personality, and he acknowledges that standard tests seldom reveal this aberration.

"The observer is confronted with a convincing mask of sanity. We are dealing not with a complete man at all, but with something that suggests a subtly constructed reflex machine which can mimic the human personality perfectly."

The antisocial personality does not evince the thought disorder patterns that are more easily discerned; there are few signs of anxiety, phobias, or delusions. He is, in essence, an emotional robot, programmed by himself to reflect the responses that he has found society demands. And, because that programming is often so cunning, this personality is extremely hard to diagnose. Nor can it be healed.

My first niggling doubt about Ted's personality came when he forgave Meg so quickly for betraying him to the police. True, he had loved her to the extent he was capable of loving, and Meg had never humiliated him. *He* was the dominant partner in their relationship, and he had humiliated her again and again. But he never viewed her betrayal as an act of revenge on her part. I think she may have been the one woman in his life who helped to fill even a small corner of his barren soul. Although he could not be faithful to her, neither could he exist without her.

And so, because he needed her so much, he seemed able to obliterate any vestiges of resentment toward her. Because it was essential to have her emotional support, he could forgive her for her weakness. But it was such a flat response, so eerily unhuman for him to be able to simply forget that it was Meg who had caused him to be caught. I am quite convinced that without Meg's interference the identity of "Ted" would still be a mystery today.

Ted's psyche so dominated Meg's that I am amazed that she was ever able to break free, and I don't know how free she is—even though she is married to another man.

Sharon Auer was merely expedient; she was there in Utah when he needed someone to run errands and bring supplies into prison, but he left her behind when he left Point-of-the-Mountain. Carole Ann Boone soon filled the gap; Ted has never been without a woman at his beck and call since his legal troubles began. Carole Boone has endured. She refers to him as "Bunnie," and plainly adores him. I could not presume to evaluate what his feelings are for her. I talked at length to his other women; Carole Ann said only five words to me. As he told me, "She has thrown in her lot with me," but it is certainly a blighted romance.

There is, within all imperfect mechanisms, a tendency to self-destruct, as if the machine itself realizes that it is not functioning correctly. When the mechanism is a human being, those destructive forces writhe their way to the surface from time to time. Somewhere, hidden deeply in the recesses of Ted's brain, there is a synapse of cells that is trying to destroy him.

Perhaps that first Ted, the small-child-Ted who could have become all that was promised, knows that the Ted who has taken over must be done away with. Or is that too farfetched? The fact remains that Ted has constantly struck out at the very people who have tried to defend him. Over and over, he has fired his attorneys—sometimes within sight of victory. He chose the most dangerous state in the union to flee to, knowing that the death penalty was a real threat there. Given a chance to plea bargain for his very life, he tore up the motion that would have saved him and virtually dared the state prosecutors to convict him—a challenge they were only too willing to accept. I think he wants to die. I don't know if he realizes that he does.

In my opinion, Ted is not a Jekyll-Hyde. I have no doubt at all that he remembers the murders. There may be some overlapping, some blurring—just as a man may not remember distinctly every woman he has ever slept with. How many times has he told me that he is able to put the bad things that have happened to him out of his mind? The memories may lie hidden like festering boils—but he does remember. The memories can no longer be left behind, because he has no place left to run, and they must haunt his cell in Raiford Prison.

My own memory haunts me. The precognition of the dream—the nightmare—I had in April of 1976 frightens me. Why did I dream that the baby I tried to save bit me? That dream where I saw the bite mark on my hand was *two years* before the bite mark on one of Ted's Chi Omega victims became the prime piece of physical evidence in the Miami trial.

If only Ted had talked to me during our last meeting in Seattle in January of 1976, it might have been different. When he said, "There are things I want to tell you . . . but I can't," was there something I could have said that would have allowed him to talk to me then? Could I have changed any of the events that were to come? Although Ted insists he bears no guilt for any of the killings, I am sure there are many others who, like I, carry feelings of guilt because we should have known more, done more—before it was too late.

Ted would have lived if he had confessed to me in the state of Washington. We had no death penalty here in 1974. He would have lived in the state of Colorado. The state of Florida will never let him go—not even to stand trial for Caryn Campbell's murder in Colorado. Colorado let him escape twice, and Florida authorities are scornful of their security. Ted Bundy belongs to Florida.

Killing Ted will accomplish nothing at all; all it would assure is that he could never kill again. But looking at the broken, confused man in the courtroom, I knew that Ted was insane. I cannot justify executing a man who is insane. Placing him in a mental institution—with the tightest security possible—could perhaps do more toward psychiatric research into the causes and, hopefully, cures for the antisocial personality than the evaluation of any other individual in history. It might save the potential victims of antisocial personalities still being formed. Ted can never go free; he is dangerous and he will always he dangerous, but there are answers to vital questions locked in his mind.

I don't want him to die. If the day comes when he is led into the death chamber at Raiford Prison, I will cry. I will cry for that long-lost Ted Bundy who might have been, for the bright, warm young man I thought I knew so many years ago. It is still difficult for me to believe that the facade of kindness and caring I saw was only that, a thin veneer. There could have been—should have been—so much more.

But if Ted is to die, I think he will muster the strength to do it with style, basking for the last time in the glow of strobe lights and television cameras. If he is relegated to the ranks of prisoners—the General Population—that will be the worst punishment of all. If he is not killed by his fellow prisoners, who have been vocal that "Bundy should fry," the emptiness inside himself will destroy him.

When I grieve for Ted, and I do, I grieve for all the others who bear no guilt at all.

Katherine Merry Devine is dead . . .
Brenda Baker is dead . . .
Joni Lenz is alive . . .
Lynda Ann Healy is dead . . .
Donna Manson is gone . . .
Susan Rancourt is dead . . .
Roberta Kathleen Parks is dead . . .
Brenda Ball is dead . . .
Georgeann Hawkins is gone . . .
Janice Ott is dead . . .
Denise Naslund is dead . . .
Melissa Smith is dead . . .
Laura Aime is dead . . .
Carol DaRonch Swenson is alive . . .
Debby Kent is gone . . .
Caryn Campbell is dead . . .
Julie Cunningham is gone . . .
Denise Oliverson is gone . . .
Shelly Roberton is dead . . .
Melanie Cooley is dead . . .
Lisa Levy is dead . . .
Margaret Bowman is dead . . .
Karen Chandler is alive . . .

Kathy Kleiner DeShields is alive . . .

Cheryl Thomas is alive . . .

Kimberly Leach is dead . . .

One day, the earth and the rivers may give up more remains, all that is left of the young women whose names are still unknown— the women Ted referred to when he said, "Add one more digit to that and you've have it . . ."

None of them could fill the hollow soul of Ted Bundy.

Epilogue

The trials and hearings of Ted Bundy had become akin to a Broadway play, its long run ended, replaced by a road company. Only the star remained in the lead role, surrounded by a new cast. And the star was tired. He had lost much of his enthusiasm. Ted's trial in the Kimberly Leach case puzzled laymen. "How many times can you kill a man?" they asked incredulously. Since Ted Bundy had already been sentenced to death—twice—they could not see the need for yet another trial. The State, of course, was covering its bets. If there should be a reversal on appeal in the Chi Omega killings, they wanted the back-up of a third death sentence. Legally, it made sense.

The Leach trial was postponed again and again, finally settling in Orlando, Florida on January 7, 1980. Orange County was a grudging host; they didn't want Ted or the hoopla that seemed to accompany him, but Judge Wallace Jopling, the sixty-two-year-old jurist who would preside at the Leach trial, had determined he could not find an impartial jury in the Lake City area.

The roster of attorneys had changed; only Lynn Thompson remained of the original defense team. Thompson was joined by Julius Victor Africano, Jr. The man who might have defended Ted was Milo I. Thomas, Public Defender for the Third Judicial Circuit—but Thomas excused himself; he was a close friend of the Leach family.

Jerry Blair of the State Attorney's Office—Jerry Blair who had vowed to himself in June of 1979 that, if Ted wanted a trial, Ted would get a trial—and Bob Dekle, a down-home, good-ole-boy lawyer with a perpetual chaw of tobacco tucked in one cheek, a special prosecutor, would speak for the state.

There was a pronounced malaise among the reporters who had covered the Miami trial; nobody really wanted to go through a second trial. Tony Polk of the *Rocky Mountain News* wasn't going. A Seattle reporter had to go on assignment, but he dreaded it. A Miami reporter called me and said, "Yeah ... I'm going, but not until I have to. I'm just going up for the kill." And then he gasped and said, "God, that sounds awful, doesn't it? But it's the only way to describe it."

I didn't go. I knew what the evidence was, I know what the witnesses were going to say, and I could not bear to see Ted again in the state he had come to. Instead, I watched the Orlando trial on television and saw a man who might well have been a complete stranger to me.

Ted was no longer as handsome as he'd been at the Miami trial. His weight hovered near 190 pounds, his jowls bulged, and his eyes were sunken. The lean, cleanly defined good looks were gone, along with his tenuous grasp of reality. He flared with temper easily, and seemed about to blow into fragmented pieces. He took offense when a court stenographer, a woman who smiled naturally, appeared to him to be making light of the proceedings.

"Would you please take this seriously!" he shouted at her.

But no one seemed to take it seriously; they had come to see the show. A local disc jockey had set the tone of the trial by opening his morning broadcast with "Watch out, girls! Ted Bundy's in town."

A female impersonator from Pennsylvania made a dramatic entrance, swirling his fake leopard jacket and tossing his platinum wig as he sashayed to a seat. Ted never looked up. A young man removed his jacket to reveal a tee shirt reading "Send Bundy to Iran." And, in the front row, were the ever-present Ted groupies, anxious for a smile from the fading star.

The television camera might as well have focused on the inmates of Bedlam.

Neither Louise or Johnnie Bundy made the trip back to Florida. There was only Carole Ann Boone, sitting beside the wife of an inmate from Raiford. Carole Ann, still flashing Ted looks of love and encouragement.

The prospective jurors, available from a seemingly endless pool, appeared willing to say almost anything so that they might be chosen. Judge Jopling had ruled that even those potential jurors who believed Ted guilty might be chosen if they indicated they could put aside their opinions and remain objective. Several of those prospective veniremen made the jury. There was nowhere else in Florida where the trial could go. Prosecutor Blair said a change in venue would be an exercise in futility. "This man is a cause célèbre here and he would be a cause célèbre in Two Egg, Pahokee, or Sopchoppy as well."

Twice, Ted stalked out of the courtroom, a demonstration against the jury being seated. "I'm leaving. This is a game and I won't be a party to it! I'm not staying in this kind of Waterloo, you understand?"

Returned and calmed down until he had a modicum of control, he blew up again, slamming his hand on Judge Jopling's desk. "You want a circus?" he cried to Blair. "I'll make a circus. I'll rain on your parade, Jack. You'll see a thunderstorm."

Ted headed for the door and a bailiff blocked his way. Ted set down the beer carton he carried his files in on a railing and removed his jacket. The television camera caught, for the first time, a Ted Bundy out of control. He was backed to the wall, a snarling fox caught in a circle of hunters. It may have been the face contorted with open-mouthed rage that his victims had seen, and it shocked me. He appeared to be about to come out swinging at the five court officers who surrounded him. He stood panting, trapped. A moment passed . . . two . . . Ted and his tormentors were frozen.

"Sit down, Mr. Bundy!" Jopling ordered.

"You know how far you can push me!"

"Sit *down*, Mr. Bundy!"

Slowly, he came back to himself, slumped, all the fight gone out of him. He walked back to the defense table and slid into his chair, eyes downcast.

"It's no use," he stage-whispered to Africano. "We've lost the jury. There's no point in playing the game."

He may well have been right.

Day after day, Ted sat in confusion and anger as sixty-five prosecution witnesses took the stand. Africano and Thompson fought it all, diggiling their heels in for some kind of foothold as they were forced back and back. This time, they would not allow Ted himself to speak, although he was allowed to participate in legal arguments away from the jurors' ears.

Three weeks into the trial, Ted made a twenty-minute plea for acquittal in Jopling's chambers. His voice quavering, he seemed on the edge of tears as his monologue drifted, a far cry from his ordered, precise arguments in Utah four years earlier. He insisted that there was no evidence that a murder had even been committed.

The defense presented two witnesses who had allegedly seen Kimberly Leach hitchhiking "near Jimmy's Buttermilk Chicken place" on the morning she disappeared. But they faltered when asked to identify her picture absolutely as that of the girl they'd seen two years before.

Even the testimony of Atlanta Medical Examiner, Dr. Joseph Burton, backfired. He had apparently been retained to bolster the defense claim that Kimberly Leach could have died of other causes, and he clearly could not do that.

"While my study of findings could not rule out accidental, suicidal, or natural causes, all three were way down on the list."

On February 6th, the most startling rumors in the courthouse concerned Carole Ann Boone. Ms. Boone had applied for a marriage license! Whether there was any way she could, indeed, marry the man she called Bunnie was questionable. Major Jim Shoulz, County Director of Corrections, was adamant that there would be no wedding in *his* jail. But Judge Jopling authorized a blood test for Ted to fulfill an initial requirement for the license.

Carole Ann admitted that she fully expected Ted to be convicted, but she was determined to marry him anyway. The odds were not on the chance of acquittal; spectators were betting on whether Ted and Carole Ann could get married. Ted himself had bet Africano that the jury would find him guilty in three hours. He lost. They took seven and a half hours, a half-hour more than the Miami jury had.

This time there was no weeping mother begging for her perfect son; there was only Carole Ann Boone. It was two years to the day since twelve-year-old Kimberly Leach had vanished: February 9, 1980. Carole Ann took the stand to plead for Ted's life.

But first, and seemingly foremost, she had a mission; she wanted to become Mrs. Ted Bundy. She had meticulously researched how one got married in Florida, given the peculiar circumstances. She knew that public declaration, properly phrased, in an open courtroom in the presence of court officers would make the "ceremony" legal. A notary public, holding the marriage license in the names of Carole Ann Boone and Theodore Robert Bundy, sat watching as Ted rose to question his fiancée.

The bride wore not white, but black—a skirt and sweater over an open-necked blouse. The groom, who had always favored bowties, wore one with blue polka dots and a blue sports jacket. The jury wore looks of utter bemusement.

The couple smiled at each other, as if they were the only two people in the courtroom, as he began to question her formally.

"Where do you reside?"

"I am a permanent resident of Seattle, Washington."

"Could you explain when you met me . . . how long you have known me, our relationship," he said, leading her.

Carole continued to smile happily as she recalled their meeting in Olympia at the Department of Emergency Services office, of the closeness they had achieved as Ted's legal problems increased. "Several years ago, our relationship evolved into a more serious, romantic sort of thing."

"Is it serious?" Ted asked.

"Serious enough that I want to marry him," she said to the jury.

"Can you tell the jury if you've ever observed any violent or destructive tendencies in my character or personality?"

"I've never seen anything in Ted that indicates any destructiveness towards any other people, and I've been associated with Ted in virtually every circumstance. He's been involved with my family. I've never seen anything in Ted that indicates any kind of destructiveness . . . any kind of hostility. He's a warm, kind, patient man."

Over the prosecution's objections, Carole Ann stated that she felt it was not correct for either an individual or a representative of the state to take the life of another human being.

She turned toward the jury and spoke with an intensity, "Ted is a large part of my life. He is vital to me."

"Do you want to marry me?" Ted asked.

"*Yes.*"

"I do want to marry you," Ted said, as the state lawyers and Judge Jopling froze with surprise. It took Dekle and Blair a few beats before they were able to rise and object.

Ted turned to confer with his attorneys. He'd almost blown it; he'd used the wrong terminology. They told him marriage was a contract—not a promise. He would have one more chance on re-direct to make his verbal contract.

State Attorney Blair questioned Carole Ann, suggesting that there might be a less romantic reason than true love behind her desire to marry Ted. He hinted that there might be financial reasons, but Carole remained unmoved. He questioned the timing of the proposal, coming as it did just as the jury was about to deliberate on the death penalty. Carole Ann would not be shaken. As Blair cross-examined her, Ted conferred frantically with his lawyers.

He rose to question her on re-direct. This time he knew what he was supposed to say to be sure the marriage was valid.

"Will you marry me?" Ted asked Carole Ann.

"Yes!" she replied with a giggle and a broad smile.

"Then I do hereby *marry* you."

Ted grinned expansively. It was done before the prosecutors realized it. Carole Ann and her Bunnie were now man and wife.

Most of the eyes in the courtroom were decidedly dry, and there would be no honeymoon. The second anniversary of Kimberly Leach's death was now Ted Bundy's wedding day. Carole Ann had prevailed; she had remained loyal and omnipresent. Stephanie, Meg, and Sharon were now relegated to Ted's dim past. One got the impression that Carole Ann's tenacity was such that she might indeed wrest Ted from the very arms of the electric chair if it came to that.

And it seemed that it would come to that. After listening to Jerry Blair's characterization of the wedding as "a little Valentine's Day charade," and to Ted's own forty-minute rambling plea for his life, the jury retired for forty-five minutes to deliberate on the question of the death penalty.

It was 3:20 P.M. on February 9th when they announced their decision that Ted must die. He rose in his chair and shouted, "Tell the jury they were wrong!"

On February 12th, Judge Jopling sentenced Ted to die—for the third time—in the electric chair in Raiford Prison. As Ted stood to receive that sentence, he carried a red envelope in his hand: a valentine for his bride.

Within an hour, Ted was in a helicopter lifting off the courthouse roof, headed back to Raiford Prison. In the language of Florida state law, he had been convicted once again of a crime "extremely wicked, shockingly evil, and vile."

There would be appeals ahead, predicted to take years, but for all intents and purposes, the Ted Bundy story was over. Locked away from the rays of the limelight, the rays that for Ted seem necessary to sustain life, I know that he will continue to sink deeper and deeper into the compulsive madness that grips him. He will never again be the Golden Boy beloved by the media.

Ted Bundy is a killer. A three-times convicted killer, a throwaway man now.

I cannot forget his phone call in October, 1975, the call where he said calmly, "I'm in a little trouble—but it's all going to work out. If anything goes wrong, you'll read about it in the newspapers."

Afterword

As I write this, it has been six years since Ted Bundy was sentenced—for the third time—to die in Florida's electric chair. In my naiveté in 1980, I ended *The Stranger Beside Me* by suggesting that the Ted Bundy story was at last over. It was not. I vastly underestimated Ted's ability to regenerate in both spirit and body, to pit his will and mind continually against the justice system. Nor was I able to extricate Ted from my mind simply by putting him and my feelings about him on paper. The relief that I felt when I wrote the last line was immense. This book was a healing catharsis after a half-dozen years of horror.

But the next half-dozen years have forced me to accept that some significant part of my consciousness will be inhabited by Ted Bundy and his crimes—for as long as I live. I have written five books since *The Stranger Beside Me*, and yet when my phone rings or a letter comes from somewhere far away—several times a week still—the questions are invariably about "the Ted book."

My correspondents fall generally into four categories. Laymen have contacted me from as far away as Greece, South Africa, the Virgin Islands—consumed with curiosity about Ted Bundy's eventual fate. Most of them ask, "When was he executed?" Police investigators call wondering where Ted Bundy might have been on a particular date (Ted's comments to Pensacola detectives that February night he was captured in 1978 are well-remembered by homicide detectives all over America. Although officially a murder suspect in only *five* states, Ted told Detective Norm Chapman and Don Patchen that he had killed "in six states" and that they should "add one digit" to the F.B.I's victim estimate of 36).

The calls that surprised me most were from Ted's burgeoning "fan club"—unofficial but passionately vocal. So many young women who had "fallen in love" with Ted Bundy and who wanted to know how they could contact him to let him know how much they loved him. When I explained that he had married Carole Ann Boone, my words fell on deaf ears. I finally asked them to read my book once more, asking, "Are you sure that you can tell the difference between a teddy-bear and a fox?"

Almost as fervent were the religious readers who hoped to get word to Ted so that they might prevail upon him to repent before it was too late.

Finally, there were the callers that Seattle policemen refer to as "220's"—people deranged to greater and lesser degrees—who imagined that they had some bizarre connection to Ted.

The latter were the most difficult to deal with. An elderly woman came to my door near midnight, regal and impeccably dressed—and yet distressed because. "Ted Bundy has been stealing my nylons and my panty-hose. He's been coming into my house since 1948—and he takes my personal files. He's very clever; he puts everything back so that you can scarcely tell it's been moved. . ."

It did no good to point out that her "thefts" had begun when Ted was still a toddler.

Her visit did, however, make me realize that I could no longer have my home address printed in the phone book.

In ways that I could never have imagined, Ted Bundy changed my life. I have flown two hundred thousand miles, lectured a thousand times to groups ranging from ladies' book study clubs to defense attorneys organizations to police training seminars to the F.B.I. Academy—always about Ted. Some questions are easy enough for me to answer; some may never be answered and some provoke more and more questions in an endless continuum.

If, indeed, Ted claimed to have murdered in six states—then *which* state was the sixth? Had there really been a sixth state—a hundred and thirty six victims or, God help us, three hundred and sixty victims? Or had it been, for Ted, a game to play with his interrogators in Pensacola? His cunning jousts with police were always akin to Dungeons-and-Dragons, and he so delighted in outwitting them, watching them scurry around to do what he considered his bidding.

There may well have been myriad other victims, and yet it is an almost impossible task to deduce precisely where Ted Bundy was on a particular date in the late sixties and early seventies. I have tried to isolate periods of that time almost 20 years ago now, and so has Bob Keppel, the one-time King County detective who knows as much about Ted as any cop in America. But Ted was always a traveler, and an impulsive wanderer at that; he would say he was going one place, and head somewhere else. He hated to be made accountable for his whereabouts—by anyone—and he reveled in popping up to surprise those who knew him.

1969 found Ted visiting relatives in Arkansas, and attending classes at Temple University in Philadelphia, his childhood home. In 1969, a beautiful dark-haired young woman was stabbed to death far back in the "stacks" of the library at Temple. That case, more than a decade unsolved, came back to a Pennsylvania homicide detective when he traced Ted's journeys in my book. In the end, he could only conjecture; no one could place Ted in that library on that evening.

Even more haunting is the unsolved murder of Rita Curran in Burlington, Vermont on July 19, 1971. Each born in Burlington, Rita Curran and Ted Bundy were twenty-four years old that summer. Ted had, of course, been raised on the opposite coast while Rita grew up in the tiny community of Milton, Vermont, daughter of the town's zoning administrator.

Rita was a very lovely—but shy—young woman. Her dark hair fell midway down her back. Sometimes, she parted it on the left side; sometimes in the middle. A graduate of Burlington's Trinity College, she taught second grade at the Milton Elementary School during the school year. Like Lynda Ann Healy, Rita spent much of her time and energy working with deprived and handicapped children. Although she was well into her twenties, she hadn't really lived away from home until the summer of 1971. She had worked as a chambermaid at the Colonial Motor Inn in Burlington for three previous summers, but this year was the first she'd taken an apartment there rather than commuting from her parents' Milton home ten miles north.

She was attending classes in teaching remedial reading and language at the University of Vermont's graduate school, and shared the apartment on Brookes Avenue with a female roommate. Rita Curran had no steady boyfriend—and that was probably one of her reasons for spending the summer in Burlington. She was hoping to meet a man who would be right for her. She wanted to be married—to have children of her own—and she'd laughed to friends, "I've gone to three weddings this year—all the bachelors in Milton are taken!"

On Monday, July 19, 1971, Rita changed bedding and vacuumed rooms at the Colonial Motor Inn from 8:15 a.m. to 2:40 p.m. That evening, she rehearsed with her barbershop quartet until ten. Rita Curran's roommate and a friend left her in the apartment on Brookes at 11:20 to go to a restaurant. Both the front and back doors were unlocked when they left. Burlington, Vermont was hardly a high-crime area.

People didn't lock doors.

When Rita's friends returned, the apartment was quiet and they assumed she had gone to sleep; they talked for an hour, and then Rita's roommate walked into the bedroom. Rita Curran lay nude . . . murdered. She had been strangled manually, beaten savagely on the left side of the head, and raped. Her torn underpants were beneath her body. Her purse, contents intact was nearby.

Burlington detectives traced the escape route of the killer, and found a small patch of blood near the back door leading off the kitchen. He had, perhaps, dashed through the kitchen and out through the shed beyond even as Rita's roommate came in the front door. A canvass of neighbors was fruitless; no one had heard a scream or a struggle.

In 1971, there were approximately 10,000 homicides in America. What intrigued John Bassett, a retired F.B.I. Special Agent—and also a native of Burlington—when he read about Ted Bundy was the remarkable resemblance between Rita Curran and Stephanie Brooks, the fact that Rita had died of strangulation and bludgeoning to the head . . . *and* the proximity of the Colonial Motor Inn where Rita worked to an institution that had wrought so much emotional trauma in Ted Bundy's life: the Elizabeth Lund Home for Unwed Mothers. The Lund home was right next door to the motel.

I had always assumed that Ted's trip to Burlington had occurred in the summer of 1969 when he journeyed East, but John Bassett's call made me wonder. It was in the Fall of 1971 when Ted spoke to me of "finding out who I really was."

If Ted was in Burlington in July of 1971, if he walked past the building where he was born, if he—perhaps—even checked into the Colonial Motor Inn, there are no records whatsoever to confirm or deny it.

There is only a blurred notation in the Burlington "dog-catcher's" records that note a person named "Bundy" had been bitten by a dog that week. . . .

In talking with Bassett, with Rita Curran's parents, and with a detective from the Burlington Police Department, I too was fascinated by so many similarities—but there was little I could do to confirm their suspicions about Ted Bundy. Meg Anders writes in her book *The Phantom Prince* that she saw Ted sometimes that summer, and sometimes he didn't show up for dates. She had begun to notice a moodiness in him.

But was Ted gone long enough to make a trip to Vermont? And is it simply too easy to imagine Ted Bundy's shadow wherever a beautiful dark-haired woman died by strangulation and blows to the left side of the head?

There are many commonalities between Rita Curran's murder and those that came later and *were* attributed to Ted.

How many victims were there for Ted Bundy? Will we ever know?

A dozen or more young women have called me since 1980, absolutely convinced that they had escaped from Ted Bundy. In San Francisco. In Georgia. In Idaho. In Aspen. In Ann Arbor. In Utah . . . He could not have been everywhere, but, for these women, there are terrified memories of a handsome man in a tan Volkswagen—a man who gave them a ride, and who wanted more. *They* are sure that it was Ted who reached for them, and declare that they never hitchhiked again. For other women, there is a man with a brilliant smile who came to their door, ingratiating, and then angry when they would not let him in. "It was him. I've seen his picture, and I recognized him."

Mass hysteria? I think yes, for most. For some, I wonder.

There have been other calls that left no doubt in my mind. Lisa Wick, nearing forty now, called me. Lisa was the stewardess who survived a bludgeoning with a two-by-four as she slept in a basement apartment on Queen Anne Hill in Seattle in the Summer of 1966. Her roommate, Lonnie Trumbull, died. Like so many of the later victims who were struck again and again on the head as they slept, Lisa Wick lost weeks of memory forever.

Lisa did not call to tell me that she had read my book; she called to say that she could not read my book. "I try to pick it up and read it, but it is impossible. When my hand touches the cover, when I look at his eyes, I get sick to my stomach."

Somewhere, buried in her deepest forbidden memory, Lisa Wick knows that she has seen those eyes before. But long after he physical injuries have healed, her mind remains bruised, and protects itself. "I know that it was Ted Bundy who did that to us—but I can't tell you how I know. . . ."

There have been no calls from Ann Marie Burr—who would be thirty-one if she was alive. From the night she disappeared from her own home in Tacoma in August of 1962, there has been no sign of Ann Marie. And yet I have had more calls—with information, and with questions—about Ann Marie than any of the other victims.

A young woman, whose brother was Ted Bundy's best boyhood friend: "We lived right across the street from the Bundys—and when that little girl disappeared, the police were all over our street. They searched the woods up at the end of the street many times—they questioned everybody because we lived so close to the Burr's house."

An older woman, now living in a retirement home, who lived near the Burrs in 1962: "He was the paper boy, Ted was—the morning paper boy. That little girl, Ann Marie, used to follow him around like a puppy—she really thought he was something. They knew each other all right. She would have gone with him if he asked her to crawl out the window."

It is so long ago. 24 years.

A young woman called from Florida one day, an assistant in the State Attorney General's Office. "I'm a Chi Omega," she began, "and I read your book."

"I was a Chi Omega too—" I said, and she interrupted, "no. I mean I was a Chi O at Florida State—I was there in Tallahassee—that night—in the house when . . . he got in."

We talked about how it could have happened—with all those girls—39 of them—and a housemother. How could anyone have done so much damage—so quietly—in such a short time?

"He had already scouted it out—that afternoon—I think," she mused. "For some reason, we were all gone Saturday afternoon, even the housemother. The house was empty for a couple of hours. When we came home, the housemother's cat was acting spooked, and its hair was standing on end. It ran through our legs and out the door—and it didn't come back for two weeks."

She said some of the girls had felt the presence of a kind of evil that night. The Chi O's had wondered only a little while about the cat's behavior, but, later that night, at least two of the girls who were upstairs in the sleeping area had experienced stark terror, a free-floating dread with nothing to pin it to.

"Kim had a sore throat, and she went to bed early. She got up sometime during the night to go down to the bathroom to get a drink of water because she was coughing. She saw that the lights were out in the hallway. They were almost always on, and it was pitch dark—but she just had a little way to walk to touch the switch. But she said she suddenly felt such unreasoning terror—as if something awful was waiting for her. She had a terrible cough and she really needed a drink of water—but she backed into her room and locked the door. She didn't come out until the police banged on the door later. . . .

"And—it must have been a little bit after that—Tina started down the back stairs—to the kitchen to get a snack. It was the same kind of thing. She couldn't seem to make her feet go down those stairs. She started to shake, and she ran back to her room too. She'd felt something—or someone—waiting down below. . ."

I had always believed that Margaret Bowman had been Ted's designated victim that January night in 1978. Margaret looked very much like Stephanie Brooks; she was a beautiful girl with the same long silken dark hair. It would have been easy enough for Ted to have spotted her on the Florida State Campus, or walking near The Oak and the Chi O house—or even at Sherrod's. But how could Ted have known which room Margaret Bowman slept in?

I asked my Chi Omega caller that. "How did he know just where to go?"

"We had a room plan posted—"

"A room plan?"

"Like a blueprint of the house. Each room had a number, and the names of the girls who had that room were written in."

"Where was it?"

"In the foyer. Near the front door, on the wall there. We took it down after."

Posted on the foyer wall, right there in the one area of the sorority house where dates and delivery men . . . and strangers could read it and pinpoint exactly which room each girl occupied. It would have been propitious for a man stalking a particular girl.

The Chi Omegas, besieged by the press, ousted from their rooms by investigators dusting for prints, gathering evidence, and testing for blood, were evacuated from the huge house on West Jefferson and farmed out around Tallahassee with alumnae. They came back two weeks later, just about the same time the housemother's cat deemed the house safe again.

I have not been back to the Chi O house in Tallahassee, but I have returned many times to the Theta house on the University of Washington campus in Seattle—with screen writers or magazine photographers—who want to *see* where Georgeann Hawkins vanished. It looks the same—the alley behind Greek Row with students constantly moving back and forth. Night or day, fraternity boys are still shooting basketballs at hoops nailed to telephone poles. The cars parked along there are newer models than those in the police photos—but otherwise, nothing has changed—not even the sorority itself that was Georgeann's destination.

But when one considers an extrasensory awareness of danger or evil, I know I felt it in the narrow space between the Theta House and the fraternity just to do the south of it. On the hottest, sunniest days, the air is icy, the pine trees there are crippled and blunted, and I want very much to be away from it, from the cement steps where Georgeann was to have perched while she threw pebbles at her roommates' window.

Fear made some of Georgeann's sorority sisters drop out of school for a time. A dozen years later, Georgeann Hawkins is still missing. The sorority girls inside the Theta House seem oblivious to what happened to her. They were only five or six in 1974; for them, Georgeann Hawkins might well have vanished in the 1950's.

Ted Bundy's rooming house on 12th. N.E. looks exactly the same as it did the day he moved out and headed for Salt Lake City. The old rooming house the next block over—where the woman was raped by a man in a dark watch cap—has been razed to make room for the University of Washington's new law school buildings.

Farther north on 12th N.E., the green house where Lynda Ann Healy disappeared in 1974 has been painted a dull brown. The main floor is a pre-school now, and, in the front window, someone has pasted a decal of—eerily—a huge smiling teddy bear.

Donna Manson has never been found. The campus at Evergreen State College is even more heavily thicketed with fir trees today. In Utah and Colorado, the missing are still gone: Debby Kent and Julie Cunningham and Denise Oliverson.

No more evidence has been found. Not an earring. Not a bicycle. Not even a faded piece of clothing. All things that were secret a dozen years ago remain hidden.

When Ted was delivered by helicopter back to the bleak walls of the Florida State Prison northwest of Starke, he joined over two hundred inmates on Death Row, the building housing more condemned men than any other state prison. Compared to Utah's "Point of the Mountain" and the jails where he'd been incarcerated in Colorado, "Raiford" was a long step down in the amenities of prison life.

Starke, Florida, is the closest town of any size, with a population of about a thousand people. Approaching from the east, it appears to be a shanty town, economically depressed. The houses move from shack to middle-class closer to the hub of Starke—where the main intersection is marked by a Western Auto Store.

About three miles west of town, the prison looms on the left, and there is a neat sign reading "Florida State Prison." Just past the sign, a visitor turns into the main driveway and proceeds one hundred yards to the parking lot and the brick administration building.

The prison is fifty yards beyond. It is not a modern concrete fortress; it is an old prison, stucco and faintly greenish white—not unlike the pallor of the inmates it holds.

The grounds are perfectly manicured, with bright flower beds; the driveway and the parking lot paved with carefully troweled cement.

Richard Dugger is the Superintendant of the Florida State Prison. He is, in a sense, a "lifer" too. Dugger was born on the prison grounds when his father was the warden. He was raised here. He is Ted Bundy's contemporary, a tremendously fit, tautly muscled athlete—the antithesis of the standard movie portrayal of the pot-bellied, semi-comedic southern warden. Dugger has been described as a rigid man who goes by the book. He is certainly a no-nonsense prison superintendant.

Dugger runs his prison meticulously. Trusties keep the flat grounds of Florida State Prison a tentative oasis in the midst of inhospitable sandy soil. There is a farm—as all prisons have farms—cows, pigs, whatever will grow to add to the prison menu.

For Ted—born on Lake Champlain, nurtured on the Delaware River, raised on Puget Sound—Ted who craved water and trees and the smell of salt air coming off *some* sound or bay or ocean, this last stop on his downward spiral had to be hell. Raiford sits smack dab in the middle of a triangle of roads surrounding nothing. There are no waterways at all; the air outside dries the membranes of the nose and throat, or smothers with mugginess. Beyond the grounds, the vista is endless and barren; there is a factory down the road, the vegetation is scrabbly palms, and whatever will grow without water and with too much sun.

The Okefenokee Swamp is approximately fifty miles north of Raiford. Gainesville (the city Ted once dismissed when his pin stuck there on a map because it had no large waterways) is thirty-five miles south. The Gulf of Mexico and the Atlantic Ocean are east and west, each an easy hour and a half's drive for a free man.

It probably didn't matter at all what it was like around Raiford. Ted Bundy would not spend time *outside* the walls. With his history and expertise at escape, every precaution would be taken that he would not demonstrate his talents at Raiford. This was something of a disappointment to a number of burly guards who muttered that they'd sure as hell like to see the bastard make a run for it—as they'd "enjoy splattering Bundy all over a wall."

Ted was not destined to be a popular prisoner. Not so much because of the crimes for which he'd been sentenced—but because of his attitude. Ted Bundy was a STAR, and that rankled both guards and fellow convicts.

When he wrote to me from the Utah State Prison, Ted had confided that he was welcome in the "general population"—a sought-after "prison lawyer." He had not done very well for himself when he played lawyer in Miami; his counsel was tainted now. Besides, in this southern prison, he was isolated among all those men struggling not to die. He was alone in a cell most of the time, a cell once occupied by John Spenkelink—the convict who had been executed six days before Ted chose to tear up his "admission of guilt" on May 31, 1979, throwing away what proved to be his last good chance to elude the death penalty. He would have been locked up forever—but he would have lived.

If it was a gamble, Ted had lost.

Less than a year later, Ted sat in the dead Spenkelink's cell, a short walk from "Old Sparky"—the electric chair that would soon hold the record for electrocuting more convicted killers than any other since the Supreme Court lifted its ban on the death penalty in 1976.

But Ted was *not* alone in this ugly life he'd come to. When Carole Ann Boone spoke her surreptitious vows of marriage in Kimberly Leach's murder trial on February 9th, she had meant them. She would stick by her "Bunnie."

Carole Ann did not, however, take Ted's name; she remained "Boone." After the two widely-publicized Florida trials, that was notorious enough. She and her son, Jamey, who was in his early teens—a dark, good-looking young man, who impressed news-people at the Miami trial as being an exceptionally nice kid—chose to live—not in Starke—but in Gainesville.

Carole Boone is an intelligent woman, with advanced degrees and an impressive job résumé. However, she had spent her financial as well as her emotional reserves in her fight to save her new husband. Ted at least, was housed, fed and clothed. Carole Ann and Jamey were on their own.

No one has ever questioned that Carole Ann believed in Ted's innocence, unquestioning. I have often wondered if she had truly expected that Ted would be freed, that they would one day be able to settle down like a normal family. Her obsession with him had landed her in Gainesville, Florida on public assistance—at least temporarily. She became only one of hundreds of prisoners' wives clogging the employment market.

But it did not seem to matter. Nothing mattered but the fact that she was still close to Ted. She was Mrs. Theodore Robert Bundy, and each week she could journey up through Starke, turn at the Western Auto Store, and go three miles out the dusty two-laned road to see her husband. From time to time, she would write to Louise Bundy to tell her how Ted was doing. But in essence, Carole Ann had become everything to Ted, as he had been for her for so many years now.

Whatever he asked for, she would try to give him.

The Stranger Beside Me was published in August of 1980. I had not written to Ted; he had not contacted me—not since his ebullient phone call just before his Miami trial. As I wrote this book, I had been startled to find a great deal of anger surfacing from someplace inside *me* where I had unknowingly repressed it for years. I thought that I had juggled my ambivalence about Ted very well. But listing the murders, detailing the crimes, and being closeted for months in my office where the walls were papered with the photographs of young women who had died grotesquely changed me.

I thought that sometimes I would write to Ted—but I wasn't ready when I finished the book. And I wasn't ready when I went out on a media tour for "Stranger" in August of 1980.

In seven weeks, I flew to 35 cities, and, in each, talked to interviewers from radio, television, and newspapers about Ted Bundy. Some of them—back in 1980—had never heard of him. Some, in surprisingly distant cities, had watched his trials on television.

The night shows were different. People listening to their radios out there in the darkness somewhere are unable to sleep—most of them—for one reason or another. The callers' voices were more emotional than daytime listeners', opinions were expressed more freely. Many of them were angry—but their rage was polarized.

In Denver, on a midnight to three A.M. talk show, the host left me on the phone—and on the air—for fifteen minutes with a man who bragged that *he* had murdered nine women "because they deserved it"—disconnecting him only when the man threatened to "blow me away" with his .45 because I was being "unfair" to Bundy. The host walked me downstairs, pointing out the bullet-proof glass in the lobby—and helped me into a cab with a perfect stranger—who, fortunately, turned out to be most protective as he raced me to my hotel. (Later, the host of that late-night talk show was shot down and killed—in front of his own apartment house.)

In Los Angeles, I had a similar threat—because I was "too kind" to Ted Bundy.

But, for the most part, readers understood what it was I was trying to convey, and I was grateful for that.

My itinerary took me to Florida in September. The closest I came to the Florida State Prison was the day I was in the Tampa-St. Petersburg area. Just as I went off the air in a radio station in Tampa, an urgent call came in from a man. The host said that I could not talk, but gave the caller the number of the next station where I would be interviewed.

But, when I arrived in St. Petersburg, there was only a message. A man who would not give his name had said it was urgent that he speak with me—that I would know why, but that he could not stay on the phone.

The next day, I was in Dallas. I never found out who the caller was. Ted? Or possibly just a "220?"

The St. Petersburg Times' interviewer had told me that he'd come up with a novel approach for reviewing my book. He had sent it to Raiford and asked Ted to criticize it—on its literary merits only—promising the usual thirty-five-dollar payment that book critics received.

Ted would have loved that, I thought—if Vic Africano let him do it. Ted had not responded, but the book had not been returned.

In late September, after weeks on the road, I came home to Seattle for a few days to rest up for the second half of the tour.

There was a letter waiting for me, a letter postmarked "Starke, Florida" and dated the day after I had been in Tempa. The handwriting was as familiar to me as my own.

It was, of course, from Ted.

> "Dear Ann,
> Since you have seen fit to take advantage of our relationship, I think it only fair that you share your great good fortune with my wife, Carole Ann Boone. Please send her $2500—or more— to: (he gave her address) as soon as possible.
>
> Best regards, ted."

Curiously, my immediate reaction was one of guilt. Emotion without rationale: *What have I done to this poor man?* And then I remembered that I had never once lied to Ted. I had my book contract months before he was a suspect, I told him about it when he became a suspect, and I reiterated the details of my contract to him many times in letters. He knew I was writing a book about the elusive "Ted," and still *he* had chosen to keep in touch with me, to write me long letters and to call often.

I believe that Ted felt that I could be manipulated into writing the definitive "Ted Bundy is innocent" book. And I would have done that—if I could have. But the Miami trial had exposed his guilt with such merciless clarity. I had written what I had to write. Now, he was furious with me, and demanding money for Carole Ann.

That he had lied to me—probably from the first moment I met him—had not occurred to him.

When I reconsidered, I had to smile. If Ted thought that I was basking in riches, he was woefully mistaken. My advance payment for the book that one day became *The Stranger Beside Me* had been ten thousand dollars—spread over five years—with a third of it going to pay my expenses in Miami.

I glanced in my checkbook. I had twenty dollars in the bank. There would be more coming, of course; my book was selling very well, but I was learning as all authors do that royalty payments come only twice a year. In 1975, I had offered Ted a portion of book royalties—if he should choose to write a chapter or two from his viewpoint, and he had declined.

I reduced his request to a simple equation. I had four children to support; Carole Ann Boone had only one. Even if I had had the money Ted requested, it did not seem fair, somehow, that I should help support Carole Ann.

I started to write to Ted to explain my feelings, and then—for the very first time—I truly realized that he could not, would not, understand or emphathize or even care what my situation was. I had been meant to serve a purpose in his life; I had been the designated Bundy P.R. person—and I had failed to produce.

For six years, I didn't write to Ted again. Nor he to me.

Ted Bundy, who had been all over the news for five years, virtually disappeared for months. The word was that he was in his cell, poring over law books, preparing for appeals. There were three books published about Ted in 1980—mine included—and the man who once yearned to be governor of Washington became instead a nationally-known criminal, his chilling eyes staring back from newstands and bookshelves all over America.

There was yet another book in 1981. The woman I called "Meg Anders"—Meg the woman who had been with Ted longer than any other—published her story, entitled *The Phantom Prince: My Life With Ted Bundy*.

Meg's real first name is Liz. She used that and a fictitious surname "Kendall" as her pen name. She did not realize, perhaps, that becoming an author had made her a public figure. Seattle papers immediately printed her true name, and her hope for anonymity for herself and her daughter—fifteen in 1981—was destroyed.

Liz/Meg had received a call from Ted at Pensacola Police headquarters on the same Thursday night in February, 1978 when I did. In her book, she intimated that Ted confessed to her the kidnapings of Carol Da Ronch and Debbie Kent—and the murders of Brenda Ball, Janice Ott and Denise Naslund. She quoted Ted as saying that the police were "years off" when they speculated about *when* he had begun to kill. . . .

Liz wrote that she asked Ted if he ever wanted to kill her, and said he admitted he had tried to kill her once. He had allegedly left her asleep in her hide-a-bed after closing the damper on the fireplace and putting towels against the door crack. She had awakened, she wrote, with streaming eyes, choking in a smoke-filled room.

Liz Kendall's book, published by a Seattle firm, may well have caused her more grief than comfort. Families of the victims bombarded radio stations where she was interviewed, demanding to know why—if Ted had confessed to her—she had not told the police. Many callers reduced Liz to tears, as she tried to explain that everything was being taken out of context. No, Ted had never actually confessed to her.

At the end of June, 1980, Liz got a last letter from Ted, mailed—not from the Florida State Prison—but forwarded by Carole Ann Boone (Bundy.) Oddly, Ted berated Liz for going to the police and telling them "fairly uncomplimentary" things about him. Why would be have been so angry at that late date? I can remember so well having lunch with Ted in January, 1976 when he told me that he knew it had been Liz who turned him in to the Salt Lake County Sheriff—"but I love her more than ever."

Whatever Ted's reason was for castigating Liz, he called her weeks later and apologized. That, she wrote, in the ending of her book, was the last time she heard from him.

Of all the lives that Ted Bundy damaged irrevocably—beyond those of the women he murdered—Liz's may head the list. She was—is—a very nice woman, fighting a hostile world. She loved Ted for a long time. She may still.

There are no authorized conjugal visits in the Florida State Penitentiary, no cozy trailers or rooms where inmates may share intimacy with their spouses. The visitors' room in Death Row is well-lighted, utilitarian, with tables and stools bolted to the floor, redolent of wax, cigarettes, disinfectant and sweat.

But there are ways around the rules. One of my periodic callers is a woman who visits a relative on the Florida State Penitentiary's Death Row. Like most visitors, she was fascinated to catch a glimpse of the infamous Ted Bundy. And she has learned a great deal about how certain activities are accomplished in the Death Row visitor's area.

"They bribe the guards," she explains. "Each prisoner who wants sex with his wife or girlfriend puts up five dollars. After they get a kitty of about fifty or sixty dollars, they draw lots. The winner gets to take his lady into the restroom or behind the water cooler and the guards look the other way."

"Have you seen Ted?" I asked her. "What does he look like now?"

"You bet I have. He's real thin. Some of them say he's just gone crazy in there . . . just purely crazy . . . that they have to keep him doped up with Thorazine all the time. . . ."

My caller was afraid of Ted Bundy. "His eyes. He just kept staring at me and staring at me and he never blinks."

But Ted had not gone crazy. He was planning and studying and working things out in his head—just as he always had. There was the mythic "Ted" who terrified female visitors—and there was the real Ted, who, if he'd had a white shirt, a tie, and a suit, could still have sat easily at the governor's right hand.

During the summer of 1982, Carole Ann Boone wore a jacket when she went to the prison to visit her husband, despite the baking heat of northern Florida's July and August. Tall and large-boned, it was easier for her to hide a growing secret than it would be for a more petite woman.

She was putting on weight. That in itself wasn't unusual. Women whose men are locked behind bars, who subsist on low incomes, frustration and meager hope, often eat too much. But Carole Ann's weight was all around the middle, and to their chagrin, prison authorities saw that her silhouette was unmistakable.

Carole Ann Boone was pregnant, carrying Ted Bundy's child.

The two of them, together against the world, had managed to marry by subterfuge. Now, they had accomplished the conception of a child the same way.

October, 1982, was a landmark month for Ted Bundy. First of all, his new attorney, Robert Augustus Harper Jr. of Tallahassee, asked the Florida Supreme Court to overturn Ted's conviction in the murders of Lisa Levy and Margaret Bowman: Supreme Court Case No. 57,772 (Circuit Court No. 78–670) Harper cited the controversial bite-mark evidence and deemed the hypnosis of a prosecution witness highly suspect. Further, Ted's attorney claimed that his client had had inadequate legal help at the time of the Miami trial. (This, when Ted had told me so gleefully just before trial that that was one area in which he would never have an appeal. He had been delighted with his attorneys then. . . .)

"Bite-mark evidence is here to stay . . . but at the same time, there are certain standards that have to be set out," Harper argued. "Richard Souviron was out to get famous on this case."

Harper also attacked Nita Neary's testimony because it came after hypnosis. "You can see that a creation of memory occurred. That point where her memory has been created by a pseudo-scientific process is improper."

Assistant Attorney General David Gauldin argued for the State that fairness of the trial was the bottom line, "I think he got a fair trial, and I think the jury was untainted. . . . He hired and fired lawyers at will, all of them publicly provided."

The six Florida Supreme Court justices did not say when they might make a judgment on whether Ted would get a new trial in the Chi Omega killings.

A new cycle had begun. Ted was attacking again, seeking a new trial—back in the game. Carole Ann, ponderously—and proudly—pregnant, visited him regularly that October. As the month neared its close, she entered a private birthing center where she bore Ted his first child: a daughter. That was all even the most assiduous reporter found out. No birthweight. Certainly no name. Only "Baby Girl Boone."

Carole took the infant along when she visited Ted. He was very proud of his progeny. Ted's genes had prevailed; the baby looked just like him.

On May 11, 1984, James Adams, a black sharecropper's son, died in the electric chair in Raiford Prison. He was the fourth man to die since John Spenkelink.

A month later, the Florida Supreme Court Announced its findings on Ted Bundy's appeal in a thirty-five page document.

Ted had lost. Justices Alderman, Adkins, Overton, McDonald, and Ehrlich swept Harper's arguments away; Ted had not been, in their opinion, denied the right to a fair trial because the public and press had attended pre-trial hearings. He had been granted a change of venue from Leon County, and the jury had already been selected and sequestered when the crucial pre-trial hearings were held. But then again Ted had claimed he'd been deprived of a fair trial because he had to ask for a change of venue—the press's fault—and lost his right to be tried in the locality where the charged crimes were committed. His two complaints were at counter-purposes. But they were both denied, making it a draw.

On a more salient issue, the Court ruled that Nita Neary's description of the man she'd seen in the Chi Omega house had not materially changed after she was hypnotized. The hypnotist could not have suggested that she describe Ted Bundy; Ted Bundy wasn't even a suspect when Nita Neary was hypnotized. Nor did the Court feel that the newspaper pictures she saw later of Ted Bundy had influenced her. The man she saw opening the front door—with an oak club in one hand—had been in profile. The news photos were all full-face.

Ted had also argued—through Harper—that he had been unfairly tried when the Dunwoody Street attack on Cheryl Thomas was being joined with the Chi Omega crimes. The Court found the crimes were "connected by proximity in time and location, by their nature, and by the manner in which they were perpetrated."

Point by point, Ted Bundy lost in this appeal. No, the Grand Jury had not been prejudiced against him when they handed down the original indictment; he had had adequate opportunity to raise his objections in a timely manner. He had always, always had legal counsel. No, he could not have a new trial because he'd been denied Millard Farmer. Nor could he have a new trial because the jury had known that he was an escapee when he arrived in Florida.

The Florida Justices disputed Ted's claim against the Forensic Odontologist, Richard Souviron—that Souviron had erred in saying that it had been Ted Bundy's teeth that left the imprints in Lisa Levy's buttocks. ". . . We find that it was proper for the expert to offer his opinion on the issue of a bite-mark match; this was not an improper legal conclusion. All facets of appellant's argument on the bite mark evidence are without merit. . . ."

In the sentencing phase, the dry legal terminology cannot hide the horror: "Next Bundy claims that the trial court erred in finding that the capital felonies were especially heinous, atrocious, and cruel. There is no merit to this argument. The victims were murdered while sleeping in their own beds . . . The trial court also recounted the gruesome manner in which the victims were bludgeoned, sexually battered, and strangled. These circumstances are more than sufficient to uphold the trial court's finding that the capital felonies were especially heinous, atrocious, and cruel. . . ."

Although it would seem a moot point—now that Ted knew that there would be no new trial in the Chi Omega and Cheryl Thomas cases—he proceeded with his appeal on the Kimberly Leach case: Case No. 59,128.

But his mind was obviously working on other levels—other possibilities too.

Ted was thin, but he was probably in the best shape he'd been in in years. He did wind sprints, one-hundred yard dashes, whenever he was allowed out in the exercise yard, or into the long corridors.

And he cultivated his neighbors, tuning in on the grapevine that blooms so lushly with information throughout a cellblock.

Gerald Eugene Stano resided on the cell to one side of Ted; Ottis Elwood Toole was on the other side. Stano, 32, had admitted to killing 39 young women—mostly hitchhikers and prostitutes— between 1969 and 1980. It was rumored that many of his victims wore blue—a color often favored by Stano's brother—whom he hated. Convicted of ten murders, he had, like Ted, been sentenced to death three times over. Toole, 36, most infamous as Henry Lee Lucas' sometime lover/sometime murder partner, had admitted to Jacksonville Detective Buddy Terry that it was he who had kidnapped and murdered Adam Walsh.

Adam was six years old when Toole spotted him near a Sears store in Hollywood, Florida. Toole had, for some reason known only to him, decided that he wanted to "adopt" a baby. He had searched all day and found no little babies—so he'd taken Adam. When the little boy resisted, Toole told Terry that he'd killed him and thrown his body into an alligator-filled canal. Adam's father, John Walsh, searched tirelessly for his child, and then relentlessly lobbied before Congress until they passed the Missing Children's Act.

The movie "Adam" has been shown many times on television.

Ted's I.Q. alone nearly equaled Stano's and Toole's combined.

In the summer of 1984—following Ted's heavy losses to the Florida Supreme Court—he came perilously close to repeating his Houdini-like Colorado escapes. Prison officials arrived to do a surprise shakedown of his cell just in time. They found hacksaw blades secreted there. Someone from the outside had to have brought them in to Ted; that person was never named.

But somehow, someone had gotten the metal blades through all the security checks. The bars in Ted's cell looked secure, but careful perusal showed that one bar had been completely sawed through at both the top and bottom, and then "glued" back with an adhesive whose main component was soap.

Could Ted have ever reached the outside? Even if he'd managed to cut through another bar or two, and wriggled free of his cell, there were so many obstacles. The entire prison is surrounded by two ten-foot-high fences, with electric gates that are never opened at the same time. Rolls of sharp barbed wire bales top the walls and occupy much of the "pen" around the Death Row cellblocks. The guards are in the tower . . . waiting.

And that is what Ted would have faced *after* (and if) he managed to get past all the safeguards inside Death Row itself, a building a separated from the rest of Raiford Prison.

If he had somehow managed to shed his bright orange tee-shirt that marked him a resident of Death Row and obtained civilian clothing, how would he have passed through the electric gates. When one gate opens, the other was already clanged shut. How would he have gotten the hand-stamp? Every visitor into these dangerous bowels of the Florida State Prison is required to have his hand stamped—like teenagers leaving a dance. But the colors change from day to day, without any discernible pattern.

When the visitor leaves, he must hold his hand under a machine that reveals "the color of the day." Without the stamp—or with the wrong color, the alarm bells sound. . . .

The hacksaw blades were confiscated, Ted was moved to another cell and it was "tossed" more frequently than before.

He had been "inside" for more than four years. His child was almost two. There had been no execution date set. He waited, and studied, and played the games that all prisoners play—but that Ted Bundy, in particular, played. Anything to put something over on those in authority.

On May 9, 1985, the Florida Supreme Court ruled once again on Ted's request for a new trial—this time in the case of Kimberly Leach.

Ted's points of law were essentially the same that they had been in the Chi Omega case. Only the characters were different. An eyewitness had been hypnotized, prospective jurors had been excluded because they opposed the death penalty. Ted claimed the judge couldn't have determined if the child's murder was "heinous and atrocious" because Kimberly's body had been too decomposed to tell, having lain so long in an abandoned pig sty.

Supreme Court Justice James Alderman wrote the unanimous decision. "After weighing the evidence in this case, we conclude that the sentence of death imposed was justified and appropriate under our law."

In that May of 1985, I was on Hilton Head Island, South Carolina—scarcely a hundred miles away from Raiford—talking—still talking—about Ted Bundy, showing the same one hundred and fifty slides that I have shown so many times. To cops this time—a two-day seminar on "Serial Murder," sponsored by the University of Louisville's School of Justice Administration. The term "serial murder" was relatively new, and seemed to have been coined for Ted Bundy, even though there had been a few dozen more men who had racked up horrific tolls since Ted's incarceration. Ted Bundy remained *the* celebrity serial killer.

As I spoke to the three dozen detectives on the South Carolina island in the Atlantic Ocean, I mused that Ted had truly become a coast-to-coast antihero. Less than a month before, I had given the same presentation—on the *Pacific* Ocean—to the American College of Forensic Psychiatry.

Hilton Head marked a reunion of sorts. The University of Louisville had gathered many of the players from the long search for Bundy. Jerry Thompson and Dr. Al Carlisle from Utah, Mike Fisher from Colorado, Don Patchen from Tallahassee. Myself.

Bob Keppel would have been there too—except that he was weighed down by his duties as advisor to a task force mobilized to find yet another serial killer in Washington State: The Green River Killer.

It was ironic. Keppel had moved on from the King County Police's Homicide Unit to be the Chief Criminal Investigator for the Washington State Attorney General's Office. He liked his new job. On a long flight to Texas a few years ago—when we were both headed for a VI-CAP (Violent Criminal Apprehension Program) conference—Keppel had confided, "One thing I never want to do again is to work under that boiler-room pressure of a serial killer task force."

Starting in January of 1984, he had been doing just that, looking for the murderer of—not eight—but at least forty-eight young women. Tracking Ted Bundy, Keppel had been through the fire, and the knowledge he'd gained made him invaluable to the Green River Task Force. He could not say no—and he hadn't.

He went back to "the boiler-room."

Ted Bundy was alive. He was several years older than I was when I first met him, but despite everything that had happened, he looked far younger than his chronological age. If he were free, he could still stroll a college campus and not look out of place. Whatever sins might excoriate his soul, they did not mark his handsome face. Only the grey strands that threaded through his still-thick wavy hair betray that he would soon be forty years old.

After seven years with no date set for execution, it seemed that Ted wasn't going to die. At least not in the electric chair in Raiford Prison. The threat of the chair was somehow so much more palpable in Judge Cowart's courtroom in the long summer of 1979.

Ted gave interviews to writers, and talked occasionally to judiciously selected criminologists. Led down endless corridors, through myriad electronic devices and doors into a little room with one door and one window looking out toward the guard Captain's office, Ted expounded for hours on his opinions, theories, feelings. He considers himself an expert on the mind of the serial killer, and offered to share his expertise with detectives in current investigations. If Warden Dugger would allow it, Ted would be happy to appear on videotape for conferences and seminars.

He was considered an escape risk—always. Within the next year, he had his cell changed once again because he was found with contraband—this time a mirror. Mirrors can be used for all manner of activities in prison.

When I visited him in the Utah State Prison in 1976, he had been neither cuffed nor shackled. In the Florida State Prison, he left his cell on Death Row only after his hands have been cuffed behind him, and his ankles shackled. Once he was safely in the tiny room where he was allowed interviews, his hands are cuffed in front of him. He wears jeans, brand-name running shoes, and the ubiquitous orange t-shirt of the Death wing.

He seemed open and cooperative, but there are things he would not speak of, and he ducks his head and laughs nervously as he demurs, "I can't talk about that." He would not talk about Carole Ann—he is most protective of *his* daughter—who is almost four years old now.

He had "forgiven" me. He described me now to questioners as "a decent-enough person—who was only doing her job."

Suddenly, on February 5, 1986, after it seemed that Ted would be caught up in the maze of legal proceedings forever, Florida Governor Bob Graham signed Ted Bundy's Death Warrant. The date for his execution was announced: March 4th.

One month to live.

The media, who had virtually forgotten Ted Bundy, pursued him as avidly as ever. I had a lecture to give the night the news broke. My topic was, again, Ted Bundy.

But before and after—because they could not talk to Ted—and because some comment seemed necessary, I was interviewed by the Seattle affiliates of ABC, NBC, CBS. What did I think? How did I feel?

I wasn't sure. I felt shocked mostly. And I felt removed from Ted, almost as if I had never known him—as if he was some invention, some fictional character I had once written about. And I knew, leadenly, that it must be. If Ted was not executed, he would some-how, find a way to escape.

Ted had fired his last lawyer—Harper—just as he eventually dismissed all the others. He had been representing himself, and he had filed an appeal for new trials with the U.S. Supreme Court—which was to have been heard on March 7—three days *after* he was now scheduled to die. On February 18, he represented himself again before the Supreme Court by delivering a hand-written appeal for a stay of execution. Justice Lewis R. Powell refused to block the execution, but he gave Ted a second chance. He turned down Ted's somewhat amateurish request "without prejudice" and instructed him to obtain proper legal counsel "to file an application that complies with the rules of this court."

No one had ever gone to the Florida electric chair on the first death warrant signed—but that was no guarantee that Ted Bundy would not set a new record.

In Lake City—where Kimberly Leach had been kidnapped—thousands of residents signed a petition supporting Ted's execution. A nurse whose daughter had attended Lake City Junior High with Kimberly said, "Many of those who signed said they would like to sign twice and would pull the switch if given the chance. . . ."

Richard Larsen, the *Seattle Times* reporter (and now Associate Editor) who wrote one of the 1980 Bundy books, received one of many letters sent to newspapers around America. It appeared to be an official communique from the "Office of the Governor, Florida State Capitol, Tallahasse, Florida, 32304."

It was two pages long, beginning, "Florida Gov. Bob Graham today signed a cooperative agreement with the Tennessee Valley Authority for more electricity to be used in the coming execution of convicted killer Theodore Bundy . . . The power sales contract with TVA will provide ten additional megawatts of energy to Florida Power & Light in order to ensure Bundy is executed using the maximum voltage and amperage allowed . . .

"In addition to the temporary contract for electricity, Graham urged Florida residents to reduce their electrical usage for a five-minute period beginning at 6:57 a.m. EST March 4, 1986. Bundy is scheduled to be executed at 7:00 a.m. on that date.

"If citizens of the state can turn off all non-vital air conditioning, televisions, electric dryers and washers during that brief period, we could have as much as five additional megawatts to pump into the chair . . .

"Reddy Communications of Akron, Ohio—owners of the popular Reddy Kilowatt logo—will prepare a special gold medallion for the event with the inscription, 'Die Quicker Electrically.' The medallions will be on sale . . . Proceeds will help defray the tremendous costs associated with Bundy's prosecution, incarceration, and ultimate execution . . ."

It was, of course, a macabre prank, and had not come from Graham's office. Yet, it reflected that the feeling in Florida about Ted had not changed much since his Miami trial.

As the March 4th date drew nearer, it seemed that Ted *was* going to die within the week.

And then, on February 25th, a Washington D.C. law firm announced that it would represent Ted without payment. However, Polly J. Nelson, an attorney from the firm, said that they had not yet decided if they would request a stay of execution.

". . . We're investigating whether it's advisable . . ."

On February 27, the U.S. Supreme Court granted a stay of execution—until April 11, 1986.

Assistant State Attorney Jack Pottinger—who was Chief of Detectives in Leon County in January 1978, when the Chi Omega attack took place—predicted that it would be a long time before Ted was actually electrocuted. "Ted's used to manipulating the system all along. He'll do nothing until the 11th hour and come forth with a flurry of things."

Inside Raiford Prison, the word was that Ted Bundy would probably be executed sometime in the Fall of 1986. One week before the date listed on his final death warrant, the lights will dim in Raiford—as the chair is tested. That is not a macabre prank; that really happens.

In the early morning of the date itself—whenever that date would be—Ted would be led down the long, long walk to "Old Sparky," and a black rubber mask pulled down over his face. So that he would not see death coming? Or, more likely, so that witnesses would not glimpse his face as the electricity jolts through his body.

It seems ironic that Ted Bundy is in such superb physical condition. He has become a vegetarian. Because Florida State Prison dieticians do not cater to individual requests, it was necessary for him to change his religious affiliation once again. Born and raised a Methodist, converted to Mormonism just before his first arrest, he is now an avowed Hindu. He admits that it is a pragmatic conversion; as a Hindu, he has the legal right to be served a vegetarian and fish diet.

His muscles are defined, his lung capacity is excellent, and his vegetarian diet prevents atheromic deposits from clogging his arteries. When he dies, Ted Bundy will be in perfect health.

Ted touched so many, many lives—in one way or another. Since this book was published, I have met a hundred people who once knew him—in one segment of his compartmentalized world. All of them look a little stunned still. Not one has confided that he seemed destined for a bad end. And I have met a hundred people—more— who knew the victims. As I bend my head to autograph a book, someone murmurs, "I knew her—Georgeann . . . or Lynda . . . or Denise." Once someone said, "That was my sister," and twice, "She was my daughter. . . ."

I did not know what to say to them.

Nor did I know what to say to Ted when I wrote to him for the first time in six years. I wasn't even sure *why* I wrote, except that it seemed to me that we had unfinished business. I mailed my letter the day after his death sentence was announced. I have had no answer. He may have torn it up.

People go on as best they can. Several of the parents of Ted's victims have died early—succumbing to heart attacks. The remains of Denise Naslund and Janice Ott were lost when the King County Medical Examiner's Office moved; their bones were cremated mistakenly with those of the unidentified dead. For Eleanor Rose, Denise's mother, it was only the last in a series of blows. She had waited years so that she could give her daughter a proper burial. Denise's room and her car remain as they were on July 14, 1974. Shrines.

One of my callers about Ted was the Mormon friend who persuaded Ted to join the church in Utah in 1975. Even though Ted had not obeyed the no-smoking/ no-drinking/no-drugs tenets of the Mormons, he had seemed earnest and sincere and good. The

Mormon missionary remembered how incensed they had both been over the murders of Melissa Smith and Laura Aime.

"We sat there at my kitchen table, and the newspapers were spread out between us, with all the headlines about the dead girls. And I remember how angry Ted was. He kept telling me that he'd like to get his hands on the man that would do something like that—he'd see he never had a chance to do it again. . . ."

—Ann Rule
March 2, 1986

The Last Chapter—Update 1989
PART ONE

When I wrote the foregoing update in 1986, I never expected to hear from Ted again. Shortly after I'd mailed my update manuscript, the letter I had sent to Ted in prison was returned marked "Refused." I was not surprised. I assumed that Ted was still very angry with me. By refusing to even open my letter, he was letting me know that he no longer had any interest in my opinions. So be it.

I tossed the still-unopened letter into a drawer. Ted certainly was within his rights to remain annoyed with me.

I don't know what made me pick that letter up—weeks later—and stare at it. As I did, I detected an almost invisible strip of cellophane tape along the top of the envelope. Curious, I looked closer; the letter *had* been opened, but then someone had obviously resealed it! Had Ted been curious to see what I had to say—only to reseal my letter and mark it "Refused"?

I peeled the tape off and looked inside. There was an institutional form letter tucked into my stationery. It read, "Reason for refusal: Contraband. See item checked below."

What possible contraband could *I* have sent to Ted? I saw that "Cash/or Personal Check" had been marked. A notation stipulated that only money orders could be sent to prisoners. I had sent Ted a small check to buy cigarettes, along with some stamps. He was facing the electric chair in the immediate future, or so it seemed; money for cigarettes seemed a humane gesture. But my check had made my letter unacceptable at Raiford Prison. Maybe they'd had too many bad checks in the Florida State Prison mail room, and the prison's commissary had been stuck with them.

The question of whether Ted would read my letter was still open. With nothing to lose, I tried one more time to reach him. Time was growing short. I replaced the check with a money order and re-sent the letter.

He answered.

Indeed, Ted answered my letter on March 5, 1986. He was to have died the day before. His life was measured now in such short increments of time.

Although I am skeptical of what can be read into our handwriting (and—because of the sheer number of requests—have long ago had to stop sending samples of my subjects' writing to graphoanalysts), I must admit that I could see a rather profound change in Ted's writing. I had not had a letter from him since 1980. In six years, during which he was locked in a single cell on Death Row, Ted's hand had become even more cramped than before, with letters pushed together like the shoulders of too many men scrunched tight in a small space.

The first letter of what would prove to be a handful was a classic study in passive-aggression. I had written to try to explain to Ted what I *knew* was unexplainable. I wanted him to know that his death would not go unnoticed—or completely unmourned—by me. I had tried to say all that, without really saying it, not writing the words that seemed apparent, "Now that you are about to die—"

In Ted's reply, he thanked me politely for the stamps I'd sent. He then set about putting me in my place, slapping me down verbally—while still appearing above it all.

"As far as I'm concerned there's nothing to be gained by trying to sort through a lot of faded memories about what did and did not transpire between us, about your book, about your numerous public statements on serial murder. That's water under the bridge. I have other matters to deal with.

"In all candor, I must say this much to you, Ann. Judging from the statements I have heard and read about you making on serial murder, I suggest you seriously re-evaluate the opinions and conclusions you've formed. For whatever reason, you seem to have adopted a number of over-simplified, over-generalized and scientifically unsupportable (sic) views on the subject. The net result of this is that by disseminating (sic) such views, no matter how well-intentioned you are, you will only succeed in misleading people about the true nature of the problem and thereby make them less able to effectively deal with it."

Ted continued by saying that he "wouldn't mind" talking to me again, "for the sake of talking," but that he would not contribute to "any more books about Ted Bundy."

He ended this first short letter:

> I have no animosity toward you. I know you to be an essentially good person. I wish you the best.
>
> Take care.
>
> > peace,
> > ted

His style had grown ponderous and self-conscious. Locked up, virtually powerless at last, it was desperately important for Ted's self-esteem that he be the *best* at something.

All he knew was serial murder, and I had trampled on his territory.

Anyone interested in the problem of serial murder undoubtedly *had* heard my views on the subject. At the invitation of Pierce R. Brooks, former captain of Homicide in the Los Angeles Police Department, and the creative mind behind the VI-CAP (Violent Criminal Apprehension Program) Task Force, I had joined the group in 1982 as one of five civilian advisors. Ted was only one of many, many serial killers I had written about—but it was the Ted Bundy case that was slated to be the prototype for the VI-CAP program—the clever, charismatic, roving killer. I presented my four-hour slide seminar on Bundy to the Task Force at Sam Houston State University in Huntsville, Texas.

Brooks believed that a central computerized tracking system could cut short the killing careers of serial killers who stalked America. So did representatives from the United States Department of Justice, the F.B.I., and state, county, and local law enforcement agencies. After years of work and lobbying, VI-CAP became a reality in June 1985 in Quantico, Virginia, where it was linked to the F.B.I.'s National Crime Information Center's computers. No longer could killers such as Ted Bundy travel and kill with impunity.

VI-CAP followed them as they left a scarlet trail across America. And VI-CAP would be instrumental in stopping then before that trail became tragically long and convoluted.

I often spoke on the need for the VI-CAP system, testified before a U.S. Senate judiciary sub-committee on serial murder, and had become a certified instructor for law enforcement, probation, parole, and corrections officers in both Oregon and California. I spoke not only on serial murder, but on victimology, and on women who killed.

Ted and I were each so far removed from our nights at the Crisis Clinic, fifteen years behind us now. I thought I detected a faint sound of a gauntlet being thrown down. He fancied himself the definitive expert on serial murder, and he was telling me that I was simplistic and misinformed.

I was perfectly willing for Ted to find me inept—if it meant that he might open up. Ted Bundy might *well* be the all-time champion expert on serial murder. I was more than happy to listen. I wrote him a letter on March 13, 1986. In it, I listed my assessment of characteristics serial killers appeared to have in common—noting that it was impossible to line up serial killers in a row like so many ducks. My overview was only a general guideline, I stressed, drawn from commonalities I had winnowed out of the life stories of a number of killers who seemed to fit. I asked him to point out the areas where he found my reasoning and conclusions off-base.

To Ted, I wrote that I found serial killers were:

* Exclusively male.
* More likely to be Caucasian than black, and very rarely Indian or Oriental.
* Brilliant, charming, and charismatic.
* Physically attractive.
* Hands-on killers who used their hands as a weapon: to bludgeon, choke, strangle, or knife victims.
* Killers who seldom used a gun (with the exception of David Berkowitz and Randy Woodfield).
* Travelers—men who moved constantly either around the city where they lived, or around the country, trolling for victims,

putting many times the mileage on their vehicles than ordinary men did.

* Men who were full of rage, who killed to take the edge off that rage, and who employed sex in their murder scenario principally to demean their victims.
* Men *addicted* to murder—as an addict is addicted to drugs or liquor.
* Men who are fascinated by police work—who either spend time hanging around the police station, or who actually work as reserve officers or commissioned policemen.
* Men who seek a particular type of victim: women, children, vagrants, the elderly, homosexuals. Vulnerable victims.
* Men who employed a ruse or a device to lure victims away from help.
* Men who had suffered from some kind of child abuse *under the age of five.* I believed serial killers were very bright, sensitive children who were abused, abandoned, humiliated, rejected—during the time when their consciences should have been developing.

It was a risky ploy, and I knew that I was right on the edge of offending Ted—angering him to the point that he would not respond. I explained that I felt that serial killers could not voluntarily *stop* killing, and that they stopped only when they were no longer able to overpower victims or when they were in prison or dead. I was telling him exactly what I told classes I spoke to, or what I had said on television dozens of times.

I was most curious to hear what Ted had to say about serial killers, just as other experts in this criminal aberration were. Ted Bundy was a gold mine of a sort. I had always believed that he had some cogent answers to the growing problem locked up inside him. If he chose to, he still had the capability to do a modicum of good in the world—if only by admitting his *badness* and offering help to criminologists, psychiatrists, and psychologists who were trying to staunch the flow of more "Teds."

He was not ready to do that . . . yet.

Once again, I waited for a response to my letter. There was none. Either I had finally alienated him, or he was too busy to reply.

He was busy. And he could pick and choose whom he might favor with his knowledge and philosophy. Everyone from Connie Chung to 20/20 to *People* Magazine to *60 Minutes* and on down an endless media list had sought an audience with Ted. From his cell, Ted announced he would grant an interview to the most prestigious in his mind: *The New York Times*. While a Florida official commented that Ted was playing "a very dangerous game with his gambles to defeat the process. . . . Even a lot of anti-death penalty people don't lose sleep over his case," Ted calmly spoke to the *Times*.

He was, as he was with me, above it all. "If anyone considers me a monster, that's just something they'll have to confront in themselves.

"It has nothing to do with me because they don't know me. If they really knew me, they would discover I am not a monster. For that matter, for people to condemn someone, to dehumanize someone like me, is a very popular and effective way of dealing with a fear and a threat that is just incomprehensible.

"It's sort of like the old cliche of the ostrich sticking its head in the sand. When people go to those cliches that someone is a monster beyond help, that he's demented, that he's got some kind of defect, then they're sticking their heads in the ground out of ignorance. . . ."

Like so many other serial killers, Ted needed to be considered a normal person. He did not want to be thought a *pervert*. So full of defect that one wondered how he kept his mind marginally intact, he certainly did not want to be seen as a monster. And like any number of sociopaths I have listened to, Ted so often spoke in cliches, even as he derided them. "Water under the bridge . . . stick its head in the sand." The cliche seems to give a sociopath something to cling to—a verbal anchoring place that allows him to communicate, to speak the language of *normal people*.

Ted did not want to be seen as a monster, and I strived, as I always had, to see Ted as something other than a monster. That was the only way I could write to him. My intellect clung tenaciously to "monster," but, working on sheer emotion, I wondered if there might not be some recessed part of him with a vestigial conscience.

That was why I wanted the dialogue with him. As many times as I told myself Ted Bundy was a monster, as many times as I told others the same thing, it was still the hardest thing for *me* to believe. Not only Ted; my work placed me next to so many "monsters."

After almost two decades of writing about sadistic sociopaths, I still found it well nigh impossible to grasp *emotionally* that there were those of my own species who truly felt no speck of compassion or empathy for another's pain. I cannot step on a spider. I couldn't swat a fly until I became a mother and one too many landed on my baby. How could someone torture and kill an innocent victim and not feel remorse?

Was that what I wanted Ted Bundy to tell me? Did I want him to say, after so many years, that yes, he did feel bad—that he did spend sleepless nights thinking about his victims? And if he did say—or write—the words, could I believe him?

Spring of 1986. In six months, Ted would be forty—if he lived that long.

It looked as if he would. Polly Nelson took an appeal all the way to the United States Supreme Court. Ted was asking for a new trial in the Chi Omega cases, based, again, on the fact that eye-witness Nita Neary had been hypnotized to help her remember.

On May 5, 1986, the Court turned the appeal down. The high court denied Ted's appeal 7–2 with no comment. Justices William Brennan and Thurgood Marshall dissented, adhering to their long-held opposition to the death penalty. A spokesman for Florida Governor Bob Graham said that the governor would probably sign a new warrant immediately for Ted's execution.

The timing was all show-biz perfection. The Court's answer was announced during a break in a two-part mini-series about Ted. Mark Harmon (*People* Magazine's "Sexiest Man Alive") played Ted as Ted was portrayed in Richard Larsen's book, *The Deliberate Stranger*. Physically, Harmon was a good choice, but he played Ted Bundy as confident from the beginning, as a young Kennedy clone.

To Harmon's credit, he could not have known that Ted Bundy had begun his 20s as the man I knew, the socially inept man, the man who felt he didn't fit into a world of wealth and success. It was the latter-day infamous Ted who was smooth and charismatic. Infamy became Ted. Only as his crimes made black headlines did he become the Ted Bundy portrayed by Mark Harmon. That one-dimensional man was the "Hollywood T.V. Ted." Harmon's Ted was so charming *and* sexy that he sometimes seemed almost heroic.

And that was the Ted that a whole new generation of teenage girls fell in love with. I was appalled at the letters and phone calls I got from young girls who wanted to rush to Florida to "save Ted Bundy."

Finally, I said—or wrote—firmly to each one: "*You are not in love with Ted Bundy*. You are in love with Mark Harmon."

I was gratified when several girls responded, "You know, you're right. I got carried away seeing Mark Harmon."

Ted's latest stay of execution had expired on May 6th, but Polly Nelson announced that she would continue the fight to save his life on two fronts. She would protest the Supreme Court's decision, arguing that they had not properly dismissed the appeal on its merits, *and* she would file a new appeal with the Supreme Court in the case of the murder of Kimberly Leach.

While Polly Nelson scrambled for legal footing, Governor Graham set a new execution date: July 2, 1986. The word was that this would be it; Ted had slid by on his first warrant. But this was the second.

Ted was scheduled to die at 7 A.M. on that first Wednesday in July, and all of Polly Nelson's determined efforts to save him might not be able to stop his inexorable progression toward "Old Sparky," the electric chair.

While Nelson's fight was slated toward appealing the conviction, she admitted that she was "willing to try any avenue" to spare Ted. Even an insanity defense.

Would Ted cooperate in such a defense? He has always been so rational, so *determined* to be rational. I had always believed he would literally rather die than admit to any weakness of mind, any aberrance. Ted was so dedicated to being sane; to give up his sanity—even to live—might not be worth it.

But Polly Nelson and James E. Coleman Jr. began to make noises about the sanity issue. Coleman, a personable, brilliant young black attorney, tentatively tested the waters. He suggested that Ted's competency was an area that had never been "fully explored."

Coleman said that the only attorney who had believed that Ted was incompetent—Mike Minerva—had been prevented from participating in Ted's competency hearing way back in the Spring of 1979. Ted, of course, had torn up the agreement that would have plea-bargained him into three consecutive 25-year terms. In effect, Ted had chosen the very real threat of death by execution rather than admit that he was less than competent.

Coleman believed that Ted was his own worst enemy. By insisting on running the show, Ted had set himself on this deadly path. Coleman argued that Ted, only a second-year law student, had frequently tried to direct his own defense, demanding that his attorneys be replaced and unknowingly undermining his right to effective representation. "Mr. Bundy was represented by a total of fourteen lawyers," Coleman said. "He was also represented by himself. We think . . . he was denied effective counsel."

Could Coleman and Nelson *now* convince an appeals court that Ted Bundy was crazy? You cannot execute a crazy man, even if his descent into madness had occurred while he waited on Death Row.

Vic Africano, Ted's defense attorney in the Kimberly Leach case, believed that Ted was "a split personality."

"In all the time I was with Ted Bundy, I never saw anything that would indicate he could commit these crimes," Africano reflected in June of 1986.

But then, neither did I. Ted kept that side of himself hidden.

Bob Dekle, the prosecutor in the Leach trial, had a blunter, less charitable opinion. He saw Ted differently. He had seen too many sociopaths in his career to believe the mask. "A sociopath is a person who, if you sit down and talk to that person, you would like him. And the longer you listen to him, and he tells you about how society—how *everybody's* out to get him—you start to believe him. At times, Bundy had me believing him. But he's just another sociopath—except he has a pretty face."

It looked as if it was really coming down. The death watch began in Starke, Florida. Nelson and Coleman filed appeals, requests for clemency hearings and stays of execution. Each was refused. Ted and Gerald Stano, 34, also linked to dozens of sex slayings of young women, were scheduled to die, in tandem as it were, two days before Independence Day.

I believed that Ted was going to die this time. I was so sure of it that I somewhat naively attempted to phone him. Personal phone calls are not favored in Raiford Prison. However, Superintendent

Dugger's office did assure me that they would pass on the word to Ted that I had called.

Carole Ann Boone was there for Ted, as loyal and faithful as always. She and her son, Jamie Boone, spent the waiting hours with Ted whenever they were allowed. Carole Ann, an unwilling subject caught by the cameras, was much thinner than she had been at Ted's 1979 trial, and she was blonde rather than brunette. She looked so different that she almost seemed to have taken on her husband's chameleon-like aspect.

Early on Tuesday, July 1st, Carole Ann, Jamie, and Rose, Ted and Carole Ann's four-and-a-half-year-old daughter, visited in a sealed visitor's room. Carole Ann left Raiford Prison shortly after noon, holding a green plastic trash bag over her head. Jamie guarded her protectively, shouting "Shut up . . . shut up!" to the reporters who called out questions.

Ted, moved to a holding cell, the last step before the walk to the death chamber, did not betray fear. "Except his eyes. There was something about his eyes," one guard said, "that made you wonder if he was getting frightened." Ted ate his breakfast of oatmeal and hotcakes. The guards watched over him, careful that he would not commit suicide and cheat the electric chair.

He had no reason to do that. Maybe Ted sensed that this wasn't the time. Both he and Gerald Stano were given first a twenty-four-hour reprieve, and than an indefinite stay of execution. Ted had come within fifteen hours of dying, and he never spoke of fear; he never let them see so much as a quiver of his jaw muscle.

His dignity intact, Ted moved from the holding cell back to his regular cell on Death Row. All the machinations of his attorneys and the courts had, once again, ended in a delay. While U.S. District Judge William Zloch of Fort Lauderdale rejected a petition from Ted's attorneys challenging Ted's murder conviction in the Chi Omega cases, Nelson and Coleman appealed to the 11th U.S. Circuit Court of Appeals in Atlanta. A three-judge panel would evaluate Zloch's decision and the appeal. That could take months, and some said it might take years.

On August 4th, Ted wrote to me again in response to the letter I'd sent him in March. His writing looked more out of control than I'd ever seen it, staggering over the pages up and down, words crossed out, over-writes. He was safe for awhile, but his writing didn't show that.

"I received the message you sent through Superintendent Dugger. Thank you very much. And thank you for the money and stamps you sent back in April. Now that things have calmed down some I can concentrate on doing some letter writing."

The niceties dispensed with, Ted started in once more on my general ineptitude in understanding serial murder. He found me "sincere," but "trapped and limited."

"You simply don't have a broad and complete enough data base to be making such judgements," he chided. "The best I can do for you is refer you to the summary of the findings of a study done through the Behavioral Sciences (sic) Unit and reported in the August 1985, edition of the *F.B.I. Bulletin*. General though the report is, it is by far the best and most accurate study in the area I have ever seen, and I have seen many. It is only a beginning, but a solid beginning."

The F.B.I., once "overrated bastards," to Ted, now *almost* had his stamp of approval. I had the F.B.I. bulletin Ted referred to, and I knew two of the contributors well from the VI-CAP days. It *was* an excellent study—a study that has now become a book: *Sexual Homicide: Patterns and Motives* by Robert K. Ressler, Ann W. Burgess, and John E. Douglas.

In this letter, Ted asked me not to put his words into print—and I decided within myself that I would not, as long as he lived and fought his legal battles. He clearly didn't trust me, and mentioned several times that he rarely trusted anyone.

He ranted for pages about a man who had given public statements about things Ted allegedly had confessed to him. Ted denied this vociferously. Caught off guard by the deviousness of someone else, Ted was as outraged as I had ever known him to be.

"He came on as such a decent, sincere, qualified, academic type," Ted wrote, anguished. "And turned out to be not only a shallow fraud but a liar. I don't use the word light. It shocked me. Really. I've met all kinds of people over the years. 'X' was not the kind I'd expect to lie as he did, and yet he fabricated things as no one else ever has. . . . It's so sad, Ann. I never talked with that man about any case in which I was a suspect. Never. I'm no fool. I didn't speculate or do anything along those lines. . . . We talked only in the most general terms. Nothing was tape recorded. . . . I have never had anyone lie to me like that before. Not even a cop.

Ted was hoist on his own petard. But he was right in his assessment.

Ted asked me to write, and to send money and stamps.

There's no way my family can help me now.
Be good.

peace
ted

I answered that letter and a month later, he answered me. It was to be his last letter to me. It was friendlier than the first two of this trio of letters from him, letters written after a space of seven years. He talked about my having a word processor to write with, and said he wouldn't mind having one himself even though it sounded so "primarily mechanical."

The bulk of his letter, the central part of it—perhaps the reason for the letter itself—was about the unsolved Green River Murder cases in the Seattle area. Seven years after Ted was arrested in Salt Lake City, the most prolific serial killings to date in America began in a terrible pattern. At least four dozen (and probably twice that many) young street girls—"Strawberries" in street lingo for baby prostitutes—had been murdered, and their bodies left in clusters in wooded areas near both Seattle and Portland.

Three thousand miles away, Ted had theories.

"It would seem that the case is about as cold as such a case can be. The folks on the Task Force must be spinning their investigative wheels. The way the person responsible dropped out of sight is truly fascinating. Of course, who knows, he may well be dead. There's just no telling.

"I've accumulated quite a lot of material on the case and developed many observations about it. A couple of times I've been tempted to express my views about the case. The public has been misled about the case. Public posturing by police officials is understandable but keeping the people ignorant about the essential nature of such crimes will in the end make a solution even less likely. And despite their best efforts, I can see that the investigators were limited by conventional concepts in an unconventional case.

"Anyway I thought of making public my specific observations and ideas but decided people weren't ready to accept my statements at face value. I didn't need the publicity anyway. . . ."

I had written to Ted about the scores of women who had contacted me about their "encounters" with him, although I didn't give specific times or names or places. I commented that he would have had to have been super-human to have been everywhere people "remembered" him. There had been a flurry in the press when campers found a tree in Sanpete County, Utah with Ted Bundy's name carved in it, and the date: " '78."

"I too am familiar with the phenomena of Ted Bundy sightings," he wrote. "Tells you a lot about the reliability of eye-witness identification, doesn't it. Eye-witness id (sic) is the most inherently unreliable evidence used in court.

"It also tells you a lot about fear.

"The business about the tree in Utah with the name Ted Bundy carved in it is bizzare (sic). The Utah authorities know very well that I wasn't in Utah in 1978. There is probably nothing more certain than my whereabouts in 1978, and yet the Utah police act out their little farce. I believe it was done to assure people that the police are still actively investigating the case. I can't say why, exactly. Is this an election year?"

His humor was still caustic. I had asked Ted if he wanted something to read, and he explained that he could not receive books—even sent directly from the publisher. The exceptions were religious books or books that came in one of our package permits a year. Each package could contain four books, but Ted had used all of his permits for 1986.

I had asked him too if he was busy working on his case, and he explained that he no longer concerned himself with legal pursuits. "I leave that all to my attorneys now. I don't find legal work to be a positive, uplifting experience for me to say the least. Now that I have attorneys who have the ability and resources to handle the cases, I keep my involvement to a minimum. I have other things to do."

He did not say what those other things were.

Write soon.
Be good.

peace,
ted

I never heard from him again. I am sure that I wrote back to him. But then, the fall of 1986 was the beginning of a frenetic two years for me. I was finishing up my book on Diane Downs, *Small Sacrifices*, I was lecturing in California, and preparing for a month-long publicity tour. (That tour would somehow never slow down between the hardcover and the paperback editions of *Small Sacrifices*, and I seemed to be running faster and faster.)

With Ted, there always seemed to be time. His life was like the Perils of Pauline; something always saved him in the final hour. I always thought I would write to him again, and see if he would answer. And I always wondered if maybe someday he would tell me the truth—or truths—he kept hidden so well.

Ted had written that he no longer indulged in the semi-practice of criminal law, that he had other things to do. I suspect that a voluminous correspondence system took up much of Ted's days. I was to learn that Ted wrote to many, many people—including women all over America. To those I have talked with, he wrote of his need for stamps, money orders, research.

He answered an eloquent, poetic letter from a man who had grown up in Tacoma at the same time Ted did. The man was a gentle soul, a lover of animals, who lived on an island in Puget Sound. He was also a talented writer of nostalgia, and I cannot imagine that Ted could resist the letters that must have evoked bittersweet memories of his own youth. Ted wrote back, and gradually built a little web—or thought he had.

His island correspondent told Ted about himself, about his work. And bells must have rung. This man was in a position to provide Ted with information that he had sought for years: Meg's address. Ted's long-time lover had moved often enough so that she had finally freed herself of him, even of his letters. He did not know where she lived. And he wanted to know that.

Ted's correspondent worked in personnel; although his letters sounded guileless, he was very shrewd. He could see Ted's mind working in his letters. He knew his value to Ted was in the fact that he could tap a code into a computer and come up with information on Meg. He deduced that Ted wanted to be able to send a letter to Meg's secret address, to say to her in effect, "See, you will never be able to hide from me. Even though I am three thousand miles away on Death Row, I have the power to find you."

Knowing it would be the end of his correspondence with Ted Bundy, the personnel man refused Ted the intelligence on Meg.

Ted never wrote to him again.

To a registered nurse in the South, a woman who felt a little sorry for Ted because she had a friend in prison, he explained that his wife had too much to do to run errands for him. He needed information on serial killers, and he needed stamps and a little money. In 1984, unknown to me, Ted also asked the nurse to locate *my* address. He explained to her that he barely knew me, that I had exploited him—but, for whatever reason, he wanted to find me. I had never changed my mailing address—I still have not. He could have written to me easily, but perhaps he had lost the post office box number. Or, more chillingly, he may have wanted to prove that he could find *me* too. Ted knew that I never revealed my street address; it would have been a subtle psychological ploy if he was able to send a letter directly to my house.

By the time I learned he was trying to reach me, I had already written to him. I have no idea what he had in mind in 1984. He never mentioned his search for me in 1984. I could imagine all kinds of things. In reality, I suspect he only wanted times and dates of other serial murders I had written about in the Northwest; he was trying to blame his crimes on other men, and I had all the specifics in my research files.

As Ted explained to at least a dozen women correspondents who contacted me later, he needed help with errands. Carole Ann Boone had run errands for Ted for years without complaint. She was, of course, a very visible presence as he awaited execution in July of 1986.

But, so gradually that no one in the media really picked up on it, Carole Ann was slipping out of Ted's life. Unless she chooses to write about her life with Ted one day, or to give interviews—which she has *not* done for years—no one can do more than speculate on why Carole Ann was seldom there for her "Bunny."

Perhaps the emotional agony she went through in July 1986, counting down the hours until her husband would die, was too much to go through again. Perhaps the glamour of being the infamous defendant's special woman faded to ashes as Carole Ann must have realized that Ted was never going to walk free. Possibly life in Gainesville, Florida, with little money, a toddler, and a teen-ager to support, surrounded by palpable hatred for her husband, was all too gritty and real.

How many people did Ted Bundy write to? I would guess thousands. A hundred or more people wrote or called me for his address. More often they must have simply written to him in care of Raiford Prison.

One very, very important correspondent was a man who was once anathema to Ted Bundy. And yet it was inevitable that they should come together at some point. Bob Keppel had published the definitive book on an area that interested Ted mightily: *Serial Murder—Future Implications for Police Investigations.* Ted had written to Keppel in 1984 to offer himself as a consultant in the Green River Murder Case. It was so typical of Ted's manipulation that he said he *might* offer to help the Task Force when he wrote to me in 1986. He had been in touch with Keppel for two years by then. Later, Bob Keppel told me that he welcomed Ted's Green River advice; it gave the Washington detective an opening to talk to Ted. If they began talking of Green River, they might also talk about the unsolved cases attributed to Ted Bundy.

Although I suspected that Ted and Bob Keppel were in touch with each other in 1986, I wasn't sure. These two men had never met during Keppel's determined investigation into the "Ted" murders. They had met—first in November 1984, in Raiford Prison—and they would meet again. Keppel, the intellectual detective, and Bundy, the intellectual serial killer, were engaged in dialogue. Keppel had been deemed worthy, and Ted was giving his theories to him. I had heard rumors but I never asked Bob Keppel directly. If he was to get a confession—or a series of confessions—out of Ted Bundy, it was going to be a delicate game, and one that Keppel needed time and discretion to carry out.

Bob Keppel and I occasionally had lunch, and infrequently I interviewed him for articles about other cases. There were subtle, tantalizing references to Ted, but I didn't pursue them because I could sense the inscrutable Keppel would clam up. After two decades as a crime writer, I had long since learned to wait until detectives were ready to talk.

And Keppel was not yet ready.

While Bob Keppel cautiously established some tenuous rapport with Ted Bundy, the legal mechanisms ground on. It could well be that Keppel might finally come to a place where Ted would talk to him frankly about the Northwest murders, and, even more importantly, the Northwest *disappearances*—only to run out of time. And yet Keppel knew that Bundy could not be rushed; anyone who wanted to talk with him must not appear too eager for information. Ted had to call the shots, as galling as that might be for those who waited.

On October 21, 1986, Governor Graham signed Ted's third death warrant, setting the next execution date for November 18th for the murder of Kimberly Leach. But three federal appellate judges made it clear on October 23rd that Ted would get another hearing in federal court on the Chi Omega case. The three-judge panel said that Judge William Zloch had erred in not reviewing the Bundy trial record before making his decision the previous July to deny the petition of Ted's attorneys. They also told Florida Assistant Attorney General Gregory Costas that *he* should have asked Zloch to accept the trial record before issuing an opinion.

"I can't understand your behavior," chided Judge Robert Vance. "This case is going to be reversed and sent down there because of a stupid error. If you had called it to the attention of the judge at the time, it could have been corrected in four days. It's wrong. It's clearly wrong, counsel. It's not arguable by an attorney of integrity."

That period in July had been wild. Polly Nelson and Jim Coleman had spent consecutive nights without sleep, racing the clock set by

Ted's pending death warrant. Zloch, who was considering his first capital punishment appeal since becoming a federal judge in January, had rejected the six-month stay, and then had also dismissed Ted's petitions without hearing arguments from attorneys on the issues involved. The trial record remained in the trunk of Greg Costas' car.

Costas was shaken by the vehemence of his verbal lambasting by the three judge-panel, and later the judges softened a bit. Vance explained he was simply frustrated by the morass of mistakes he'd seen. "Maybe the Court has been a little too harsh on your personally, counsel."

It was becoming a merry-go-round. When Ted managed to get stays on the Chi Omega murders, some legal experts said he could not then be executed in the Kimberly Leach murder. Conversely, he would next manage to get a stay on the Leach death warrant, and there was the question of electrocuting him for the sorority murders.

He might be able to continue this legal balancing act until he was an old man.

Ted didn't die in November 1986 either. Less than seven hours before he was to be executed, the 11th Circuit Court ordered a stay. The Florida attorney general's office asked the U.S. Supreme Court to overrule that decision, but all the legal jargon really meant only that there would be another delay of many months.

Ted's attorneys had now filed eighteen different appeals over his two murder convictions in Florida. The appeals were reportedly being paid for by a Washington, D.C. law firm. However, the State of Florida had to pay to argue against all those appeals and delays, and the tab was running into the millions.

Florida residents were getting restless. Reader boards read, "Fry Ted Bundy," and "I'll Buckle Up When Bundy Does." Disc jockeys played parodies about Ted: "Bye, Bye, Bundy, Bye Byeee!" and "I Left My Life in Raiford Prison."

Carole Ann Boone had left her husband in Raiford Prison. Very quietly, she had left town. She was not there with Ted as he awaited death on November 18th. The official reason given to the press was that Carole Ann had left six weeks earlier for Everett, Washington, to visit a sick relative. It would seem that her relative must have been in extremis for Carole Ann to opt for that visit—rather than stand by her man as he waited for the third time to die.

Perhaps her reason for leaving Florida was illness in the family. But she never came back.

Initially, the November 18th date didn't seem as threatening as the July date had been—even though Ted was coming uncomfortably close to his slow walk to the electric chair. The public was simply getting used to Ted Bundy's execution dates. Maybe Ted was too.

Vernon Bradford, spokesman for Florida's state corrections department, said that Ted "began the day in a very good mood." He watched television, and listened to a radio placed at his cell door—the holding cell just thirty paces from the death chamber. "He was confident."

Ted betrayed no fear at all. Rather, witnesses said, "He was mad, incensed—but he didn't seem scared. It was as if he was outraged that anyone could do this to *the* Ted Bundy. . . ."

Maybe everyone involved—including Ted—knew that it was far from over. He seemed to consider the preparations for executions as a charade, an inconvenience and a deliberate humiliation.

As the long Tuesday dragged by, Ted's confidence slipped, and he got angrier and more agitated. However, when one of his new wave of friends, John Tanner, a Florida criminal defense attorney and spiritual counselor to Ted, visited him that night, he found Ted calm. "There was a peace about him. . . ."

Ted knew he wasn't going to die.

Back in Seattle, I wasn't as comfortable about Ted's escape hatch as he apparently was. CBS Morning News called to say they had a limousine waiting to rush me to the Seattle affiliate station, KIRO. They wanted to interview me at 7 A.M. *if* Ted was executed. At 1 A.M., they called to say the execution was off.

I was vastly relieved. I would not have stopped the execution if I could have. But I was quite willing to have it postponed, accepting only vaguely that, when the time really came (if it ever did), I would have emotions yet unfathomable to deal with.

In November 1986, the pressure was off again.

The spring of 1987 brought a small rash of articles about Ted. Millard Farmer, of the Atlanta Defense Team, speaking in Portland

Oregon at the Oregon Criminal Defense Lawyers Association, discussed the Bundy case with an *Oregonian* reporter.

"Either Bundy didn't commit the crimes or he's suffering from one of the deepest mental illnesses I've ever seen," Farmer said.

Farmer said it was relatively common for the mentally ill to receive death sentences in the "Old South." Farmer also blasted the media in the courtroom. "(Television) makes clowns out of the lawyers, jesters out of the judges, and injustice out of the proceedings."

Farmer said that the judges and witnesses in the Chi Omega trial had preened before going into court and would rush to the press room on the ninth floor of the Metro Justice Building in Miami to see how they looked on television.

That wasn't true. I was there on that ninth floor in the summer of 1979, and Millard Farmer was not there—at least, I never saw him. Nor did I ever see a judge or a lawyer there with us on the press floor looking at television. One time I saw Larry Simpson, for the State, comb his hair before his opening argument. But he wasn't "preening."

Ted's correspondents continued to flood the Raiford prison mail room with letters for him. In April 1987, the Associated Press reported that Ted and John Hinckley, the would-be assassin of President Reagan and White House press secretary James Brady, had exchanged a number of letters! Hinckley had written to Ted to "express sorrow" about "the awkward position you must be in."

The pen-pal arrangement was enough to cancel a proposed furlough for Hinckley, who had also written to Lynette "Squeaky" Fromme. Fromme had allegedly asked him to write to Charles Manson. Hinckley reportedly declined to write to Manson, but had gone so far as to obtain Manson's address.

I have always considered that John Hinckley was legally and medically insane. In the years since I wrote the first draft of this book where I stated that I thought Ted Bundy *was* insane, my subsequent research and enlightenment have convinced me that Ted was never psychotic.

But how Ted would have relished his correspondence with John Hinckley; it would have given him a chance to explore his own studies of the criminal mind, and I am sure he thought his "credentials" as an expert on multiple and serial murder would be greatly enhanced by any inside track to Hinckley.

But there was more. Ted's research into the reasons behind serial murder was fueled, I think, by his own desperate need to figure out what was wrong with *himself*. He knew full well he was not insane, but he also sensed there was something deeply aberrant in his actions, although he didn't know what—or why.

One thing is clear; Ted never wrote to anyone or granted interviews to anyone without having reasons, pay-offs, or hidden agendas.

By the summer of 1987, Ted Bundy was no longer front page news in Northwest papers—except during the week preceding each new execution date. The Green River Killer had supplanted Ted.

On July 7, 1987, an old picture of Ted appeared in the "Local/ Region" section of the *Seattle Post-Intelligencer*. The article suggested that Ted would be around for years, possibly for decades.

"He is really in the *infancy* of his litigation," Carolyn Snurkowski, chief of criminal appeals for the Florida attorney general, explained. She estimated that Ted was probably no more than one third of the way along the route to conclusion!

If that were to be translated into time in direct proportion, then Ted—who had already survived eight years beyond his first sentences of death—would live sixteen more. Until he was fifty-seven-years old.

That formula was probably simplistic. But then . . .

Governor Bob Graham had been defeated in his bid for re-election, and Ted Bundy's name—*and* continuing survival—were subjects raised often in both the gubernatorial and attorney general races in Florida. If Graham couldn't seem to sign a death warrant that would stick, perhaps his successor, Bob Martinez, could.

Just four of the hundreds of prisoners on Florida's death row had survived three death warrants. Sixteen men had been executed since 1979. There was only one prisoner who evoked rage and frustration in the citizens of Florida the way Bundy did. For many of them, he was no longer a human being; he was a cause.

The first day of August 1987, brought sad news to all of us who covered Ted's Miami trial. With bleakly ironic timing, Judge

Edward Douglas Cowart, 62, suffered a heart attack exactly eight years and one day after he had sentenced Ted Bundy to die for the Chi Omega murders.

On July 31, 1979, Judge Cowart had told Ted to "take care of yourself." On Saturday, August 1, 1987, Judge Gerald Wetherington who succeeded Cowart as chief judge of the 11th Judicial Circuit in 1981, called Cowart to discuss some routine court business, and found him in good health and great spirits.

Ed Cowart then went out to work in his yard. Overheated, he came in for some cold water and suffered chest pains. His family took him to Coral Reef Hospital, more as a precaution than anything. The husky Cowart was first put into intensive care, but was then moved to a private room. It seemed that nothing was seriously wrong. Tests were scheduled for Monday morning.

But Ed Cowart died suddenly Sunday night of a massive heart attack.

His death was a tremendous professional—and personal—loss to the judicial system of southern Florida. Flags flew at half-mast outside the Metro Justice Building on Monday morning as co-workers whispered the sad news that spread like wildfire throughout the building.

Judges cried along with secretaries and bailiffs. Ed Cowart was the kind of a judge who always tempered hard justice with his personal compassion. When he'd had to send a policeman to jail for perjury, bribery, and weapons convictions, he'd granted the rogue cop a two-week delay before starting his sentence—because the man had promised his little girl he'd take her to Disneyland. Cowart's "May God have mercy on your soul" admonitions to condemned killers always sounded as sincere as a preacher's sermon on Sunday morning. I can still hear him saying, "Bless your heart" to both Ted and the attorneys from both sides of that trial ten years ago.

He was a good man.

Cowart left his wife of forty-one years, Elizabeth, and two daughters, Susan and Patricia.

Judge Cowart, who had no history of illness, was dead. Ted Bundy, who had had his life threatened for eight years, was alive and well.

And liable to stay that way.

A new legal fight was about to begin. James Coleman and Polly Nelson had hinted for some time that they might attack the verdicts from the angle of Ted's mental competency. It now looked as if that would be the new thrust in this long process.

It made some kind of sense when they said it out loud. Ted Bundy couldn't have had fair trials because he wasn't in his right mind as they were going on.

That was the next campaign to keep Ted from the electric chair. While Polly Nelson and Jim Coleman put forth their theories that Ted had been incompetent during the Kimberly Leach trial, the Florida Attorney General's office prepared to argue for the other side. They felt Ted had been sane, competent, and capable throughout all his trials. Indeed, he had defended himself, as an attorney, in the Miami trial. He had managed to legally marry Carole Ann Boone during the Orlando trial. He had seemed sane.

Early in October 1987, I received a call from the Florida attorney general's office. Assistant Attorney Generals Kurt Barch and Mark Minser asked if I would consent to being an expert witness for the State of Florida in the matter of Ted Bundy's competency at the time of his trials in 1979 and 1980.

I thought back to the time in 1976 when Ted weighed the possibility of having me testify as a character witness for him. I could not have done that, and luckily, he chose to ask someone else. Now, I was being sought by the other side. Competency is always a dicey judgment call. Even a psychiatrist cannot truly say what was in the mind of a killer at the moment of a crime, or during trial. It was true that I had been in continual contact with Ted from September 1975 through the Miami trial—a vital four-year period. And I had known him for years before that. The last time I had actually talked with him in any depth was, of course, his collect phone call to me in late June/early July of 1979. His mind was clicking along as smoothly as computer software at that point. And, watching him in trial, I had seen a man in exquisite control.

I could testify to my perceptions. That was all.

I had to say yes. If Ted was deemed "retroactively" incompetent, the Kimberly Leach verdict—and possibly the Chi Omega verdicts would probably be voided, and new trials ordered. There would be a very real threat that Ted Bundy could work his way back through all his legal thickets, back to Colorado where the State had rather "iffy" physical evidence in the Caryn Campbell murder case, and possibly even back to Utah. If his attorneys were skilled enough, and if luck was with Ted, he might find himself at Point-of-the-Mountain again, with only the sentence of the attempted kidnapping of Carol DaRonch to serve out. Incredible as it seemed, Ted's life and times in the court systems of America had proved to be almost mythic; he was *alive* still, and that alone suggested he might be eerily indestructible.

I agreed to testify in Florida in Ted's competency hearing. At that moment, I realized that I would have to be in the same courtroom with Ted as I told a judge that he should not be allowed to avoid penalty for his crimes because I believed him competent. What an unsettling thought that was. Ted would be furious, but then he had been angry at me before. My value to the team was, essentially, that I had known him *when*. I had no choice.

I received the contract from the Flordia Department of Legal Affairs. It asked me to appear on my birthday: October 22, 1987.

WHEREAS

The Department is representing the Department of Corrections (Richard L. Dugger) in the case of Bundy v. Dugger and requires expert services for assessing Theodore Bundy's competence at the time of his trial and providing expert testimony at trial, and Ms. Ann Rule is willing and able to provide needed testimony in this regard, now therefore the parties agree as follows. . . .

The contract was ten pages long. And moot. I never had to sign it; in the last analysis, they didn't need *me* to prove that Ted Bundy was sane and competent.

The competency hearing proceeded in Orlando during the third week of October before U.S. District Judge G. Kendall Sharp but without any testimony from Ted. Polly Nelson said that his current state of competency would be relevant only if a new trial should be ordered.

Mike Minerva, one of Bundy's earlier attorneys, testified that Ted had insisted on directing his own defense. Minerva stayed on to help him, tried to get psychiatric help for his client, and was rebuffed.

"He said talking to most psychiatrists is no better than talking to truck drivers."

"Would you say Mr. Bundy was qualified to represent himself?" Jim Coleman asked.

"No sir," Minerva said evenly. "I would say he was not qualified to represent himself. . . . He couldn't do it. The amount of evidence was staggering. To try to conduct a defense in those two cases simultaneously, given the complexity and details, required a staff of lawyers with full access to investigators and law books. To do both from a jail cell with no investigator and no law books was impossible. No one could have done it."

A paradox. Minerva testifying for Bundy—who must have been an ultimately frustrating client. Ted had called Minerva incompetent because he wouldn't allow Ted to call the shots. Now Minerva was trying to save him.

Ted was in the courtroom in Orlando, listening. He wore a blue and white striped sports shirt and white pants. His wavy hair was close-cropped, but the short cut didn't hide the gray hair that wasn't there seven years earlier.

The question of Ted's competency would drag on for months. Testimony in December was more interesting. Donald R. Kennedy, an investigator for the public defender's office, and former public defender Michael Coran testified that Ted had been *drunk* and otherwise compromised at the trial in the murder of Kimberly Leach! Ted had frequently used pills and alcohol during the trial, according to the witnesses. Kennedy said that the alcohol had been discovered in a juice can that had been "doctored up" and provided by Ted's then-fiancée, Carole Ann Boone.

Coran said the juice cans with flip tops had been in the defense office. Kennedy testified that he had found "one or two pills in a bag of goodies" brought into Ted during trial.

If Ted chose to cloud his mind with drugs and alcohol while he was on trial for his very life, he showed, at the least, a lack of judgment. One wonders why Carole Ann would help him do that.

Assistant State Attorney Bob Dekle, who prosecuted Ted in 1980, differed with the defense team's recall. "If there had been any doubt that Mr. Bundy was incompetent to stand trial, *I* would have made a motion to that effect."

Dekle told Judge Sharp that he had found Ted to be reasoned, articulate and persuasive in presenting legal arguments and carefully orchestrated defense efforts to sway the Leach jury.

His wedding to Carole Ann in court wasn't "crazy" at all; Dekle found it to be a failed attempt to gain sympathy from the jury.

Ted Bundy had the ability to pull new supporters continually to him, like so many rabbits out of a magician's top hat. Art Norman, the forensic psychiatrist who spent countless hours with Ted in Florida, and who now practices in Oregon, commented to me in January 1989, "I have never encountered an individual who could move from one relationship to the next so easily, being seemingly deeply involved with someone, and then dropping them completely and moving on. . . ."

Norman hadn't wanted to talk to Ted in the first place. The first time he met with Ted, the experience was so jolting that he came home and cried. His wife and family didn't want him to be involved, but he finally agreed to work with Ted.

Ted would often tell Norman details—but no names—of what were surely his crimes. He would say, "You guess."

Norman wouldn't play the game with this prisoner who was obsessed with Nazis and torture. "He was devastated for a week after seeing 'Friday the 13th,'" Norman recalls. The slice-and-dice movie stimulated Ted to the point that he was almost out of control.

Eventually, like all those Ted was close to, Art Norman pulled away.

And now, in December 1987, a new voice was heard from. Dorothy Otnow Lewis, 51, a professor at the New York University Medical Center, educated at Radcliffe and Yale, happened to be studying juveniles on Florida's death row. She was asked by Bundy's defense team to meet with him and evaluate him.

Lewis testified that she had spent seven hours talking with Ted himself, had read "boxes" of legal and medical documents from his past, interviewed most of his relatives, and now had a diagnosis.

Lewis felt that Ted was manic-depressive, subject to drastic mood swings. Another term for this disorder used in the Diagnostic Statistical Manual (DSM-III, the "bible" of psychiatrists,) is "Bipolar Disorder." Subjects can be "Bipolar Disorder, Mixed" (with periods of both elation and depression), "Bipolar Disorder, Manic" (with only the highs), or "Bipolar Disorder, Depressed" (with only the lows). Once thought to be a rare disorder, manic-depression is now rather widespread, and occurs with varying degrees of severity. Lithium is the drug of choice to treat manic-depression.

Ted Bundy, to my knowledge, had never been adjudged manic-depressive before. *Was* he? I don't know, but I doubt it.

Forensic psychiatrist Dr. Charles Mutter disagreed with Dr. Lewis. "His arguments were brilliant. He *is* brilliant. He has defied and beaten three death warrants. Is that insanity?"

Whether Dr. Lewis had diagnosed Ted's mental disorder correctly or not, she did, however, present testimony that I found fascinating. Ted had told me about his grandfather, Sam Cowell of Philadelphia, Pennsylvania. This was the grandfather whom Ted told me he thought was his *father* for much of the early part of his life. Ted and Louise, of course, lived with the elder Cowells, Sam and Eleanor, for the first four-and-a-half years of his life.

The grandfather-father Ted described to me at the Crisis Clinic so long ago was a Santa Claus kind of grandfather. Ted clearly adored him, or so he recalled him to me. When Louise brought Ted out to Tacoma in 1951, Ted said he had been torn away from Grandfather Sam, and he missed him terribly. Indeed, Ted also told Dr. Lewis that his grandfather was "wonderful and loving and giving, and that all his memories were favorable."

The Grandfather Sam that Dr. Lewis described after interviews with family members (not including Louise Bundy) was a volatile, maniacal man. Sam Cowell, a talented, workaholic landscaper, allegedly terrorized his family with temper tantrums.

He was the sort of breadwinner whose homecomings sent his family scattering for shelter. He shouted and ranted and raved. His own brothers feared him, and reportedly muttered that somebody should kill him. His sister Virginia thought him "crazy." Sam Cowell was described as a bigot who made Archie Bunker look liberal; he hated blacks, Italians, Catholics, Jews.

And Cowell was sadistic with animals. He grabbed any cat that came near him and swung it by the tail. He kicked the family's dogs until they howled in pain.

A church deacon, Sam Cowell was said to have kept a large collection of pornography in his greenhouse. Some relatives said that Ted and a cousin snuck in there to pore over the pulp magazines. Since Ted was only three or four, that may be a creative memory talking. And it may be true.

The picture emerging from Lewis's testimony on Ted's grandmother, Eleanor, was that of a timid, obedient wife. Sporadically, she was taken to hospitals to undergo shock treatment for depression. In the end, Grandma Eleanor stayed home, consumed with agoraphobia (fear of open places), afraid to leave her own four walls lest some unknown disaster should overtake her.

There were three daughters born to this ill-matched pair. Louise was the eldest, and then Audrey, and, ten years later, Julia.

This then had been the household where Ted Bundy spent his first, vital, formative years—the years when a child grows a conscience. For fourteen years, I have wondered if there was not something more to know about Ted's childhood, something beyond his illegitimate birth, beyond his mother's deception (if, indeed, Ted was even telling me the truth about that), something traumatic back in Philadelphia. It finally spilled out in Dr. Lewis's testimony in Orlando.

When Louise Bundy discovered she was pregnant, seduced by that shadowy man whose real identity grows more blurred with every years that passes, she must have been terrified. More than most families in 1946, hers would not welcome a bastard grandchild.

Her church failed her; she was ostracized by her Sunday School group. One can only imagine her father's reaction. Her mother must have wept and crept still further into herself.

Louise went off to Burlington—without her family—and gave birth to a husky baby boy.

*And then she went home leaving Ted behind. Ted waited in the
Elizabeth Lund Home for three months while his mother agonized
over what she would do. Could she take him home to Philadelphia?
Should she put him up for adoption? The nurturing, cuddling—
the bonding, so necessary to an infant's well-being was put on
hold.*

He was only a tiny baby, but I think he knew.

It was not Louise Cowell Bundy's fault. I have always maintained
that she did the best she could. With the new information coming
from Dr. Lewis's testimony, it is obvious she did the best she could
under horrendous circumstances. But she brought little Ted Bundy,
a sensitive, brilliant little boy, into a household dependent on the
whims of a tyrannical patriarch. The fact that Ted Bundy could
never remember his grandfather as anything less than a kindly,
wonderful man indicates, I think, just how frightened Ted was. He
must have repressed all those emotions, virtually wiping out
normal responses.

He survived—but I think his conscience died back then, a casu-
alty of Ted's flight from terror. Part of him closed off before he was
five years old.

Some of the Bundy relatives recall that Sam and Eleanor Bundy
said they had adopted the baby boy in 1946. Adults in the family
didn't believe such a story. Eleanor was too ill to be cleared as an
adoptive parent. They all knew the child was Louise's, but no one
talked of it aloud. That might well substantiate the story that Ted
told me. *He* believed, at least for a time, that Sam and Eleanor
were his parents. I know he did; he was so intense and disturbed
when he said he never really knew who he was, or who he belonged
to.

The fact that Ted was damaged early on comes out in a most-
telling incident that Dr. Lewis related in Ted's December 1987
competency hearing. It occurred when Ted was three years old. His
Aunt Julia, then about fifteen, awakened from a nap to find that her
body was surrounded by knives. Someone had placed them around
her as she slept. She wasn't cut, but the glitter of the blades made
Julia's heart convulse.

Julia recognized that the knives had come from the cutlery
drawer in their kitchen, and she looked up to see her

three-year-old nephew. The adorable, elfin Ted Bundy stood by her bed, grinning at her.

Three years old.

Thirty-eight years later, Ted sat in Judge Sharp's courtroom and listened with equanimity as Dr. Lewis described his fearsome childhood. He was relaxed, even affable as he chatted with his attorneys.

Next, prosecutors played a videotape of the courtroom rhetoric Ted employed in February 1980—after a jury had found him guilty of abducting and murdering twelve-year-old Kimberly Diane Leach. The younger Ted on the flickering screen seemed anything but crazy as he strutted before Judge Wallace Jopling in Orlando.

"I was not convicted by the jury," Ted argued. "A publicity-created symbol was convicted. I bear none of the onus. I bear none of the responsibility. I did not kill Kimberly Diane Leach."

Ted smiled slightly at his image. Despite how he blamed the media for metamorphosing him into a "symbol," he'd already proven earlier in this day that he still loved the cameras. As he was led from jail to the security van that would take him to the Orlando courthouse, Ted had spotted the cameras. With a grin, he wheeled and nimbly turned a backward somersault into the waiting van.

Judge Kendall Sharp, white-haired, jut-jawed, Naval Reserve, and no nonsense about him, ruled on Ted's competency on December 17, 1987. Sharp was swift, impatient and firm. Sharp was convinced that Ted had been "fully competent" during the Leach trial.

"I consider that Mr. Bundy was one of the most intelligent, articulate, coherent defendants I have ever seen."

He added that Bundy was "a very self-assured individual who was well acquainted with legal procedures. . . . Whenever Bundy presented legal arguments, he did so cogently, logically, and coherently."

The tab was getting steeper. Florida Attorney General Bob Butterworth's office computed the total bill for the state's legal battles against Ted Bundy had reached $6 million!

There was no end in sight. Judge Sharp could see appeals going on and on. "I could be seeing him for the rest of my life—or his."

It would be far more economical to keep Ted in prison than for the State of Florida to keep dashing through the mine fields of legal battles. It cost $33.70 a day to keep an inmate behind bars—including meals, laundry, prison maintenance, guard salaries and other costs. If Ted, 41, should live to be 80, it would cost approximately $492,000 to keep him alive.

The majority of the people of Florida seemed not to care. They wanted the state to enforce the death penalty, whatever it might cost.

Thirty days after Judge Sharp's ruling, the U.S. Supreme Court upheld his decision that Ted was competent during the Kimberly Leach trial.

And then began a strangely quiet year. Legal maneuverings were surely taking place, but not in the headlines. It was easy not to think about Ted Bundy.

Bob Keppel thought about him. Indeed, Keppel flew to Florida and had a second meeting with Ted in February of 1988. Reporters never picked up on that.

Their dialogue and correspondence continued.

One person who thought about Ted continually, obsessively perhaps, was Eleanore Rose, Denise Naslund's mother. Eleanore could not bury her daughter in the pink casket she had purchased back in 1974. Denise's remains were still lost.

She had been allowed to "borrow" Denise's bones in 1974 to place them in the casket for a religious memorial service. But they had to be returned to the police evidence area, and now they were gone.

In December 1987, Mrs. Rose and other family members won an unspecified amount in damages in an out-of-court settlement from the county over the loss of Denise's remains. Shortly after that, officials at Yarrington's Funeral Home in West Seattle suggested that Eleanore might want to think about burying the casket. They had stored it for thirteen years.

Rose, 50, looked two decades older. She seemed to survive on the need to avenge Denise's death. Nothing more.

On March 30, 1988, Eleanore placed a collection of mementos into the pink coffin: Denise's favorite floral print dress, a poem, a pink silk rose, photographs of Eleanore and Denise, a rosary, and a crucifix—and a note,

Dear Denise,
    God forgive them for what they have done. I love you.

She didn't say *he*; she said *they*. Eleanore did not explain what she meant to reporters. A short item appeared under "Paid Notices: Funerals" in the *Seattle Times* and *Post-Intelligencer*.

DENISE MARIE NASLUND
    Final memorial service will be Wednesday, March 30, 2 P.M., graveside committal at Forest Lawn Cemetery, West Seattle. Denise died July 14, 1974. Her remains were recovered the following September. Rosary and Mass of Christian Burial were celebrated October 10, 1974 at Holy Family Church. She is the daughter of Eleanore and Robert Naslund; sister of Brock Naslund; granddaughter of Olga Hansen, all Seattle. Arrangements,
                                        YARRINGTON'S FUNERAL HOME

I went back to Florida for the first time in many years in July 1988. I was on a promotion tour for my book, *Small Sacrifices*. Eight years had passed since I'd been in Miami and Tampa-St. Petersburg. Although interviewers wanted to talk about Diane Downs, the murderess in *Small Sacrifices*, they never failed to ask questions about Ted Bundy. Odd, somehow, that his impact had faded in the Northwest while he was a living, breathing reality in Florida.

In Orlando, the site of the Leach trial in 1980, I appeared in a bizarre early morning show: the "Q-Zoo." It was a radio station where the show consisted of a disc jockey playing records and greeting guests. It was the definitive "wild and wacky" radio show. Fairly standard, except that the entire program was televised at the same time it was broadcast over radio.

This was the station that had popularized the sound of frying bacon sizzling—to remind listeners that Bundy should "fry." An entire cassette caddy was filled with Bundy parodies. While I was the morning guest, the host dedicated songs to Ted. I wondered if he was listening. He might well have been. We were not that far from Raiford Prison.

Once again, just as he had been in Colorado, Ted Bundy was a macabre kind of folk hero—or anti-hero. It may have been that his crimes were *so* heinous that no one could bear to stop and reflect on their reality.

And so they laughed.

I could never see anything funny about what Ted had done. The best I'd ever been able to muster was to occasionally see the black irony in his saga. But here in Orlando, on July 19, 1988, the sun already beating hot on the pavement at 8 A.M., the radio blasted out, "Hang down your head, Ted Bundy/hang down your head and cry/ Hang down your head. Ted Bundy/poor boy, you're bound to die . . ."

Part of me wanted to lean toward the microphone and say, "Ted, this isn't *me* playing this song. I just happen to be here to plug my book."

I said nothing. Being a Bundy biographer meant having to listen to sick Bundy jokes.

Throughout the summer and fall of 1988, there were short little columns of information on Ted. Mostly the headlines began, "Bundy Loses An Appeal . . ."

I think those of us who followed the case were almost surfeited on that sort of news. It was growing hard to follow—from circuit court to federal appeals court to the U.S. Supreme Court. I remember saying to a young Florida Assistant A.G., "It almost seems as though Ted can take one issue all the way to the Supreme Court, and it gets turned down, and then he can find another issue and start all over again."

"You got it," he said succinctly.

PART TWO

Gene Miller of the *Miami Herald* called me during the first week of December 1988. We had talked sporadically over the decade since we met at the first Florida trial in Miami.

"Ted's going to go," he said.

". . . *what?*"

"The word is that he will be executed by early spring 1989."

"I've heard the word before," I said.

"This time, they sound positive."

I thanked him. He said that he had a young reporter, Dave Von Drehle, who was only 27, but a natural. "Dave's doing a long piece on Bundy. Can he call you?"

"Sure."

Not believing that it was really going to happen in the foreseeable future, I talked with Von Drehle. He seemed to feel too that the time was at hand. Von Drehle's excellent article appeared in the Herald's Sunday edition on December 11th.

"This is Bundy's last stand," he began.

I mused that the reporter who now knew every facet of Ted Bundy's history had been only twelve years old when Lynda Ann Healey died. He was not even born when Ann Marie Burr vanished from her Tacoma home in 1961.

Ted's attorneys had taken what might well be their final appeal to the U.S. Supreme Court. Should the court deny that appeal—already denied by judges in Orlando, Tallahassee, and Atlanta—Governor Bob Martinez would be free to sign another death warrant. This would be Ted Bundy's fourth death warrant.

On January 17, 1989, the Supreme Court denied, and Martinez immediately signed that death warrant.

The warrant had a seven-day lifespan, beginning at 7 A.M. EST on Monday, January 23. Plans were underway to carry out the execution on Tuesday, January 24.

There was a different chill in the wind. My phone rang off the hook with calls from television and radio shows. Fort Lauderdale, Albany, Calgary, Denver. How could everybody *know* that this was the time?

It was the fourth death warrant. Maybe that was it.

The wheels of justice had been given a squirt of lubricating oil, and they raced, faster and faster and faster.

Bob Keppel, who had already journeyed twice to see Ted Bundy in the Florida State Prison, waited for a call from Florida. So did the Salt Lake County Detectives, and those in Pitkin County, Colorado.

And so did the parents who had never had truthful answers to haunting questions. Those whose daughters were still gone vacillated between wanting it over at last, and knowing that once Ted was gone, they would probably never find their daughters' remains.

Ted had played his luck out, running it perilously down to the end of the line. I remembered how scornful he had been of Gary Gilmore, but also how he had been almost envious of the news blitz at the end when Gilmore faced the Utah firing squad. Ted could not, would not, go quietly. He could not turn his back on the fanfare.

I knew that. There would be fireworks and revelations.

A day after the fourth death warrant was signed, word surfaced in Florida that Ted Bundy *might* be willing to tell what he knew about unsolved murders. It was beginning to look as if he had little, if anything, to lose—and much to gain by confessing. He could hope, possibly, for a delay; as long as he kept confessing, it seemed unlikely that he would be executed. Too many people had been waiting too long to hear the secrets only he knew.

Beyond that, Ted could move back into the sunshine of the strobe lights once again—*if* he talked. He had been telling me, and I'm sure a number of other people how much more he knew about serial murder than anyone else did. This might be his last chance to prove himself the all-time expert.

Governor Martinez was not impressed. His office said that Ted could confess if he wanted to, but it wasn't going to buy him any time. "He's got six days to do it," John Peck, Martinez's press secretary said.

Polly Nelson said she planned to file another appeal in state court in Lake City. Jim Coleman said he was aware that there was the possibility of a deal to delay—confessions for time—but that he was not involved in it, and would not comment.

Ted Bundy was suddenly headline news again, but he was in danger of being pushed off the front pages of American papers. Riots in Miami burned through the nights in Overtown and Liberty City and threatened the Super Bowl; a drifter fired into an elementary schoolyard in Stockton, California, and killed five children; Seattle's Mayor, Charles Royer, announced that he would not run for re-election; and the Republicans—Ted's old party—were about to stage a presidential inauguration.

But the *word* was right. Ted Bundy *was* headed for the electric chair, and now, after fourteen years of denial, Ted Bundy was prepared to talk to detectives.

Perhaps as surprising as his sudden accessibility to the men who had stalked him for so long was the announcement that Ted had agreed to meet with Dr. James Dobson, president of Focus on the Family, a Pomona, California, minister and member of President Reagan's commission on pornography. Beyond a general press conference, Ted had the right to pick one solo interviewer and he had chosen Dobson. Ted reportedly had been corresponding with the conservative preacher for years. Their meeting was to be videotaped, but that tape would not be released until such time as Ted was no longer alive. There would be no press conference.

On January 18th, Ted changed his mind about giving a press conference. He would hold a press conference on Monday, the day before he was to be executed, for a pool of reporters who would draw lots to win one of the much sought-after spots.

Jim Coleman and Polly Nelson, Ted's criminal attorneys, remained—at least on the surface—optimistic as they filed legal motions. Ted was also being advised by Diana Weiner, his "civil attorney." Weiner is an attractive woman with long, almost-black hair, some years younger than Ted. The Sarasota, Florida, attorney and Jack Tanner, his "spiritual advisor," a lawyer and Christian prison minister were the team who had approached Governor Martinez to plead for time for Ted in exchange for confessions.

Diana Weiner, obviously deeply committed to Ted emotionally, called Bob Keppel at home at 3 A.M. on Thursday morning, January 19th. "Why are you calling me *now*?" he asked.

Weiner was feeling panicky, desperate to somehow slow the plummet toward Ted's execution. She wanted Keppel to call the governor and plead Ted's case, to ask for a delay. For Keppel, now back as chief investigator for the criminal division of the Washington State Attorney General's Office, Weiner's request seemed at once premature and too late. Fighting off sleep, Keppel told Diana Weiner that he would be leaving in a few hours to fly to Florida. He was in no position to make any plea to the governor—if he should be so inclined—until he heard what Ted Bundy had to say.

An interview with Bob Keppel was high on the list of coups for reporters; he had been deluged with calls and he looked forward to some time in the air with peace and quiet. Reporters from Seattle, holed up in motels around the prison in Starke, tried to guess where Keppel might be staying once he got to Florida. They asked me what I thought the likely hotels might be.

I had no idea.

Nobody knew where Bob Keppel stayed in Florida—not even his wife. If she didn't know, reporters couldn't catch her off guard. In actuality, Keppel flew into Jacksonville and stayed the first night at Motel 6, the first spot he could find near the airport. Later on, he hooked up with Bill Hagmaier of the F.B.I.'s Behavioral Science Unit, and they stayed at the Sea Turtle on Jacksonville Beach. "I never got to see that beach, however," Keppel recalls. "We left early in the morning in the dark, and came back after dark."

Bill Hagmaier had come to know Ted Bundy too. As Ted had written to me, he approved—at least partially—of the F.B.I.'s Behavioral Science Unit's approach to serial murder. Those special agents would be men he would seek out. Hagmaier was coordinating the last-minute confessions; he had a calming influence on Ted, and he would serve well as an advisor to the detectives arriving, men so anxious to have their questions answered before time ran out.

Keppel was scheduled to talk to Ted at 11 A.M. Friday morning until 2:30 that afternoon. But he had lost half an hour going in. Diana Weiner and Jack Tanner wanted to brief him before he talked to Ted. That took to 11:30. Then there was another visitor, and Keppel had to wait ten more long minutes. It was almost noon when he finally faced Ted.

Diana Weiner was present at the interview with Ted, and that prevented Keppel from having a "contact" visit. The "no-contact" visit meant there would be a glass panel between Bundy and Keppel. A tape recorder was on Ted's side of the partition. Weiner listened carefully to what was said, hovering nervously. The prison interview rooms were either lime-green or mustard-colored, and neither enhanced Ted's facial pallor. He had not been out in the sunshine for years. But he smiled at Keppel, greeting him confidently. He trusted Keppel as much as he trusted anyone; Keppel had never lied to him.

"The first day I talked to him he was pretty well prepared to talk," Keppel recalls. "It didn't dawn on me the first day I went in there—Friday—that he wasn't going to confess that day. He wanted to lay the groundwork for the next three days. He had notes—preparations to cover those days. He started on that with me, got about halfway through it, and got off-track. He realized he'd better start confessing, otherwise I wasn't going to appreciate all this. Because I didn't have any time set with him after that."

Keppel had expected that his previous visits to Ted would allow them to "cut all the B.S. and get down to it." But the Washington detective saw that there was a game being played. "It was all orchestrated. They were going to do some things, but not all."

Keppel realized he was going to have to figure out a way, "real quick-like to get Ted to talk about one murder—but to admit to all the others."

It was not the ideal interrogation situation. Far from it. To take a good, solid statement on *one* murder, any detective would like to have at least four hours. Keppel needed information on eight or more murders—all in the space of ninety minutes.

And time was draining away while Ted continued to attempt to manipulate the thrust of their meeting. There was no time left to play to Ted's ego. . . .

"The easiest way to do it," Keppel recalls, "was to ask him about the sites. And it turned out to be *five* bodies left on Taylor Mountain—not four as we thought."

Ted told Keppel that the fifth body was that of Donna Manson, the girl missing from Evergreen State University in Olympia since March 12, 1974.

"He said there were *three*—not two—at the Ott and Naslund site."

Detectives had found an extra femur bone, and extra vertebrae beside that rutted road two miles from Lake Sammamish State Park. But they had not known whose they were.

Ted finally admitted they had found all that was left of Georgeann Hawkins.

Keppel's last-hour technique worked well. He mentioned the body sites, and if Ted didn't refuse to talk about it, the interview moved ahead smoothly. Ted gave Keppel *real*, verifiable information. Keppel watched the tape twist and curve and saw it coming to the end. They were in the midst of a vital confession—but but he had to slow Ted down, and ask him to turn the tape cassette over. He saw pure gold as the tape rolled on, recording what he had sought for so many, many years. What Keppel was hearing was ugly, and Ted choked up, paused, gulped, and sighed heavily. But the truth was coming out. At last.

The most fortuitous turn of their talk was when they got into talking about *numbers*.

The numbers didn't come out even. Finally, Keppel said, "Who are these other ones? Is there somebody out there that I don't know about?"

Ted answered quickly. "Oh, yes. Three more."

But the time was up. Keppel didn't know if he'd ever get to talk to Ted again. He knew that Utah had questions and Colorado. His allotted time was over.

As it happened, he had one more shot. Keppel was offered a slot on Sunday evening, after the Dobson interview which took place between 5:30 and 7:30 P.M., after Detective Dennis Couch from Salt Lake City, and before Mike Fisher of Colorado.

Ted was exhausted. He hadn't slept for several nights. His face was washed of color, stained with tears. He was thin, even frail-looking, and he wore two shirts as if he were already trying to shut out the chill of death. He no longer looked like the charismatic young politician; Ted looked old and worn out.

Ted had spent hours with Bill Hagmaier on the first night of the marathon interrogations, with Hagmaier helping Ted to isolate the information that the detectives were going to need. He had talked to Dobson and to his attorneys, and he was starting again on the detectives.

Asked if he thought Ted was going without sleep to savor the last days of his life, Keppel shakes his head. "No, I think he really thought he had some kind of a chance to live longer—if he played out his scenario right. He wanted to save his own life. He didn't want to die. He had the expectation that his efforts would be realized."

This was undoubtedly true. Ted's team had asked for three years more. If Martinez would give Ted just three years more to live, then Ted would tell it all.

All through Keppel's meetings with Ted, he could see that Ted had an ear cocked for the phone. Messages were coming in from Polly Nelson and Jim Coleman all through Friday, Saturday, Sunday, and Monday. There was still a chance as long as the U.S. Supreme Court was considering an emergency request aimed at keeping Ted alive until another formal appeal could be filed. Nelson and Coleman now were prepared to argue that the jurors in the Leach case were misled about the importance of their role in determining whether Ted would receive the death penalty or life in prison for his crime.

"The phones were ringing," Keppel recalls. "And they woke Ted up. Whatever he was doing, he heard the phone ringing. That's what he was really concentrating on."

Ted knew he was getting no reaction from Governor Martinez. No matter what Ted and Tanner and Weiner offered, Martinez said no.

Diana Weiner had asked Bob Keppel to intercede with Martinez, but Keppel would not. The next avenue of intercessions was to ask the victims' families to fax letters to the Florida governor, *asking for mercy for Ted!*

Keppel had arranged for Linda Barker, a victims' advocate, to call the victims' relatives and ask how they felt about delaying Ted's execution so they could know the truth about their daughters' last moments on earth, and, in some cases, so they could know where their daughters' remains lay.

To a person, the families refused to intercede for Ted Bundy.

"The timing was all wrong," Keppel said. "Ted was giving us spots where victims were buried, but we couldn't check it out. Not then. There was seven feet of snow in those areas in Utah and Colorado. Even in Washington, we had a foot of snow."

Bob Keppel had forty-five minutes with Ted Bundy on Sunday night, January 22, 1989. He got a few more details. But when Keppel attempted to joust a bit with Ted, he saw that the man before him had no fight left. Ted stared at him, his eyes dropping with the effort; he was almost asleep. He roused himself and said, "I know what you're trying to do—but it won't work. I'm just too tired."

The phone rang and Ted was awake and alert. The news was bad. The Supreme Court had turned him down.

"He didn't have any energy after that," Keppel remembers.

There were no more answers for Keppel's questions.

Bob Keppel talked to reporters and the strain of the past few days was evident on his face. Not a man easily shockable, Keppel had been shocked. He had been poleaxed to look, finally, into the dark mind of a man "born to kill."

"He described the Issaquah crime scene (where Janice Ott, Denise Nalund, and Georgeann Hawkins had been left) and it was almost like he was just there. Like he was seeing everything. He was infatuated was the idea because he spent so much time there. He is just totally consumed with murder all the time. . . ."

Bob Keppel was also shocked to see Ted Bundy beg for his life— to see at last the tears that flowed for himself as he scrabbled and scurried to live. Ted had maintained such exquisite control for so long.

Keppel answered some of the reporters' questions, and promised to answer more later. He said there were some things he had learned that he would never discuss.

The news services carried the story in the next editions. Bundy had confessed. Bundy would confess more in all likelihood. The headlines flashed in all languages.

"Bundy Admits 'Ted' Slayings!"

"Aplaza Bundy Varias Entrevistas Para Confesar Otros Asesinatos!"

Bob Keppel drove the sixty miles to Jacksonville, and boarded a plane for Atlanta where he would change planes and fly back to Seattle.

He had done all he could, and he was probably as satisfied with the results as he could possibly be. By Monday night, he would be sleeping in his own bed.

He had no plans to be awake at 4 A.M. P.S.T., the hour that Ted Bundy was scheduled to die.

Dr. Dorothy Lewis arrived from Connecticut to talk with Ted again. If she found him incompetent, the governor would have to appoint three psychiatrists to examine him. They would have to be in the same room at the same time, a mass psychiatric examination. If two of the three should agree that he was incompetent, there would be a delay.

There was none.

At this eleventh hour, there was the knowledge that Ted knew he was probably not going to get a stay of execution, that he'd probably sensed it over the past several days. And yet he had confessed and confessed and confessed. He had finally given details that would link him irrevocably to so many murders.

Ted told Bob Keppel he had left Janice Ott's yellow ten-speed "Tiger" bike in the Arboretum in Seattle shortly after he killed Janice in July 1974. No one ever had reported finding it. Keppel assumed that "some kid picked up the bicycle and rode off on it."

If anyone should still have that bike, its serial number is PT290.

Although Ted has always been linked to Donna Manson, who vanished from Olympia, only now could detectives be sure. Ted said that Donna's was the fifth body left on Taylor Mountain. When the snows go away, searchers will move once more into the area.

Who were the three victims Ted steadfastly refused to name?

Ted denied killing Ann Marie Burr, the little girl from Tacoma.

But his excuses were so weak. He said that he couldn't have killed Ann Marie because, "I was too young at the time," and "I lived too far away from her house."

Ted was fifteen when Ann Marie vanished. Old enough. And he lived only blocks away. Ann Marie took piano lessons next door to the house where Ted's Uncle John lived. Ted could very well have seen her there.

The early morning Ann Marie disappeared is locked into her family's memory. It was August 31, 1961. There had been a tremendous storm during the night, and they had to get up twice to tend to Ann's little sister, Julie. Julie had broken her arm and the cast woke her up with itches that she couldn't scratch.

Ann Marie was there the first time. The second time, her bed across the hall was empty.

Ann Marie's aunt recalls that the little girl liked to get up early and go downstairs in her nightgown to practice the piano in the living room. "The window there didn't quite shut. There was a T.V. antenna lead coming in through that window and the latch couldn't quite catch."

When Beverly and Donald Burr came down in the morning, the window was open—and so was the front door.

And Ann Marie never came home.

During the late-hour confessions, Ted shied away from talking about child victims. Or he made faint excuses.

I think he killed Ann Marie. I think that, quite probably, she was his first victim.

I also think he killed Katherine Merry Devine—although he would not admit to that. Ted did tell Bob Keppel that he had picked up a hitchhiker in 1973 near Olympia. He said he murdered her and left her body in the trees somewhere between Olympia and Aberdeen on the Washington coast. But he could not pinpoint the spot from a map Keppel showed him. Kathy Devine was *found* near Olympia. It is possible that the ride she hitched in the University District let her out sixty miles south of the freeway. And that Ted was the one who picked her up near Tumwater.

And that Ted was the man who killed her in December 1973.

I think the third victim was Lonnie Trumbull, the stewardess attacked in her bed in 1966.

Ted would not say.

The list of the victims Ted Bundy did acknowledge is long and tragic. He confirmed to Bob Keppel that he had killed Lynda Ann Healy, Donna Gail Manson, Susan Elaine Rancourt, Brenda Carol Ball, Roberta Kathleen Parks, Janice Anne Ott, and Denise Marie Naslund.

And finally, as the fifteenth anniversary of Georgeann Hawkins' disappearance looms, Ted filled in the missing scenario of the bleak drama played out in the alleyway behind Greek Row at the University of Washington in June, 1974. Georgeann's disappearance without a scream, in the space of a minute or so, has baffled detectives—and me.

In my head, as I lectured and showed the slides of that alley, I had pictured a hundred times what might have happened. As it turned out, it happened very much the way I had imagined.

Georgeann had laughingly called "Adios" to her friend in the window of the Beta House at the north end of the alley. She'd walked down toward the shiny yellow Buick convertible parked on the west side of the alley—

And met Ted Bundy.

The tape of his confession is hard to hear; there is a steady thunk-thunk-thunk, where the recorder malfunctioned slightly. And Ted's voice itself is so tired, raspy with stress. It is hard to hear and it is *difficult* to hear. I know the voice. I have never heard that voice say such ugly things before.

". . . I was ahhh—at about midnight that date (June 10, 1974) in an alleyway behind, like—I may have my streets wrong here—the sorority and fraternity houses, it would have been 45th—46th . . . 47th? . . . In the back of the houses, across the alley and across the other side of the block, there was a Congregational Church there, I believe . . . I was moving up the alley, ahhh, handling a briefcase and some crutches. This young woman walked down—all around the north end of the block into the alley. She stopped for a moment and she kept on walking down the alley toward me. About half way down the block, I encountered her. And asked her to help me carry the briefcase. Which she did—and we walked back up the alley, across the street, turned right on the sidewalk—in front of I think the fraternity house on the corner there. (This would be the Beta house where Georgeann's boyfriend lived.)

"Around the corner to the left—going north on 47th, part way in the block, there used to be one of those parking lots they used to make out of burned-down houses in that area. The University would turn them into instant parking lots. There was a parking lot there at ahhh . . . no lights, and my car was parked there."

"About that day—" Keppel prompts.

Ted sighs deeply. "Ahhh, awwwww . . . Basically—when we reached the car, what happened was I knocked her unconscious with the crowbar—"

"Where'd you have that?"

"By the car."

"Right outside?"

"Outside—in back of—the car."

"Could she see it?"

"No. And then there were some handcuffs there, along with the crowbar. And I handcuffed her and put her in the driver's—er, I mean the passenger side of the car and drove away."

"Was she alive or dead then?"

"No. She was quiet—she was unconscious, but she was very much alive."

Ted's sighs on this tape are those of a man in the grip of deeply painful emotion. He groans, gasps, draws in breaths. And the flaw in the tape goes on as steady as a clock ticking. Thunk. Thunk. Thunk.

Ted tells of driving down the alley to 50th N.E. "The street going east and west. I turned left—I went to the . . . freeway. Went south on the freeway, turned off on the old floating bridge—90—(the I-90 Freeway). She regained consciousness at this time—basically—ahh, Well, there's a lot of incidental things that I'm not getting into. I'm not telling you about them 'cause they're just— anyway, I went across the bridge to Mercer Island, past Issaquah. Up a hill. Down a road to a grassy area. . . ."

At this point, Keppel tested Ted, and mentioned a barricade in the road that would keep Ted from crossing both lanes. Ted insisted there was no barricade in 1974. And he was right.

"At that time, you could make a left hand turn. Illegal as it may have been because of the double yellow line. And that was crazy of me—talk about craziness—if there'd been a state patrolman there, he probably would have arrested me. (Ted laughs.) But, you know, nevertheless, at that time, there was no divider going down the middle of the road at that point ... All you had to do was make an illegal left-hand turn all the way across—well, the two west-bound lanes of 90 and right into that side road that ran parallel to 90.

"... I took the handcuffs off her, and ... took her out of the van and took the handcuffs off her. Took her out of the car."

Keppel interjected. "*Van?*"

"No, it was a Volkswagen."

"You said van."

"Well, I'm sorry if I—it was a Volkswagen. Ahhh ... anyway, this is probably the hardest part—I don't know ... We were talking abstractly before, but we're getting into—we're getting right down to it. I will talk about it but, it's just—I hope you understand—it's not something that I find easy to talk about, and, after all this time, ohhh, awwwww."

Ted sighs so deeply that his breath whistles into the tape recorder. He seems to try to pull away from himself, and groans as he does so.

"One of the things that makes it difficult is that, at this point, she was quite lucid, talking about things ... Funny—it isn't funny, but it's odd—the things that people say under those circumstances. And she thought—she said that she thought that—she had a Spanish test the next day—and she thought that I had taken her to help get ready for her Spanish test. Odd. Things they say. Anyway ... the long and short of it was that I again knocked her unconscious. And strangled her, and dragged her into about ten yards into the small grove of trees that was there."

"What'd you strangle her with?" Bob Keppel's voice is soft, drained of emotion. He would ask these questions and suspend his own feelings. At least five hours were unaccounted for.

"A cord—er, an old piece of rope that was there."

"... then what happened?"

There was another spate of sighs and groans. "... started the car up. By this time, it was just about dawn. The sun was coming up.

And I went through my usual routine. I went through this routine—I would go through this—where I was just absolutely—on this particular morning, I was just absolutely, again just shocked—again just shocked, scared-to-death—horrified. I went down the road, throwing everything I had—the briefcase, the crutch, the rope, the clothes. Just tossing them out the window. I was—I was in this sheer state of panic, just absolute horror. At that point in time, is . . . ahhhhh . . . consciousness of what has really happened. It's like you break out of a fever of something . . . I would. I drove northeast on 90 throwing articles of clothing out the window—shoes—as I went—"

Keppel cut in, asking Ted if Georgeann had disrobed.

"*What?*" A flat irritated tone.

Keppel asked again.

Ted tossed it aside. "Well, after we got out of the car—well, I skipped over some stuff there—and we'll have to get back to it sometime, but I don't feel—it's just too hard for me to talk about right now."

And some of those things that Ted "skipped over" he did get back to. But they will remain with Bob Keppel. Keppel wondered why no one had found the things Ted had tossed out in his alleged frenzy of panic. The answer came. Ted had gone back and picked everything up, once he calmed down.

The confessions came in bursts and despite long silences. They were horrific. Ted Bundy proved to be, as he had said years before in Pensacola and Tallahassee, a "voyeur, a vampire," a man whose fantasies had taken over his life. His aberrations and perversions were as ugly and sick and as deeply entrenched as those of any killer I have ever written about.

They must have been there all the time I was spending Sunday and Tuesday nights alone with the clear-eyed young man of 24 named Ted. That thought makes me shiver, as if a rabbit had run over my grave.

Beyond the Washington crimes, Ted confessed to more and more murders.

He admitted that he had killed Julie Cunningham in Vail, Colorado in March of 1975. She would have been crying, walking alone toward the comfort of her friend. Ted met Julie on that snowy street, and he asked her to help him carry his ski boots. At his car, he hit her with a crowbar, and lifted the unconscious woman inside. Like Georgeann had, Julie came to—and he hit her again. He left her body behind, but he came back later to bury it.

Yes, he had varied his pattern; he had buried some of them, left some in woods, tossed some of his victims away in rivers.

There were so many. There were probably more victims than we will ever know. Bob Keppel thinks Ted has killed at least a hundred women, and I agree with him.

Ted Bundy, who was voted the "shyest" boy in his class at Hunt Junior High School in Tacoma, began to kill, I think, in 1961 with the disappearance of little Ann Marie Burr. He was free, moving through his intricately compartmentalized life, until October 1975. After his escape in December 1977, he was free again for a deadly six and a half weeks. We know that he attacked seven women during that time, killing three of them. How many more are there that we do not know about?

When the confessing was over, the dreadful toll of dead girls filled a page of a newspaper—top to bottom.

Ted Bundy confessed to killing:

IN COLORADO
Caryn Campbell, 24.
Julie Cunningham, 26.
Denise Oliverson, 24.
Melanie Cooley, 18.
Shelly K. Robertson, 24.

IN UTAH
Melissa Smith, 17.
Laura Aime, 17.
Nancy Baird, 23. (A young mother who vanished on July 4, 1975 from a Layton service station where she worked.)
Nancy Wilcox, 16. (A cheerleader last seen on October 3, 1974 in light-colored Volkswagen bug.)
Dehi Kept, 17.

Other suspected victims in Utah:

Sue Curtis, 15. (Disappeared June 28, 1975, while attending a youth conference.)

Debbie Smith, 17. (Disappeared February, 1976. Her body was found at the Salt Lake International Airport on April 1, 1976.)

IN OREGON

Roberta Kathleen Parks, 20.

Although Oregon detectives were not given time to question Ted in Florida, they believe he is responsible for the disappearance of at least two more women in their state:

Rita Lorraine Jolly, 17. (Vanished from West Linn in June, 1973.)

Vicki Lynn Hollar, 24. (Disappeared from Eugene in August, 1973.)

IN FLORIDA

Margaret Bowman, 21.

Lisa Levy, 20.

Kimberly Leach, 12.

The State of Idaho had had no reason to send detectives to Raiford Prison. However, Bob Keppel phoned Russ Reneau, Chief Investigator from the Idaho Attorney General's Office and suggested that it might be a good idea for that state to send investigators to Florida.

Attorney General Jim Jones dispatched three detectives to Starke. Russ Reneau had not the foggiest notion what he would learn. However, after meeting with Ted, he found the Idaho connection.

According to reports, Ted admitted that he had stopped off near Boise during his Labor Day weekend move to Salt Lake City. He had seen a girl hitchhiking near Boise on September 2, 1974, and picked her up. He bludgeoned her, and threw her body into a river, the Snake River, he thought. Idaho authorities were unable to find a missing person report to match the description Ted gave.

However, the next confession sounded too much like a known unsolved disappearance to be coincidental. And the story that emerged was a study in calculated cruelty. Ted reportedly told Reneau that he made a trip up into Idaho with no other purpose—beyond finding someone to murder. He made sure that he would not have to buy gas that might mark his trail. He chose Pocatello as his turnaround point. The trip to Pocatello and back to Salt Lake City was 232 miles; a Volkswagen could manage that handily without refueling.

The area was high traffic, a spot where people came for outdoor recreational activities. Strangers passing through.

Ted drove his Volkswagen bug up Highway 15, looking for his quarry, for some unknown female to kill.

It was May 6, 1975.

He spotted a girl in a junior high school playfield during the noon hour. He picked her up, murdered her, and disposed of her body in a river. Again, he thought it was probably the Snake River.

Lynette Culver, 13, of Pocatello *had* been missing since May 6, 1975. Missing thirteen and a half years, longer than she had been alive, Lynette's body was never found.

His mission fulfilled, Ted had headed back to Salt Lake City. The entire trip took only four hours driving time.

Without the bodies of the missing girls, Idaho could never prove that what Ted Bundy had told them was true. But, in Lynette's case, it seemed as though the questions were answered. The other girl, who surely must have existed, was never reported missing. Somewhere, someone may remember a young girl who disappeared over Labor Day of 1974 in Idaho.

How many more? Because Ted murdered so many, many women, he did more than rob them of their lives. He robbed them of their specialness too. It is too easy, and expedient, to present them as a list of names; it is impossible to tell each victim's story within the confines of one book. All those bright, pretty, beloved young women became, of necessity, "Bundy victims."

And only Ted stayed in the spotlight.

The time between my first call from Gene Miller in December 1988, and the eye of Ted's electrocution went so swiftly. I spent Monday, January 23rd, racing from one talk show to another. Each new interviewer seemed so convinced that the execution was going to happen. There was an other-worldly sense to that time period in my life. We had a new president in the White House, the weather had finally begun to warm up in Seattle after an unseasonal winter of bitter cold, and Ted was going to die.

This time, he really was.

Given a choice, I would have preferred to stay home, where things were familiar, and where my family and friends were. I needed a comfort zone.

For good and bad, Ted Bundy had been some part of my life for eighteen years. Indeed, he had *changed* my life radically. Now, I wrote books instead of magazine articles. This book—which turned out to be about him—started it all. Now, I had enough income to live comfortably, without worrying about bills.

I had worked to stop people like Ted Bundy, and I had worked with the victims and the survivors of people like Ted Bundy. Ninety-five percent of my brain power detested Ted, and what he represented. But one part of me still thought, "Oh my God, he is going to walk down a hall and get into an electric chair, and he is going to have electricity surging through him, leaving burn marks on his temples and his arms and his legs."

It was a thought that ran through my head over and over as I sat very still on a plane carrying me to San Francisco. I gazed out at the clouds and down below to the Golden Gate Bridge. Since my first flight to Miami to cover Ted's trial—a flight where I was so bedazzled at the thought of actually flying all night—I have flown a thousand or more times. I'd been to San Francisco eight or nine times a year. Now I flew to New York, or Los Angeles or Chicago the way I used to drive to Portland, Oregon.

But, on this night, how I wished I could have been home.

First, I was going to do the Larry King Show, and San Francisco was the closest CNN affiliate where they could hook up a satellite. A limousine met me at the airport and delivered me to a skyscraper.

I sat under hot television lights and tried to talk at a camera lens as if I really saw Larry King there. Anybody who had ever known or encountered Ted Bundy was being interviewed somewhere in America on this night. We were newsworthy, although we wouldn't be particularly sought-after within a day or so.

Somewhere in the southeast, Karen Chandler, now a young wife and mother, was telling King about that night in January 1978. She seemed remarkably normal, and I thought that was nice. To know that even a handful of the girls who survived Ted could live happy, everyday, *normal* lives was a comfort. Karen didn't mention that she still pays $300 a month for dental bills to try to repair what Ted did to her with an oak log.

Karen's sorority roommate Kathy Kleiner's jaw hurts too, but there seems to be no surgical remedy guaranteed to help it.

I had talked to another Florida State Chi Omega, Susan Denton, when she called earlier in the week, just as I had called or been called earlier in the week, just as I had touched mine because of Ted Bundy. She said that a reporter named Amy Wilson had done an article about the girls of Chi Omega in *Sunshine: the Magazine of Southern Florida*. It had summed everything up, about their nightmares, and how they were trying to forget.

But not one of us had forgotten, and we all knew we never would.

In that hot little studio in San Francisco, I watched the cues of the cameraman and listened to Karen Chandler's sweet voice, and to Jack Levin, a Boston professor, discuss serial murder.

I felt a little faint.

My mind kept circling back to the execution and the thought of how electricity must burn.

And even so, I also thought: Ted had absolutely nothing to give to this world any longer, and the world certainly has nothing more to give to him. It's time.

It was cool and fresh in downtown San Francisco. The limo driver took me to the best hotel in town, where the *20/20* staff was waiting for me. There were also thirty-four phone messages waiting, all marked "Urgent." I wondered how I could answer them all, and it made me crazy until I realized there was no way I could do that.

For the next forty hours, I would be living with *20/20*, with Tom Jarriel, Bernie Cohen, the producer, and Bob Read, the man who made everything mesh smoothly. We would talk about Ted.

The other-worldliness feeling came back stronger than ever, and I felt a schism in my attention. I was aware of a clock ticking inside, the sure steady march toward the little room in the Florida State Prison—the room with the rough-hewn oak chair with the leather straps and the electrodes, the room where the witnesses' chairs were shiny black and white with backs shaped like tulips—chairs that seemed frivolous given their location.

20/20 took me downstairs to a gourmet dinner that cost more than any meal I'd ever partaken of. My mouth was too dry to enjoy it. Tom and Bernie and Bob were very nice, and funny. They were working on an interesting story; there was no personal involvement for them. I had done the same thing myself a thousand times.

Tomorrow, Ted was going to die. January 24th.

I had finally come to the place where I *had* to acknowledge my reactions. I could not coast through the next twenty-four hours. I had a feeling much like the last time I ever saw my brother, Don. My new husband and I drove him to the Seattle airport, terribly worried by how depressed he was. Ironically, he and my father were headed for San Francisco, where I was now, so that Don could go back to Stanford. As soon as they were out of sight of the gate, I started to cry.

I knew that I would never see Don again. There was nothing I could do about it. There was no way I could stop Don from dying. It was just one of those things that was going to happen, and nothing anyone could do to make it be different. At 20, I felt that fatalism for the first time.

Don was 21 years old when he committed suicide the next day. And Ted was a year older than that the first time I met him. My brother was goodness and kindness personified, and Ted Bundy was the opposite. And yet, I had probably always identified with Ted because I had lost Don.

And now, thirty years later, Ted was going to die, and nothing anyone could do was going to stop it. And nothing should stop it.

I tried hard to focus on the dinner conversation. I owed nothing to Ted, the monster. The rapist-killer-monster. He had lied to me, and he had destroyed more lives, horribly, than anyone I had ever written about. I was remembering a myth.

Far away in Florida, Ted's life was winding down rather quietly. He had cancelled his press conference. He was visited by Jamie Boone, his stepson, now a grown man and a Methodist preacher. Jamie had always believed in him. Ted reportedly felt some remorse about having deceived Jamie.

Carole Ann Boone did not visit.

Louise Bundy had always doted on and trusted in her "precious darling boy" too. Her anguish at his revelations to detectives was incomprehensible. The media had found her and hounded her until she shut her doors on them.

Louise had talked to the *Tacoma News Tribune*, her hometown paper. "It's the most devastating news of our life," she said on hearing that Ted had confessed eight—possibly eleven—murders to Bob Keppel. "If indeed, it was a confession (it's) totally unexpected because we have staunchly believed—and I guess we still do until we hear what he really said—that he was not guilty of any of those crimes . . . I agonize for the parents of those girls. We have girls of our own who are very dear to us. Oh, it's so terrible. I just can't understand. . . ."

Ted called his mother on the night of January 23rd. He told her over and over that she had done nothing wrong. "He kept saying how sorry he was, that there was 'another part of me that people didn't know.'" But Ted had rushed to assure his mother that "the Ted Bundy you knew also existed."

In a house filled with friends, Louise pressed the phone to her ear to block out extraneous noise, listening for the last time to her son's voice.

"You'll always be my precious son," she said softly. "We just want you to know how much we love you and always will."

In Raiford Prison, the long night passed too swiftly. Ted spent four of his last hours praying with Fred Lawrence, a Gainesville clergyman, and with the Tanners. Reportedly calmed by massive tranquilizers, Ted went through the final preparations. There was no last meal. He had no appetite. His wrists, right leg and head were shaved to facilitate the electrodes that would carry a peak load of two thousand volts in three surges, until he was dead. He was given clean blue pants and a light blue dress shirt to wear.

In San Francisco, we sat up all night. While the cameramen adjusted lights and camera angles, I talked for hours about Ted, and what he was like—or what he seemed to be like and, in truth, was not.

The phone rang seventy-five more times. Even the hotel operator, who was married to a Bay Area probation officer, asked about Ted.

When it was 7 A.M. in Starke, Florida, it would be only 4 A.M. in San Francisco.

Not even sunrise.

At about 2:30 A.M., I stretched across the top of the bed-spread and slept for half an hour. At 3 A.M., the camera crew woke me up. They were ready to start filming.

Tom Jarriel and I sat in silk-covered chairs in front of a television set. The screen showed the Florida State Prison, and then it focused on the crowds who sang and drank beer and celebrated the coming execution. Three hundred people wore costumes and masks and held banners up that said "Burn Bundy!" and "It's Fry-Day!" A man in a Reagan mask kept popping in front of the cameras. He held an effigy of a rabbit in one hand, his "Bundy Bunny," he explained.

They all seemed quite mad. They had no more humanity than Ted.

Parents had brought their children to witness the happy event. There was a holiday feeling that appalled me.

The *20/20* cameras were on us. Tom Jarriel asked me questions, and I watched the screen. I wanted again to be home. The green building that housed the death chamber was only dimly visible against the first rays of Florida's sunrise.

At seven, we all gazed at the screen. There could be no reprieve now. It was really going to happen. I thought that I was probably going to throw up. I had not felt that particular visceral turmoil for a decade. I felt exactly as I had in Miami when I realized that Ted was guilty.

The cameras seemed focused up my nose, and I could hear Tom's soft southern voice asking me a question. I shook my head. I couldn't talk.

We saw the lights outside the prison dim for what seemed a long time, and then they came back on bright. The expectant crowd murmured and hooted.

At exactly 7 A.M., a door had swung open in the death chamber. Prison Superintendent Tom Barton stepped in. Escorted by two guards, Ted came next; his wrists were hand-cuffed. He was quickly strapped into the electric chair.

Ted's eyes were said to be empty, perhaps the result of no sleep or of large dosages of sedatives. Or perhaps because he no longer had any hope or expectation. He looked through the plexiglass partition at the twelve witnesses who sat on the shiny black and white chairs. Did he recognize all of them? Probably not. Some he'd never known, and some he hadn't seen for years. Tallahassee detective Don Patchen was there, and Bob Dekle, and Jerry Blair. State Trooper Ken Robinson, who found all that was left of Kimberly Leach, was there.

Ted's flat eyes locked onto Jim Coleman and Reverend Lawrence, and he nodded.

"Jim . . . Fred," he said. "I'd like you to give my love to my family and friends."

Barton would have one more call to make. He called Governor Martinez from the phone inside the death chamber. His expression unreadable, Barton nodded to the black-hooded executioner.

No one knew who the executioner was, but one witness saw thick, curled lashes fringing his/her eyes. "I think it was a woman."

I watched the television screen in San Franscio. The lights dimmed outside the prison once more. Once again.

And then a blurry figure came out from somewhere in the green building and waved a white handkerchief in wide, sweeping motion.

It was the signal. Ted was dead.

It was 7:16 A.M.

A white hearse moved slowly from somewhere behind the prison. The crowds cheered and whistled joyfully as it picked up speed, officials worried that the mob might stop it and turn it over. Bill Frakes, of the *Miami Herald*, shot a picture of it, the same Bill Frakes who had captured the only image of Ted Bundy out of control. That photograph was shot at the Leach trial nine years ago. When Ted decided to leave the courtroom and deputies blocked his path, he had suddenly flown into a towering rage. *That* Ted was out of control, the Ted his victims saw. I use that slide to end my Bundy seminar, and the audience never fails to gasp.

But the Ted Bundy who walked under his own power to the electric chair was in control. He died the the way I always thought he would: without letting the witnesses see his fear.

I flew back to Seattle with the 20/20 group, and, without sleep, spent the next twelve hours doing radio and television interviews. Everywhere I went, I saw the instantly-released videotape of Ted and Dr. James Dobson. In the tape, Ted, looking pale yellow, his face lined and exhausted, earnestly confided to Dobson that his crimes could be attributed to pornorgraphy and alcohol.

Two agendas were met with that videotape. Dr. Dobson believed that smut and booze triggered serial killers, and he had the premiere serial killer to validate his theories. Ted wanted to leave behind a legacy of his wisdom and humanity's guilt. He was guilty, yes, but *we* were guiltier because we had allowed pornography to be sold. *We* walked by newsstands and did not demand that filthy literature be confiscated and outlawed. Tired as he was, Ted was brilliant, persuasive, and self-deprecating. He lowered his head and looked sharply up at the cameras as he responded to Dobson's question of what had happened to him, "That's the question of the hour and one that . . . people much more intelligent than I will be working on for years. . . ."

Ted was charmingly humble as he said he was no expert—this man who had told me, Kappel, Art Norman, Bill Hagmaier, and anyone who would listen that he was *indeed* the definitive expert on serial murder and psychopathology. He was only offering his opinion, tentatively, modestly, on the Dobson tape.

"This is the message I want to get across, that as a young boy, and I mean a boy of 12 or 13 certainly, that I encountered— outside the home again, in the local grocery store, in a local drug store, the soft-core pornography—that people called soft-core. As I think I explained to you last night, Dr. Dobson, in an anecdote, as young boys do, we explored the bad roads and sideways and byways of our neighborhood, and oftentimes people would dump the garbage. . . . And from time to time, we would come across pornographic books of a hard nature . . . of a more explicit nature. And this also included such things as detective magazines."

With Dobson seeming to lead him, Ted talked of his alleged addiction to pornography, of his warping by printed matter that involved violence and sexual violence.

Ted was very convincing, a drained, repentant man about to die—yet still warning the world.

I wish that I could believe his motives were altruistic. But all I can see in that Dobson tape is another Ted Bundy manipulation of our minds. The effect of the tape is to place, once again, the onus of his crimes—not on *himself*—but on us.

I don't think pornography caused Ted Bundy to kill thirty-six or one hundred or three hundred women. I think he became addicted to the power his crimes gave him. And I think he wanted to leave us talking about him, debating the wisdom of his words. In that, Ted succeeded magnificently.

The blunt fact is that Ted Bundy was a liar. He lied most of his life, and I think he lied at the end. He talked to Dobson of stumbling across detective magazines, of reading them avidly and "fueling his fantasies." Yesterday, I came across a letter Ted sent me almost exactly twelve years before he died. It is dated January 25, 1977.

I had written to tell him I had done a "Ted" article for *True Detective* magazine.

"I wasn't surprised or disappointed to hear about the detective magazine story," he wrote. "I rather anticipated such stories would surface or, in the case of the detective reading public, sub-surface. I hope I won't offend you and I don't intend to malign the detective magazine press, but who in the world reads these publications? I may have led a sheltered life, nevertheless I have never purchased such a magaine, and on of the two or three occasions I have ever picked one up was at the Crisis Clinic that night you brought some to show us some of your articles.

"Come to think of it, I have never known anyone who subscribed or regularly read these magazines. Of course, I don't qualify as your typical American either.

". . . If the article was being published in *Time, Newsweek*, the *Denver Post, Seattle Times* or even the *National Inquirer* (sic), I would be concerned. . . ."

Which was it? Either Ted never, ever read fact-detective magazines and shuddered at the thought, as he wrote me—or, as he told Dr. Dobson, he had been corrupted by them and other reading material to the point he had become a serial killer.

Ted Bundy's interview with James Dobson accomplished one thing that troubled me. During the weeks after Ted was executed, I heard from a number of young women. Sensitive, intelligent, kind young wrote or called me to say that they were deeply depressed because Ted was dead. One college student had watched the Dobson tape on television and felt moved to send flowers to the funeral parlor where Ted's body had been taken. "He wouldn't have hurt me," she said. "All he needed was some kindness. I know he wouldn't have hurt me. . . ."

A high-school student said she cried all the time, and couldn't sleep because a good man like Ted Bundy had been killed.

There were so many calls, so many crying women. Many of them had corresponded with Ted and fallen in love with him, each devoutly believing that she was his only one. Several told me they suffered nervous breakdowns when he died. Even in death, Ted damages women. They have sent for the Dobson tape, paying the $29.95 fee, and watch it over and over. They see compassion and sadness in his eyes. And they feel guilty and bereft. To get well, they must realize that they were conned by the master conman. They are grieving for a shadow man that never existed.

There were other calls—calls from women who were so afraid of Ted Bundy that they had not been able to call me while he still lived. They all believed that they had narrowly escaped from him during the killing time in the seventies. Some of them were clearly mistaken; others were impossible to dismiss. There are so few actual Bundy survivors that it is illuminating to hear their stories.

Brenda Ball disappeared from The Flame Tavern on Memorial Day Weekend, 1974. A week or so after Brenda vanished, a young mother named Vikky spent the evening at a tavern just down the street, Brubeck's Topless Bar. Twenty-five, petite, with long brown hair parted in the middle, Vikky drove there in her convertible, and left before midnight.

Her car wouldn't start, so she accepted a ride home with friends. At 4 A.M., just as the sun was beginning to light the eastern horizon, Vikky went back to try to start her car. She didn't want to leave it vulnerable and open in the tavern lot.

"I was fiddling with the car, trying to get it started—and it wasn't responding—when this good-looking man walked out from behind the tavern. I don't know what he was doing there at that time of the morning, and it didn't occur to me then that he might have deliberately disabled my car.

"He tried to start it, and then he told me that I needed jumper cables. He didn't have any, but told me he had friends in Federal Way who did. We went to this store and he sent me in to get some. The guy inside thought I was nuts, and said he didn't have any jumper cables. Well, the man who was 'helping' me said, 'I know someone who has jumpers.'

"Before I could say no, we hit the freeway in his car, heading someplace north—toward Issauah. We were driving along, and I thought he knew where he was going, but I was worried because my five-year-old daughter was home alone. All of a sudden, the guy said, 'Do me a favor,' and I looked at him and he pulled a switchblade from between his legs and held it to my neck.

"I started to cry, and he said, 'Take your top off,' and I said, 'It's coming off,' and he said. 'Now, your pants' and then he made me take off my underclothes.

"I sat there stark naked, and I tried to talk to him—to use psychology. I told him he was a nice-looking guy and he didn't need to do something like this to have a woman. He said, 'I don't want that—I want a little variety.'

"I grabbed for the knife, and he was furious. He shouted. 'Don't do that.'

"Finally, I said, 'My five-year-old's home alone, and she's going to wake up and she'll be all alone.'

"He changed all of a sudden. Just like that. He drove onto a street with tall trees. He said, 'This is it—this is where you get out.' I shut my eyes, thinking he was going to stab me, and said, 'Not without my clothes.' He threw my clothes out of the car, but he kept my purse and shoes.

"I got to a house and they let me in, and called the police. They found that someone had pulled the distributor cap on my car. They never located the guy who pulled the knife on me.

"But a year or so later, I was watching the news on television and I saw the man on the screen. I yelled to my friend, 'Look! That's him. That's the guy who almost killed me.' When they said his name, it was Ted Bundy."

Ted Bundy had passed into the criminal folklore of America. There will be stories and recollections and reports and anecdotes about him for years to come. There are truths to be winnowed out of his life and his crimes, and hopefully, criminologists and psychiatrists will find some knowledge from so much horror, some intelligence that will help us prevent criminal aberrance like his from developing.

Ted wanted to be noticed, to be recognized. He accomplished that. He left this earth a man almost as hated as the Nazis who intrigued him. When Ted's representatives announced that they planned to scatter Ted's ashes over the Cascade Mountain range in Washington State, there was a swell of outraged protest. The question was dropped, and no one knows what has become of his earthly remains.

It no longer matters. It is over.

The Ted who might have been, and the Ted who was, both died on January 24, 1989.

I remember back to 1975 when Ted was first arrested in Utah. My New York editor at the time didn't see that there would ever be a book about Ted Bundy. "Nobody's ever heard of Ted Bundy," he said. "I think it's just a regional story—there's no name recognition at all."

Tragically, there is now.

At long last, peace ted.

And peace and love to all the innocents you destroyed.

—Ann Rule
April 27, 1989

Acknowledgments

I have been fortunate indeed to have had the support of many individuals and organizations in writing this book. Without their help and emotional backing, it would have been impossible, and I would like to thank them: The Committee of Friends and Families of Victims of Violent Crimes and Missing Persons; the Seattle Police Department Crimes Against Persons Unit; the King County Police Department Major Crimes Unit; former Sheriff Don Redmond of Thurston County; Lieutenant James Stovall of the Salem, Oregon Police Department; Gene Miller of the *Miami Herald*; George Thurston of the *Washington Post*; Tony Polk of the *Rocky Mountain News*; Rick Barry of the *Tampa Tribune*; Albert Govoni, editor of *True Detective*; Jack Olsen; Yvonne E.W. Smith; Amelia Mills; Maureen and Bill Woodcock; Dr. Peter J. Modde, and my children, Laura, Leslie, Andy and Mike, who gave up months of their mother's companionship so that I might write.